Literary History in and beyond China

HARVARD-YENCHING INSTITUTE MONOGRAPH SERIES 137

Literary History in and beyond China

Reading Text and World

Edited by
Sarah M. Allen, Jack W. Chen,
and Xiaofei Tian

Published by the Harvard University Asia Center
Distributed by Harvard University Press
Cambridge (Massachusetts) and London 2023

© 2023 by the President and Fellows of Harvard College
Printed in the United States of America

The Harvard-Yenching Institute, founded in 1928, is an independent foundation dedicated to the advancement of higher education in the humanities and social sciences in Asia. Headquartered on the campus of Harvard University, the Institute provides fellowships for advanced research, training, and graduate studies at Harvard by competitively selected faculty and graduate students from Asia. The Institute also supports a range of academic activities at its fifty partner universities and research institutes across Asia. At Harvard, the Institute promotes East Asian studies through annual contributions to the Harvard-Yenching Library and publication of the *Harvard Journal of Asiatic Studies* and the Harvard-Yenching Institute Monograph Series.

Cataloging-in-Publication Data is on file at the Library of Congress.
ISBN 9780674291270 (cloth)

Index by the editors

♾ Printed on acid-free paper

Last figure below indicates year of this printing
28   27   26   25   24   23

To Stephen Owen

Contents

List of Tables	ix
Acknowledgments	xi
Chronology of Chinese Dynasties	xiii
Thinking through Literary History: An Introduction / Xiaofei Tian	1
1 Search and Intent: Early Chinese Literature for Now / David Schaberg	20
2 Ghost Poetry as a Problem for Literary History / Jack W. Chen	51
3 Northern Halls and Western Gardens: Literary History by Topic / Christopher M. B. Nugent	71
4 The Creation of a Genre: The Long, Slow Rise of Tang "*Chuanqi*" / Sarah M. Allen	98
5 The Case for Outsiders / Tina Lu	125
6 Theoretical Reflections on Literary History and Middle Period Chinese Poetry / Michael A. Fuller	150

viii   *Contents*

7   Poetic Omens and Poetic History / Lucas Rambo Bender   176

8   Tuning Literary Histories to World Time / Wiebke Denecke   205

9   When Literary Relations End—and Begin Again / Jing Tsu   232

Works Cited   259

List of Contributors   277

Index of Personal Names and Titles of Works   281

Tables

1	Poetic Omens in the Standard Histories	180–181
2	Poetic Omens in the *Gujin tushu jicheng*	182

Acknowledgments

The idea for this book originated with the April 2018 conference "Reconsidering Chinese Literature in the World: An International Symposium in Honor of Stephen Owen." We are deeply grateful to all the panelists, participants, and institutions that made this conference possible. Inspired by the exchanges at the conference, we decided that instead of editing a conference volume, we would invite fresh contributions on the issues, problems, and methods of writing a new kind of literary history. Because we were not able to have a workshop about our collective undertaking in crafting this volume, it took numerous communications and many rounds of revision to bring it to fruition. We thank all of the contributors for enthusiastically embracing our proposal of writing new papers specifically for this volume and persevering through this stimulating yet arduous process.

We are grateful to the Chiang Ching-kuo Foundation for International Scholarly Exchange, the Fairbank Center for Chinese Studies, the Harvard University Asia Center, and the Harvard Yenching Institute, as well as the Department of East Asian Languages and Civilizations and the Department of Comparative Literature at Harvard University, for sponsoring the conference that led us to conceive of this volume. We thank Bob Graham and the Harvard Asia Center Publications Program for taking an interest in this project, and Deborah Del Gais for gently and expertly steering the project through the publication process; we also thank Laura Poole for her meticulous copyediting. We thank Ronald Egan and the other, anonymous reviewer for their thoughtful comments xii *Acknowledgments*

and suggestions that made the essays collectively more coherent and individually stronger. We thank Liu Tao at the Central Academy of Fine Arts, Beijing, China, for gracing the book cover with his calligraphy. We are grateful to the Williams College Oakley Center for the Humanities and Social Sciences for generously providing a subvention to underwrite publication costs. A part of Jing Tsu's essay, "When Literary Relations End—and Begin Again," first appeared in *Journal of World Literature* 5, no. 2 (May 2020); the author modified this essay for the present volume. We thank the publisher for permission to adapt the essay here.

Finally, on behalf of all of the contributors, we thank the scholars, friends, and family members who have allowed us to carve out time to read, think, and write, to allow ourselves the solitude that is only achievable when we are part of families and networks. We are grateful to all of the people who make scholarship possible, from our teachers to our students, from our parents to our partners, from our colleagues to our fellow travelers. On this note, we affectionately dedicate this volume to Stephen Owen, a scholar who has spent nearly half a century teaching, contemplating, and often dramatically remapping Chinese literary history. His profound care for the field of Chinese literary studies at large as well as for the people who make up the field has contributed immeasurably to creating and sustaining the scholarly community of which we are all fortunate to be a part.

S.M.A.

J.W.C.

X.F.T.

Chronology of Chinese Dynasties

Zhou dynasty 周 (ca. 1046–256 BCE)
    Western Zhou 西周 (ca. 1046–771 BCE)
    Eastern Zhou 東周 (771–256 BCE)
        Spring and Autumn Period 春秋 (770–481 BCE)
        Warring States Period 戰國 (481–221 BCE)
Qin dynasty 秦 (221–207 BCE)
Han dynasty 漢 (206 BCE–220 CE)
    Former/Western Han 前漢 / 西漢 (206 BCE–8 CE)
    Later/Eastern Han 後漢 / 東漢 (25–220 CE)
Wei 魏 dynasty (220–265) / Three Kingdoms 三國 (220–280)
Jin 晉 dynasty (265–420)
    Western Jin 西晉 (265–316)
    Eastern Jin 東晉 (317–420)
Sixteen Kingdoms and Northern Dynasties 十六國/北朝 (304–581)
Southern Dynasties 南朝 (420–589)
    Song 宋 (420–479)
    Qi 齊 (479–502)
    Liang 梁 (502–557)
    Chen 陳 (557–589)

xiv *Chronology of Chinese Dynasties*

Sui dynasty 隋 (581–618)
Tang dynasty 唐 (618–907)
Five Dynasties 五代 (907–960)
Song dynasty 宋 (960–1279)
    Northern Song 北宋 (960–1127)
    Southern Song 南宋 (1127–1279)
Yuan dynasty 元 (1271–1368)
Ming dynasty 明 (1368–1644)
Qing dynasty 清 (1644–1912)

Thinking through Literary History

An Introduction

Xiaofei Tian

First Opening: A Ghost Story

People love a good ghost story, and we open with one from ninth-century China.

On a moonlit night in the year 806, Mr. Lu Qiao 陸喬, a well-to-do scholar and poetry lover living in the Danyang area (near modern Nanjing), was visited by the ghost of Shen Yue 沈約 (441–513), a courtier poet and historian well known in the southern Qi and Liang dynasties. Shen Yue first invited his good friend Fan Yun 范雲 (451–503), also an eminent writer, to join them. As the party went on, he summoned his young son Qingxiang 青箱, whose name literally means "green book-box," because, as Shen explained, the boy loved reading. Shen told the host that his son had composed a poem the other day lamenting the ruins of the former Southern Dynasties capital Jiankang (modern Nanjing). Like any proud parent, he proceeded to recite the poem for his host. The host, as expected, lavished praise on the poem but could not help wondering why the poem, instead of being in the "Qi-Liang style" of Qingxiang's lifetime, was composed in the "modern style," that is, as a "regulated poem," after the Tang dynasty court poets Shen Quanqi 沈佺期 (ca. 656–ca. 716) and Song Zhiwen 宋之問 (d. 712). Shen replied, somewhat defensively, "He wrote it in modern times, so he used the modern style. What's so surprising about that?" 今日爲之, 而爲今體, 亦何訝乎?[1]

---

1. The story is from Zhang Du 張讀 (833–889), *Xuanshi zhi* 宣室志, in Li Fang 李昉 et al., *Taiping guangji* 太平廣記, 343.2717–18.

Like Mr. Lu Qiao, Qingxiang is not attested in extant historical records and was probably invented for the story. We might well imagine that, had his ghost composed a poem in the twentieth century, he would have done so in the vernacular free verse of New Poetry. Qingxiang's poem, concluding with "mourning the current age and remembering the past" 傷時與懷古, is the focal point of this whimsical little tale, and the fact that even a ghost would change with the times is the punchline. The story shows that a sense of change, period style, and poetic history was intimately bound up with a sense of the chronological progression of history itself.

For a volume on the question of literary history and China, this is an emblematic story and the choice of Shen Yue as the main character is fortuitously apt in several ways. Shen Yue was one of the writers credited with theorizing and advocating the tonal awareness that laid the foundation for Tang "regulated verse," but more important, he lived in a time of literary historical consciousness. As the compiler of the dynastic history of the Liu-Song dynasty (420–479), he composed the "historian's comment" on the biography of the great poet Xie Lingyun 謝靈運 (385–433), which offers one of the earliest literary historical accounts in the Chinese poetic tradition. For more than one thousand years since that time, Chinese writers, readers, and scholars have written, read, and understood the literary tradition in essentially literary historical terms.

Second Opening: Literary History as a Modern Genre versus Literary History as a Way of Thinking

In Martin Kern and Robert E. Hegel's unsparing review of *The Columbia History of Chinese Literature*, literary history is upheld as the "ultimate" form of literary scholarship. The authors go into an ecstatic litany of the virtues of an ideal literary history:

> The genre of literary history has often been the place of the finest scholarship available: a place where authors rise above and beyond their chosen specializations in order to provide a balanced, comprehensive, and reliable survey of disparate phenomena; a place that accommodates a vast number of texts and genres that become related to one another in a historically meaningful way

and recognizable in their change and development over time; a place where the history of texts becomes intertwined with history writ large: the history of cultural, political, social, economic, and religious change.[2]

Barely twenty years later, in a review essay on several disparate volumes grouped under the title "Chinese Literary Histories in English," Haun Saussy expresses a deep-seated mistrust of literary history that is expected to "tell a *story* and tell *one* story," because literary history, just like Kern and Hegel's "history writ large," is a "more or less continuous narrative." Saussy cautions that this story dimension is "where this genre shows the greatest fragility, where it becomes most nakedly ideological and thus most liable to rejection from readers who do not share its interests and perceptions."[3] For that reason, he feels that a literary history written as a set of topical essays—on the condition that "the table of contents be rigorously thought through at the planning stage and the authors be held to a specific brief," and also with "the availability of inclusive, chronological histories like *The Cambridge History of Chinese Literature*" that has relieved the demand for a framework of making sense of the topical essays—can indeed work. As a matter of fact, he clearly believes that such topical essays (provided they satisfy his stringent conditions) are superior to the chronological histories.

Each review has a clear standpoint and a persuasive way of carrying through its agenda. One looks for historical coherence, whereas the other finds it rather oppressive and stupefying. Yet we can discern at least two commonalities. First, both are opposed to the kind of literary history filled with "simplifications and just-so stories," "quick platitudes," "unreflective use of traditional labels and categories," and "strong reliance on what one may call the commonplace version of Chinese literary history."[4] Second, both speak of literary history as a genre in a matter-of-fact manner, indicating that the transparency of this particular label is taken for granted.

This genre of literary history, regarded as a more or less continuous narrative, is widely established in Chinese-language publications today. It is a modern genre, and when the first histories of Chinese literature

2. Kern and Hegel, "A History of Chinese Literature?" 179.
3. Saussy, "Recent Chinese Literary Histories in English," 232–33.
4. Kern and Hegel, "A History of Chinese Literature?" 174, 175; Saussy, "Recent Chinese Literary Histories in English," 239.

XIAOFEI TIAN

were written, the genre of literary history was barely a century old in Europe. The earliest history of Chinese literature by Huang Ren 黃人 (Huang Moxi 黃摩西, 1866–1913) and the first literary history published in full by Lin Chuanjia 林傳甲 (1877–1922) were originally lecture notes for a college class, and both explicitly acknowledge foreign influences.[5] Moreover, these are explicitly *Chinese* literary histories, Zhongguo *wenxue shi* 中國文學史. This genre of narrative literary history was thus born in the national university system, along with the concept of "Chinese literature" or "China's literature" (*Zhongguo wenxue* 中國文學), and became closely tied to nation building. The story it tells is familiar to anyone who knows something about modern China, with the victory of vernacular Chinese declared over classical Chinese in a modernized Chinese state.

However, this particular genre is certainly not the only kind of literary history available in the Chinese tradition. As Jack W. Chen writes in this volume, "Although national literary history may be a modern institution . . . it is informed by the cultural logics and the histories of the traditions that precede modernity and by the repression of these cultural logics and histories" (69). It behooves us to historicize literary history itself, and to recognize that, as in the tale about Shen Yue's ghost, Chinese writers, readers, and scholars have written, read, and understood the literary tradition in essentially literary historical terms for more than a millennium. They traced ancestry and constructed lineages for writers as in a family tree; they wrote literary criticism in terms of dynasties, reign periods, and eras; they offered theories on literary history. They thought, and think, literary-historically. How does this affect our own thinking about and writing of literary history?

Although we need to recognize that any "historically meaningful" pattern is an artificial construction, which is bound to leave out many things that do not fit, disdain for chronological histories may not be entirely justified either. Instead, what we need is a new kind of chronological history, and the use of such a history should go far beyond treating it as a dictionary or reference guide that represents an interruption of a more intellectually charged mental process. Instead, we believe in writing literary history that leads to more questions than answers, and we believe in thinking

---

5. Xu Sinian, "Huang Moxi de *Zhongguo wenxueshi*"; Zhou Xinglu, "Dou, Lin, Huang sanbu zaoqi Zhongguo wenxueshi bijiao," 140.

through literary history that itself must be defined as a way of thinking, rather than merely as a modern genre, in a historicist culture.

One Story, Many Stories, Stories within Story

In "Histories within History," Stephen Owen defines "historicist" as meaning that "particular phenomena are understood through their historical specificity in the context of a continuous narrative of culture."[6] Although not all cultures are historicist, China certainly remains a historicist culture. But one quickly realizes this phenomenon is not limited to China: with regard to, say, English literature, whenever we speak of "Victorian novels" and "Romantic poets," we are conceiving of the novels and poets in literary historical terms, and our very judgments and attitudes toward the novels and poems are tinted by the knowledge of their historical origins. We are so accustomed to using the historical framework to understand everything that we are often unaware we are using it. When Brian Boyd summarizes *On the Origin of Stories: Evolution, Cognition, and Fiction*, an "evo-critical" work that attempts to explain a human being's natural attraction to narrative from a biological point of view, he writes a wonderfully self-reflective sentence: "Narrative allows us to understand where we have come from and where we are so that we can predict or plan where we might soon move."[7] That is, this very statement reflecting on narrative is woven with the warp and weft of time—past, present, future; chronology; temporal flow—the essence of a narrative. Thus, if we discover that we have made a mistake about when a text was written and about its author, it could entirely change our understanding of the text.

If literary history, like "history writ large," is essentially a story, it is not *one* story but a story infinitely complicated by the multiple stories embedded inside it. The bits and pieces of information are not stationary and stable elements waiting to be assembled, like bricks and beams, into a solid "palace of knowledge," but are highly variable and mediated elements that form a constantly changing pattern. To claim that we in the present may

---

6. Owen, "Shi zhong you shi (xia)" (History within History: Part II), 98.

7. Boyd, *Why Lyrics Last*, 3.

arrange those elements into meaningful patterns and sequences that belong to us somehow misses the fact that we are constrained by historical forces in the making of the patterns and sequences: the demonstration of such historical forces and our own constraints in the storytelling must become part of the story we tell. These abstract principles will become more perspicuous with a concrete example and some statistics.

The example takes us back to the early seventh century and what I call the twin biases against the literary legacy of the Period of Disunion (317–589). The early seventh century marks the beginning of the Tang dynasty (618–907), successor of the short-lived Sui (581–618), in ruling over a unified Chinese empire. Like the Sui, the Tang was a northern dynasty and similarly condemned the literature of the Southern Dynasties, the last of which was conquered by the Sui in 589. While the official judgment on the literature of the south by early Tang historians is harsh and unforgiving, at the same time there was an equally strong bias against the literature of the north in the act of selection and preservation of literary writings. In my chapter in *The Cambridge History of Chinese Literature*, I offer a detailed account of how early Tang encyclopedias, which are among our most important sources of pre-Tang literature, showed an overwhelming preference for southern writings against their northern counterparts. For instance, the early seventh-century *Classified Extracts of Literature* (*Yiwen leiju* 藝文類聚) "contains more than 900 selections from [southern] Liang poetry, but only four selections from Northern Wei poetry." For perspective, we may add that the Liang dynasty (502–557) lasted a little more than fifty years, whereas the Northern Wei (386–534) was about three times that length. This bias was not unique to one early Tang compilation. In *Grove of Texts from the Literature Office* (*Wenguan cilin* 文館詞林), a partially extant massive anthology of pre-Tang literature completed in 657, we find two poems from the Northern Wei and not a single poem from the Northern Qi and Northern Zhou. In contrast, we have thirty-one poems from the Southern Dynasties—Song, Qi, Liang, and Chen—with eighteen of them being Liang poems.[8]

One might imagine that, with the contemporary ideology praising the Northern Dynasties literature for its "substance" (*zhi* 質) and earthiness, the north might have fared better in prose genres, but this is not the case. *Classified*

---

8. Tian, "From the Eastern Jin through the Early Tang," 1:275.

Extracts of Literature includes more than 600 selections from Liang prose, but only 43 from the Northern Wei and Northern Qi, and the Northern Zhou and Sui prose selections are almost entirely dominated by southern court writers who came to the north in adulthood. In the fragmentary *Grove of Texts from the Literature Office*, we find one prose piece from the Northern Wei and one from the Sui, as opposed to five from the Liang.[9]

We know for sure that the extreme underrepresentation of Northern Dynasties writings in these sources was not due to a lack of literary productivity in the north, nor was it caused by textual losses (at least not at that time). However—and here the plot thickens—these biased selections in encyclopedias and anthologies are wholly responsible for the subsequent loss of the majority of the northern writings; as a consequence, today it is difficult, if not downright impossible, to give any balanced and comprehensive account of Northern Dynasties literature. An anecdote from the period relates that the prominent northern writer Wei Shou 魏收 (507–572) once requested Xu Ling 徐陵 (507–583), a great writer of the south, to take his literary writings to the south and circulate them there. As soon as Xu Ling boarded the boat, he dumped Wei Shou's collection in the Yangzi River. When an alarmed attendant asked him what he was doing, Xu Ling answered, "I am getting rid of an embarrassment for Mr. Wei" 吾爲魏公藏拙.[10] The story summarizes the fate of Northern Dynasties literature in its encounters with the south. In this volume, Christopher M. B. Nugent argues that even though early Tang encyclopedias do not make any theoretical statements about literary history or literary criticism, they nevertheless pass implicit judgment on the works of preceding generations by their selections and omissions, thus constituting a particular form of literary history. Literary histories, he states, "manage abundance" (71). Sometimes they manage so well that it becomes impossible to look beyond them for the past as it was then.

Although southern writings were held up as models, ideological prejudice against southern literature was all the rage in the seventh century and has been carried on well into modern times, leading to a slew of dubious, unexamined claims about southern literature regardless of available

---

9. For a discussion of these statistics and discrepancies, see Tian, "From the Eastern Jin through the Early Tang," 1:274–77.

10. Liu Su, *Sui Tang jiahua*, 1:116.

evidence. For instance, the view that the Palace Style poetry composed by Xiao Gang 蕭綱 (503–551; Liang Emperor Jianwen, r. 549–551) was all about erotic sensibilities and boudoir themes, first defined as such by early Tang historians in denouncing the effete "sounds of the fallen state," has been mindlessly repeated for 1,400 years. From the upright northerner courtier Wei Zheng 魏徵 (580–643) to the equally upright poet-scholar Wen Yiduo 聞一多 (1899–1946), we witness a remarkable consistency in their moral outrage. The only change—or, dare we say, "progress"?—is that poems depicting beautiful women are no longer automatically considered decadent today.

A new kind of literary history should foreground the very biases as demonstrated by the specific example above. Such a literary history is not the kind that prizes fragments over coherence, but the kind that acknowledges the gaps and holes in any coherence, looks honestly at the multiple strands of the fabric of history, and takes into consideration the historical contingencies of the literary historian's own vantage point.

The Essays

This volume contains nine essays on the question of literary history, since "literary history," or "literature" itself, is not a given, nor can it be taken for granted. We do not presume, nor is it our intention, to cover each and every aspect or period of Chinese literary history in this volume. Rather, the essays offer critical reflections on crucial organizing principles and concepts of the history of Chinese literature; as a whole, they represent a theoretical intervention in the field of Chinese literary studies and in the broader debates over the concept and practice of literary history.

AUTHORSHIP AND LITERARY PRAGMATICS

We begin with the notion of authorship, the most basic constituent of literary historical narrative. Literary history is organized around authors and their fixed place in the flow of time. The author is traditionally seen as the authoritative source for the meaning of a literary work, even though, as Wai-yee Li points out, the "purported retrieval of the author's state of mind as the goal of interpretation represses other possible readings."[11] Author-based interpretations can be immensely popular, as many general readers—and some students of literature—relish a good story invented around a poem without wanting to bother about the cultural-historical and intellectual implications of such a story or its invention. If one does not know what to say about a poem, talking about the state of mind and circumstances of its author, purported or not, is a sure way of rescuing a hapless literature professor from the plight of making the poem seem compelling to students. Biographical criticism dies hard, perhaps because, as Stephen Owen notes, "The Chinese author cannot 'die,' as Foucault would have it, if only because, in the context of Chinese poetics, authorship has become a necessary systematic function. Without the contextualizing cultural narrative, replete with authors, many poetic texts become unreadable. Such a claim, however, needs itself to be historicized: this was not necessarily true in all forms at all times."[12]

In his essay, "Search and Intent: Early Chinese Literature for Now," David Schaberg gives a deeply historicized, and hence iconoclastic, reading of the single most authoritative statement in the Chinese tradition, "Poetry bespeaks the intent" (*shi yan zhi* 詩言志). From the Western Han on, this statement has been taken to refer to poetic composition and become a central tenet in Chinese poetics underlying the importance of the author. Schaberg, however, shows that in ancient China, *shi* poems were used to teach persuasive speech and oratory and that a young member of the elite learned to convey his own intent through poems—the "intent" in the statement was not the author's. Schaberg's essay brackets the whole "author" question and empties out the author concept thought to be implied in the early canonical statements on the relationship between intent and expression by looking at the pragmatic function of literary texts in "learning to speak." The separability between the speaking and the spoken, as any "user" could inhabit the language of *shi* and use it to convey their own *zhi*, has long-lasting consequences for the issues of person and voice, authenticity and insincerity, that became so prominent in the later tradition.

11. Wai-yee Li, "Concepts of Authorship," 371.
12. Owen, *The Making of Early Chinese Classical Poetry*, 219.

The emptied-out author returns in Jack W. Chen's essay, "Ghost Poetry as a Problem for Literary History," as a troubled and troubling entity: a ghost. Chen uses ghost poetry (*guishi* 鬼詩), poems authored by ghosts, to interrogate the category of author and the generic concept of the poem to organize literary history. What does it mean, he asks, to attribute authorship to a ghost in premodern times? Why did ghosts tend to compose poems rather than prose pieces, so that "ghost prose" (*guiwen* 鬼文) never took off as a popular phenomenon? In one of the cases he examines, the ghost of Murong Chui 慕容垂 (325–396), a Xianbei/Särbi ruler of one of the "barbarian" northern kingdoms, composed a quatrain upon appearing to Tang Emperor Taizong 唐太宗 (r. 626–649) during the latter's military campaign against Korea. The poem, recorded in a contextualizing account in an eighth-century work, was eventually included in the largest collection of Tang dynasty poems, *Complete Tang Poems* (*Quan Tang shi* 全唐詩), commissioned by and compiled under the aegis of the Manchu ruler of the Qing dynasty, Emperor Kangxi 康熙 (r. 1654–1722). By virtue of the time of the composition of the poem, "Murong Chui" became not only a Tang dynasty poet but an early Tang poet at that. How does that destabilize the period style that has become established and well known in the standard modern literary histories? How are such ghosts, both inside and outside of time, subsumed, however uncomfortably, into literary history? We think back to Shen Qingxiang, the ghostly son of the historical poet Shen Yue who composed a "modern" poem in the early ninth century and inserted himself/itself back into the stream of time, in conformity with the living. These spectral presences, as Chen's essay suggests, serve to reveal the fissures and gaps in the apparently seamless cultural projects of empire building and, later on, nation-building, both of which require a teleological narrative. That the ghosts' preferred genre should be *shi* poetry is not surprising: after all, in the imperial history, *shi*, with its claim to immediacy and presence, is the privileged genre believed to channel authorial intent.

Schaberg also makes the point that it is valuable to consider literary texts for their pragmatic effects because these texts always train the reader in useful forms of communication. Christopher M. B. Nugent's essay in this volume, "Northern Halls and Western Gardens: Literary History by Topic," resonates with the issue of literary pragmatics from a different angle and in a different period by focusing on the educational and pedagogical purpose of encyclopedias, known as *leishu* 類書 ("writings arranged by category"), compiled in medieval times. These compilations, assembled for the edification of imperial princes and members of the elite, offer resources and technologies for acquiring competence in composing literary works as demanded by various social occasions. Nugent demonstrates that in the selections of the literary texts therein, and in the very structures the compilers used in arranging and presenting the texts, we can identify implicit judgments. Thus, these encyclopedic compilations constitute a kind of literary history that serves the practical needs of the present. The sense of utility, Nugent argues, may best account for why the courtiers selected so many poems from the defeated Southern Dynasties that they must by necessity condemn. Such a paradox, borne out of the irreconcilable political and cultural ideologies of the time, not only plagued the early Tang courtiers but also, through their selections and writings, continues to trouble literary historians today. Because our present is mediated by the Tang *leishu* compilers' mediation of their recent past, it is only fitting that David Perkins's model of the needs of the present intervening in the literature of the past becomes more nuanced and complicated.

STEPPING ASIDE: GENRES AND OUTSIDERS

Genre is the next staple constituent of literary historical narrative. It is, however, no more a stable category than authorship. It is always an afterthought, a historical construct, and a process of becoming—every innovative work defines that genre anew—that should be studied in the performance. Sometimes a retrospectively imposed generic label does great violence to the body of diverse texts harnessed under its rubric.

In the early twentieth century, the modern, Western-inspired national history of Chinese literature (*Zhongguo wenxue shi*) strenuously looked in the native tradition for equivalent concepts and categories that could match European and American counterparts. Since fiction enjoys a privileged place in the hierarchy of modern literature, early twentieth-century Chinese scholars decided to seek the origin of fiction—an important step in identity formation—in past literary culture, and not surprisingly they found it. Lu Xun 鲁迅 (1881–1936), the preeminent modern writer and scholar, declared the short tales from the Tang dynasty, which he called *chuanqi* 傳奇 ("transmitting the marvelous"), to represent the genesis of modern Chinese fiction, *xiaoshuo* 小説, in *A Brief History of Chinese Fiction (Zhongguo xiaoshuo shilüe* 中國小説史略, preface dated 1923). Sarah M. Allen's essay in this volume, "The Creation of a Genre: The Long, Slow Rise of 'Tang *Chuanqi*,'" asks us to reconsider a narrative that ever since Lu Xun's landmark work has become familiar to any student of Chinese literature. As the story goes, *chuanqi* were short tales that evolved from simpler antecedents known as *zhiguai* 志怪 ("recording the strange" or "anomaly accounts") over the course of the Tang dynasty, matured in the ninth century, and declined in popularity and quality in the late ninth and subsequent centuries. In this story, *chuanqi* is considered a crucial landmark in the long development of Chinese fiction.

But what if there were no "Tang *chuanqi*"? Posing this provocative question implicitly, Allen's essay offers an illuminating account of the gradual formation and reification of *chuanqi* as a genre. Just as important, she shows what new insights can be gained into Tang narratives, and Tang cultural and social history, by breaking free from the familiar mold of thinking within the *chuanqi* box. Taking up three Tang stories about remarkable women, one of which was upheld as an exemplary *chuanqi* tale while the other two were excluded from the *chuanqi* category, she demonstrates that liberation from the *xiaoshuo*/fiction model allows us to reconstruct these stories' textual ecology by seeing their connections to a much broader range of texts and understanding them better in their contemporary contexts. Thus Allen performs a double service in her historicizing move: she deconstructs "*chuanqi*" and opens up space for making new kinds of inquiries.

Sometimes it takes a latecomer and an outsider to see something more clearly, and to ask questions that could not have been posed by contemporaries or insiders because they stood too close, lacked the language for formulating the questions, or—even though they may not always be cognizant of this or willing to admit it—had a stake in it. When we consider genres in the field of late imperial Chinese literature, especially a southern-style drama fortuitously also called *chuanqi*, we witness a remarkable continuity between the sixteenth-century playwrights' concerns and the modern scholars' interests, which veer strongly and overwhelmingly toward formal elements and performance styles. Tina Lu's essay, "The Case for Outsiders," gives an eloquent critique of a lopsided focus on the formal properties of a genre at the expense of critical issues that, although never articulated explicitly and in such abstraction, lie at the heart of those plays and are barely disguised: class, gender, and power.

This kind of uneven focus on formal and stylistic aspects of a genre is not limited to the study of late imperial drama; it can also be seen in the studies of *shi* and *ci* poetry. The tendency appears to have been intensified in recent years, as the Chinese state has been investing enormous resources in encouraging its citizenry in mastering traditional Chinese arts. Many Chinese researchers of classical Chinese poetry nowadays seem to feel that somehow, being a practitioner with the ability to produce a classical-style poem or sing a *kunqu* libretto is a certificate of sorts, lending credibility to their research credentials. Of course we cannot fault, say, a Petrarch scholar for trying their hand at a Petrarchan sonnet in their spare time, but there seems to be a troubling desire in the Chinese case not only to study the premodern scholarly elite but also to be—or become—that elite, even though there is hardly any room for that elite in contemporary Chinese society except perhaps in the increasingly rarefied space of those well-funded universities and research institutes ranked as key (*zhongdian* 重點) by the Ministry of Education.

Nowadays, however, the community of outsiders exterior to the Chinese-speaking world is diverse: unlike fifty, forty, or even just thirty years ago, it includes an abundance of scholars who are ethnically Chinese and have grown up in the Chinese-speaking world; they work and live as immigrants, but they retain various close ties with their native places and some choose to retain their original citizenship. Unlike fifty, forty, or even just thirty years ago, everything written in English on classical Chinese literature is being translated into Chinese at an astonishingly rapid rate, reviewed in national journals and newspapers (often before the Chinese version is printed), and eagerly consumed by an audience, in and out of academia, of an impressive magnitude—certainly much larger than what an academic book usually gets in the English-speaking world, and this is not just thanks to the size of the Chinese population.

The topography of interiority and exteriority is further complicated by the outsiders inside Chinese-speaking academia: women scholars, especially young women scholars, who still routinely encounter gender bias in matters such as publication, promotion, and honors, and who are often unable to participate in the lively socializing and networking of their male counterparts. There is much discontent brewing barely beneath the surface, as attested by numerous conversations with our female colleagues based in China. As a result of the changed and constantly changing dynamics in the field and in the world, there are many fuzzy edges and blurry boundaries.

Because of these vibrant dynamics, and perhaps precisely because of the different viewpoints provided by the outsiders to the Chinese university system and the structure of power of the Chinese state, what is being done outside the Chinese-speaking world has the potential to matter to that world in a profound way. In another thirty, forty, or fifty years, in some areas the distance between the insiders and outsiders will perhaps have closed, while in others there may be new distinctions. Toward the end of her essay, Lu proposes that the way to understand literary history should be "as always in the process of making" (149). Indeed. And we are all in it together.

TAKING THE LONG VIEW

Michael A. Fuller's essay in this volume, "Theoretical Reflections on Literary History and Middle Period Chinese Poetry," represents the best of one kind of literary history: a neat and enclosed narrative about a single genre, namely, *shi* poetry, designed in dialogue with certain forces in social life and intellectual culture. Fuller offers a lucid account of the belief that literary creativity cannot be separated from other aspects of social life and that literary history must be able to account for its changes by drawing on the larger patterns of human experience and cultural transformation. Grounding his story of literary historical development in such a belief, Fuller outlines the trajectory of *shi* poetry in correspondence to epistemological change following the collapse of the medieval world order after the An Lushan rebellion of the mid-eighth century through the end of the Song dynasty (960–1279).

Fuller's essay makes an instructive counterpart to Lucas Rambo Bender's "Poetic Omens and Poetic History." Bender likewise stresses the need to sometimes turn our attention away from purely aesthetic concerns and instead explore topics that may seem to lie on the margins of literature but, as he argues, eventually turn out to be useful to literary history. He subsequently gives an original treatment of the relationship between poetry and omens, a relationship that he contends moved from the margins of the literary toward its center over the course of the medieval period and transformed how literature related to history. Through a consideration of the developmental history of verses considered to be poetic omens, ranging from vaguely "folk" ditties (especially by children) of an earlier time to Tang and Song poems by members of the scholarly elite, Bender questions the traditional model of regarding the Tang-Song transition as an epochal rupture and suggests that the largely continuous history of poetic omens should perhaps encourage us to no longer think about continuity and rupture as mutually exclusive models of literary history.

WHOSE LITERARY HISTORY AFTER ALL?

Wiebke Denecke's essay, "Tuning Literary Histories to World Time," focuses on the modern genre of literary history. Proposing that it is time to historicize the practice of literary historiography, Denecke examines the new forms and methods of literary history that have appeared since about 2000, providing full evidence that this academic genre, time and again declared as either "dead" or "impossible," is far from having disappeared from the scholarly community or having fallen outside the interest range of general readership. Instead, it has elicited all kinds of innovative responses and critical reflections. Denecke's essay ends with East Asia, which she finds to be a premier case for examining the origins, motives, and consequences of writing literary histories. She introduces the coined word "letterature," based on "letters" 文 (Ch. *wen*; J. *bun*) and "literature," which is used in the title of a new Japanese literary history that she coauthored with a Japanese colleague to include a broad range of practices and conceptualizations that formed around *wen* in social and political life, in material culture and knowledge transmission, and in interactions between people of different classes and sexes. This conception of literary history represents a historiographical approach that is much more tuned in to the expansive premodern discursive field of *wen/bun* in East Asian cultures. It also hearkens back to the not-so-distant past in Europe: *The Cambridge History of English and American Literature* published between 1907 and 1921, spanning eighteen volumes and 303 chapters, exhibits a catholic incorporation of "a wide selection of writing on orators, humorists, poets, newspaper columnists, religious leaders, economists, Native Americans, song writers, and even non-English writing, such as Yiddish and Creole," and the essay topics range from the staples of literature—poetry, fiction, drama, and essays—to history, theology, and political writing.[13]

The term "letterature" is cast in a new light when juxtaposed with Jing Tsu's essay in this volume, "When Literary Relations End—and Begin Again," in which the letters home written by Chinese immigrants in Cuba become one of the figures Tsu uses in proposing the restructuring of the very framework of literary value as we know it. Tsu's essay takes us well beyond the national borders of China. It begins with a retrospective look at a book review by Stephen Owen titled "What Is World Poetry?" which was published in the *New Republic* in 1990. The reviewer points out that the book of poetry under review is written to "travel well": it has no particular characteristics, and could be just as easily translated from a Slovak or an Estonian or a Philippine poet, and "this version of 'world poetry' turns out, unsurprisingly, to be a version of Anglo-American modernism or French modernism. . . . And this situation is the quintessence of cultural hegemony, when an essentially local tradition (Anglo-American) is widely taken for granted as universal."[14] In 2003, Owen once again stated the reality we face—albeit not as something we should be complacent about—in unequivocal terms: "For a young Korean poet to be translated into Tagalog and acclaimed in Manila is, no doubt, a matter of satisfaction; but it has less cachet than to be translated into English or French and invited to New York or Paris. It is unfair, but it is a fact."[15]

In her essay, Tsu presents a strong case that the system of valuations has changed a great deal since the early 2000s, painting a picture of the majority of literary humanity that, she contends, stays largely undifferentiated in the backdrop of world literary space and does not care much about the idea of world literature. She celebrates smallness because it enables a focused attention on "local literary ecologies that do not aspire to be canonized in literary history" (239). In this field of vision, being small

---

13. For the description cited here, see https://www.bartleby.com/cambridge/. This colossal encyclopedic work was put online in 2000 by Bartleby.com.

14. Owen, "What Is World Poetry?" 31, 28.

15. Owen, "Stepping Forward and Back," 533.

Thinking through Literary History

and going local are prized over the big, metropolitan, and global; some of the literary products serve an immediate pragmatic purpose and never intersect with the kind of world literature space where New York or Paris are front and center.

To the small ecologies recounted by Tsu, one might add the vibrant scene of Chinese Internet literature consisting of poetry, fiction, essays, and criticism. These digital texts cross national boundaries easily. They are often anonymous. They are fragile and ephemeral unless scholars make a conscious effort to capture and archive them. They are fragmented, appearing as numerous interest groups and fan forums of all kinds. They are largely democratic, bypassing the authority of cultural establishments like universities, presses, and peer-reviewed journals. In the realm of poetry, the web has played a crucial role in making visible numerous practitioners of classical verse genres alongside individuals writing poems in the modern vernacular, enabling an alternative account of modern Chinese poetry outside the framework established by the May Fourth generation declaring the "death" of old poetic forms.[16] But these digital texts can also be censored and policed; they can be co-opted by and stay in comfortable complicity with the governing forces just as easily as Chinese science fiction has been, whose top writers' international fame "has become a source of national pride."[17] When we can look beyond canonization as a main purpose or function of literary history, we will see the very fact that small ecologies are being seen and heard and commented on by an international community of scholars as, paradoxically, the quintessential gestures of literary historical documentation. Literature's relations with the world are indeed never closed off. Just as the present is constantly changing, the past is changing in response to the changing present—in this, premodern literature and contemporary literature are not so different.

* * *

In 1975, renowned Chinese literature scholar James J. Y. Liu asked in a state-of-the-field review published in the *Journal of Asian Studies*: "if the

16. Tian, "'Each Has Its Own Moment,'" 520–23; and "Muffled Dialect Spoken by Green Fruits."

17. Jiayang Fan, "Liu Cixin's War of the Worlds."

historians are now able to produce the *Cambridge History of China*, are we in literature so far behind that we cannot even contemplate a similar undertaking?"[18] Some scholars indeed contemplated such an undertaking. In 1979, David R. Knechtges and Stephen Owen published an article in *Chinese Literature: Essays, Articles, Reviews* (*CLEAR*), which relates how they were approached by Yale University Press to produce "an authoritative and detailed history of Chinese literature" in the spring of 1974, and how a planning conference was subsequently held in the summer of 1975.[19] In this article, the authors, still at the early stages of their careers, sketched out a series of general principles for a history of Chinese literature. There is the expected "Who wrote what when," with a good dose of commonsensical levelheadedness shown in declarations such as, "For example, there is no longer any reason to consider all the traditional attributions to Qu Yuan as authentic."[20] There is also the less obvious, as the authors define the social context of literature as "the function of literature in society," but not as historical determinism, cautioning literary historians against "determining 'causes' or explaining 'why' an event in literary history occurred by exclusively resorting to the 'external order' of literature."[21] There are statements that at the time were revolutionary and subsequently proved prophetic: "In some periods it would be useful to explore the relation between encyclopedias and literary composition"; and "period style should be based on an analysis of more than just the major poets."[22] The meticulously planned twenty-one volumes never materialized except in much transfigured forms in a few cases, and Yale University Press turned out to be too optimistic in their generous estimation of "a minimum of ten years" to finish the project. But thanks to this document, which reads at times like minutes of a meeting, one sees just how much the field has changed since then.

18. James J. Y. Liu, "The Study of Chinese Literature in the West," 30.

19. Knechtges and Owen, "General Principles for a History of Chinese Literature," 49.

20. Knechtges and Owen, "General Principles for a History of Chinese Literature," 50. I have converted the Wade-Giles transliteration into pinyin in these citations.

21. Knechtges and Owen, "General Principles for a History of Chinese Literature," 50–51.

22. Knechtges and Owen, "General Principles for a History of Chinese Literature," 51–52.

In the past decades, several histories of Chinese literature and a number of reference works and handbooks on classical and modern Chinese literature have been published in English. With new discoveries, advances, and theoretical underpinnings, and with the effects of digitization and computational methodologies profoundly felt in many subfields of cultural, historical, and literary studies inside and outside China, it is time not just to write literary history but also to write "about" literary history, to approach the problem of literary history on a theoretical level, and to reflect on the concepts and frameworks we have received from the May Fourth generation, who established the modern disciplines in a national university system. The essays in this volume address various aspects of literary history in the Chinese cultural tradition, from the epistemological bases for literary historical understanding to the problem of what such a term as "China" might mean in terms of literary history. As such, the essays consider what it means to think through literary history.

CHAPTER I

Search and Intent

Early Chinese Literature for Now

DAVID SCHABERG

The migration of literary historical research activity toward digital platforms and media since about 1990 has brought unprecedented access to texts of all kinds and raised new questions and possibilities of method.[1] As the accessible online corpus has grown, advances in user interfaces and other tools have also given investigators of searchable corpora more control over their materials. An advanced search using regular expressions, for example, or a search performed across a whole digitized library of texts is remarkable for how intentional it can be, how precise in its targeting of results and its exclusion of irrelevancies from consideration. A scholar researching a question in her field, say, early Chinese literature, may consider the results in full awareness of existing configurations of information in that field, such as narrative histories, anthologies, encyclopedias, and the like, all of them demonstrating their own principles for selecting, arranging, and connecting data points.[2] These other frameworks will figure in the interpretation of search results and may allow the scholar to recognize shortcomings and distortions in search results and correct for them in some measure. The resulting representations of early Chinese literature will be richer for how they take existing scholarly perspectives into account while accessing their supporting data ever more nimbly, on demand, and at will.

---

1. See Tian, "Introduction," in this volume.
2. Jack W. Chen et al., *Literary Information in China*.

Search and Intent 21

Along with the amassing of digitized research materials has come the spread of connectivity and the amassing of users of these materials. The search window of an internet browser like Chrome, for example, is pointedly open to anyone with a connection and is the very image of an invitation to ask—an empty, entirely undetermined space in which anything you type will become a question to the amorphous, ever-growing corpus of searchable pages. When we conduct these sorts of searches, especially as we pose queries and interpret results beyond our own areas of expertise, we enjoy some of the power of the scholarly search, but without much awareness of alternative contextualizations and therefore without much possibility of precision. Transmediation of cultural legacies opens them to the sort of discipline-informed questioning a scholarly query entails and to free, playful, unprefigured, or uninformed questions that might draw trivial, illuminating, or revolutionary results out of the corpus.

Transmediation has also brought a concentration and a consolidation of the scene of inquiry. However different the preparation behind them, the scholarly search and the casual search may start from the same search buffer, and users may enjoy access to many of the same collections of information, paywalls and memberships permitting. The results of the scholar's research are increasingly likely to be accessed online, whether in a digital reflex of a print form, an article or monograph, or in a form (blog, online annotation) that belongs more squarely in the new medium, and they will appear alongside other sources of information about the same subject. Under these circumstances, academic disciplines have lost some of the arbitrating role they had in the era when peer-reviewed print publication dominated. The consequences are at the moment especially clear in the case of peer-reviewed medical research, which finds itself pitted, in a general market of online information, against rumors and claims that have a different appeal for searchers. The freedom implied by the open search window is also the freedom to access the corpus with little prior information or understanding of any kind, whether academic or other—that is, in an entirely ad hoc construction of knowledge from the results. Arguably, every discipline or profession that produces knowledge now does so in the same recently recontextualized way. As scholarly research has become more accessible and more public, it has come into new competitions and collaborations and has become one voice—not always a corroborating voice—among others.

22 DAVID SCHABERG

To practice some literary history while also reflecting on it, I consider these new research powers and this new rhetorical and political situation in terms of an old question in the history of Chinese poetics: the question of what is meant in "poetry bespeaks the intent (*zhi* 志)" and "poetry is that to which the intent (*zhi*) goes," formulas that have been touchstones of thought about poetic language and meaning since the Han dynasty (206 BCE–CE 220). Focusing especially on meanings of the word *zhi* and following the lead of Zhu Ziqing 朱自清 (1898–1948), I examine the origins of these chestnuts in the context of pre-Han rhetorical activity and focus on the sense of *zhi* as a willful reuse of existing language in debate and persuasive speech. In poetics, the two formulas came in post-Han times to stand for the putative sincerity of the historical poet, the absolute correspondence of the words of the poem to the emotions in the poet's heart. This understanding was also shadowed by a very different definition of *zhi* that is apparent in its early rhetorical contexts. In some cases, the word seems to denote not just an intention but an intention that has already been articulated in language and that has a normative authority. It therefore reflects how language is reappropriated and how one may speak sincerely about one's intention but in language not one's own, and this duly becomes a problem in poetics. Finally, reflecting on a strange contradiction in the writings of Zhu Ziqing's final years, I argue that because of its origins in the context of practical persuasion, the problematic of *zhi* in Chinese poetics can guide the work of the researcher in our time of public knowledge. The complicated history of giving voice to *zhi* offers a conceptual framework for our own moment of intentional speaking.

Zhu Ziqing on Zhi *and on Revolutionary Poetry*

In the twentieth century, Chinese scholars began to write literary histories that were informed by existing traditions and resources and by European approaches. Zhu Ziqing's 1947 monograph *Poetry Bespeaks Intent: An Analysis* (*Shiyanzhi bian* 詩言志辨) is, as the title suggests, a discerning investigation of the motto *shi yan zhi* 詩言志 ("a poem bespeaks the intent") and three other foundational ideas of Chinese poetics, as well as

Search and Intent

how these ideas evolved through reinterpretation in accordance with specific contextual needs over the long history of classical Chinese *shi* poetry writing.[3] Zhu notes in his preface that exposure to Western approaches to literature had been reflected in new histories of Chinese literature, elevating fiction, drama, and literary criticism to near parity with traditionally prestigious forms, such as *shi*. After citing some existing modern histories of Chinese literary criticism, he writes that although he is certainly eager to see efforts of that kind, he is even more eager for there to be "many people separately gathering materials, seeking out the emergence and evolution of every critical concept—seeking out their historical traces." He dreams of a project as painstaking and exhaustive as Qing dynasty Han learning (*Han xue* 漢學) approaches to the Confucian classics, anticipating the meticulous collective work of "combing and picking through" (*pashu tijue* 爬梳剔抉) that will be required in consulting all relevant texts.[4]

Besides *shi yan zhi*, the three other guiding threads or precepts (*gangling* 綱領) Zhu follows are metaphor (*bixing* 比興), *shi*-based political didactics (*shijiao* 詩教), and the dichotomy of "correct" and "changed" (*zhengbian* 正變). The presentation is vernacular and sometimes colloquial, apart from its numerous citations from classical texts. In its ordering and argumentation, it is often reminiscent of literary criticism and literary history as written in Western languages. In every case, the threads Zhu pulls lead to a beginning—a moment when a notion rose to utility and prominence in the explanation of poetic activity, typically through a transformation that obscured original meanings and contexts—and to an extended, philologically inflected review of the varying ways poets and critics remade the notion in constant use over centuries. This approach to literary history feels familiar partly because it proceeds through keywords, going straight to the texts as if searching a corpus and making sense of the results. In the reference to combing and picking through, Zhu implies a sort of public crowdsourcing of research efforts. Concordances were just becoming available at the time, but Zhu already envisions the literary legacy—that massive corpus of inherited texts—as

---

3. Zhu Ziqing, *Shiyanzhi bian*. I am grateful to Xiaojing Miao for reminding me of the importance of this study.

4. Zhu Ziqing, *Shiyanzhi bian*, v.

notionally in the hands of readers and users ready to discover new truths in it. A revisionist impulse to reveal hidden connections and impose a new construction on the history of culture bespeaks a newly activist orientation of author to material and may echo Zhu's reading in Western histories of literary criticism.

Zhu ends his book with some pages on the process by which the word "changed" (*bian* 變) came to have a positive value in accounts of originality and innovation, and on how, in a cyclical alternation of "correct" and "changed" that some literary historians had discerned, "The appearance of New Poetry (*xinshi* 新詩) during the Literary Revolution is truly a case of the 'changed' reaching its extreme and turning point. New Poetry has mainly to do with affective expression (*shuqing* 抒情) and more or less corresponds to the so-called 'elevated airs and distant rhymes' [of the ancients]. It could probably count as a matter of changing and 'returning to the correct.'"[5] With these allusive words, perhaps meant playfully, Zhu identifies the New Poetry of his day with "restoration of antiquity" (*fugu* 復古), in the specific case of the Tang and Song movement and as a general phenomenon in literary historical cycles. Although he addresses ancient *shi*-based political didactics in this account, he makes no space for a politically inflected or efficacious New Poetry in his time. Intent is solely a matter of subjective construction and expression. It is as if earlier uses of poetry such as the Spring and Autumn period (770–476 BCE) practice of recitation (*fushi* 賦詩), with its distinctly practical and political potential, had long since disappeared behind an emphasis on the poet's individual intents and meanings and on the problem of speaking sincerely, politically or otherwise.

In a remarkable departure from this *Shiyanzhi bian* account, in other writings from the same years Zhu was making a place for a very different poetry, "recitational poetry" (*langsong shi* 朗誦詩) as he called it, that he saw as revolutionary and entirely disconnected from poetic occasions and poetic language of the premodern past. In his *Voices in Revolution: Poetry*

---

5. Zhu Ziqing, *Shiyanzhi bian*, 183; compare 173 on "elevated airs and distant rhymes" (*gaofeng yuanyun* 高風遠韻), which was Zhu Xi's 朱熹 (1130–1200) characterization of the quality of antiquity. "Returning to the correct" (*gui yu zheng* 歸於正) (compare 170) alludes to Su Shi's 蘇軾 (1037–1101) description of the effect of Han Yu's 韓愈 (768–824) writings on the world of his contemporaries.

and the Auditory Imagination in Modern China, John Crespi has explored this version of recitational poetry and the "situational poetics" that Zhu espoused during his final years. Recitational poetry presumes performance aloud in the literal presence of live hearers in a group setting, claims to speak directly to and for the audience as a collective, incorporates disparate voices as novels and plays do, and plays on the aesthetic possibilities of real and implied audiences that are ripe for political mobilization.[6] Crespi borrows a metaphor from revolutionary poet He Da 何達 (1915–1994), a favorite of Zhu's: the words of a situational poem are like machine-gun rounds forcing the hearers to action.[7]

A new possibility for the poetic voice is especially important in this form's break with the past. In recitational poetry, Zhu wrote in 1947, "There is no 'I,' only 'we,' and there is no center, only the collective. This is a revolution in poetry, and it can be said also to be a poetry of revolution."[8] As Crespi puts it,

> When set in its immediate historical context, understanding a poem designed for recitation becomes, not a question of what the poem "means" or "expresses," but a question of what it does, that is, how its *tropic structure* reaches into the audience at a specific historical moment and reconfigures the intersubjective network constituted by reciter and audience. . . . Zhu's aesthetics of recitation extended poetic form into a spontaneous and fluid revolutionary moment.[9]

This poetry pointedly projects the circumstances of its reception, diminishing the role of author as individual separate from the collective and emphasizing the mobilizing force of the voice for and from the crowd. In this form, according to Zhu, the atmosphere of the public setting of recitation is key and is characterized by strong emotions rather than tranquil

---

6. For Zhu's allusion to Wen Yiduo's 聞一多 (1899–1946) insistence that new poetry take on the heteroglossia of novels and plays, see Zhu Ziqing, "Jintian de shi" 今天的詩, in *Zhu Ziqing quanji*, 4:501.

7. Crespi, *Voices in Revolution*, 136.

8. Zhu Ziqing, "Jintian de shi," in *Zhu Ziqing quanji*, 4:502. Translation modified slightly from Crespi, *Voices in Revolution*, 140.

9. Crespi, *Voices in Revolution*, 140–41, emphasis added.

recollection. As in theater, there is dialogue, but here it is not contained on the stage but addressed directly across the fourth wall to a mass audience. "The listeners are the mass of people who have something to say," Zhu writes, and the author serves as spokesperson for the audience, whom he envisions as poised on the verge of an explosive, revolutionary political response that the poet's speaking seeks to structure and detonate.[10] He saw recitational poetry as the product of an industrialized and collectivized era and as the future of new poetry, though he also expressed the hope that it would not be the only form to survive. It is a most ambitious vision of the literary speech act.

What shall we make of the rupture implied by Zhu's separate treatment of early recitation in *Shiyanzhi bian* and of revolutionary recitational poetry in other writings? The chapter on "correct" and "changed," with its conclusions on New Poetry of affective expression, was written in the years just before 1947, when he was tracing the replacement of that New Poetry by recitational poetry.[11] Can the latter truly be regarded as disconnected from earlier literary history? If not, where does one search in the earlier stretches of literary history for something like recitational poetry's characteristic engagement with situation and audience? Zhu points to an easy link when, writing about recitational poetry, he recalls that Confucius too had seen a message of undeviating (*wu xie* 無邪) political work as the through-line of the earliest collection of poetry, the *Classic of Poetry* (*Shi jing* 詩經).[12] But Zhu specifies that that kind of poetic exhortation was narrowly directed to scholar-officials while recitational poetry addresses the masses and their revolutionary work.[13] He therefore leaves this connection underdeveloped and identifies no antecedent for contemporary recitational poetry along *Shiyanzhi bian*'s lines of inquiry.

That exclusion was presumably necessary to establish the vision of a truly revolutionary poetry for a time of political and cultural transformation, but as read against *Shiyanzhi bian* it invites new questions about the political status of poetic expression before the rise of revolutionary recitational poetry. Granting that early episodes of recitation were normally

10. Zhu Ziqing, *Lun yasu gongshang*, 48.
11. For Zhu's account of writing the book, see Zhu Ziqing, *Shiyanzhi bian*, viii.
12. *Analects* 2.2; Liu Baonan, *Lunyu zhengyi*, 2.39–41.
13. Zhu Ziqing, *Lun yasu gongshang*, 48.

Search and Intent 27

elite court affairs rather than mass assemblies, we can nonetheless ask how an early reciter's intent was understood to inform the act of recitation itself and to project a "tropic structure" upon the surrounding hearers and their situation. We can further ask how this initial rhetorical and political framing of poetic performance informed later understandings of *shi yan zhi* and prepared the way for Zhu's ideal of recitational poetry. How does language concretize the connection between this speaker's intent and the intents of others, including past speakers and present listeners?

Shi yan zhi *in Persuasive Speech*

The two formulations mentioned above, tags that more than any others have been cited as capturing the relationship between intent and poetry, both appear in ancient works that were canonized during the Han, though in what appear to be relatively late additions to those works. In a *Classic of Documents* (*Shang shu* 尚書) passage that many have read as the earliest reference to *shi* composition, the sage king Shun addresses Kui, commissioning him to oversee music:

> Kui, I command you to be director of music. Teach the descendants' sons to be frank but warm, broad-minded but cautious, strict but never cruel, great but never overbearing. Poems (*shi*) bespeak the intent (*zhi*); singing (*ge*) prolongs speaking (*yan*). The sounds (*sheng*) follow according to the length (*yong*) [of the chants]; the pitch pipes (*lü*) harmonize the sounds (*sheng*). When the eight tones bear the harmony, so that they do not clash with one another, spirits and humans thereby are harmonized.
>
> 夔, 命汝典樂, 教冑子, 直而溫, 寬而栗, 剛而無虐, 簡而無傲. 詩言志, 歌永言, 聲依永, 律和聲, 八音克諧, 無相奪倫, 神人以和.[14]

The text from which the passage is taken, the "Canon of Yao" ("Yao dian" 堯典), is now typically dated to the Warring States period, that is, as late

---

14. Karlgren, "The Book of Documents," 7.

as or possibly later than materials collected in the *Zuo Tradition* (*Zuo zhuan* 左傳), and the command to Kui is one in a series of parallel appointments in an idealized early administration. "Teach the descendants' sons to be" could just as credibly be translated as "In teaching the descendants' sons, be"; the qualities mentioned might equally well be those of the teaching itself or of the desired result, and the ambiguity about the subject may imply that the goal of this teaching is to transmit these qualities from the teachers who embody them to the students. Only a few of these qualities could relate directly to music, but rhetorically, in the balancing of contrasting qualities, the list recalls some other early pronouncements about the music of *shi*.[15]

This treatment of *shi* reads as fundamentally pedagogical in tenor. The relation of *zhi* and *shi* is immediately placed in a musical context, with music representing order in the social and natural world. Parallel construction in the key series of three-character phrases (from "poetry" to "harmonize the sounds") suggests that what is envisioned is an orderly sequence or a mechanism. The parallelism is complex in that on top of a straightforward grammatical pattern in four iterations on the model "poetry bespeaks the intent," a separate pattern emerges, in which the verb of one phrase (e.g., "bespeak," *yan*) becomes the object of the verb in the following phrase ("singing prolongs speaking"). The interlocking effect is marred by the final phrase, where "sounds" rather than "following" (*yi*) is made the object of "harmonize." Nonetheless, there is a sequence, prescriptive or descriptive, that connects an origin in intent (*zhi*) with a *shi* poem that "speaks" and provides words, then with singing that prolongs these words, then with sounds that follow up on the singing, perhaps in accompaniment, with the pitch pipes and musical standards that bring singing and instruments into harmonious order.

The other canonical statement on poetics comes from the "Great Preface to the Mao Recension of the *Classic of Poetry*" ("*Mao Shi* daxu" 毛詩大序), a text tentatively associated with various pre-Han and Han

---

15. See *Analects* 3.20 (Liu Baonan, *Lunyu zhengyi*, 4.116–19), where the first poem in *Shi jing*, "Guanju" 關雎, is "joyous but not to excess, mournful but not to the point of injury," and Ji Zha's comments on a musical performance (including performance of *Shi*) in *Zuo zhuan*, Xiang 29.13. For a translation of the latter reference, see Durrant, Li, and Schaberg, *Zuo Tradition*, 2:1246–47.

Search and Intent

figures and thought to have been completed no later than the time of Wei Hong 衛宏 (fl. first century CE), who may have had a hand in the editing:

> The *shi* is that to which the *zhi* goes. When it is in the heart it is *zhi*, when uttered as speech it is *shi*. An emotion (*qing*) stirs within and takes form in speech; when speaking is not enough (*zu*) one then sighs about it; when sighing about it is not enough one then sings long about it; when singing long about it is not enough, one unknowingly gestures about it with one's hands and dances it with one's feet. The emotion issues forth as sound, and when sound forms patterns it is called tone.
>
> 詩者、志之所之也. 在心爲志, 發言爲詩. 情動於中而形於言, 言之不足, 故嗟歎之, 嗟歎之不足, 故永歌之. 永歌之不足, 不知手之舞之足之蹈之也. 情發於聲, 聲成文謂之音.[16]

For the generations of readers who have—mistakenly, in Zhu's view—read this passage as a guide to the composition of *shi*, the intent, heart, speech, and emotion all belong to the poet, and the *zhi* gives rise to *shi* the way an emotion gives rise to speech and a whole range of nonverbal expressions. In what looks very much like a commentarial move, the text explains the laconic declaration that "*shi* is that to which the *zhi* goes," with its sense of movement and its hint of an etymological or graphic analysis, by tracing a drive from the inception of emotion to its various expressions in and through the body. Separated from the solemn topics of *zhi* and *shi*, this account of *qing* consequences could be a description of music's organizing and communal effects, even trance (*bu zhi*, "unknowingly"), and it comes after a linking of *shi* and *zhi*, just where the "Canon of Yao" offered a more social and cosmic vision of music's role. The image of emotion overflowing one mode of expression after another, until at last it takes over the body and is perhaps exhausted in singing and dancing, may reflect early notions of sufficiency of expression that will reappear.

In the opening pages of *Shiyanzhi bian*, Zhu Ziqing makes the case that in the centuries before the appearance of the "Great Preface," *zhi* was not simply another word for the emotions of the poet. Instead, to the extent

---

16. *Mao Shi zhengyi*, 1.13.

that it denotes personal motives in early works, *zhi* seems to relate specifically to political views and political teachings. Citing the several *Shi jing* pieces that refer internally, as if in the voices of their authors, to the reasons for their composition, Zhu understands these as examples of "presenting" or "offering" poems (*xian shi* 獻詩), where praise or (more commonly) critique addresses a specific situation from a specific subject position. He distinguishes them from *fu shi* recitation, in which the speaker invites a reading of a present situation by performing an existing poem or selection and opening its words to reinterpretation and application.[17] He argues that certain poems, including some in the "Airs" section of *Shi jing*, in early times would not have been thought of as having any teachings or any *zhi* of their own to convey outside of a specific *fu shi* application; preserved solely because of their music, they were later recuperated and connected with *zhi* through the historicist interpretations of the Mao school.[18]

One of the effects of Zhu's rereading is to suggest that in its connections with poetry, *zhi* did not only, always, or primarily denote a psychological or emotional motive for composition. In early times *zhi* may not even have been understood as preverbal or entirely separate from the body of material that would come to be called *shi*.[19] Zhu argues that the graphs *zhi* 志 and *shi* 詩 represented the same word, and the latter appeared during the Zhou to designate a specific sort of *zhi* material that might be "offered" or "presented" in speech.[20] Although *zhi* has a long and complicated association with *shi* behavior and was what noble diplomats were invited to "speak of" (*yan*) through poetic recitation at banquets described in the *Zuo zhuan*, Zhu points out that the graph could also denote "awareness," "knowledge," "aphorism," and "record" or perhaps "didactic record."[21] The declarations that the *shi* is what the *zhi* "goes to" or that the *shi* "bespeaks" the *zhi* may reflect an early sense that the *zhi* gravitates to existing *shi* as its most prestigious and transmissible

17. Zhu Ziqing, *Shiyanzhi bian*, 4–5, 16.
18. Zhu Ziqing, *Shiyanzhi bian*, 26.
19. I admire Steven Van Zoeren's treatment of *zhi* in *Poetry and Personality*, 12–13 and 56–79, but he does not seem to have engaged with Zhu's views on the early history of *zhi*.
20. Zhu Ziqing, *Shiyanzhi bian*, 11–12.
21. Zhu Ziqing, *Shiyanzhi bian*, 14.

Search and Intent

expression.[22] *Zhi*, so clearly associated with pedagogy, normative aims, and didactic language, may overlap with emotion as in the "Great Preface," but it appears that it was understood to have some connection with exemplary verbal activity and with the situational needs of new composition.

As Zhu notes, the formula *shi yan zhi* in "Canon of Yao" echoes and may even have been drawn from *Zuo zhuan*, where ministers of the state of Zheng are asked to recite *shi* poems so that their honored Jin banquet guest can "observe" (*guan* 觀) their *zhi*. In conversation following the recitations, the guest observes that "poems are for speaking of intent" (*shi yi yan zhi* 詩以言志).[23] This contextualization must shift our attention from the role of *zhi* in the original composition of *shi* poems to its role in the use of these poems and in new occasional prose composition, especially speeches.

The uses to which the educated elite of the Spring and Autumn period put *shi* poems are well known, at least if *Zuo zhuan*, *Discourses of the States* (*Guo yu* 國語), and the anecdotes scattered among other Warring States texts are to be trusted. Some children were educated in *shi* as a regular part of their training for adulthood; trading recitations of whole *shi* poems or excerpts from them was common at banquets like the one mentioned above; and many a deliberative speech was built around citations from the *shi*, interpreted and adapted to shed light on the policy issue at hand. *Shi* pedagogy seems to have connected knowledge of *shi* language with effective speech in official interactions. As Confucius is supposed to have said, "He may recite the three hundred *shi* from memory, but if you entrust governing to him and he is not up to it, or if you send him on a mission in some distant place and he cannot make response on his own initiative, then however many he may know, what is he to do with them?" 誦詩三百; 授之以政, 不達; 使於四方, 不能專對; 雖多, 亦奚以爲.[24]

Although Zhu implies it rather than stating it, it seems to have been mainly in connection not with *shi* but with (prose) speaking, especially

---

22. Zhu Ziqing, *Shiyanzhi bian*, 25f., cites passages from *Xunzi* 荀子, *Zhuangzi* 莊子, and other pre-Qin and Han texts that make the *shi* an instrument for speaking the *zhi*, although apparently not through composition of new *shi*.

23. Zhu Ziqing, *Shiyanzhi bian*, 1. See Xiang 27.5a (Durrant, Li, and Schaberg, *Zuo Tradition*, 2:1201–2).

24. *Analects* 13.5; Liu Baonan, *Lunyu zhengyi*, 16.525–27.

32 DAVID SCHABERG

with practical and diplomatic oratory, that the early Chinese developed their ideas about composition. The formulations that were brought together in the "Canon of Yao" and the "Great Preface" echo claims made elsewhere, in connection with a range of practical, occasional compositional activity that might make calculated use of the *shi* corpus but was hardly confined within it.

When Prince Zhao 王子朝, a son of King Jing 景 (r. 535–520 BCE), contended with his brother, King Jing 敬 (r. 519–477 BCE), for the Zhou succession, he sent envoys (*shi* 使) around to the lords of the various states (*zhuhou* 諸侯) to make a proclamation (*gao* 告) of his case.[25] The speech is rhetorically distinctive in that it exaggerates certain tendencies found in many court addresses, showing a more pronounced archaism, a strong preference for a prosody based on four-syllable phrases, and a penchant for generation-by-generation rehearsal of stylized historical precedent. As the words of the speech make clear, these envoys were embodying Prince Zhao in the sense that they spoke in his voice, adopting the first-person pronoun as if referring to him and serving as his bodily representatives or voice transmitters in the capitals of the other states; this body substitution is not unusual in envoy speeches.[26] They would have begun:

In times past, after King Wu prevailed over Yin, King Cheng pacified the four quarters, and King Kang gave the people their ease. Both of them set up their younger full brothers as vassals to serve as a bulwark for Zhou. Indeed, they said, "We would by no means care to enjoy the exclusive possession of the lands won by the achievements of Kings Wen and Wu. What is more, should our successors lose their way and fail, capsizing and drowning in troubles, these men will come to their rescue." When it came to the reign of King Yi, that king suffered a serious illness, and every one of the princes hurried about to offer all the prospect sacrifices in order to pray for the king's health. When it came to the reign of King Li, that king was cruel, and the myriad people could not tolerate him, so they settled the king at Zhi, at which point the princes left their own posts to join the royal gov-

25. As other episodes in *Zuo zhuan* show, it was quite possible just to send a letter. Prince Zhao is clearly thought to have sent an individual or individuals to make this proclamation on his behalf.

26. I have collected some examples in my "Functionary Speech" 19–41.

Search and Intent

ernment. Only when King Xuan reached the age of awareness (*you zhi*) was he given his official position.

昔武王克殷, 成王靖四方, 康王息民, 並建母弟, 以蕃屏周, 亦曰:"吾無專享文, 武之功, 且爲後人之迷敗傾覆而溺入于難, 則振救之."至于夷王, 王愆于厥身, 諸侯莫不並走其望, 以祈王身. 至于厲王, 王心庚虐, 萬民弗忍, 居王于彘. 諸侯釋位, 以間王政. 宣王有志, 而後效官.[27]

Readers of Western Zhou texts, including early portions of *Shi jing*, will hear the echoes of royal and sacrificial rhetoric in this piece. "Pacifying the four quarters" (*jing sifang* 靖四方), for example, is a phrase found in the hymn "Wo jiang" 我將, and there are other touches of archaic usage and form, including the vocabulary of bulwarks (*fan* 蕃) and the pervasive tetrasyllabic phraseology.[28] The diction and prosody do indeed serve to claim for Prince Zhao some of the authority and prestige that is concentrated in speech and texts associated with the old royal court. But they do not separate *shi*-style archaizing language out as if it belonged to another time or another author. Instead, this would-be king and his representatives speak as if this older voice belongs to them in the present, and indeed, it is the medium of many communications relating to the Zhou royal court.[29]

In a remark recounted just after the speech, Lu official Min Mafu 閔馬父 characterizes what the prince has done as "making speech elegant":

Min Mafu heard Prince Zhao's declaration (*ci*) and said, "Speeches (*ci*) are made elegant (*wen*) for the sake of implementing ritual. Prince Zhao has violated the command of King Jing and alienated himself from Jin's greatness in his single-minded pursuit of his own ambitions (*zhi*), and this is a great failure of ritual propriety. What will he accomplish by making his speech elegant?"

閔馬父聞子朝之辭, 曰:"文辭以行禮也. 子朝干景之命, 遠晉之大, 以專其志, 無禮甚矣, 文辭何爲?"[30]

---

27. *Zuo zhuan*, Zhao 26.9 (translation modified from Durrant, Li, and Schaberg, *Zuo Tradition*, 3:1664–65).

28. See Cheng Junying and Jiang Jianyuan, *Shi jing zhuxi*, 857, 945.

29. See my "Speaking of Documents," 320–59.

30. *Zuo zhuan*, Zhao 26.9 (translation modified from Durrant, Li, and Schaberg, *Zuo Tradition*, 3:1666–67). Min Mafu otherwise appears only at *Zuo zhuan*, Zhao 22.5 (Durrant, Li, and Schaberg, *Zuo Tradition*, 3:1610–11), where he predicts that Prince

34   DAVID SCHABERG

"Elegant" here captures only part of the semantic range of *wen*, which stretches from material patterning and decoration to a cultural attainment associated especially with early Zhou rule. "Ambition" is the translation appropriate here for an intention (*zhi*) that is monomaniacal and thus disconnected from the normative intentions of others.

In another episode, Confucius is the one commenting on a piece of elegantly made speech (*wenci* 文辭). Zichan 子產 of Zheng, the head of Zheng's government and stalwart defender of the state against the aggressive interests of Jin and Chu, leads the troops of his state in a successful but unsanctioned punitive attack on Chen. He then justifies the campaign to the leaders of Jin, the head of the alliance, in a speech that is highly formal and full of historical justification and notes of archaism. His Jin listeners are convinced, finding that "his words follow smoothly" (*ci shun* 辭順) and it would therefore be inauspicious to go against them.[31] Confucius comments:

> As the *Records* (*zhi*) has it: "Use words that are adequate to the intent (*zhi*); use elegance (*wen*) that is adequate to the words." Without words, who can know the intent? Words without elegance cannot go far. When Zheng entered Chen while Jin was overlord, there would have been no merit had it not been for elegant speeches (*wenci*). Speeches require the greatest care!
>
> 志有之: "言以足志, 文以足言." 不言, 誰知其志? 言之無文, 行而不遠. 晉為伯, 鄭入陳, 非文辭不為功. 慎辭也.[32]

Zichan's words have restructured the situation for the Jin hearers, who recognize that his good sense—the patent order of his prose and

---

Zhao will not prevail, and in one episode in *Guo yu*, where he comments on ritual practice in covenant ceremonies on the basis of a citation from the Shang hymns (*Shang song* 商頌) section of *Shi jing* (see Xu Yuangao, *Guo yu jijie* 國語集解, 5.205–6).

31. Zhao Dun 趙盾 of Jin has the same response to a brief remark from Zhu leaders. *Zuo zhuan*, Wen 14.8 (Durrant, Li, and Schaberg, *Zuo Tradition*, 1:538–39). Compare the notion of "guiding him with words of instruction" (*dao zhi yi xunci* 道之以訓辭), where because of the early interchangeability of the graphs *shun* 順 and *xun* 訓 we are invited to imagine that the flow and smooth following in the words may be what makes them words of "instruction" or "taming" for their hearers, who are being "guided" (*dao*) in a way that may already imply speaking (*dao*).

32. *Zuo zhuan*, Xiang 25.10 (translation modified from Durrant, Li, and Schaberg, *Zuo Tradition*, 2:1152–53).

Search and Intent

reasoning—is a reason to heed him. This success opens the way for these pragmatic observations from Confucius on the value of *wen*, and this association of Zichan's success with Confucius and *wen* suggests that there is something singularly important about compositions of this kind.

What invalidated Prince Zhao's declaration, in Min Mafu's view, and made all its elegance irrelevant was the disruptive *zhi* ("ambition") that lay behind the words. For Confucius, Zichan's speaking shows the alternative, the matching of words to a laudable *zhi* (here translated as "intent") for the purpose of expressing that intent, and matching elegance to the words for the purpose of making the words "go far." The matching is to be adequate or sufficient (*zu* 足); speaking or ornamentation is calibrated to the purpose at hand, and excess in either is to be shunned. The grammatical parallelism in the *Records* (*Zhi*) passage Confucius cites underscores the aspirational order of the precept: the analogy implied in the couplet (*wen* is somehow to *yan* as *yan* is to *zhi*) suggests that what is envisioned is a sort of mechanism for producing effective prose; the parallelism distantly recalls the series of trisyllables in the "Canon of Yao," but without extending the mechanism to its social or cosmic effects.[33] The terms are far from neutral, given the specific cultural associations of *wen* and possibly of *zhi* itself.

These episodes shift the discussion somewhat. Questions that in the "Great Preface" seem to have squarely to do with original *shi* composition—specifically, questions around motivation, expression, and ornamentation—arise not only in episodes where *Shi jing* poems are cited or recited but in a broader realm of speech activity with a less determinate relation to *shi*. Some of these speeches are referred to as *ci* 辭, which is suggestive of their character. *Ci* can refer straightforwardly to an utterance, a series of spoken words, as it seems to do here, where the Jin leaders find that Zichan's words "follow." More broadly, it designates a class of situational utterances in which words respond directly to a given need, whether in the form of ritually prescribed formulae (*lici* 禮辭) or as high-stakes explanations, especially those given by people declining some offer.[34] Mentions of

---

33. Elsewhere Confucius comments admiringly on the process by which decrees in the state of Zheng were drafted, debated, and finalized, with Zichan applying the final embellishments (*run se* 潤色). See *Analects* 14.8; Liu Baonan, *Lunyu zhengyi*, 17.560–62.

34. For *lici*, see *Zuo zhuan*, Xiang 12.5 (Durrant, Li, and Schaberg, *Zuo Tradition*, 2:996–97).

"elegant" or "patterned" utterances (*wenci*) come typically in connection with ritual elements of governance and sometime imply the concern with implementation and success (*xing* 行) that are also clear in Min Mafu's and Confucius's remarks.[35] Elsewhere, Confucius reiterates the notion of sufficient and effective communication in *ci*: "The words should get across, no more" 辭達而已矣.[36] Later uses of the words *ci* and *wenci*—during the Han sometimes applied to *fu* 賦 (rhyme prose) and to the historical narrative of the *Zuo zhuan*, respectively[37]—may inherit from these early uses the sense of a prestigious performative genre of embellished speech.[38]

Let *ci* stand for all the ways *shi* would have come directly and indirectly into persuasive language, through recitation, citation, and the specific kinds of ideas and forms *shi* exemplified. *Shi* had an important place in the practical affairs of certain Spring and Autumn period officials. As Confucius put it, competence in using *shi* was defined by success in governing at home or in speaking during a mission abroad. The *wenci* said to have been uttered by Prince Zhao's envoys and by Zichan were two examples of such speech, which is represented as arising from and corresponding to a normative *zhi*; as being embellished sufficiently but not excessively; as incorporating or echoing *Shi jing* language, Zhou themes, and archaism in various ways; and as answering a specific political need. In this broader arena of composition, *shi* and high-register language are

---

35. See *Zuo zhuan*, Xiang 25.7 (Durrant, Li, and Schaberg, *Zuo Tradition*, 2:1148–49); Zhao 13.3c (Durrant, Li, and Schaberg, *Zuo Tradition*, 3:1502–3). Confucius's admiration for *wenci* in the context of interstate covenant meeting ceremonies is mentioned at Xiang 27.4b (Durrant, Li, and Schaberg, *Zuo Tradition*, 3:1194–95).

36. *Analects* 15.41; Liu Baonan, *Lunyu zhengyi*, 18.642.

37. See Ban Gu, *Han shu*, 30.1755–56. For *wenci* in the sense of the excesses of *fu* ornamentation, see *Han shu*, 65.2863. Ban Gu also refers to Liu An's 劉安 (179–122 BCE) excellence at writing *wenci* (44.2145), reminding us of Martin Kern's argument that the final chapter of *Huainanzi* may have been presented at court in the form of a *fu* recitation. See Kern, "Creating a Book and Performing It." For *wenci* in reference to the materials of *Zuo zhuan*, see Sima Qian, *Shi ji*, 14.509 and 47.1943.

38. In a compelling study, David Lebovitz has illuminated a broader range of early *shi*-related compositional activity in the form of rhyming tetrasyllables and has argued that narratives in the form of "verse albums" may have influenced the formation of the Mao recension and commentary, with their fundamentally historicizing approach. See his "Historical Poetry, Poetical History, and the Roots of Commentary."

Search and Intent

prestigious artifacts for interested reuse. This recontextualization of pre-existing verbal material, a practice that encompasses recitation, imitation, citation, allusion, and any other detectable echo of earlier text in later, I call *revoicing*.

Read in light of this larger account of persuasive speech, the "Canon of Yao" and the "Great Preface" appear to have taken on notions of the relation between *zhi* and expression that had been articulated in connection with oratory—that is, with the use of *shi* and other tools in persuasion—and narrowed and recast them as having to do with the original composition of *Shi jing* poems. Traces may remain in the "Great Preface," particularly in the perplexing passage on the "six principles" (*liu yi* 六義). This mixed bag of terms makes little sense as a list of the parts of the *Shi jing* or of individual poems, and the variants of the list, applied in slightly different ways to the practices of court music, make the "Great Preface" look like one version among several.[39] In the context of the *wenci* ideas developed already, the six terms appear to name oratorical practices connected with *shi* learning. *Feng* 風 has long been identified with *feng* 諷 or *fengjian* 諷諫 (sometimes written *fengjian* 風諫), "indirect remonstrance." *Fu* 賦 is the recitation of a *shi* or a section thereof for specific oratorical effect, especially but not exclusively for encoding *zhi*, in a setting that requires formal speech. *Bi* 比 is the use of analogy and is attested as a rhetorical and oratorical technique in the *Zhuangzi* 莊子 and the *Han Feizi* 韓非子.[40] *Xing* 興, before all the effort that went into explaining how it could denote the imagistic "stimulus" in a poem, was plainly an effect of speech, perhaps including *shi* citation or recitation, necessarily

39. *Institutes of Zhou* (*Zhouli* 周禮) gives the same list as the "Great Preface," but for the name *liu yi* it substitutes *liu shi* 六詩, which cannot mean "six poems" but must denote something having to do with poems or something one does with poems; see Sun Yirang, *Zhouli zhengyi*, 7:45.1842, under "Music Master" (*da shi* 大師). But compare the entry for "Musician-in-chief" (*da siyue* 大司樂) (6:1724), where well-born young people are instructed, in terms derived from music (*yue yu* 樂語), in the following six activities: *xing* 興, *dao* 道, *feng* 諷, *song* 誦, *yan* 言, and *yu* 語. These activities might still involve *shi*, but they seem to go much further.

40. See the specifically historical approach of "comparing to antiquity" (*shang bi* 上比), explained in the "Renjian shi" 人間世 chapter of *Zhuangzi* (Guo Qingfan, *Zhuangzi jishi*, 1:143) and the more general technique of "linking types and comparing things" (*lianlei biwu* 連類比物) in the "Nan yan" 難言 chapter of *Han Feizi* (Chen Qiyou, *Han Feizi jishi*, 1:1.48).

38 DAVID SCHABERG

in the presence of an audience.[41] *Ya* 雅 was, like *feng* and *song*, the name of a part of the *shi* collection, but in the context of the six principles perhaps related to a markedly archaic way of speech.[42] *Song* 頌 has often been glossed as *song* 誦, to recite from memory.[43]

If the six principles describe ways of speaking that somehow involve the *shi*, then hidden in the "Great Preface" and its apparent account of composition is a fossilized version of an old order of pedagogy in which the student learned to speak with and through the *shi* and at the same time had his *zhi* cultivated through contact with the words he was learning to use.[44] The model depends on speaking aloud the words of the *shi*; the six principles can have their effect only when pronounced aloud in the presence of an audience. To learn *shi* was to cultivate oneself for speech and through speech. Later readings of *shi yan zhi* as an account of private meaning-making in composition tended to obscure this early model, turning moral cultivation into a private and perhaps silent matter of reading and reflection.[45] Still, the pedagogical sense of the voice that cultivates the speaker did survive in Chinese literary practice.

---

41. *Xing* is among the uses of *shi* Confucius mentions at *Analects* 17.8 (Liu Baonan, *Lunyu zhengyi*, 20.689–91), where he encourages his followers to study the poetry collection. There it seems to mean "stimulate," "arouse," or perhaps "encourage." *Analects* 8.8 ("be stimulated by the *Shi*" 興於詩; Liu Baonan, *Lunyu zhengyi*, 9.298–99) frames this stimulation as a phase of self-cultivation. In *Li ji* 禮記, *xing* can mean "to set in motion" ritual dance and music (*xing yuyue* 興羽籥), and it can describe the effect of the words of the *junzi* 君子 (*qi yan zu yi xing* 其言足以興); see Sun Xidan, *Li ji jijie*, 3:49.1273, and Zhu Xi, *Sishu zhangju jizhu*, 36.

42. Confucius is said to have used *ya* speech (雅言) for *shi*, *shu* (writings of the kind associated with *Shang shu*), and conducting ritual (see *Analects* 7.18; Liu Baonan, *Lunyu zhengyi*, 8.269–70).

43. See Jiao Xun's 焦循 (1763–1820) commentary on *Mengzi* 孟子 5B.8, "Is it permissible to recite their *shi* and to read aloud their books, yet not to know their persons?" 頌其詩, 讀其書, 不知其人, 可乎 (Jiao Xun, *Mengzi zhengyi*, 2:16.726).

44. Qian Zhongshu 錢鍾書 (1910–1998) held that *zhi* equally denotes something that has been externalized in set language (as in the "Records" Confucius refers to) and its inner, unformulated, and unspoken form. See Qian Zhongshu, *Guanzhui bian*, 1:173. Although he does not equate *shi* and *zhi* as Zhu Ziqing does, he connects *shi* with *chi* 持 and *zhi* 止 in the sense of self-restraint and emotional discipline, playfully citing lines on the cruel strictness of constraint in later regulated verse; see Qian Zhongshu, *Guanzhui bian*, 1:57–58.

45. Such a consequence would be consistent with the trajectory Jack W. Chen has traced in "On the Act and Representation of Reading in Medieval China."

Revoicing and Zhi

Seen in the light of this reinterpretation of *shi yan zhi*, the situational, revolutionary poetry that Zhu Ziqing came to admire is not without precedent in the tradition. Instead, it is an intensification of that early vision. It is a live performance aiming to spur political action or even transformation, as in the speech of Prince Zhao, the words of Zichan, or an urgent persuasion that relies heavily on language from the *Shi jing*. Situational poetry extends this prospect of political transformation to a mass audience, although Zhu seems to have envisioned this audience in gatherings small enough to witness recitations live. Situational poetry also imagines not a simple change of policy in response to persuasion but a thoroughgoing revolution. It eschews allusion, relying on a new configuration and situational projection of language—"tropic structure," in Crespi's formulation—to shape and evoke the revolutionary possibilities of the situation, that is, to mobilize the hearers to action.[46] Considered in terms of *shi yan zhi*, the rejection of inherited language underscores the connotations of willfulness in the word *zhi*. What the recitational poet recites most certainly asserts a normative political will, but it does so in a revolutionary way, de novo and in a voice made for the moment.

Where the two visions meet is in the questions we have about the voice we hear or read, the actual words that emerge in performance. Is this voice repeating things we have heard before? If so, to what end does it reconfigure them in connection with the situation, and how? Is it, on the contrary, entirely new, something without parallel in anything we have heard before? The speakers in *Zuo zhuan* prized the appropriation and recoding of lines from the *Shi jing*. That strong mode of revoicing, by which a new person in a new situation takes on the precise words of a prestigious and well-known poem and turns them to new and unexpected rhetorical uses, seems to reveal a positive pleasure in and rhetorical advantage to a witty, creative aptitude in reusing language. Revoicing is a way of describing a persistent theme in the longer life of the *shi yan zhi*

---

46. As Zhu Ziqing notes in "Jintian de shi," revolutionary poetry avoids the difficult, idiosyncratic language of tradition poetry and adopts ordinary, natural language. See *Zhu Ziqing quanji*, 4:503–5.

DAVID SCHABERG

idea and, I argue, of thinking about what we do when we do literary history these days.

Episodes of willful revoicing have a special place in influential narrative representations of early Chinese political relations, even where these have little or nothing to do with the persuasive use of *Shi jing* materials. To borrow the terms of Zhu's description of revolutionary poetry, early narratives idealize moments in which an adviser, working through the medium of speech, imposes a strong interpretation on perceived reality and reconfigures it toward a specific political end. For example, the *Zuo zhuan* records that in 534 BCE, "A stone spoke in Jin, in Weiyu" 石言于晋魏榆.[47] The ruler of the state of Jin looks into the news with his court preceptor of music, Shi Kuang 師曠, whose responsibilities seem to encompass not just musical sounds but all things heard abroad in the state.[48] Shi Kuang declares that stones cannot speak and that some entity, a ghost or spirit, might be "availing itself of" or "possessing" the stone (*huo ping yan* 或馮焉) and speaking through it. But he seemingly sets that explanation aside and goes on. If it is not a case of possession, Shi Kuang says, the report must arise from an "excess" or "error" (*lan* 濫) in the people's hearing. Such things can happen, he notes, when the people are pressed into untimely public works projects. *Zuo zhuan* adds that the ruler of Jin was building his extravagant Siqi 虒祁 palace at the time and then cites a Jin contemporary who predicted disasters for the state once the palace was complete.

Often the indirect remonstrance is opportunistic, seizing on an aberration from the norm and slyly insisting on its relevance to the political crisis at hand. But here the figure of speech becomes more literally a figure—of speech itself. In Shi Kuang's explanation, an excess in the people's "hearing" (*ting* 聽) is secondarily an excess in their "heeding" or "obedience," and their credulity is a consequence of their oppression and their exploitation for the Siqi project. Shi Kuang insinuates that this excess in hearing/heeding can produce a corresponding excess in speech: "When grudges and enmities stir among the people," he explains, "then

---

47. *Zuo zhuan*, Zhao 8.1 (Durrant, Li, and Schaberg, *Zuo Tradition*, 3:1436–38).
48. Compare *Zuo zhuan*, Xiang 18.3c, 18.4b (Durrant, Li, and Schaberg, *Zuo Tradition*, 2:1052–53, 1058–59) for similar exercises of hearing.

things that do not speak speak" (怨讟動于民, 則有非言之物而言).[49] What the people cannot say, a stone will seem to say, and even if the stone's words are not transmitted, the fact of the voice itself will convey the complaint. The voice that in the report of the prodigy seemed to originate beyond the human world is made to belong to the people themselves, who through their report possess the stone and use it as their means of expression, and to Shi Kuang, who is able to shape their report as political critique. Something *is* speaking through the stone.

Starting from the figure of the speaking stone, we can imagine a spectrum that stretches from the perfectly disembodied voice, so minimally human that it has only sound and no words, right across to a voice perfectly integrated with and obligated to the body that produces it. Gods and ghosts are fantasies of sense-making without a body, and that may be the point of them. The other extreme, the integrated voice, entirely authentic and sincere, would be a denial of the dynamic of alienation inherent in sense-making. Any system of signification must be capable of signifying apart from, and above and beyond, the body that produces it or the medium that carries it. Anything that can signify must be capable of lying. On one hand, speaking stones and gods; on the other hand, dumb brutes and impossible earnestness. Left in the middle is the whole range of accommodations between real historical voice-producing human bodies and the sorts of things they say. As expressed in Hesiod's *Theogony*, one of the oldest reflections on the voices of poetry, the muses (themselves not human, not real) "know how to speak lies like to truths" and know, too, when they wish, "how to sing true things."[50] Composers and singers always face these questions around revoicing and the unverifiable match of singer and song, the inner intent, and the external signs of it.

The theme of the separable voice and its imagined integration with the historical person of the speaker has figured heavily in recent decades'

---

49. Elsewhere in *Zuo zhuan* (Zhao 22.5, Durrant, Li, and Schaberg, *Zuo Tradition*, 3:1610–11), *feiyan* 非言 means something like "inappropriate language," and *Shi jing*, "Bin zhi chu yan" 賓之初筵 includes the line *fei yan wu yan* 匪言勿言, "inappropriate words should not be spoken"; see Cheng Junying and Jiang Jianyuan, *Shi jing zhuxi*, 701. Shi Kuang's words may somehow echo that *shi* line. More tentatively—and more threateningly to the ruler—Shi Kuang may here hint at something like "unspeakable things are spoken."

50. Hesiod, *Hesiodi Theogonia*, 6 (ll. 27–28), translation mine.

writings on the history of Chinese poetry. Writing about the function of repeated language in the "Daya" 大雅 poems' representations and performances of ritual, Stephen Owen sees the durability of voice as a figure for and practical instrument of cultural continuity, with poetry serving as mnemonic and as orderly image of an orderly social and ancestral hierarchy. "At the top of the social hierarchy is the master, and, above him, the invisible ancestors above him, who fade off toward origins. In the system words play an essential role. Something is complete only if it is declared so. . . . The poem of the rite repeats the cycle in words."[51] In this world and in its poetry, the primacy of the voice approaches a limit. Human singers come and go and, at least in the ideals of the poetry itself, flourish only when they personify the roles prescribed for them. The imaginary subordination of person to voice is strongest in these earliest preserved texts. Whatever else was being sung at the beginning of the Western Zhou, these pieces grew up as the voice of a transgenerational phenomenon, Chinese governance, and were well suited to thrive in its institutions, including pedagogy and writing.

After the "Great Preface" and its recasting of speech-composition's *shi yan zhi* as an account of *shi* composition, the later tradition lived with an awareness of the problem of body and voice, of representing emotions and intents in a new composition that drew somehow, uncertainly, on the poetic language that preceded it. Writing about poetry that purports to be autobiographical, Owen reiterates the idea, derived from the "Great Preface," that *shi* poetry assumes an involuntary bond between the poet's inner life and the poem that is produced. He focuses on the tensions between the inchoate historical self and the limited, determinate roles through which it is enabled to speak.[52] Although he does not dwell on the language available for making these roles, it is clear that the roles are stable because the language has its own continuities and longevity. Elsewhere he writes of the problem of the voice as performance by persona, that is, the voice as something that can in no way demonstrate its own fidelity to the speaking self. In Song dynasty love songs in the form of lyric (*ci* 詞), for example, where paid professionals sing words of love that may or may not represent their true inner feelings, "The genuineness of

51. Owen, "Reproduction in the *Shijing* (*Classic of Poetry*)," 292.
52. Owen, "The Self's Perfect Mirror," 75.

Search and Intent   43

repeatable words is inherently suspect. And yet the song lyric was a form in which repetition in performance was essential."[53] As Owen distinguishes between the *shi*, in which genuineness is assumed, and the *ci*, in which it is a problem,[54] it becomes clear that these two most prestigious genres of Chinese verse were defined, in the world of letters and against each other, by their engagement with revoicing and the voice-body problem.

The moment a real individual speaker chooses and arranges the voices and revoicings that constitute a new utterance—the moment of composition—must be understood as a moment in which the real-world situation supplies the immediate conditions of the literary and rhetorical act's relevance. Scholarly investigations of the moment of composition in recent years have sought to reconnect literary discourse with ordinary language discourse, especially through reflections on the implications of speech-act theory and the development of notions of literary pragmatics. When Hans-Georg Gadamer and Hans Robert Jauss had stressed an abstract notion of dialogue as key to the hermeneutic relationship in general and to literary reception and response in particular, Mary Louise Pratt drew explicitly on the philosopher Paul Grice's treatment of logic in ordinary talk and held up conversation and its conditions of appropriateness as offering fundamental insights into literary discourse. In an apt summary, she writes: "The kind of relation that holds between reader and literary work need not and cannot be viewed as resulting from a suspension of or an immunity to the rules governing other discourse; rather it is a relationship that commonly characterizes discourse outside literature and that must be accounted for by the general rules of talk, rather than by special rules for literary discourse."[55] Publications in the area of literary pragmatism have focused on the "consubstantiality" of literary works with the many other revoicing processes of discourse that surround them and have elaborated how the meaning of the work comes into existence, is created or re-created, only through each new, situated act of reading or other reception.[56] That

53. Owen, "Meaning the Words," 42.
54. Owen, "Meaning the Words," 45–46.
55. Pratt, *Toward a Speech Act Theory*, 149. On dialogue as a model for inquiry in the human sciences, see Gadamer, *Truth and Method*, 356–63.
56. Sell, "Literary Pragmatics," xiv, xxi; Engler, "Textualization," 179–85.

44   DAVID SCHABERG

is, meaning is situated in and contingent on the circumstances of reading or hearing. The attention here (explicitly in Pratt's case) is on use and how literary works serve their purposes by the same means as nonliterary texts and utterances. But the issues of voice and revoicing that Owen treats, the old rhetorical questions of the selection and arrangement of materials, do not seem to come into consideration. The reader's return to speaking and writing after reading is beyond the consideration of this pragmatics.

With considerations like those of Owen in the background, how should we approach the question of composition and practical creativity? It is valuable to consider literary texts from this perspective because these texts always potentially, and often quite literally, train the reader in forms of communication that may be of use to him or her. They show a specific intentional response to the situation of utterance, and (as Confucius saw) their *wen* is a quality built in to make them go far, that is, to survive as distinct, repeatable examples of voice. Figuring the individual literary text as among other things a manual for live human speech and writing (a manual registered in writing or memorization) helps us understand the attractiveness of works in the course of their uptake and transmission while also suggesting a more complete understanding of the hermeneutic act. Beyond the culturally and historically situated moments of a text's original composition, beyond the myriad situated moments of individual readings of that text, there are the productive moments in which earlier voices inform new-made language in some way—through citation, recitation, allusion, imitation, or even plagiarism. This broader field of productivity, of exercising the value of our readings, matters for our understanding of literary activity just as oratory and other *shi*-related speech matter for our understanding of the origins of Chinese poetics.

Walter Benjamin, in his essay "The Storyteller," made a fetish of the living voice and of the tale as a "mouth-to-mouth" transmission of experience. In his world, experience was fast being displaced by information, whose genre is the novel, a form dependent on the technology of printing:

> What can be handed on orally, the wealth of the epic, is of a different kind from what constitutes the stock-in-trade of the novel. What differentiates the novel from all other forms of prose literature—the fairy tale, the legend,

even the novella—is that it neither comes from oral tradition nor goes into it. This distinguishes it from storytelling in particular. The storyteller takes what he tells from experience—his own or that reported by others. And he in turn makes it the experience of those who are listening to his tale. The novelist has isolated himself.[57]

Benjamin argues that storytelling thrives in association with crafts of various kinds: the small-scale workshops where boredom and tedious labor were a standing occasion for telling and retelling experiences. He also notes that for Leskov, the writer he puts at the center of his investigation, storytelling was itself a craft.

If storytelling conveys experience in connection with craft, and if storytelling is a craft, then it must at the very least convey something about itself. More generally, it must teach something about speech: about effective narration and, within narration, effective speech of all kinds. Anyone who listens to a storyteller learns something about what one might say in this or that context, how one might decorate one's speech, how speech might be presented as genuine or exposed as false. Benjamin could not have made this point without undoing much of his sociological and historical model, however, because the novel—whatever its comprehension of the magical category of experience—is a treasury of model speech. Benjamin opens the way for this reading of the novel, but resists it: "It has seldom been realized that the listener's naive relationship to the storyteller is controlled by his interest in retaining what he is told. The cardinal point for the unaffected listener is to assure himself of the possibility of reproducing the story."[58] A few pages later: "A man listening to a story is in the company of the storyteller; even a man reading one shares this companionship. The reader of a novel, however, is isolated, more so than any other reader. (For even the reader of a poem is ready to utter the words, for the benefit of the listener.)"[59] Granting Benjamin's points about the novel's uniqueness and its ties with the age of information, we can still temper his views with a Bakhtinian acknowledgment of the novel's capacious inclusion of voices from across the social scale. The concepts of

57. Benjamin, *Illuminations*, 87.
58. Benjamin, *Illuminations*, 97.
59. Benjamin, *Illuminations*, 100.

heteroglossia and the speech genre imply a vision of the novel that puts it at the frontier between stilled, textualized, composed speech and the impromptu speech of living discourse. If, as Benjamin insists, the hearer of a tale is interested in retaining what was heard, if the reader of the poem is always ready to utter the words aloud, and if novels trade in examples of a particular craft—that of speech—then the novel is not especially divorced from companionship and the world of everyday social interaction.

Given the importance of possible later adaptation and reperformance in this vision of the literary text, one might compare it with a musical score. Although it is silent, it is a trove of sounds that can be reproduced accurately and effectively if you know what you are doing. The literary text tells you what it can about the voices it has captured, and it invites you to take them on in your own voice, for whatever use you might make of them. The training that we begin by sounding out letters and words when we learn to read does not quite end at that stage, and we are also to some extent trained to the longer units: the sentences and the speeches and the narratives we read through. No reading, not even of the novel, can occur without a mental voice, however attenuated and hasty, to test out the words and identify the modulations of tone that make any language richer than its written representation. As it reads, that inner voice learns something about how to speak like the voices in the text, and will have good cause to note and remember those things that are of known or likely pragmatic and situational value for when it is called on to perform under some new set of circumstances.

That literature has thrived, that it has a history at all, owes something to the role of literary works as treasuries of exemplary and distinctive composition that new generations of readers could make valuable for their own uses in their own situated, intentional acts of speaking and writing. Their act of connecting with the past in the course of composition might be conceived of on the model of a hermeneutic dialogue such as Gadamer envisioned, but the implications for composition are that that dialogue and the resulting composition take place in the given situation of what the pragmatists called consubstantiality, that is, in a more or less conscious, situated, observable set of interactions with existing text, including revoicing earlier text. In Shi Kuang's case and in the allusive practice of generations of Chinese writers in the classical tradition, the delight of citation and allusion could lie simultaneously in the connection with past language and in the marked repurposing for present aims.

Shi Kuang is exemplary for our purposes because of his willful, situational handling of a voice. A stone spoke in Jin, or some entity was possessing it and speaking, or the people were hearing voices, or the voice imputed to all of them was Shi Kuang's own voice of critique. Literary works considered in their pedagogical and pragmatic reception are somewhat like the stone and its voice, and readers and users of a text or a corpus are like Shi Kuang, acknowledging at the outset the otherness of that voice but finding ways to adapt it to their own needs. Prince Zhao, Zichan, and other orators of the Spring and Autumn period did something similar in their compositions, taking on for themselves forms of elegance that resonated with earlier texts while speaking to present circumstances. Literature is for learning to speak and, more than that, for learning to speak for oneself, with as much of a voice as one can invoke.

Conclusions: Zhi *and the Literary Historical Thesis*

Zhu Ziqing was intrigued by the possibility of a poetry that would be pragmatic in the strongest sense of that word, that would be a making (*poeisis*) of not just words but worlds. His ideas on recitational poetry reflect a conception of the masses as a field of potential, as the powder that could be ignited by a spark of new poetic speech. The language of this poetry would be colloquial, speakable, separate from poetic language of the past. Its art lay in its connection with the details of the situation in which it was spoken aloud, specifically in the way it could move its hearers to revolutionary action. In marking the language of this poetry as separate from the past, though, Zhu assumes that the form of this activity likewise has no meaningful precedent. He does not look back to the context of *wenci* and other forms of spoken persuasion, in which poems had been used for speaking of a normative intent (*shi yi yan zhi*) long before poets were writing new work with the thought that poems were for expressing their own intents (*shi yan zhi*).

But this ancient oratorical activity truly was the antecedent of recitational poetry as Zhu presented it. It put a speaker before an audience

48 DAVID SCHABERG

in an attempt to speak for that audience in some way, to make that audience—often power-holders—"listen" and "heed" (*ting*), to go with the flow (*shun*) of the words, to find themselves spoken for in the language. Although the early speeches typically upheld ideals of repetition and continuity and showed this orientation by frequently revoicing older language, here too there are continuities on the formal level. What these speeches exemplify is the matching of ancient language, through citation and allusion, with current situations, and the structuring of the reality of these situations through exposure to this language. Zhu's recitational poetry differs in that its voice must be entirely new and its audience the masses gathered as such, but in both cases the glory of the language is its effective normative informing of audience and situation.

The construction of a reasoned representation of something in literary history, whether as narrative or in some other form, whether in a specialized study or in more summary scope, is an act of situated revoicing. It may on some level resemble the revoicings that go on in *shi* under the aegis of a compositional notion of *shi yan zhi*, that is, where the poem is understood to embody the author's or implied author's intent and to do so through an awareness and manipulation of the resources of preexisting voices. But it resembles even more closely the contexts *Zuo zhuan* supplies for our understanding of *shi yan zhi* as a description of and occasional prescription for live speech performance, including prose persuasions. Constructing a historical narrative or any other guide to the materials of the past is a supremely interested, intent-driven, situated act, and its rhetorical character is not diminished in the slightest by its specific methodological principles or their validity. Its interests and intents reflect, perhaps in the structured way Crespi envisions, the moment and setting of its composition and performance, and it aims to reconstruct a situation, both in the sense of capturing it and making it intelligible in language and, very often, with the intent of thus displacing some alternative construction of the situation. The medium is both the new language of the new construction and whatever older language, revoiced as it were, is incorporated into the new construction as relevant and useful to the historian's purpose.

To draw this comparison is to follow Pratt in defying the artificial separation of literary speech from its terroir of everyday speech, and it takes us back to the starting point of this essay. The advances in the accessibility of texts and the power of digital research tools, especially search, have driven all kinds of new extensions of research in the discipline of early Chinese literary studies, and they have brought this specialist research into a global context of knowledge creation and exchange. This new context for specialist work, this new situation for the arguments of literary historians, cannot but be reflected in the approaches and concerns and subjects we adopt, because we cannot help but live in and speak to our own time and because the internet has become the place of consubstantiality, in the literary pragmatists' sense, of our work with public knowledge. As the situatedness of our work makes itself more apparent, the work will come to reflect inwardly the circumstances, opinions, and questions it is answering.

To the extent that literary history is faced with a new rhetorical situation, it will register its own rhetorical character. The intentions specialists have brought to our construction of literary and cultural history will necessarily respond to other intentions and other rhetorical constructions. On the one hand, this confrontation is likely to have an isolating effect, as conclusions founded in the disciplinary constraints of specialists come up against the critiques and alternate conclusions that nonspecialists can easily arrive at on the basis of access and search. The implicit promise of the search window seems to be that a question will bring an answer. That may mean a default to common accounts or a new life for creative and contrarian accounts, but it is unlikely to ensure greater authority and influence for scholarly accounts. On the other hand, the new situation of our work may allow that external setting of argumentation, with all its multiplicity of users and uses, to express itself in the way specialist representations are built. On the level of specifics, these representations will respond to the sorts of claims that are being founded on appeals to early texts and will seek to provide specialist answers to the kinds of questions arising about the past. The external profusion of users and intentions may further lead to specialist representations that support multiple approaches to and interpretations of the historical data and in this way honor the diverse constructions and appropriations of the heritage. Finally, a true consummation of the potential of search would mean the creation of tools that open the legacy to free, interested, intention-driven questioning from specialists and nonspecialists alike, allowing them to reconfigure the legacy through their queries, while still incorporating the kinds of disciplinary strictures regarded as necessary for producing accurate representations. If literary history concerns itself with the reception of a tradition and the handing over of this tradition to the present and future generations, then changes in medium and audience matter, and it will be the specialist's work to build tools to carry the transmission onward.

CHAPTER 2

Ghost Poetry as a Problem for Literary History

Jack W. Chen

To speak of ghosts (*gui* 鬼) is to speak of the souls of the dead who return to haunt the living, a phenomenon that is found across historical periods and cultural traditions. Yet ghost poetry (*guishi* 鬼詩), or poems composed or performed by the returning dead, is a literary phenomenon that—as far as I know—exists only in the classical Chinese tradition.[1] Ghost poetry has been examined previously (and most prominently) by Judith T. Zeitlin in a study that focuses on seventeenth-century literary representations of female ghosts.[2] Her study provides new insight into the gendering of the ghost and the haunting nature of female sexuality across a remarkable range of sources, periods, and disciplinary perspectives. What I propose here is more modest, but I take aim at a broad theoretical issue: how the existence of ghost poetry problematizes the categories through which we conceptualize literary history. For example, what does it mean to attribute authorship to ghosts, that is, to the souls of the dead? Which is to say, what is the concept of authorship if the souls of the dead and the (once) living might both be considered authors? What exactly is this medium of poetry if it may serve as a privileged

---

1. There are poems written in the voices of the dead in other literatures, but these are not treated as poems authored by ghosts in the same way that they are in the Chinese literary tradition. See Linton, "Blithe Spirits."

2. Zeitlin, *The Phantom Heroine*.

communicative form through which ghosts may express themselves? On this point, why isn't there such a thing as "ghost prose" (*guiwen* 鬼文)? This essay examines the ghost as a liminal figure in literary history, the ghost's manifestation as an author of poetry, and the challenge that this poses for the theoretical frameworks and conventional assumptions of literary history.

At the outset, it is important to clarify what is meant by "ghost" in this context, given the range of paranormal entities in the Chinese cultural imagination.[3] Ghosts exist alongside various other kinds of spirits (*shen* 神), daemons (*jing* 精), and weirds (*guai* 怪). *Gui*, the term most commonly used for ghost, shares semantic space with terms for aspects of the soul (*hun* 魂, *po* 魄) and for spiritual intelligence or potency (*ling* 靈). However, ghosts are distinguished from these other categories as deceased souls who have returned to haunt the living. Indeed, one of the early pseudo-etymologies for *gui* derives from *gui* 歸, "to return," in the Han dynasty *Explaining Graphs and Analyzing Characters* (*Shuowen jiezi* 説文解字), where we find the statement, "A ghost is that as which a human being returns" 人所歸爲鬼.[4] This equation of *gui* (ghost) and *gui* (to return) is built on the family resemblance of paronomasia, in which phonetic coincidence becomes semantic necessity, but it nonetheless comes to define the concept of the ghost in traditional China as a revenant.

The question of ghostly return has been theorized by Jacques Derrida, who coined the term "hauntology" (*hantologie*), a portmanteau that

---

3. I bracket the larger question of mapping the Chinese *gui* on to the Western concept of "ghost," as well as the question of how ghosts and *gui* have changed over time and under the influence of various different traditions. For a discussion of how ghosts are represented in early medieval narrative accounts, see Campany, "Ghosts Matter." For a broader discussion of ghosts and fiction, see A. C. Yu, "'Rest, Rest, Perturbed Spirit!'." On ghosts as religious phenomenon, see Poo, "The Concept of Ghost in Ancient Chinese Religion" and "The Culture of Ghosts in the Six Dynasties Period"; and Teiser, *The Ghost Festival in Medieval China*. On ghosts in the early period, see B. Hu, *Believing in Ghosts and Spirits*.

4. Xu Shen, *Shuowen jiezi*, 9A.15a.186. See Schuessler, *ABC Etymological Dictionary*, 267. Note that Schuessler gives *wei* 威 as the primary etymon, based on Childs-Johnson, "The Ghost Head Mask." It should be further noted that Childs-Johnson identifies the etymon *wei* 畏 as primary and only gives *wei* 威 as a variant form.

Ghost Poetry   53

foregrounds the haunted nature of ontology. Hauntology names how the dead/past always returns to haunt the living/present and how the living/present cannot be exorcised of the dead/past. At the same time, its nearly indistinguishable pronunciation from "ontology" (particularly with the French *ontologie*) marks how the ghost is the uncanny double of the living as that which is neither present nor absent, neither now nor past.[5] Indeed, the ghost stands in ambivalent relationship to time, being always out of time, both in the sense of being unmoored from time and in the sense of having no time left, marking a domain that should be our ontological future but haunting our past and our present. That is, as our uncanny double, the ghost reminds us of how we (the living) are also haunted by our pasts, how our present is shaped by pasts that we cannot exorcise, and how we move toward the same future state of death that is the ghost's domain.

There is a ghostliness that also haunts literary history, which depends on its own set of ontological assumptions to construct viable frameworks for classifying and organizing its data.[6] Authorship, genre, and text may seem to be firm, stable concepts at first, but they become ghostlike under scrutiny, phantasmal categories that waver in the light of historical, transmedial, and philosophical analysis.[7] To speak of ghost poetry, then, is to speak of poetry in general, for what marks ghost poetry as ghostly is also already present in poetry. In this way, I am concerned less with the representation of the ghost and more with how attention to the literary production of ghosts forces us to rethink what we take for granted in the tellings of literary historical narrative.

I discuss three examples of early and medieval ghost poetry: the first from the pre-Qin (before 221 BCE) narrative chronicle *Zuo Tradition*

---

5. Derrida introduces the term in *Specters of Marx*. This term has come to define an entire field of cultural theory and aesthetic production; see Fisher, "What Is Hauntology?"; and Blanco and Peeren, *The Spectralities Reader*.

6. See Huters, "Literary Histories."

7. For different statements on authorship, see Burke, *Authorship*. On textual instability in manuscript culture, see Cerquiglini, *In Praise of the Variant*. On the question of genre, consider how recent work on lyric as a genre has emphasized its historical nature, recasting the lyric genre as a process of lyricization. See Jackson, *Dickinson's Misery*.

(*Zuo zhuan* 左傳);[8] the second from a set of Southern Dynasties (420–589) Music Bureau (*yuefu* 樂府) songs that bear the name of an otherwise unknown female singer named Ziye 子夜;[9] and the last, from the Tang dynasty (618–907), an exchange between the Tang Emperor Taizong 唐太宗 (r. 626–649), second ruler of the Tang (often credited as its co-founder), and the ghost of Murong Chui 慕容垂 (326–396), founding ruler of the Later Yan 後燕 (384–407). In many ways, these examples are not exceptional but are illustrative of a not-insignificant corpus of ghost poetry that spans the entirety of the classical literary tradition. Such poems may be said to constitute a minor literature, perhaps not quite in the sense defined by Gilles Deleuze and Félix Guattari of "that which a minority constructs within a major language" with its attendant political program of emancipation, but one that performs a similar kind of deterritorialization, undoing and defamiliarizing the orthodox categories and narratives of literary history.[10]

How Hun Liangfu (Almost) Became an Author

I begin with what might be considered the earliest extant ghost poem, a short text that is recorded in the *Zuo zhuan*. Let me qualify this immediately by noting that this piece is treated as a poem only late in its life, a concession that I will return to later in this section.

In 480 BCE, exiled crown prince Kuaikui 蒯聵 from the state of Wei 衛 plotted with Hun Liangfu 渾良夫, a servant of the Kong family in Wei, to seize the state from Kuaikui's own son.[11] Hun Liangfu made Kuaikui promise that Hun would not be executed unless he committed three capital offenses. But after Kuaikui was installed as the ruler of Wei (he was known posthumously as Duke Zhuang of Wei 衛莊公, r. 480–478 BCE), he had his one-time ally

---

8. The *Zuo zhuan* covers the years 722 to 468 BCE and is dated to the fourth century BCE. It is traditionally treated as a commentary to the *Springs and Autumns* (*Chunqiu* 春秋), though it is perhaps better understood as a related historical work.

9. The genre of *yuefu* poetry is complicated. In English, see J. Allen, *In the Voice of Others*; and Owen, *The Making of Early Chinese Classical Poetry*, 301–7.

10. See Deleuze and Guattari, *Kafka*, 16.

11. This was the fifteenth year of the reign of Duke Ai of Lu 魯哀公 (r. 494–468 BCE).

Ghost Poetry

eliminated on the pretext of having committed three ritual infractions. Two years later, Kuaikui reencountered his former vassal in a dream:

The Lord of Wei had a dream in the northern palace.[12] He saw a person climbing the watchtower atop Kunwu.[13] With unbound hair and facing north, he shouted out:

I climb up this Kunwu ruin,
spreading, spreading grow the gourds.[14]
I was Hun Liangfu,
I call to Heaven that I am without blame.

The lord personally cast a milfoil divination, and Xumi She interpreted it, saying, "No harm." The lord bequeathed him a township, but Xumi She gave it up and fled to Song.

衛侯夢于北宮. 見人登昆吾之觀. 被髮北面而譟曰:

登此昆吾之墟.
縣縣生之瓜.
余爲渾良夫.
叫天無辜.

公親筮之. 胥彌赦占之, 曰: "不害." 與之邑, 寘之, 而逃奔宋.[15]

Ghostly dream visitations are common in traditional China and other parts of the world, and the boundaries between dreaming and haunting are often ambiguous.[16] We recognize Hun Liangfu as a ghost not only because he is fixated on proclaiming his wrongful death but also because

---

12. The "northern palace" is glossed by classicist Kong Yingda 孔穎達 (574–648) as a "detached palace" (*biegong* 別宮). Yang Bojun, *Chunqiu Zuo zhuan zhu*, 17.5.1709.

13. Kunwu is an old name for the region around the Wei capital of Diqiu 帝丘.

14. This line echoes the *Classic of Poetry* (*Shi jing* 詩經) poem "Spreading" ("Mian" 縣; Poem 237), which begins with the lines, "Spreading, spreading, grow the melons, / when the folk were first born" 縣縣瓜瓞, 民之初生. One of the "Greater Odes" (*daya* 大雅), this poem describes the building of the first Zhou capital. See *Mao Shi zheng-yi*, 16.545–51; and Wang Xianqian, *Shi sanjia yi jishu*, 21.834. I discuss this image later.

15. Yang Bojun, *Chunqiu Zuo zhuan zhu*, 17.5.1709. This is also translated in Durrant, Li, and Schaberg, *Zuo Tradition*, 3:1959.

16. See Campany, *The Chinese Dreamscape*; Wing, Lee, and Chen, "Sleep Paralysis in Chinese"; and Lohmann, "The Night I Was Attacked by a Ghost."

of his unbound hair.[17] Yet Kuaikui, who should know full well why his former retainer has returned to haunt him, suspects that there is more to this. He personally casts a divination that he then orders the divination scribe Xumi She 胥彌赦 to interpret. Xumi She realizes that this haunting is an omen that portends the fall of Kuaikui and, fearing for his own life, lies about the meaning of the dream and flees to Song. The *Zuo zhuan* goes on to relate the destruction of Kuaikui, who is ousted during an attack by the state of Jin at the end of that year.

What Hun Liangfu says to Kuaikui is presented by the verb *zao* 譟 (to shout, or as a noun, noise), a word not typically used for poetic compositions. Yet the "shout" clearly belongs to the small corpus of rhymed pieces, songs, and couplets preserved in the *Zuo zhuan* and other early texts. David Schaberg has pointed out that these "non-canonical songs of the Warring States and Han periods . . . closely resemble songs in *Shijing* or *Chuci*, sharing prosody, diction, and themes," but they are almost always "shorter than the typical *Shijing* or *Chuci* song."[18] Hun Liangfu's shouted utterance is indeed short, but it is prosodically rougher than most pieces in the *Classic of Poetry* (*Shi jing* 詩經). Four lines are distinguishable by the end-rhymes (*xu* 墟, *gua* 瓜, *fu* 夫, and *gu* 辜), which conform to a rhyme scheme of AAAA and belong to the reconstructed Old Chinese rhyme category of *yu* 魚.[19] The lines are irregular in length, consisting of syllabic counts of six, five, five, and four. There is one other dream composition in the *Zuo zhuan*, and it is similarly brief (four lines), with irregular syllabic count (four, five, four, and six) and a monorhyme (rhyme category of *wei* 微). However, this is explicitly marked as sung (*ge* 歌) by

17. Mark Edward Lewis points to "the wearing of hair unbound (*pi fa* 被髮)" as signaling "figures outside the human community: barbarians, madmen, ghosts, and immortals"; Lewis, *Flood Myths of Early China*, 89. For a more sustained treatment of unbound hair, see Brindley, *Ancient China and the Yue*, 143–49.

18. Schaberg, "Song and the Historical Imagination in China," 321–22. Also see various studies on the relationship between poetry and the *Zuo zhuan*, such as Tam, "The Use of Poetry in *Tso Chuan*"; Schaberg, *A Patterned Past*, 234–43; Sanders, *Words Well Put*, 29–72; and Nienhauser, "Qing Feng, Duke Xian of Wey, and the *Shijing*."

19. See the entries for *xu* 墟, *gua* 瓜, *fu* 夫, and *gu* 辜, respectively, in Wang Li, *Wang Li gu Hanyu zidian*, 167, 729, 178, and 1414. Wang Li divides Old Chinese rhymes into twenty-nine categories, relying on evidence from the *Shi jing*; see his *Shi jing yundu*.

Ghost Poetry 57

the dreamer himself, who also treats the experience as an omen and meets his death soon after.[20]

As for the content of what Hun Liangfu shouts, the statement begins by locating the speaker in space, as climbing up "this Kunwu ruin," a site identified by the *Zuo zhuan* as a watchtower near Kuaikui's northern palace. Hun Liangfu's use of the term *xu* 墟 in place of *guan* 觀 follows the rhyme scheme and might refer to the hill on which the tower is presumably set (*xu* meaning "earthen mound"), but given the ghostly context, it might also refer to the current or future ruined state of the watchtower. The second line introduces the image of growing gourds, with the reduplicative *mianmian* 綿綿 phrase found in the opening couplet of the *Shi jing* poem "Spreading" ("Mian" 綿; Poem 237).[21] On this image and its function in Hun Liangfu's utterance, the late Ming playwright Mei Dingzuo 梅鼎祚 (1549–1615) wrote:

> "Spreading, spreading grow the gourds" is when it [the gourds/enterprise] first grows. Liangfu is praising himself for how he achieved a great deed from a small [beginning]. This is just like when a gourd first grows, and it refers to how he made it possible for the Lord of Wei to obtain the kingdom. Originally [the Lord of Wei] had a compact pardoning [Liangfu] for three capital offenses, but [the Lord] added up what were the events of a single incident and killed him. Therefore [Liangfu] said of himself that he was "without blame."
>
> 綿綿瓜, 初生也. 良夫善己有以小成大之功, 若瓜之初生, 謂使衛侯得國也. 本盟免三死, 而并數一時之事殺之. 故自謂無辜.[22]

Thus, by evoking this particular topical image, which is connected to the establishment of the Zhou, Hun Liangfu is paradoxically insisting on his role in establishing Kuaikui and foretelling Kuaikui's destruction. Hun Liangfu concludes by revealing his identity and protesting his blamelessness.

---

20. This dream song is found in the seventeenth year of Duke Cheng (574 BCE). See Yang Bojun, *Chunqiu Zuo zhuan zhu*, 17.8.899; and under the title "Dream Song" ("Meng ge" 夢歌), in Lu Qinli, *Xian Qin Han Wei Jin nanbeichao shi*, 7.

21. See note 14.

22. Mei Dingzuo, *Caigui ji*, 1.2–3. See also the comments on Mei's anthology in Zeitlin, *The Phantom Heroine*, 6, 77–78.

It is worth noting that the great Song dynasty (960–1279) encyclopedia *Imperial Digest of the Taiping Era* (*Taiping yulan* 太平御覽) includes this story under three categories: "Inauspicious Dreams" ("Xiongmeng" 凶夢), "Milfoil Divinations" ("Shi" 筮), and "Spirits and Ghosts" ("Shen gui" 神鬼).[23] The informatic ontologies of the *Taiping yulan* do not require that the dream be sorted into one category to the exclusion of others, but rather represent metatags that identify the episode as belonging to different overlapping contexts: a ghostly visitation that takes the form of an inauspicious dream and requires divinatory interpretation. Another major Song dynasty encyclopedic compilation, the *Historical Exempla from the Storehouse of Volumes* (*Cefu yuangui* 冊府元龜), includes the episode, though only under the category of "Dream Portents" ("Mengzheng" 夢徵).[24] As encyclopedic works concerned primarily with organizing textual material into normative categories, neither the *Taiping yulan* nor the *Cefu yuangui* is particularly interested in the relationship between the ghost of Hun Liangfu and what he shouts out—which is to say, between the author and the text the author produces.

If I have refrained thus far from referring to this shouted utterance as a poem, it is because I am mindful of how, despite its rudimentary literary qualities, it remains noncanonical (in Schaberg's words) for much of the tradition. By this I mean that the utterance is not treated as a literary text and thus does not belong to the literary canon, broadly understood. Once Mei Dingzuo includes the piece in his anthology *Record of Talented Ghosts* (*Caigui ji* 才鬼記; preface dated 1605)—a collection of sixteen scrolls' worth of anecdotes and tales about poetry-composing ghosts from the pre-Qin period to the Yuan and Ming dynasties—what had simply been a rhyming shout by Hun Liangfu's ghost is now a poem. Moreover, the poem nicely fits the orthodox model of poetic interpretation articulated by the "Great Preface to the Mao Recension of the *Classic of Poetry*" ("Mao Shi daxu" 毛詩大序), presumably completed in the first century CE, where the poem (*shi* 詩) is the means by which what is on the speaker's mind (*zhi* 志, "fixed intention") is articulated.[25] In other words, by anthologizing Hun Liangfu's shout alongside other poems,

---

23. Li Fang et al., *Taiping yulan*, 400.1846b, 727.3222a, and 883.3921b.
24. Wang Qinruo et al., *Cefu yuangui*, 892.10554b.
25. *Mao Shi zhengyi*, 1.13. See Schaberg, chapter 1 in this volume.

the hermeneutical framework for the shout is transformed from that of a dream omen to the autobiographical expression of a wrongly executed retainer who relies on poetic form to say what cannot remain unsaid.

The *Caigui ji*—perhaps more than any other classical work of scholarship—is responsible for the literary historical construction of ghosts as authors, although, like the Song encyclopedic works before it, what it collects are anecdotes about poetic ghosts and not just the poems. That is, the ghost poems are not presented as stand-alone literary works but as embedded in narrative accounts that showcase ghostly poetic talent. Nonetheless, by organizing these anecdotes by ghost (rather than by topic), the anthology elevates the ghost to the level of informatic ontology. In many ways, the organizational structure of the *Caigui ji* anticipates the massive comprehensive anthology projects of the Qing (1644–1912), the most prominent of which was the *Complete Tang Poems* (*Quan Tang shi* 全唐詩). For this Qing anthology, ghost poems were collected *qua* poems, and the ghosts therefore were represented as authors, even as a certain sense of unease with the uncanny nature of ghostly authorship was evidenced in how the *Quan Tang shi* separated ghost poets (and other marginal authorship categories) from the main body of male poets of public record.[26]

We see a version of this discomfort over authorial ontology in modern scholar Lu Qinli's 逯欽立 (1910–1973) definitive anthology of pre-Tang verse, which arranges poetry by historical periods and lists works by author whenever possible. It is not surprising that Lu Qinli includes Hun Liangfu's piece, given the goal of the project to collect every scrap of poetry prior to the Tang, but he does not assign the piece to Hun Liangfu as author, instead including it under Mei Dingzuo's title, "Hun Liangfu zao" (without acknowledging Mei Dingzuo).[27] Indeed, Lu Qinli sidesteps the question of authorship for all pre-Qin poetry—anonymous songs and folk verses, and pieces that have speakers associated with them—in presenting them by title (or assigned title), rather than by the poem's composer. It is as if authorship cannot quite be granted to pre-Qin figures, who might make rhymed statements, sing songs, or recite poems but do not own the words they utter.

---

26. On the *Quan Tang shi* and its organizational logic, see Broadwell, Chen, and Shepard, "Reading the *Quan Tang shi*."

27. Lu Qinli, *Xian Qin Han Wei Jin nanbeichao shi*, 51.

Taking an even broader perspective on this issue, Stephen Owen has written that authorship "must . . . involve a claim that the particular words belongs to a specific person and are not merely one possible articulation of a general truth."[28] The complication for ghosts in regard to authorship has everything to do with the ghost's hauntological condition, with what it means for a ghost to have ownership over its words. However, as Owen also points out, "it is sometimes useful to think of the ascription of authorship as a property of a text." For example, in considering whether an early *yuefu* poem is by Eastern Han writer Cai Yong 蔡邕 (132–192) or if it is an anonymous composition, "the issue may not be deciding if Cai Yong was indeed the author; rather, we might ask what is at stake in these different descriptions ('Cai Yong' or 'old lyrics') appended to the title."[29] What Owen points to is how authorial ascription (and its absence) sets the hermeneutical parameters of a text and frames its literary historical possibilities. However, it remains unclear what it then means for a poem to be assigned to a ghost, for a ghostly author to be a property of the poetic text. The problem of the ghost is not only that it can be both an author and a nonauthor, that it is both in and out of literary historical temporality, but that it calls into question the stability of authorship as a property of the text in the first place.

Literary Subjectivity in the "Ziye Songs"

The question of authorship emerged with some urgency in the post-Han period, not least because of the anthological and encyclopedic projects that required coherent systems of organization. Authorship was a convenient means by which to group texts, although it was not the only one. Zeitlin, drawing on Michel Foucault, has addressed the historical emergence of authorship in the early medieval period as follows:

> In the case of Chinese lyric poetry, the need for a firm attribution to an individual author emerged during the Six Dynasties but solidified during the Tang. Once the "Author-function" had become required for lyric poetry, a

28. Owen, *The Making of Early Chinese Classical Poetry*, 214.
29. Owen, *The Making of Early Chinese Classical Poetry*, 215–16.

Ghost Poetry   61

development accompanied by the rise of occasional verse, it was no longer enough simply to know the author's name; it became imperative to know the circumstances behind the production of a poem. When these circumstances were not spelled out in the title or preface to a poem, they had to be discovered or invented. Hence the emergence during the Tang of a rich anecdotal literature to fill in the missing context behind a poem's composition.[30]

Zeitlin argues that the attribution of ghostly authorship was a function of the requirements of poetic interpretation, a retroactive discovery of the circumstances underlying the composition of otherwise uncategorizable poems. Yet the pairing of ghost anecdotes and ghost poetry can be seen already in the fourth through sixth centuries, which spans the Eastern Jin 東晉 (317–420) through the Liang (502–557), most prominently in the corpus of strange tales known as *zhiguai* 志怪 (anomaly accounts), though also elsewhere, attached to certain anonymous traditions of poetry.

Let me turn to one such poetic tradition, the "Ziye Songs" ("Ziye ge" 子夜歌). These songs comprise the largest group of the "Wu Melody Songs" ("Wusheng ge" 吳聲歌), the *yuefu* tradition that was associated with the region around the Southern Dynasties (420–589) capital of Jiankang 建康 (modern-day Nanjing), the lands of the former kingdom of Wu 吳.[31] Related *yuefu* traditions include the two "Greater Ziye Songs" ("Da Ziye ge" 大子夜歌) and the several versions of the "Ziye Songs of the Four Seasons" ("Ziye sishi ge" 子夜四時歌). While the word *ziye* means "midnight," it was traditionally understood to refer to the name of the girl who first composed the songs (though both meanings could and probably did coexist). As the eminent poet and historian Shen Yue 沈約 (441–513) relates in the "Treatise on Music" ("Yue zhi" 樂志) of his *History of the Song (Song shu* 宋書):

> As for the "Ziye" songs, this music was composed by a girl named "Ziye" [Midnight]. During the Taiyuan Reign [372–396] of Jin Xiaowudi, Wang Kezhi of Langye's house had a ghost [or ghosts] who sang the "Ziye Songs." When Yin Yun governed Yuzhang, in the Yuzhang émigré Yu

---

30. Zeitlin, *The Phantom Heroine*, 63.

31. On the topic of the south, Qiulei Hu has persuasively connected the exoticizing and erotic fantasies of northern emigrés regarding the freely displayed charms of local southern girls to a concurrent anxiety regarding ghostly singing maidens. See Q. Hu, "From Singing Ghosts to Docile Concubines."

Sengqian's house there was also a ghost [or were also ghosts] who sang the "Ziye Songs." When Yin Yun governed Yuzhang, it was also during the Taiyuan Reign. Thus Ziye was a person who lived prior to this time.

子夜歌者, 有女子名子夜, 造此聲. 晉孝武太元中, 琅邪王軻之家有鬼歌子夜. 殷允爲豫章時, 豫章僑人庾僧虔家亦有鬼歌子夜. 殷允爲豫章, 亦是太元中, 則子夜是此時以前人也.[32]

This story is also mentioned in the "Treatise on Music" (also "Yue zhi" 樂志) in the *Old History of the Tang* (*Jiu Tang shu* 舊唐書), which states, "The songs of Ziye were Jin melodies. During the Jin, there was a girl named 'Ziye' who composed this music; the music was excessively sad and bitter. In the Jin, there were often ghosts who sang them" 子夜歌者, 晉曲也. 晉有女名子夜造此聲, 聲過哀苦, 晉日常有鬼歌之.[33]

Shen Yue's discussion makes it clear that nothing is known of Ziye beyond the fact of her composition of the songs, making her something of a ghost in literary history, suspended between named authorship and effective authorial anonymity. Moreover, she is never treated as the author in later anthologies that collect these songs; her relationship to the corpus is only marked in the titling of the songs as "Ziye Songs." Because the ghostly performance of Ziye's songs took place during the Taiyuan reign (a reign period in the second part of the Eastern Jin), Shen Yue supposes that Ziye must have lived before this. However, the ghostly reperformance of Ziye's songs is what make these poems relevant here. Though the Tang account is more cursory, it supplies an explicit motive for why the ghosts would attach themselves to Ziye's music, which was the "surpassing" (*guo* 過) sense of sadness. As these Wu songs are traditionally classified as *yuefu* songs, in which the speaker of the poem is not understood as the author but as a typological figure, the songs do not represent the personal voicings of a fixed intention (*zhi*). Yet even though the ghosts do not author the songs, they nonetheless rely on the songs, borrowing Ziye's music and language to manifest themselves in the world and articulating a kind of affective intentionality shared with Ziye.[34]

32. Shen Yue, *Song shu*, 19.549. On Shen Yue's writing of the *Song shu*, see Mather, *The Poet Shen Yüeh*, 26–36.

33. Liu Xu et al., *Jiu Tang shu*, 29.1062.

34. On the need for ghosts to manifest themselves through a medium, see my essay "Poetry, Ghosts, Mediation."

Ghost Poetry 63

If the ghostly narrative is bracketed, we might note that Shen Yue's dating of the poems to the Eastern Jin probably reflects a desire to assign relatively early dates to what were anonymous poems. Indeed, as Guo Maoqian 郭茂倩 (fl. twelfth century) in his comprehensive *Collection of Music Bureau Poetry* (*Yuefu shiji* 樂府詩集) speculates, the set of poems probably evolved over the course of the Jin, Song, and Qi dynasties, and together represent a cumulative musical tradition, rather than a single poem cycle. It should also be noted that Shen Yue does not include the texts of the poems in his "Treatise on Music." Rather, Guo Maoqian first identified and collected the poems as a set of forty-two pieces. The lateness of this assemblage raises questions as to the transmission of the texts and the historical construction of the pieces as a poetic tradition.

A handful of examples from the corpus of forty-two "Ziye Songs" should provide a sense of why these poems might have been identified as being sung by ghosts. Unrelated to the topic of ghosts, these poems are marked by a prominent usage of puns, such as *si* 絲 for *si* 思. These are glossed in parentheses in the translations.

子夜歌 (四十二首)　　Ziye Songs (Forty-Two Poems)

I

落日出門前,	As the sun set, I went out before my gate,
瞻矚見子度.	gazing out afar, I see you cross.
冶容多姿鬢,	Bewitching face, gorgeous hair,
芳香已盈路.	fragrance already fills the road.

II

芳是香所爲,	As for fragrance, this is what perfume creates,
冶容不敢當.	"bewitching face"—I dare not assume.
天不奪人願,	Heaven does not snatch away one's wishes,
故使儂見郎.	thus it allows me to run into you.

VIII

前絲斷纏綿,	Previous silk [longing] breaks off from its continuous spooling [abiding passion],
意欲結交情.	but in my heart I want to form an attachment.
春蠶易感化,	Spring silkworms easily are moved to change,
絲子已復生.	Silk [longing] is already being produced again.

XXIII

誰能思不歌,	Who can long but not sing out,
誰能饑不食?	who can be hungry but not eat?

日冥當戶倚，	The sun darkens, by the door I lean,
惆悵底不憶?	full of gloom, how can I not think of him?

XXIX

歡從何處來?	My love—where does he come from?
端然有憂色.	so serious, he has a worried look.
三喚不一應，	I called thrice but got nary an answer,
有何比松柏?	how is this like "pine and cypress"?

XXXIII

夜長不得眠，	The night was long, I could not sleep,
明月何灼灼.	The bright moon—how dazzling it was!
想聞散喚聲，	I thought I caught the sound of someone calling,
虛應空中諾.	In vain I answered "Yes!" to the emptiness.[35]

As Xiaofei Tian has noted, many of the "Ziye Songs," like many of the southern *yuefu* compositions, were "paired songs" (*duige* 對歌).[36] This can be seen in the first two songs, which present male and female perspectives on a passing encounter, as well as in the eighth song, which puns on spinning silk (*si* 絲) and longing (*si* 思). The poems may be considered antiphonic, which complicates the authorial construction of the "Ziye Songs" as being in the voice of a single disappointed singer, particularly if one assumes that the feelings conveyed in the songs are the girl's personal feelings.

However the question of authorship is resolved (or not), the more interesting issue is the transference of these songs from Ziye to the ghosts who sing them during the Taiyuan reign of the Eastern Jin, which is to say, from their vague association with a mortal female composer to ghostly performers of the music. Of the forty-two songs, only the twenty-ninth makes a possible reference to death, with the "pines and cypress" (*songbo* 松柏) serving as a metonymy for steadfast love and for the grave, by which pines and cypresses were often planted. There is no way to know whether the lyrics are those sung (and presumably composed) by Ziye, yet the depth of longing and sorrow in the poems lends themselves to a hypothetical narrative that is

---

35. See Guo Maoqian, *Yuefu shiji*, 44.641–44; and Lu Qinli, *Xian Qin Han Wei Jin nanbeichao shi*, 1040–42. It should be noted that the last two poems of this set are also attributed to Xiao Yan 蕭衍 (464–549) (Liang Emperor Wu 梁武帝, r. 502–548). See Lu Qinli, *Xian Qin Han Wei Jin nanbeichao shi*, 1516.

36. Tian, *Beacon Fire and Shooting Star*, 360–62.

not provided in Shen Yue's account: one in which the separation from her beloved proved too much for the singer, and she either died of sorrow or took her own life. Indeed, this quality of sadness is hinted at by the *Jiu Tang shu*, which notes how "the music was surpassingly sad and bitter," as if explaining the transition from the woman Ziye to the ghosts who "often" (*chang* 常) performed the songs during the Jin. That is, even if the original feelings of the singer were not authentically those of the girl, the sadness expressed in the songs have an authenticity of their own. This representation of feeling can provide a communal medium—a common language—through which ghosts might express their own bitterness and loss.

I would argue that what the "Ziye Songs" represent is an allegorization of how subjectivity is produced in poetry. Just as ghosts may inhabit a living human's heartfelt lyrics, so can we as readers of the poems. That is to say, there is no difference between a ghostly borrowing of a poem and the empathetic recitation of the poem by a reader who is moved by Ziye's song. In a sense, it does not matter that ghosts take possession of these songs (or perhaps one should say the songs possess the ghosts). The capacity for the poem to be transferred from one consciousness to another is what constitutes literary subjectivity, which, in Michel Zink's words, is "not spontaneous display or real expression in a text of an author's personality, opinions, or feelings, but rather what marks the text as the point of view of a consciousness."[37] That is to say, the poem does not belong to a particular author but is authored anew each time it is performed, activating the subjectivity in the poem, whether it be as a living reader or as a ghost. Indeed, poems in later traditions of the "Ziye Songs" troped on precisely this relationship between Ziye as the subject of authentic emotion and the subject who, moved by Ziye, reperforms her words.

How Murong Chui Became a Tang Poet

I end with an anecdote about Taizong (Li Shimin 李世民, 599–649), the second emperor of the Tang dynasty, who spent the last part of his reign in a futile campaign to conquer the Korean peninsula. The story features

---

37. Zink, *The Invention of Literary Subjectivity*, 4.

66   Jack W. Chen

a poem by Murong Chui, a prince and powerful general during the Former Yan 前燕 (337–370) and afterward founder of the Later Yan dynasty. This anecdote reads:

> Tang Taizong went on campaign in Liaodong, faring as far as Dingzhou [in modern Hebei]. By the side of the road was a ghost who was wearing yellow clothes and standing atop a burial mound; its expression and demeanor were quite exceptional. Taizong dispatched someone to question it, and the ghost replied:
>
> > My past triumphed over your past,
> > Your present triumphs over my present.
> > Glory and splendor change with each age,
> > What use is there in striving to pursue it?
>
> When he finished speaking, he vanished. Taizong inquired about this, and it turned out to be the tomb of Murong Chui.
>
> 唐太宗征遼, 行至定州. 路側有一鬼, 衣黃衣, 立高冢上, 神彩特異. 太宗遣使問之, 答曰: "我昔勝君昔, 君今勝我今. 榮華各異代, 何用苦追尋." 言訖不見. 問之, 乃慕容垂墓.[38]

The anecdote is minimal; it serves only to frame the quatrain the ghost communicates to Taizong. The full significance of the encounter requires some elaboration, particularly in regard to the historical circumstances of the Tang emperor and his ghostly counterpart, Murong Chui.

Murong Chui lived during the Sixteen Kingdoms Period (302–439), when the Jin had lost the northern heartland and fled south across the Yangtze River, leaving its former territories in the hands of the so-called Five Barbarian Tribes (*wuhu* 五胡). This was an age of turbulence and constant warfare, as the various northern potentates struggled over control with each other, as well as with the Eastern Jin, which harbored designs to retake their former territories. Murong Chui's life was complicated,

---

38. In Li Fang et al., *Taiping guangji*, 328.2601, which attributes the tale to the *Collection of Spirits and Strange Matters* (*Lingguai ji* 靈怪集), a compilation edited by Zhang Jian 張薦 (744–804) that has not survived intact (though it has been reconstituted from extracts in encyclopedic works). For a bibliographic summary of the *Lingguai ji*, see Ning Jiayu, *Zhongguo wenyan xiaoshuo*, 53. Also see *Quan Tang shi*, 865.9777, which provides a very slightly different anecdotal frame.

Ghost Poetry

67

involving early military victories against the Later Zhao 後趙 (319–351) and power struggles within the Former Yan ruling house that led to him taking refuge with Fu Jian 符堅 (337–385), ruler of the Former Qin 先秦 (350–394). He soon rebelled and established his own dynasty, the Later Yan 後燕 (384–407), reigning as Emperor Chengwu 成武 (r. 384–396). Murong Chui was ethnically Xianbei 鮮卑, and his state occupied the territory that is approximately equivalent to modern Shandong. In 369, Murong Chui led his troops to resounding victory over the invading Eastern Jin armies commanded by the great general and statesman Huan Wen 桓溫 (312–373). However, the Former Yan was then conquered by the Former Qin, which managed to unify the north. About 250 years later, in 644, Taizong initiated a costly expedition against Koguryŏ, passing through Liaodong on the way to the Korean peninsula.

The poem embodies the kind of encounter between the living and dead that one finds in the medieval European *topos* of "les trois morts et les trois vifs," referred to in English as "the three living and the three dead princes."[39] The purpose of the encounter is to issue a *memento mori* ("remember that you will die"), to the heedless living, almost always a man or men of high-born status. This is, in short, the message that Murong Chui wishes to impart to Taizong. Murong Chui once stopped the Eastern Jin's dreams of reconquering the north and unifying the empire, but now lies forgotten in a tomb by the side of the road. In 644 Taizong was at the height of his power, having pacified the Turkish nations who are treated as the descendants of the Xianbei dynasties. He was also about to engage in a war that eventually led to his own death. Not surprisingly, Taizong does not understand Murong Chui's warning, which is not only a general reminder of the temporal nature of empire but also more specifically of Taizong's own imminent defeat.

The poem is a general statement—a common warning about the fleeting nature of temporal glory—and a specific warning, signifying only if the speaker is a posthumous ruler of a past historical period speaking to the living ruler of a present historical period. The pairing of Murong Chui and Tang Taizong is uncannily apt, given how the Tang dynasty was a northern dynasty that managed to last beyond a third reign (something that would not have been known to Taizong when he

---

39. See Todd, "Apropos of the Trois Morts et Les Trois Vifs," 58–59; Storck, "Aspects of Death in English Art and Poetry," 314–19; and Binski, *Medieval Death*, 134–37.

marched on the Korean peninsula), and the ruling Li clan were themselves of mixed Xianbei/Han descent. Whereas Kuaikui should have recognized Hun Liangfu in his dream (and it is somewhat odd that he doesn't), here Taizong has no reason to recognize this ghost and has to send someone to find out the ghost's identity afterward. The encounter must have been extremely puzzling to the Tang sovereign—again, such is the fleeting nature of worldly glory and power.

While the anecdote was known by the Song dynasty (960–1279), Murong Chui does not become an author, nor his poetic warning a "poem," until much later in the tradition. Like Hun Liangfu's rhymed shout, Murong Chui's poem and its contextualizing anecdote are included in Mei Dingzuo's *Caigui ji*, but the name "Murong Chui" is given as the informatic categorical heading, suggesting that the ghost of Murong Chui has become an author in a way that Hun Liangfu was unable to.[40] This subtle ontological shift is carried forward by the *Quan Tang shi*, in which Murong Chui is listed as author of the poem, and the poem is included with all other ghost poems that are experienced during the Tang dynasty in the "ghosts" (*gui*) category of the great Qing anthology. Unlike the anecdotal collections and encyclopedias that collected such tales, *Quan Tang shi* operates as much as possible on an author-based and chronological system of organization, even in the more thematic chapters that preserve encyclopedia-like categories like "transcendents" (*xian* 仙), spirits (*shen* 神), and of course ghosts. What is striking about Murong Chui's inclusion in the *Quan Tang shi* is that he is effectively made into a Tang author and his poem a Tang poem. Although Lu Qinli includes several *yuefu* by Murong Chui that had been first collected in the *Yuefu shiji*, he does not mention this piece, since it would have been composed by Murong Chui centuries after his own death.[41] This speaks to the limits of literary historical chronology, which Lu Qinli's anthology follows, and to the hauntological nature of the ghost poet, whose presence and present is always outside of its proper time. Murong Chui is a Later Yan poet, but for the editors of *Quan Tang shi*, he becomes a Tang poet because his ghost returns to haunt Taizong in the Tang

40. Mei Dingzuo, *Caigui ji*, 3.1.

41. Guo Maoqian, *Yuefu shiji*, 25.367; Lu Qinli, *Xian Qin Han Wei Jin nanbeichao shi*, 2156.

Ghost Poetry   69

dynasty, decoupling historical period and authorship in a way that cannot be accounted for in the chronological structures of literary history.

Conclusion: Hauntology and Literary History

Although national literary history may be a modern institution, emerging only in the nineteenth and twentieth centuries,[42] it is informed by the cultural logics and the histories of the traditions that precede modernity and by the repression of these cultural logics and histories. The category of author, and the concept of the poem, are units by which to organize literary history, but these do not always fit easily with the teleologies that often govern literary historiography. For example, Lu Qinli's anthology is modeled on a literary historical logic: it proceeds from a strictly chronological structure, identifying authors by dynasty and attempting to group their works in biographical order wherever possible. Yet we see how the figure of the ghost as author poses challenges to this logic. The ghost is both inside and outside of time, present and absent, and this hauntological condition makes the attribution of authorship difficult, given that authorship is how literary history assigns ontological reality. One solution, as seen in *Quan Tang shi*, is to create multiple structures of organization, which allows the privileging of exceptional categories, such as emperors, and the quarantine of more troubling ones, such as ghosts, Buddhists, and women. This is a distinctly premodern solution, one that expresses a literary historical logic through an unmarked but normative category (historical male poets). The modern solution would be to ignore the presence of ghosts and strip them of authorial capacity, which then makes possible a cultural narrative of the nation-state that is free from its ghosts.

Even the seemingly stable category of the author is troubled by its own uncertain ontology, one that is bound to the past and returns to haunt us in the present. That is, the historical author is revivified when invoked by the literary text, which binds it to literary history as the site of authorial haunting. In this way, the author always returns as a *revenant*, a ghost that inspires (or even enspirits) the text with meaning for

---

42. See Denecke, chapter 8 in this volume.

the duration of the text's reading. Poetry, in particular, has the power to reanimate the dead, a power not granted to prose, at least not in the traditional Chinese context.[43] What affords poetry this capacity may be its claim to immediacy and presence, its staging of an oral moment, and perhaps the fact that it is an occasional genre in a way that prose is not. Thus, Hun Liangfu is moved by feelings of resentment to proclaim his innocence to Kuaikui in verse; the unnamed ghosts sing the "Ziye Songs" and make known their endless grieving; and Murong Chui cautions Taizong that life leads inexorably to the grave and history repeats itself in a simple quatrain. These are moments of heightened language, when fixed intention impels a form of speech that transcends ordinary language. If these ghosts author or perform poetic texts, they do so in ways that are consistent with the poetic norms of the living, a fact that does not necessarily subsume the dead in the domain of the living but underscores just how similar (and perhaps indistinguishable) the living and the dead truly are. If ghosts trouble literary history, so do all authors, who may, in the end, become indistinguishable from ghosts. After all, what literary history narrates is the story of the dead, a ghost story that brings the dead back to life in the telling.

43. There is more to say on the nature of prose, a discursive mode that is undertheorized in traditional Chinese literary thought, as it is in other classical cultures. Often prose is simply understood as "nonpoetry," or as the unmarked ordinary of literary discourse, whereas poetry is explicitly defined and theorized. For a recent discussion in the classical Greek context, see Graff, "Prose versus Poetry in Early Greek Theories of Style."

CHAPTER 3

Northern Halls and Western Gardens

Literary History by Topic

CHRISTOPHER M. B. NUGENT

Poem after poem and document after document never got beyond images of the moon and dew; tables were heaped and chests filled with nothing more than the descriptions of the wind and clouds. 連篇累牘, 不出月露之形; 積案盈箱, 唯是風雲之狀.

Li E 李諤 (fl. 580s)

Histories manage abundance. Many people did many things in the past; histories judge which ones are worth remembering, which we in turn must examine in order to understand—and respond appropriately to—our present. Literary histories likewise manage abundance. Many people produced many texts in the past and literary histories serve, in part, to make judgments about which texts are worth reading, remembering, and alluding to in new literary compositions.

The ability to produce literary works in a range of genres was a major component of social and political life for the literate elite of medieval China, especially between the fifth and tenth centuries, after the wide spread of paper but before the prevalent use of woodblock printing. Whether drunkenly dashing off a poem at a party held by a social superior or carefully composing an essay as part of the civil service exam, elite men (and in more limited contexts, women) were expected to produce literary works that would, if not necessarily dazzle and survive through the ages, at least show that their authors were competent writers who understood the rhetoric appropriate for a given context. This skill took many years of training and required mastering a literary and cultural inheritance that was among the most voluminous and complex the world had ever known. Although our knowledge of the details of this training is limited, numerous works that played a part in it have survived, either through transmission as part of the received tradition or sealed up in the caves at Dunhuang. These works provide insights into the structure and the content of what we might call medieval China's "literary curriculum" and, through that, the literary values and judgments of the works' creators.

This essay looks at a small subset of these works of literary training and the curriculum they promote as a way of thinking about conceptions of literary history in medieval China and in the Tang (618–907) in particular. None of the texts examined here include theoretical statements about literary history or literary criticism. However, in the selections their compilers made and the structures they used in compiling these texts, we can identify implicit judgments about which parts of the literary past were worth preserving and learning—which works were not just part of the literary past but parts of the literary inheritance. A key factor in the judgments is utility. Texts of literary training had a clear and explicit purpose: to teach the literate elite how to compose their own literary works, or at least to give them instructional examples to emulate and reference.[1] The literary training curriculum is thus both prescriptive and descriptive. These works tell readers what parts of the literary past they should know; they base this not solely on aesthetic or moral judgments but also on an awareness of what parts of the literary past people do know and are thus likely to use and recognize in various literary contexts.

These implicit judgments involve complex criteria and function differently from what David McMullen has identified as an important current of literary criticism in the Tang period, what he terms a "primitive literary historicism." In this mode of criticism, "the nature of literature is related to the conditions of the society that produced it."[2] To some extent, the judgments found in works of literary training instead come closer to what David Perkins calls "critical literary history," which, he argues, "does not perceive the literature of the past in relation to the time and

---

1. David Schaberg deals with similar issues of utility in chapter 1 of this volume.
2. McMullen, "Historical and Literary Theory," 332.

place that produced it, but selects, interprets, and evaluates this literature only from the standpoint of the present and its needs."[3] However, this match is imperfect. The works discussed below indeed select and thus implicitly evaluate, but they do not make explicit interpretations. The question of the "present and its needs" is, however, crucial. In both content and structure, these works present the literary inheritance as something to be put to use.

I examine how the two most important *leishu* 類書 ("writings arranged by category," also translated as "encyclopedia") that survive from the period—*Classified Extracts from Literature* (*Yiwen leiju* 藝文類聚) and *A Primer for Beginners* (*Chuxue ji* 初學記), with my focus being on the latter—deal with a common Tang poetic topic: the moon. It is helpful to look at a single topic because this is the kind of literary history these works tell: the history of how past literary works have addressed a topic and thus how that topic should be addressed in new compositions. What emerges is something very different from a history of a particular genre or a history of belletristic literature in general. After looking at the problem of abundance and the corresponding need for selection, I move on to the specific content of these works and the way that the content builds interwoven sets of images that delineate for readers how to write about a topic. Finally, I draw some conclusions about what it means to think of these works as literary history and offer an explanation as to why poets regarded as morally suspect by important early Tang scholars and officials nonetheless feature prominently in imperially commissioned compilations.

Collecting the Blossoms and Trimming the Weeds

Concerns about textual overabundance and the challenge of proper selection date back to the earliest stages of the literary and historical tradition in China. In *Records of the Historian* (*Shi ji* 史記), Sima Qian 司馬遷 (ca. 145–ca. 86 BCE) famously portrayed Confucius as compiling the *Poems* (*Shi* 詩, also known as *Classic of Poetry*, *Shi jing* 詩經,) by taking a mass

---

3. Perkins, *Is Literary History Possible?* 179.

74 CHRISTOPHER M. B. NUGENT

of over three thousand poems gathered from various sources and culling it down to three hundred by removing redundancies and keeping only those that would "propagate ritual and correct moral behavior" 可施於禮義.[4] Sima Qian sees Confucius as editing the *Shi* to create a moral history of the Zhou, rather than a literary one, and the basis of his selection is thus presented as ethical, not aesthetic. The need for some sort of selection, however, remains clear. The chaos of overabundance calls out for principled selection to bring order.

While Confucius's editing of the *Shi* is surely the stuff of legend rather than fact, similar concerns continued to be voiced, and with more urgency, centuries later when the widespread use of paper had enabled a massive increase in textual production and survival. In writings from the Southern Dynasties period (420–589), we often find issues of aesthetic quality coming to the fore, combined with a new awareness of the temporal challenges presented by textual abundance. In Xiao Tong's 蕭統 (501–531) preface to *Selections of Refined Literature* (*Wen xuan* 文選), the preeminent surviving literary anthology of the age, he states:

> Literary men and talents: their names spill out from blue silk bags. Swift writings and moist brushes: their scrolls fill up yellow sleeves. If one does not pass over the weeds, and collect only the purest blossoms, though one doubles his effort, it will be difficult [to read] more than half.
>
> 詞人才子, 則名溢於縹囊; 飛文染翰, 則卷盈乎緗帙. 自非略其蕪穢, 集其清英, 蓋欲兼功, 太半難矣.[5]

His brother Xiao Yi 蕭繹 (508–555) uses a similar metaphor and specifically ties this effort to learning (*xue* 學), in *Master of the Golden Tower* (*Jinlouzi* 金樓子), writing:

> Master's writings arose during the Warring States and literary collections flourished in the two Han periods, to the point that every household produced [writings] and every person had a collection. The finest among them suffice to relate feelings and aims and bring order to customs. The

---

4. Sima Qian, *Shi ji*, 47.1936–37.

5. Xiao Tong, *Wen xuan*, 2. For a translation of the full preface, see Xiao Tong, *Wen xuan, or Selections of Refined Literature*, 72–97.

Northern Halls and Western Gardens

worst among them merely increase the number of books and exhaust later students. [Writings] from the past have already piled up and those to come will never end. Even if you long to set your mind to learning, when your hair is gray you won't have gotten to them all. Sometimes what was valued in the past is now scorned, and what is valued today was considered base in antiquity. Ah! May there be among us later scholars with broad and far-reaching [knowledge], those able to appraise similarities and differences, cut out and trim the weeds, making scrolls free of flaws and reading free of wasted effort. This could be called learning!

諸子興于戰國, 文集盛於二漢, 至家家有制, 人人有集. 其美者足以敘情志, 敦風俗; 其弊者祇以煩簡牘, 疲後生. 往者既積, 來者未已. 翹足志學, 白首不遍. 或昔之所重, 今反輕; 今之所重, 古之所賤. 嗟我後生博達之士, 有能品藻異同, 刪整蕪穢, 使卷無瑕玷, 覽無遺功, 可謂矣.[6]

Xiao Tong's concern is with an excess of texts and the corresponding need for careful selection. Xiao Yi expands this concern to encompass judgments: not only are there too many texts, judgments about which ones are valuable change over time, and definitive judgments thus require particularly acute discernment. One might say that the brothers ultimately had very different responses to having too much to read. Xiao Tong compiled an influential anthology, one of the most important since the *Shi* itself. Xiao Yi eventually burned his own library to the ground.[7]

Xiao Yi's was hardly the only library to suffer destruction during early medieval times, but writings from the early Tang make it clear that the problem of textual abundance remained pressing, as writings connected to the period's surviving *leishu* show. In his preface to *Yiwen leiju*, Ouyang Xun 歐陽詢 (557–641) complains, "In the Perpetual Pavilion and the Stone Canal Library, the shelves store a profuse accumulation; spreading in all directions from distant sources, they are so difficult to thoroughly explore" 延閣石渠, 架藏繁積, 周流極源, 頗難尋究.[8] The solution is to "pick out the very best, and gather up the essential" 摘其菁華, 採其指要, and "get rid of the flotsam and jetsam, and excise the redundant" 棄其浮雜,

---

6. Xiao Yi, *Jinlouzi jiaojian*, 164. See discussion in Tian, "Literary Learning," 132.

7. For the details surround this incident, see Tian, *Beacon Fire and Shooting Star*, 93–95.

8. Ouyang Xun et al., *Yiwen leiju*, 27. The Perpetual Pavilion and Stone Canal Library were Western Han imperial libraries.

删其冗長.[9] A description of the imperial order to compile *Chuxue ji*, found in the early ninth century miscellany *New Accounts of the Great Tang* (*Da Tang xinyu* 大唐新語), notes a similar concern. According to this account, Tang Emperor Xuanzong 唐玄宗 (r. 712–756) worried that even earlier *leishu*-like compilations included too much to be useful for pedagogical purposes in the education of the imperial princes:

> Xuanzong said to Zhang Yue: "My sons want to study literary composition. They need to examine historical facts and peruse literary forms. The sections and chapters of works like the *Imperial View* are vast, and searching through them is rather difficult. I would like you and some other scholars to compile important facts and important writings and group them by category, aiming for simplicity and convenience so that my sons will more easily find success." [Zhang] Yue and Xu Jian, Wei Shu, and others edited these and presented them. [Xuanzong] decreed it be named *A Primer for Beginners*.
>
> 玄宗謂張說說曰：「兒子等欲學綴文，須檢事及看文體。御覽之篇，部帙既大，尋討稍難．卿與諸學士撰集要事並要文，以類相從，務取省便，令兒子等易見成就也．」說與徐堅、韋述等編此進上，詔以初學記為名.[10]

Part of Xuanzong's concern here is with how previous encyclopedic works structured the information they contained. In his view, their organizational methods did not help the kind of rapid retrieval of relevant textual content that would ease his sons' educational burden. The issue of volume, moreover, remained. Earlier compilations were selective, but their filters were not finely meshed enough for the purpose Xuanzong had in mind. What was needed was a selection of selections.

As with the *Yiwen leiju* preface, there is no explicit description of the criteria for what should be included, beyond that the content should be "important" (*yao* 要). The context, however, makes it clear that "important" content is what would be useful to the imperial princes in learning to compose their own literary works. This could be a socially fraught activity for the elite in medieval China. A passage about the social embarrassment suffered by ill-educated aristocratic young men from *Family Instructions*

---

9. Ouyang Xun et al., *Yiwen leiju*, 27.

10. Liu Su, *Da Tang xinyu*, 137.

for the Yan Clan (*Yanshi jiaxun* 顏氏家訓) by writer and scholar Yan Zhitui 顏之推 (531–590s), who had served under Xiao Yi, shows the cost of ignorance:

> At public or private feasts, when there is conversation about ancient history or when there is composition of poetry, they just silently hang their heads, yawning and stretching. The learned bystanders would like to sink into the ground for them. Why do they begrudge spending a few years on diligent study, and instead endure shame and disgrace throughout their whole lives?
>
> 公私宴集, 談古賦詩, 塞默低頭, 欠伸而已. 有識旁觀, 代其入地. 何惜數年勤學, 長受一生愧辱哉.[11]

In spite of a prince's high social status, or perhaps because of it, success in such contexts was no minor concern. A prince's literary products were not composed merely for his own amusement; in most cases, they were performative acts that were, in part, a public manifestation of the cultural authority of the imperial family. He had to demonstrate a command of the literary inheritance showing that he not only was familiar with literature's "finest blossoms" but also understood how these model works were to be deployed in a contemporary literary/social context. Even if such performances involved only his own entourage, the entourage would be made up of members of powerful imperial clans. In making their selections, the *Chuxue ji* compilers were both judging the literary past and prescribing the literary present. The "important facts and important writings" were those that aided a prince in discussing ancient history and composing poems in ways that showed him to be informed about the past and skilled at making use of it.[12]

To achieve this goal, the *Chuxue ji* compilers needed to be selective in content—taking into account aesthetic, moral, and utilitarian concerns—and creative in how they organized that content. The structures they use for this organization, which I discuss in more detail later can be considered

---

11. Yan Zhitui, *Yanshi jiaxun*, 143.

12. It is worth noting that while it was originally compiled for the use of Xuanzong's sons, *Chuxue ji* soon spread widely among members of the elite. Indeed, its use became so common as to elicit complaints in later periods that writers became overly reliant on it.

a second level of selectivity; they emphasize certain aspects of the content by using it repeatedly in different sections of individual entries. Because it is much shorter than *Yiwen leiju*, *Chuxue ji*'s judgments are potentially more revealing: two layers of selectivity involve more filters than one. This is reflected in the judgment of the eighteenth-century authors of the *Catalogue with Critical Abstracts of the Complete Library of the Four Treasuries* (*Siku quanshu zongmu tiyao* 四庫全書總目提要), which holds that although *Chuxue ji* "does not match *Yiwen leiju* in breadth, it surpasses it in [selecting] the essence" 博不及藝文類聚, 而精則勝之.[13] In the terms and allusions that make up this essence that, we find the implicit literary history of the moon that the work presents.

In this context, it is worth briefly comparing *leishu* and the other primary form of selective work from the period, the anthology. There are similarities between these two types of works. Both bring together a range of different literary pieces (in the case of *Wen xuan*, from thirty-eight different genres). Both use a variety of organizational structures, with different anthologies ordering and categorizing their content by such criteria as genres, topics, periods, authors, and titles. Both select their content from a far greater mass of materials, implying that the content they chose is special for some reason. Indeed, some scholars have used the term *leishu*, which does not appear as a bibliographic term until the Song dynasty (960–1279), so broadly as to include anthologies.[14]

But there are distinct differences between anthologies and such works as *Yiwen leiju* and *Chuxue ji*. Anthologies typically take as their basic unit of selection full literary pieces. *Leishu* sometimes include full pieces of writing, especially brief ones such as a short *shi* poem, but more often than not they extract segments as small as a single couplet or even a single binome from complete pieces. *Leishu* use far more complex organizational schemes than do anthologies, cutting up and combining parts of literary pieces in ways that make them easier to locate and memorize. If anthologies provide a history made up of individual literary works, *leishu* tell a story made up of a much greater range of textual units. The latter's judgments can be seen as more fine-grained, choosing not only the most important works but the most important parts of those works.

13. *Siku quanshu zongmu tiyao*, 135.2786.
14. See discussion in Tang Guangrong, *Tangdai leishu*, 45–68.

Important Facts and Important Writings

Although we lack more detailed descriptions of these works' selection criteria, we have the results of the selection process in the works themselves. Selective though they may be, *Yiwen leiju* and *Chuxue ji* are both of sufficient length to provide a wealth of evidence, with the former consisting of over 1 million characters and the latter of around 600,000. *Yiwen leiju* contains excerpts from 1,431 earlier works that it arranges into 46 "categories" (*bu* 部) and 727 individual entries over the course of 100 scrolls (*juan* 卷).[15] *Chuxue ji* includes 23 categories and 313 entries in 30 scrolls total. It contains excerpts from around 1,200 earlier works. A full accounting of the contents of each *leishu* is beyond the scope of this essay, but both include excerpts from the major traditional bibliographic categories. In the case of *Chuxue ji*, the category of "classics" (*jing* 經) is represented by the fewest excerpts, whereas writings from "collected works" (*ji* 集) are greatest in number.[16] This likely reflects its specific focus on helping with certain kinds of literary composition—those that often took place in social contexts. Its compilers may also have assumed that their intended readers would already be sufficiently familiar with the important portions of the classics, as they made up much of their earlier education.

Let us turn now to a more detailed examination of how these works tell the literary history of one of their many topics, the moon. This topic is a potentially revealing one in part because it is singled out by Li E 李諤 (fl. 580s), the Sui (581–618) critic quoted in the epigraph to this essay, as problematic in its superficiality and its abundance.[17] It thus brings into sharp relief some of the intellectual tensions in the period. The moon may have come to be viewed by some as a frivolous topic, but it was still a topic

---

15. "Categories" (*bu*) represent larger topics, such as "Heaven" (*tian* 天) or "Emperors and Kings" (*diwang* 帝王). "Individual entries" refers to subcategories under a larger topic, such as "moon" (*yue* 月) under "Heaven."

16. For more details, see Ditter, "*Chuxue ji*," 52–57; and Jiang Xiumei, *Chuxue ji zhengyin*. For a fuller description of *Yiwen leiju*, see Choo, "*Yiwen leiju*," 454–64.

17. For further discussion of Li E and his views, see Bol, "*This Culture of Ours*," 90–91.

80 CHRISTOPHER M. B. NUGENT

that members of the elite would be called on to write about in various contexts. They needed to master at least some of the content of those heaped-up tables and full chests about which Li E complains.

The entries on the moon in *Yiwen leiju* and *Chuxue ji* are similar in length: the former has 2,142 characters and the latter just slightly fewer with 2,040 characters. There is also considerable overlap in terms of the cited sources, which is not surprising given that *Chuxue ji* was likely based in part on *Yiwen leiju*. But there are important differences in how each work organizes the entries, differences that reflect different levels of selectivity and ways of presenting the literary inheritance.

The *Yiwen leiju* entry opens with a lengthy section of short informational excerpts from earlier sources about the moon. At 728 characters, this section makes up almost a third of the full entry and quotes from twenty-four different sources (with some being quoted multiple times, for a total of thirty-two excerpts). The focus here is on conveying the *shi* 事—factual information—about the moon: these passages tell the reader what the moon is. The first passage concerns linguistic matters and quotes from an Eastern Han (25–220) work titled *Explication of Names* (*Shi ming* 釋名) on the origin and meaning of terms for the moon's different stages:

> *Explication of Names* says: "The moon is that which wanes. Once full, it then wanes. *Hui* [the last day of the lunar month] means 'ash.' When the moon dies, it turns to ash. The moon's light coming to an end resembles this. *Shuo* [the first day of the lunar month] is 'resurrect.' The moon dies and comes back to life. *Xian* [bowstring] is the term for the half-moon. Its shape is curved on one side and straight on the other, like a taut bow's string. *Wang* [to gaze at] is the term for the full moon. The sun and the moon gaze at each other from afar."
>
> 釋名曰: "月, 闕也. 滿則缺也. 晦, 灰也. 月死爲灰. 月光盡似之也. 朔, 蘇也. 月死復蘇生也. 弦, 月半之名也, 其形一旁曲, 一旁直, 若張弓弦也. 望, 月滿之名也, 日月遙相望者也."[18]

The most frequently cited text in this section is the Western Han (206 BCE–8 BCE) syncretic work *Master of Huainan* (*Huainanzi* 淮南子),

---

18. Ouyang Xun et al., *Yiwen leiju*, 1.7.

Northern Halls and Western Gardens   81

with five separate quotations. The first describes the basic physical nature of the moon:

> *Huainanzi* says, "The moon is an agent of heaven. The greater part of the cold *qi* of accumulated *yin* becomes water. The essence of water's *qi* becomes the moon." It further says, "The moon is the ancestor of *yin*. Because of this, when the moon is waning, fish have less cartilage."
> 淮南子曰:"月, 天之使也, 積陰之寒氣, 大者爲水, 水氣之精者爲月." 又曰:"月者陰之宗. 是以月毀而魚腦減."[19]

Two passages, one from Liu Xiang's 劉向 (79–8 BCE) *Comprehensive Meaning of the Five Classics* (*Wujing tongyi* 五經通義) and another from Zhang Heng's 張衡 (78–139) *Numinous Statutes* (*Lingxian* 靈憲), explain some of the animal lore associated with the moon:

> *Comprehensive Meaning of the Five Classics* says, "Why are there a hare and a toad in the moon? The moon is the *yin* force. The toad is *yang*, and it shines together with the hare. *Yin* and *yang* are connected."
> 五經通義曰:"月中有兔與蟾蜍何? 月, 陰也. 蟾蜍, 陽也. 而與兔並明, 陰係陽也."

> Zhang Heng's *Numinous Statutes* says, "The moon is the ancestor of essential *yin*. When it is amassed it forms animals, resembling the toad and hare."
> 張衡靈憲曰:"月者, 陰精之宗, 積而成獸, 象蜍兔."[20]

A short quotation from Ban Gu's 班固 (32–92) *History of the Han* (*Han shu* 漢書) gives a historical anecdote connected to the moon: "Empress Yuan's mother née Li dreamt that the moon entered her chest and she gave birth to the empress" 元后母李氏夢月入其懷而生后.[21] Many well-known works that became part of the received tradition are cited in this section; however,

---

19. Ouyang Xun et al., *Yiwen leiju*, 1.7.
20. Ouyang Xun et al., *Yiwen leiju*, 1.7.
21. Ouyang Xun et al., *Yiwen leiju*, 1.7. As is the case with many excerpts quoted in these *leishu*, this passage appears in slightly different wording in the received version of the work. Ban, *Han shu*, 98.4015.

82   CHRISTOPHER M. B. NUGENT

it is clear that these passages were chosen not for their particular aesthetic merit but for the information they contain. These are the facts that an educated person should know about the moon.

The *Chuxue ji* entry on the moon opens in similar way, with a section labeled "Account of the Facts" (*xushi* 敘事) that shares a number of sources with the *Yiwen leiju* section. Its second quoted passage is a slightly different version of the *Shi ming* passage quoted above. In *Chuxue ji* it reads, "*Explication of Names* says: 'The moon is that which wanes. This means that once full, it then again wanes'" 釋名云: 月, 闕也, 言滿則復闕也.[22] Like this passage, *Chuxue ji*'s full *xushi* section is much shorter than its equivalent in *Yiwen leiju*. It contains only 241 characters, with five passages from only three sources: *Huainanzi*, *Shi ming*, and *Han shu*. The emphasis here is on giving only the most basic factual information about the moon: its *yin* nature, the stages of its cycle, and some mythological lore (e.g., the name of the lunar driver, Wang Shu 望舒).

This does not mean that the *Chuxue ji* compilers did not think it important to convey to their readers a wide range of facts about the moon. Most of the facts found in the opening section of *Yiwen leiju*'s entry are not missing from *Chuxue ji*; they are almost all found, in some form, in the next and largest section of the latter work, the *shidui* 事對, "parallel matters." Recall that the moon entries in these two *leishu* are almost the same length. The difference is in the distribution of content. Although there is no *shidui* section in *Yiwen leiju*, this is the largest section of the *Chuxue ji* entry on the moon, which stands at 980 characters. This is a pattern found throughout *Chuxue ji*.

The *shidui* section takes the kind of information found in the opening section of *Yiwen leiju* and places it in a new structure that maximizes mnemonic efficiency and ease of use. This structure is organized around parallel paired compounds or very short phrases. Parallelism being a key component of many styles of traditional Chinese poetry and prose, this format not only makes the pairs easier to recall, it provides the building blocks for constructing parallel couplets in poetry and parallel structures in prose. In *Chuxue ji*, each pair is followed by quotations from a range of works that contextualize each compound or give important examples

---

22. Xu Jian et al., *Chuxue ji*, 1.8.

Northern Halls and Western Gardens

of its use. We see the former function in the following *shidui* item in the moon entry:

> **Water's *qi*; metal's essence.** *Huainanzi* says: "The sun and the moon are agents of heaven. The cold *qi* of accumulated *yin* eventually becomes water. The essence of water's *qi* becomes the moon." *Yellow River Diagram for Imperial Reading Pleasure* says: "The moon is the essence of metal."
> 水氣; 金精. 淮南子曰: "日月, 天之使也. 積陰之寒氣, 久者爲水, 水氣之精者爲月." 河圖帝覽嬉曰: "月者, 金之精也."[23]

The phrases "water's *qi*" and "metal's essence" serve as short mnemonic pegs the reader can easily set to memory. The contextualizing excerpts provide the "facts" that explain the connection between these terms and the moon. These compounds can be used as allusive ways to refer to the moon in new literary compositions (note that the word "moon" itself never appears in a *shidui* pair in the moon entry). The core facts about the moon appear in both *leishu*; *Chuxue ji*, however, gives more direct indications about how those facts can be employed in a literary context.

We find a similar situation with a number of *shidui* phrases. For example, the phrase "the toad and hare join" (*chan tu bing* 蟾兔並), which appears as part of a *shidui* pair with the phrase "the unicorn and dragon contend" (*lin long dou* 麟龍鬭), is contextualized by the same *Wujing tongyi* passage on the hare and toad's connection with the moon that appears in *Yiwen leiju* and is cited above.[24] Turning to the pair "residing toad; gazing hare" (*juchu*; *gu tu* 居蟾; 顧兔), we find the following excerpts:

> **Residing toad; gazing hare.** *Primal Destiny's Buds of the Springs and Autumns* says: "As for the moon being called 'that which wanes' and being arrayed with a toad and hare, it is that the *yin* and *yang* forces both reside there. This shows that *yang* can control *yin* and *yin* relies on *yang*." *Verses of Chu* says: "What virtue has the night's glow, / that it dies and is born again? / What advantage is there, / that it has a gazing hare in its belly?"

---

23. Xu Jian et al., *Chuxue ji*, 1.8. The *Huainanzi* passage quoted is the first of those cited in *Yiwen leiju*, though textual variants change the reading somewhat.

24. Xu Jian et al., *Chuxue ji*, 1.9–10.

居蟾; 顧兔. 春秋元命苞曰: "月之爲言闕也. 而設以蟾蜍與兔者, 陰陽雙居, 明陽之制陰, 陰之倚陽." 楚詞曰: "夜光何德, 死而又育? 厥利維何, 而顧兔在腹?"[25]

Although the first excerpt, from a Han apocryphal work, does not appear in *Yiwen leiju*, the second, from *Verses of Chu* (*Chu ci* 楚辭), does.[26] Again, we find information shared by the *leishu* presented differently. *Chuxue ji* provides the information and further selects from it the most "essential" (*jing*) element, helping the reader remember the most "important" (*yao*) facts about the moon.

Both the *Yiwen leiju* preface and the *Da Tang xinyu* passage about the compilation of *Chuxue ji* emphasize that these works contain not just "facts" (*shi*), but also "literary writings" (*wen*). This is true of the *shidui* section of *Chuxue ji* in particular, which includes several items that tell the reader nothing about the nature of the moon but rather give the most important examples of phrases and terms connected to the moon in specifically literary contexts. The following *shidui* pair contains what are perhaps the most commonly used allusions in poems about the moon:

> **Northern hall; western garden.** A poem by Lu Shiheng says: "I sleep peacefully in the northern hall; / the bright moon enters my window. / It shines there with lingering brightness; / I grasp at it, it doesn't fill my hands. A poem by Cao Zhi says: "On a clear night I wander in the western garden; / flying canopies follow one after another. / The bright moon makes a pure light, / and the constellations are just now scattered here and there."
>
> 北堂; 西園. 陸士衡詩曰: "安寢北堂上, 明月入我牖. 照之有餘輝, 攬之不盈手." 曹植詩曰: "清夜遊西園, 飛蓋相追隨. 明月澄清影, 列宿正參差."[27]

The excerpt for "northern hall" is from the poem "Imitating 'How Bright Is the Moon'" ("Ni 'Mingyue he jiaojiao'" 擬明月何皎皎), by the prolific poet Lu Ji 陸機 (261–303). "How Bright Is the Moon" is the last of the

---

25. Xu Jian et al., *Chuxue ji*, 1.9.

26. *Chu ci* is an Eastern Han anthology that includes works attributed to authors from the southern state of Chu and imitations of such works from the Han.

27. Xu Jian et al., *Chuxue ji*, 1.9.

Northern Halls and Western Gardens

well-known "Nineteen Old Poems" ("Gushi shijiushou" 古詩十九首).[28] Lu Ji's full poem as found in *Wen xuan* has three additional couplets.[29] *Yiwen leiju* also includes Lu Ji's poem in its entry on the moon under the section of exemplary *shi* poems. Though *Yiwen leiju* typically gives the full poems in this section, in this case it gives only the first two couplets. For "western garden," *Chuxue ji* supplies the second and third couplets of a poem by Cao Zhi 曹植 (192–232) that appears under the category of "Lord's Banquet Poems" ("Gongyan shi" 公讌詩) in *Wen xuan*.[30] As we shall see, both the *shidui* terms and parts of the excerpted poems can be found in many later poems about the moon. They arguably constitute the allusive core of the topic.

Another *shidui* pair connected to literary works, this one with a parallel pair of three-character phrases, functions somewhat differently:

> **Reflected on Ruan's curtains; illuminating Pan's room.** A poem by Ruan Ji says: "In the night I could not sleep, / and rose to sit and pluck my resounding zither. / The thin curtains reflected the bright moon; / a clear breeze blew my lapels." Pan Yue's "Lament for My Wife" says: "Brilliant, the moon in my window, / it shines on my chamber's south entrance. / The clear *shang* notes respond to autumn's arrival, / humid heat follows the season nearing its end."
>
> 鑒阮帷; 照潘室. 阮籍詩曰: "夜中不能寐, 起坐彈鳴琴. 薄帷鑒明月, 清風吹我衿."
> 潘岳悼亡詩曰: "皎皎窗中月, 照我室南端. 清商應秋至, 溽暑隨節闌."[31]

The quotation to match the first phrase is from a well-known poem by Ruan Ji 阮籍 (210–263) that is included in *Wen xuan*; it is the first of his series of poems titled "Intoning My Feelings" ("Yonghuai" 詠懷).[32] Unlike with most of the *shidui* section, the words in this pair appear in a different order in the quotation from that in which they are given in the "prompt" phrases. The prompt phrase thus does not truly appear in the poem to which it is connected. Indeed, the word "Ruan" is not in the poem at

---

28. Xiao Tong, *Wen xuan*, 29.1350.
29. Xiao Tong, *Wen xuan*, 30.1428.
30. Xiao Tong, *Wen xuan*, 20.943.
31. Xu Jian et al., *Chuxue ji*, 1.9.
32. Xiao Tong, *Wen xuan*, 23.1067.

all but is the surname of the poet. As is more typical of the *shidui* sections, only a portion of the poem (half, in this case) is quoted, even though the original is quite short. The second phrase in the pair functions similarly. The two excerpted couplets are the opening of a fourteen-couplet poem by Pan Yue 潘岳 (247–300), "Lament for My Wife" ("Daowang" 悼亡), also found in *Wen xuan*.[33] Again, we see an image from the original poem with the surname of the author added. The larger context here, a lament for the poet's deceased wife, is absent. These lines about the moon function as bits of literary information that can be used or alluded to in new compositions.

The *shidui* sections of *Chuxue ji* contain the kind of information found in other *leishu*, including *Yiwen leiju*, and display the selectivity that is fundamental to all such compilations. The way *Chuxue ji* structures this carefully selected information, however, is more sophisticated than what is found in most other surviving *leishu* from the period. Each *shidui* entry has two parts: the parallel terms and the excerpts from which they come. As noted already, the parallel terms can be seen as serving two functions. In all cases, they are easily memorized mnemonic pegs that help the reader recall the fuller passages to which they refer. Scholar of medieval European memorial arts Mary Carruthers writes of how many mnemonic systems divide material into short units that are put into "some sort of rigid, easily reconstructable order."[34] These units allow the learner to more quickly bring to mind the larger passages from which the units were taken or to which they point. In such a scenario in the *shidui* sections of *Chuxue ji*, the more important information is arguably found in the original texts. The parallel pairs primarily aid in their recall. As a result, these texts are best seen not as annotations to explain the *shidui* pairs but as the fuller information those pairs are meant to convey. Looked at another way, these pairs can also serve as ready-made allusions or at least examples of what forms such allusions might take. In this context, their parallel structures model how parallelism works and give indications as to how one would appropriately apply parallelism in one's own literary compositions on the moon (and other topics). From this perspective, the

---

33. Xiao Tong, *Wen xuan*, 23.1091.
34. Carruthers, *The Book of Memory*, 7.

Northern Halls and Western Gardens

pairs are intended not primarily as mnemonic aids but as compositional models or prompts.

It is important to note that these two aspects of the *shidui* pairs are not mutually exclusive. Each pair can fulfill both roles simultaneously. Indeed, one might argue that this describes an important aspect of all allusions: they are smaller bits of textual information that serve partly to bring to mind in the reader the fuller texts to which they refer.

This structure is closely tied to the selectivity function. We can identify three layers of pedagogical selectivity at work in *Chuxue ji*. The first is the selection of the topic of the entry, in this case the moon. This tells the reader that the moon is a topic about which one should know how to compose literary works. Indeed, *Chuxue ji* reduces the entire world to 313 such topics, making it more than twice as selective as *Yiwen leiju* in this respect. Within a given topic, only a limited set of previous works can be cited; this is a second level of selection that indicates to the reader what things that have been written about this topic in the past are important to know. The third layer of selectivity is the *shidui* pairs. These are the distillation, the essence, of these past works. It is this final level of selectivity, perhaps, that the *Siku quanshu zongmu tiyao* authors had in mind when they state that *Chuxue ji* surpasses *Yiwen leiju* in terms of the essence (*jing* 精).

Useful Models

Both *Yiwen leiju* and *Chuxue ji* include in every entry a section with generic models for writing about the topic at hand. In their entries on the moon, these are limited to poems (*shi*) and rhapsodies (*fu* 賦), whereas many other entries include a wider range of genres. Here I focus on the *shi* models.[35] For both genres, the section in *Yiwen leiju* is about twice as long as that in *Chuxue ji*. *Yiwen leiju* provides twenty-one poems with a total of 947 characters. For each poem, both *leishu* give the author and dynasty. This section is the first in which historical context and chronological ordering are made explicit. The earliest model poem in the *Yiwen*

---

35. The *fu* models are quite limited, with only four in *Yiwen leiju* and two in *Chuxue ji*.

leiju section is the one by Lu Ji discussed already, and the latest is by Jiang Zong 江總 (519–594). The selection is heavily concentrated on the southern Liang dynasty (502–557), with fifteen of the twenty-one poems attributed to that period, three of which are by Liu Xiaochuo 劉孝綽 (481–539). The *Chuxue ji* section includes only eleven poems for a total of 587 characters. Of these, six are attributed to the Liang and two are by Tang authors, including Tang Emperor Taizong 太宗 (r. 626–649), whose compositions are included in many entries in *Chuxue ji*. The southern Chen dynasty (557–589), the northern Zhou dynasty (557–581), and the Sui dynasty poets have one poem each. There is some overlap with the selections in the *Yiwen leiju* section, but not as much as one might expect given that the *Chuxue ji* compilers seem to have based much of their work on that earlier *leishu*. Only four of the eleven poems are in *Yiwen leiju* as well, and all of these are by Liang authors.

We can see these sections in both *leishu* as providing a brief anthological history of the moon as a literary topic. The poems in each do not necessarily include mentions of the moon; rather, they are all "about" the moon in that it is their primary topic, reflected in the fact that all include the word "moon" in their title, most commonly as some variation on "gazing" (*wang* 望, *kan* 看, *shi* 視) at the moon.[36] The poems are typically complete, with only two represented by excerpts: Lu Ji's "Imitating 'How Bright Is the Moon'" and Bao Zhao's 鮑照 (ca. 414–466) "Admiring the Moon" ("Wan yue" 翫月). For *Yiwen leiju*, this section is clearly meant to be the *wen*, the literary works, to go with the "facts" found in the first section. The facts tell the reader what they should know about the moon; the poems function as demonstrations of how these facts can be employed in a literary composition. Again, we see that the focus is on the use of appropriate information: what to use and how to use it.

This emphasis on use is even clearer in *Chuxue ji*'s model poems. These seem to have been carefully selected to serve not only as demonstrations of how to write about the moon but as examples that specifically connect to the terms and phrases in the *shidui* section. Though this is true of almost all the poems, two make particularly good examples.

---

36. The title for Lu Ji's "Imitating 'How Bright Is the Moon'" is not given in *Yiwen leiju*.

Northern Halls and Western Gardens

Chen dynasty poet Zhang Zhengjian's 張正見 (527–575) "'The Thin Curtains Reflected the Bright Moon'" ("Bowei jian mingyue" 薄帷鑒明月) reads:

長河上月桂	The moon's cassia atop the Milky Way;
澄彩照高樓	clear colors illuminate the high pavilion.
分簾疑碎璧	Through parted curtains, it seems a broken jade disk;
隔幔似重鉤	divided by the screen, like a double hook.
窗外光恆滿	Beyond the window, its glow constantly full;
帷中影暫流	within the curtains, its reflection drifts for a moment.
豈及西園夜	How can I reach that western garden night,
長隨飛蓋遊	and forever follow those flying canopies as they wander?[37]

The connections begin with the poem's title, which is the third line of Ruan Ji's "Intoning My Feelings" poem quoted for the *shidui* phrase "reflected on Ruan's curtains" discussed already. The cassia in the first line also appears in the *shidui* phrase "looking at the cassia" (*shigui* 視桂), and the moon shining on the high pavilion recalls the second half of the *shidui* pair with "reflected on Ruan's curtains," "illuminate Pan's room" (*zhao Pan shi* 照潘室), as Pan Yue's quoted lines depict the moon framed in a window ("how bright, the moon in the window" 皎皎窗中月). The "curtains" of the title reappear in the second couplet, which uses a jade disk and a hook in parallel positions, just as the *shidui* pair "Resembling a hook; like a jade disk" (*si gou; ru bi* 似鉤; 如璧) does. The final couplet brings us back to the "western garden" of the pair "northern hall; western garden," putting "western garden" in a parallel position with the "flying canopies" from the second line of Cao Zhi's poem quoted for that *shidui* term. Other terms in the poem are also found in the *shidui* section. Terms for "broken" (*sui* 碎 in this poem and *po* 破 in the *shidui*) or "doubled" (*chong* 重) in reference to the moon appear both in the *shidui* terms and in this poem.

An even more striking example of connections between the *shidui* terms and a model poem is found in the Liang poet Dai Song's 戴嵩 (fl. early sixth century, also known as Dai Gao 戴暠) "Song of the Moon's Doubled Wheel" ("Yue chonglun xing" 月重輪行):

---

37. Xu Jian et al., *Chuxue ji*, 1.10.

皇儲屬明兩	The crown prince is akin to its double brightness;
副德表重輪	matching virtue, manifest as a doubled wheel.
重輪非是暈	But that doubled wheel is not a halo;
桂滿月恆春	where cassia fills, the moon is in constant spring.
海珠全更減	A pearl in the sea, full and then diminished;
階蓂翳且新	the auspicious shrub by the stairs is withered, about to be renewed.
婕妤比圓扇	The Favored Beauty compared it to a round fan,
曹王譬洛神	the Cao prince likened it to the river goddess.
浮川疑讓璧	Floating in the river, it seems a relinquished jade disk;
入戶類燒銀	coming through the door, like a quick silver lamp.
從來看顧兔	In the past I have seen the gazing hare,
不曾聞鬬麟	but I have never heard the contending unicorn.
北堂豈盈手	In the northern hall, how could it fill my hands?
西園偏照人	In the western garden, it only shines on others.[38]

Again, the first connection between the poem and the *shidui* section is found in the title, here with the term "doubled wheel" (*chonglun* 重輪). The accompanying text for this term in *Chuxue ji* connects the image to a crown prince, reading:

> Cui Bao's *Notations on Matters Past and Present* says: "When Han Emperor Ming was crown prince, the court musicians sang four pieces to commend his virtue. The first was called 'The Sun Doubles Its Rays,' the second was called 'The Moon Doubles Its Wheel,' the third was called 'The Stars Double Their Radiance,' and the fourth was called 'The Sea Doubles Its Sheen.'"
>
> 崔豹古今注曰: "漢明帝作太子, 樂人歌四章, 以贊太子之德. 其一曰日重光, 二曰月重輪, 三曰星重曜, 四曰海重潤."[39]

The connections continue with cassia image and the "auspicious shrub," both of which appear in the *shidui* pair "observing the auspicious shrub; looking at the cassia" (*guan ming*; *shi gui* 觀蓂; 視桂). The former term is explained as follows by the accompanying text:

---

38. Xu Jian et al., *Chuxue ji*, 1.10.
39. Xu Jian et al., *Chuxue ji*, 1.9.

Master of Embracing Simplicity says: "Long ago the Yellow Emperor waited for the phoenix's call to harmonize the pitch pipes. [Emperor] Yao of Tang observed the auspicious shrub to know [the phase of] the moon." *Record of the Lineages of Emperors and Kings* says: "In the time of [Emperor] Yao there was a plant that that grew alongside the stairs. Each month it would daily put forth a single seed pod. By the midpoint of the month it would have put forth fifteen seed pods. Reaching the sixteenth day and thereafter, it would drop a single pod each day; by the last day of the month, the pods would all be gone. If it was a twenty-nine-day month, there would be a single pod left over. The ruler would use this to divine the calendar. It put forth [seed pods] in response to harmony and was taken as an auspicious omen of Yao and was called 'auspicious shrub.' One alternative name for it was the 'calendric shrub,' and another was 'immortals' cogon.'"

抱朴子曰:"昔帝軒候鳳鳴以調律, 唐堯觀蓂荚以知月."帝王世紀云:"堯時有草夾階而生, 每月朔日生一荚, 至月半則生十五荚. 至十六日後, 日落一荚, 至月晦而盡. 若月小餘一荚. 王者以是占曆. 應和而生, 以爲堯瑞. 名之蓂荚, 一名曆荚, 一名仙茆.[40]

The "Favored Beauty" (Jieyu) of the fourth couplet is Lady Ban (Ban Jieyu 班婕妤, d. ca. 6 BCE), a Western Han imperial consort whose "Song of Resentment" ("Yuan gexing" 怨歌行) is quoted in the accompanying text for the *shidui* phase "resembling a white silk fan" (*si wanshan* 似紈扇). Though that phrase itself does not appear in the line, the reference is clear:

Favored Beauty Ban's "Song of Resentment" says: "Newly cut white silk from Qi, / bright and pure as frost and snow. / Cut to make a fan of joined happiness, / so round, I take it for the bright moon."

班婕妤怨歌行曰:"新裂齊紈素, 鮮潔如霜雪. 裁爲合歡扇, 團團以明月."[41]

The terms in parallel positions in Dai Song's penultimate couplet also appear as exact or near exact matches in the *shidui* section. The *shidui* term "Gazing Hare" (*gu tu* 顧兔) quotes the aforementioned passage from *Chu ci*: "What virtue has the night's glow, / that it dies and is born again? / What advantage is there, / that it has a gazing hare in its belly?" The

40. Xu Jian et al., *Chuxue ji*, 1.8.
41. Xu Jian et al., *Chuxue ji*, 1.9.

contending unicorns of the second line in the couplet connect to the *shidui* phrase "unicorn and dragon contend," which, as the quoted passage explains, refers to an eclipse. Finally, the last couplet takes us back to those perennial favorites, Lu Ji's northern hall, where the moon does not fill his hands, and Cao Zhi's western garden. It is no mystery why the compilers chose this as a model poem: it has direct overlap with seven of the fifteen *shidui* pairs in the moon entry and shares imagery with a number of others.

These two poems and others in this section demonstrate how *Chuxue ji* functions as a literary history of a topic. The poems are not necessarily chosen primarily for their aesthetic merit (although clearly they would not have been chosen had the compilers judged them as *lacking* aesthetic merit) or for their importance in the historical development of the genre. Rather, they are presented as examples that skillfully model the technical aspects of literary composition, in this case the technique of using the literary inheritance in a way that demonstrates cultural competence. They show how the terms and phrases the reader has learned from the *shidui* can be used in new literary compositions. Because both poems allude to important works, ranging from *Chu ci* to the poems of Cao Zhi, they are encapsulations of the literary history of the moon as well. Just as important, they are useful. If one is writing a poem about the moon for a crown prince, here is how one can foreground that context through the use of the term "doubled wheel." If one wants to show a command of the key works in the literary inheritance, these poems show a range of ways to do so. One crucial aspect of this is how they work together with the *shidui* section. One reinforces the other in an interwoven network of pedagogically effective structures. In this particular context, the passages accompanying the *shidui* pairs function as annotations to the model poems. The passages explain the allusions in these models. The models, in turn, function as demonstrations on how to make such allusions, some direct (e.g., northern hall and western garden), some less so. The result is a different kind of literary history whose judgments may still involve moral and aesthetic merit but which also puts significant weight on social utility.

Not surprisingly, references to the model works and *shidui* found in *Chuxue ji* appear in innumerable later poems about the moon. There are examples of later poems that seem to be directly based on *Chuxue ji* or at least densely use the same conventions. A particularly apt example is a work by late Tang poet Li Shangyin 李商隱 (ca. 813–858) titled "On the Assigned Topic 'The Moon Shines on the Frozen Pool' in Eight Rhymes" 賦得月照冰池八韻. Li Shangyin is an interesting case in this regard because he is known to have been interested in *leishu*. Like a number of other writers in the mid- and late Tang periods, including Yuan Zhen 元稹 (779–831), Bai Juyi 白居易 (772–846), and Pi Rixiu 皮日休 (ca. 834–883), he apparently compiled a *leishu*-type work himself, the now lost *Golden Key* (*Jinyao* 金鑰). His poem reads as follows:

皓月方離海	The bright moon about to leave the sea,
堅冰正滿池	firm ice just now filling the pool.
金波雙激射	Golden waves, paired, spurt,
璧彩兩參差	jade disk's brilliance, doubled, gives an irregular [sparkle].
影占徘徊處	Its reflection occupies the spot where it lingers,
光含的皪時	its light envelops a moment of brilliance.
高低連素色	High and low joined by the hue of raw silk,
上下接清規	above and below connected by the clear compass.
顧兔飛難定	The gazing hare, hard to settle his flight,
潛魚躍未期	the submerged fish, not yet time for its leap.
鵲驚俱欲遶	The magpies startle, all about to encircle,
狐聽始無疑	the fox listens, beginning to lack suspicion.
似鏡將盈手	Like a mirror, it will fill my hand,
如霜恐透肌	like frost, I fear it will penetrate my flesh.
獨憐遊玩意	How I cherish its notion to wander,
達曉不知疲	and meeting the morning without knowing weariness.[42]

As the title indicates, this is a poem composed to an assigned topic—a topic that may have been on the exam at some point. It is doubtful that anyone would consider the work to be the pinnacle of Li Shangyin's poetic art; it may have been composed specifically as a model poem for the exam.[43] The following brief discussion focuses on the connections to references found in *Chuxue ji* rather than on the work's aesthetic value.

42. Li Shangyin, *Li Shangyin shige*, 493.
43. See Luo Jiyong and Zhang Pengfei, *Tangdai shilü*, 45–46.

The poem begins with the term *haoyuu* 皓月 "bright moon," which also appears in the first line of the second exemplary *shi* poem in the *Chuxue ji* entry on the moon by Xiao Yi titled "Gazing at the Moon in the River" 望江中月詩; it is also a poem about the moon reflected in a body of water.[44] The second couplet begins with "golden waves" *jinbo* 金波, a term that is also the first part of the ninth *shidui* item for the *Chuxue ji* entry on the moon; it quotes *Han shu* as saying "The shifting colors of the moon make golden waves" 月移彩以金波.[45] The parallel term in that *shidui* pair is "jade disc's glow," *biguang* 璧光. In Li Shangyin's poem, the parallel he uses for "golden waves" is the similar term "jade disc's brilliance," *bicai* 璧彩. Li Shangyin's next two couplets focus on the glow connecting the moon in the sky with its image reflected in the frozen surface of the pool. Though he uses terms that also appear in various parts of the *Chuxue ji* entry on the moon, such as *cenci* 參差 ("irregular") and *paihuai* 徘徊 ("to pause or hesitate"), I would not go so far as claiming they are clearly taken from the entry but rather are more general conventions that Li Shangyin uses in many other poems.

The fifth couplet, however, sees the beginning of a long string of allusions for which the argument that their use and order is guided by *Chuxue ji* or similar *leishu* is much stronger. The couplet begins with the term "gazing hare." The second line of the couplet begins with a much more specific allusion in the term "submerged fish" (*qian yu* 潛魚). Cao Zhi's poem that served as the source for "western garden" in *Chuxue ji* includes the line "the submerged fish leaps from clear waves" 潛魚躍清波, the obvious source for Li Shangyin's allusion. The next couplet similarly follows appropriate *Chuxue ji* entries. The first line reads "the magpies startle, all about to encircle." The penultimate *shidui* pair in the *Chuxue ji* moon entry includes the phrase "The Wei Magpies Fly" 魏鵲飛 for which it gives the following explanation: "Wei Emperor Wu's 'Short Song' says, 'the moon bright and the stars scattered, crows and magpies fly south; circling the trees three times, on what branch may they rely?'" 魏武帝短歌行曰: 月明星稀, 烏鵲南飛; 繞樹三匝, 何枝可依.[46] Although they are not in the same couplet in Li Shangyin's poem, he does use an allusion

44. Xu Jian et al., *Chuxue ji*, 1.10.
45. Xu Jian et al., *Chuxue ji*, 1.9.
46. Xu Jian et al., *Chuxue ji*, 1.9.

Northern Halls and Western Gardens

to Cao Zhi followed by an allusion to his father, Cao Cao 曹操 (155–220; also known as Wei Emperor Wu), in the next line (again, following the content of the *Chuxue ji* moon entry). The connection is thematic as well. In Cao Zhi's poem, the parallel line to "the submerged fish leaps from clear waves" is "a fine bird calls from a high branch," 好鳥鳴高枝, thus moving from fish to bird just as Li Shangyin's poem does (albeit across couplets in the latter case). In the second line, Li Shangyin's couplet puts a fox in parallel to the magpie: "the fox listens, beginning to lack suspicion." Though there is nothing here that connects to the moon specifically, the *Chuxue ji* entry on "foxes" (*hu* 狐) includes the *shidui* term "listening to the ice" (*ting bing* 聽冰) with the explanatory text noting, "When the north wind is strong and the ice on the Yellow River first forms, a fox must walk [on it]: it is said that this animal is skilled at listening, and when it hears that there is no sound of water beneath the ice, only then will it cross the river" 北風勁河冰始合, 要須狐行, 云此物善聽, 聽冰下無水聲, 然後過河.[47]

The poem proceeds in similar fashion to the end. The first line of the penultimate couplet reads, "Like a mirror, it will fill my hand" 似鏡將盈手. This once again connects to the *Chuxue ji shidui* pair "northern hall, western garden." Instead of Cao Zhi's poem and its submerged fish, Li Shangyin makes an allusion to the quotation provided by *Chuxue ji* for "northern hall," namely, Lu Ji's "Imitating 'How Bright Is the Moon,'" which, again, reads "I sleep peacefully in the northern hall, / the bright moon enters my window; / It shines there with lingering brightness, / I grasp at it, but it doesn't fill my hands." In Li Shangyin's poem, however, the moonlight becomes more solid: it *will* fill his hand. Rather than entering the window as it does in Lu Ji's poem, it instead becomes frost-like, threatening to penetrate flesh. This particular *shidui* pair is clearly the most important for Li Shangyin's poem, and indeed he returns to the same Cao Zhi poem quoted for "western garden" again in the final couplet, with the themes of free wandering and tirelessness, both of which play roles in Cao Zhi's piece. Allusions to Cao Zhi's poem also appear in several of the model poems in the *Chuxue ji*'s entry on the moon. It dominates allusions in the entry just as it does in Li Shangyin's own treatment.

---

47. Xu Jian et al., *Chuxue ji*, 29.717.

Although there is no way of determining that Li Shangyin was following *Chuxue ji* specifically, the important role of the conventions enshrined by the latter is clear.

Conclusion

Only with the model poems and their assigning of writers and their works to specific dynasties does chronologically ordered history come into play in the entries on the moon in *Yiwen leiju* and *Chuxue ji*. This does not mean that only in these sections do these *leishu* function implicitly as literary histories. The histories they encapsulate are not those of the development of genres; they are not explanatory histories that describe how literary trends developed and explain why. What we find instead are histories of topics, histories suffused with pedagogical concerns. I noted at the opening of this essay that histories manage abundance. They winnow down human experience to those people and events important to remember. Pedagogy functions in a similar way. The world of facts and literary works, even in the medieval manuscript culture of the early Tang, was far greater than most could master, especially imperial princes for whom distractions were no doubt numerous. Pedagogically oriented works like *Chuxue ji* present a narrowed set of topics, texts, and excerpts that promise to constitute what one really has to know to function in contemporary elite society.

All histories are in some sense pedagogical. They are all prescriptive and descriptive. What, then, sets apart the literary history found in *leishu*? I suggest that it is ultimately the issue of use. The histories these works tell of their chosen topics are meant to give readers the facts and literary works connected to these topics to use in the readers' own compositions. This is made explicit in the *Da Tang xinyu* description of *Chuxue ji*'s origin. Even if we discount the veracity of that anecdote, the structures that *Chuxue ji* uses to organize the information it presents strongly suggest that its compilers intended to make that information easily accessible. As we have seen with the *shidui*, these structures served mnemonic purposes, helping readers recall the information, and simultaneously served as models to show how that information could be used in a compositional context. The model poems are best seen not as miniature historical anthologies (though they may end up functioning as such) but as fuller illustrations of how to use the literary inheritance to produce new works in a highly literate (and competitive) social context.

To return to Perkins, we indeed find here a kind of literary history that prioritizes "the standpoint of the present and its needs." As such it potentially offers a different perspective on early Tang ideas about the literary inheritance. This is a history that is directly tied to the social reality of taste and poetic production in that period. While I have retuned again and again to the issue of utility, it should be clear that this sense of utility is not separate from aesthetic judgments but closely tied to them. These judgments, however, are always implicit, and I believe this opens up more room for including works that might have fared less well in the context of literary-historical approaches that were more focused on theoretic and moral accounts of literature. My speculation is that we have more space for poems that the princes should know because everyone (who matters) knows them.

This may partly explain the emphasis on poems from periods that many court officials of the early Tang considered morally suspect and politically disastrous.[48] The majority of the poems in entries on the moon in *Yiwen leiju* and *Chuxue ji* are from the Liang. Indeed, many of the poets who are given other dynastic designations, such as Jiang Zong, Wang Bao 王褒 (513–576), and Yu Xin 庾信 (513–581), are more accurately thought of as Liang poets who fled north after the dynasty's fall. These were exactly the sorts of poems about which Li E complained and about which Taizong's advisers warned him. Why include them in such substantial numbers? Because poetry was a social activity for imperial princes, as it was for all of the elite. It would be unacceptable for them to "silently hang their heads, yawning and stretching, unable to say anything," as Yan Zhitui described, no matter what the topic. Sometimes one was called on to write about the moon, and one had best know how to do so.

---

48. For a discussion of the disjunction between Sui and Tang official discourse on literature and the contents of contemporaneous *leishu* such as *Yiwen leiju* and *Chuxue ji*, see Tian, *Beacon Fire and Shooting Star*, 319–21.

CHAPTER 4

The Creation of a Genre

The Long, Slow Rise of Tang *"Chuanqi"*

SARAH M. ALLEN

Literary histories tell stories in which texts and genres are the main actors. To bring order to the jumble of texts that is the reality of literary production and transmission, historians seek groupings and categories. Some of these reflect groupings in play during the period in question; others are retrospective, based on likenesses perceived by the historian that may not have been recognized in prior ages. The most consequential is perhaps the category of the literary itself. All such categories reveal influences and relationships and trends, making it possible to trace changes within and among genres over time and to tell a satisfying story. But they can also obscure other relationships, narrowing the contextual background against which individual works are read; and the more appealing the story, the more effectively the categories it posits eclipse other possibilities.

The story that has been told for the past century about Chinese narratives of the eighth and ninth centuries is such a case. The chief protagonist is a genre called *chuanqi* 傳奇 ("transmitting the marvelous"): short tales that evolved from simpler antecedents known as *zhiguai* 志怪 ("recording the strange" or "anomaly accounts") over the course of the Tang dynasty (618–907). *Chuanqi*—so the story goes—reached their height in the ninth century only to suffer a decline in popularity and quality in the late ninth and subsequent centuries. In addition to being intricate and compelling texts in their own right, *chuanqi* hold an important place in histories of Chinese literature as stepping stones toward the development

The Long, Slow Rise of Tang "Chuanqi"

of more overtly fictional stories and novels in the vernacular in later centuries. Anchored in key examples that illustrate the genre's literary achievements, the *chuanqi* story posits the maturation of this new type of tale over the course of some 150 years on the foundation established by its generic ancestors, marking a milestone in the history of Chinese fiction.[1] It is appealing in offering both an explanation of *chuanqi*'s origins and an argument for their significance.

Take a closer look at the textual landscape in which these tales came into being, however, and it is not clear that texts placed in the *chuanqi* category can so easily be demarcated from other contemporaneous narratives not so designated, nor that so-called *zhiguai* are their primary antecedents. These questions only become more acute as the scope of the texts examined expands. Though it is perhaps inevitable that any attempt to apply categorical labels to historical artifacts as complex and varied as literary texts will fail when examined too closely, the fissures prompt us to consider whether there is more to the *chuanqi* story—and even whether the simpler explanation is that there were no "Tang *chuanqi*."[2]

Here I explore this possibility by proposing an alternative context in which we might read one of the most representative *chuanqi*, Bai Xingjian's 白行簡 (776?–826) "Account of Li Wa" ("Li Wa zhuan" 李娃傳). "Li Wa" tells the story of a courtesan who fleeces a young man and leaves him destitute—leading his father to disown him—but later rescues and marries her former lover and earns his family's praise, as well as that of Bai Xingjian himself.[3] The tale is a mainstay of the *chuanqi* canon, frequently anthologized and referenced in histories of *chuanqi* and Chinese fiction. As a freestanding account concerned with human behavior and human relationships, however, "Li Wa" differs markedly from its

---

1. See Li Jianguo, "Tang bai sikao lu (dai qianyan)" 唐稗思考錄 (代前言), esp. 1–60, in Li Jianguo, *Tang Wudai zhiguai chuanqi xulu*, vol. 1; and Cheng Yizhong, *Tangdai xiaoshuo shi*, 6–19.

2. I am not the first to suggest that the *chuanqi* label is an invention of later centuries that does not adequately account for the texts to which it has been applied. Most notably, Glen Dudbridge argues the point eloquently from a somewhat different perspective in "A Question of Classification." For other discussions questioning the evolutionary link between *chuanqi* and *zhiguai*, see Wang Yunxi, "Jianlun Tang chuanqi," and Pan Jianguo, *Zhonguo gudai xiaoshuo*, 27–55.

3. Li Fang et al., *Taiping guangji*, 484.3984–91.

supposed closest relations, *zhiguai,* which were stories about the occult and other anomalies gathered into collections. We can better account for key aspects of its content and form by reading it in the context of narratives ("accounts," *zhuan* 傳) commemorating noteworthy but fully human individuals, women in particular—though in some respects, "Li Wa" stands out here as well.

If the *chuanqi* story is not the true story—or not the full story—how did this vision of Tang narrative win such acceptance? In the second half of this essay, I explore the decisions and chance developments that, playing out over the course of a millennium, allowed for the gradual emergence of the idea of *chuanqi* and their placement in a key role in histories of Chinese literature. I suspect that in the ninth century when "Li Wa" was written, its kinship with other contemporaneous accounts of remarkable women would have been self-evident and natural to its first audiences. By the sixteenth century—to say nothing of the twentieth—times had changed, and other affinities stood out more clearly. The lesson is not that the story that has been told is the wrong one, but rather that literary history is an ever-shifting business. If one role of the literary historian is to interpret the literary past and preserve memory of it for a new generation, it is no wonder that reader-historians of different eras will see it differently. For that reason, it behooves us to continuously examine the texts themselves anew to see what we might discover, or rediscover.

Three Remarkable Women

Narratives recounting women's deeds had a long history by the Tang, stretching back to Liu Xiang's 劉向 (79–8 BCE) compilation of over a hundred such accounts under the title *Accounts of Exemplary Women* (*Lienü zhuan* 列女傳) in the first century BCE. The three accounts I consider here were all written around the turn of the ninth century, as *chuanqi* were coming into their own according to the dominant modern literary historical narrative. The women these tales celebrate are all remarkable for different reasons, but each receives her chronicler's commendation for what she accomplishes. One of these narratives is now labeled a *chuanqi*; the other two are not.

The Long, Slow Rise of Tang "Chuanqi"

Our first extraordinary woman is Miss Yang 楊氏, the wife of Li Kan 李侃, district magistrate of Xiangcheng 項城 (in modern-day Henan). Her deeds are celebrated in an account by Li Ao 李翱 (772–841), who credits her with rallying her husband and the people of Xiangcheng to the defense of their town when soldiers of the rebellious military commissioner Li Xilie 李希烈 (d. ca. 786) attacked in 783.[4] Li Ao's narrative is fast-paced and suspenseful, presenting Miss Yang as a resourceful leader in a moment of crisis. When Li Kan is at a loss for what to do as the rebels advance on the town, Miss Yang bluntly reminds him of the responsibilities of his office: "You are the district's magistrate. When the bandits arrive, you must protect it; and if your strength is not sufficient, then it is your duty to die here" 君, 縣令也. 寇至當守; 力不足, 死焉職也. When Li Kan bewails his lack of soldiers and money, Miss Yang tells him to use the contents of the state's granaries and storehouses to feed and reward the townspeople, so they will risk their lives to defend the town. When he returns home with an arrow wound in his hand, she sends him back to the fight with the query, "Is[n't] it better to die atop the city wall than to recover at home?" 與其死於城上, 不猶愈於家乎. Her strength of mind is highlighted by the contrast with her timorous husband. Whenever Li Kan hesitates, Miss Yang forces him into action, in one version of the text even "making" 使 him issue a defiant statement to the attackers.[5]

Miss Yang is equally forceful in exhorting the people of Xiangcheng, pointing out that Xiangcheng's fate in the upcoming battle will affect them the most:

The district magistrate is the one in charge, to be sure. Nonetheless, when his term is complete, he will be relieved of his post—not like you clerks and commoners. [You] clerks and commoners are people of this town. Your [ancestors'] graves are in this place. Together and to the death, you

---

4. Li Fang et al., *Wenyuan yinghua*, 796.4213a–14a, under the title "Yang liefu zhuan" 楊烈婦傳 ("Account of the exemplary wife Yang"). The text is also found, with slight variations, in Dong Gao et al., *Quan Tang wen*, 640.6465a–66a, and Yao Xuan, *Tang wencui*, 99.6b–7a.

5. Dong Gao et al., *Quan Tang wen*, 640.6465a–65b. In Li Fang et al., *Wenyuan yinghua*, the word order is reversed such that Li Kan "sends" (also 使) someone to issue the statement (796.4213b).

must defend your town! Could you bear to give yourselves up and become the bandits' men?

縣令, 誠主也. 雖然, 歲滿則罷去. 非若吏人百姓然. 吏人百姓, 邑人也. 墳墓存焉. 宜相與致死, 以守其邑. 忍失其身而爲賊之人耶?

Putting in practice her advice to her husband, she promises cash rewards to those who strike the rebels with roof tiles, rocks, knives, or arrows—the payments presumably drawn from the state's stores, as she had instructed Li Kan. Her appeal, and her offer of pay, persuades several hundred townspeople to join the fight. Though it is Li Kan who then leads the defense troops to ascend the town walls to fight while Miss Yang remains behind to cook, the narrative makes clear that it is she who wins them to the cause.

The text further heightens the suspense inherent in the townspeople's precarious situation by underscoring the odds against them. The defense force of several hundred atop the town wall is severely outnumbered by the several thousand rebels sent by Li Xilie to attack Xiangcheng, and their weapons and fortifications are woefully lacking. When Li Kan appeals to the attackers to desist, they simply laugh and prepare to scale the walls; it appears inevitable that they will crush the defense. It is only when their leader, Li Xilie's son-in-law, happens to be killed by an arrow that they lose momentum and scatter, and the town is saved (for which Li Kan is commended and promoted). The archer who fired the decisive shot remains anonymous, though, and Miss Yang is the hero whose impassioned words and decisive actions are the means through which the townspeople survive unscathed.

In the final third of his account, Li Ao addresses another aspect of Miss Yang's actions, namely, that they transgress (or transcend) contemporaneous normative expectations for a woman's behavior. Li Ao acknowledges that "worthiness" 賢 for a woman ordinarily consists simply of submission to her parents and in-laws, amity with her sisters-in-law, tenderness toward the young, and chastity—all qualities that operate exclusively in the domestic sphere. Miss Yang becomes remarkable when she steps out of that domestic sphere and into the public arena. By doing so, she accomplishes something "truly difficult [even] for high officials and great ministers" 固公卿大臣之所難—roles filled by men. Li Ao's discussion amounts to an argument that Miss Yang's deeds should be evaluated for

The Long, Slow Rise of Tang "Chuanqi"

their results and not through the lens of her gender. In one version of the text he asks, "Are not all people alike in receiving vital breath from heaven?" 人之受氣於天其何不同也, proposing a fundamental kinship among all people that here is most easily read as referencing gender roles.[6] Miss Yang deserves remembrance not in spite of her transgression of the usual expectations for women, but because of it, since it allowed her to accomplish so much. Li Ao's discussion suggests that her deeds collapse the distinction between feminized and "regular" worthiness, making her the equal not only of "principled women of old" 古烈女 but of "the ancients" 古人 as a whole.

Li Ao's account thus presents a story that is absorbing for both its suspenseful plot and the arresting figure at its center. Miss Yang's deeds make her stand out not only among other women, but also among men. Li Ao, who explains that he was moved to commemorate her so that her story would be known to historians, was also moved—or perhaps felt obliged—to pass judgment on her behavior and affirm that it is not only acceptable but deserving of praise.

A second remarkable woman—as it happens, connected even more closely to Li Xilie's rebellion—is a Miss Dou 竇氏, known as Guiniang 桂娘, who was captured by Li Xilie and installed as his concubine. She secretly conspired against him with his general Chen Xianqi 陳仙奇 (d. 786), ultimately helping Chen Xianqi bring him down. Du Mu 杜牧 (803–853) heard her story from a relative of hers and was inspired to record her deeds.[7] His account is not crafted for suspense in the way that Li Ao's is, perhaps because readers would have already known that Li Xilie's rebellion failed, but his heroine is equally striking.

Du Mu's account constructs a portrait of a woman adept at plotting and manipulation. Guiniang uses her beauty and her wits to win Li Xilie's trust, thus becoming privy to "all Xilie's secrets, that even his wife and sons didn't know about" 凡希烈之密雖妻子不知者. After Li Xilie suffers a defeat and is forced to retreat, Guiniang cultivates a sisterly relationship with Chen Xianqi's wife (also surnamed Dou), claiming to Li Xilie that

---

6. Li Fang et al., *Wenyuan yinghua*, 796.4213b.

7. Li Fang et al., *Wenyuan yinghua*, 796.4214a–14b, under the title "Dou lienü zhuan" 竇烈女傳; Du Mu, *Fanchuan wenji jiaozhu*, 6.561–65, written as "Dou lienü zhuan" 竇列女傳.

her goal is to secure Chen's loyalty. But to the other Miss Dou, she speaks of Xilie's unprincipled ruthlessness and suggests that his defeat is inevitable. When Xilie dies and his sons conceal his death, plotting to kill his senior generals (presumably including Chen Xianqi), Guiniang pretends to the sons that she is sending Chen Xianqi's wife a gift of peaches to make it appear that nothing has happened (i.e., that Xilie is still alive); but sealed in a wax ball colored to look like a peach, she encloses a secret message divulging the sons' plans. Her note prompts Chen Xianqi and another general to attack Xilie's family the next day: they too lie, claiming to act on orders from the emperor. They kill Xilie's sons and cut off their heads, and those of Xilie and his wife, to send to the imperial court in a gesture of loyalty.

Du Mu depicts a world of deceit, treachery, and cunning, in which a person must constantly recalibrate her loyalties to hope to survive. Like Li Ao, Du Mu represents his heroine as a quick thinker who responds adroitly in a difficult situation. Guiniang is a skilled player in this game in which the other players are men. She ingratiates herself with a traitorous general and becomes his beloved concubine; she also betrays the affection and trust he places in her by encouraging his general to plot against him and abets in the deaths of his wife and sons. Her collaboration with Chen Xianqi is an act of loyalty to the Tang that may also be a bid for self-preservation. Initially she succeeds, when she avoids the fate of Li Xilie's wife, but two months (two days in one text[8]) later, a general loyal to Li Xilie kills Chen Xianqi and Guiniang.

Also like Li Ao, Du Mu concludes his account by analyzing his protagonist's behavior. For him, the central tension Guiniang faces is between her loyalty to the husband circumstances have brought her and her loyalty to the Tang state her father serves. Du Mu argues that given Guiniang's circumstances, to throw in her lot with Li Xilie would have been an acceptable choice:

> The only way in which Xilie let Guiniang down was in abducting her. When Xilie usurped [the title of emperor], Guiniang became his consort [i.e., her position was elevated when he claimed the imperial title]. Moreover, he

---

8. Li Fang et al., *Wenyuan yinghua*, 796.4214b, reads "two months" 兩月, while Du Mu, *Fanchuan wenji*, 6.562, reads "two days" 兩日.

doted on and trusted her. As far as her woman's heart is concerned, to devote herself to Xilie would have been fine.

希烈負桂娘者但刼之耳. 希烈僭而貴娘妃, 復寵信. 於女子心始終希烈可也.

Though we might take issue with the insinuation that Xilie's abduction of Guiniang is offset by her rise in status, Du Mu's comments reflect the same expectations that a woman's duties lie in the domestic and not the public sphere that we saw in Li Ao's account.

But Guiniang chooses loyalty to the state, a choice that Du Mu locates at the moment of her abduction: "As she was about to go out the door, she looked back at her father and said, 'Don't be distressed! I'm sure to be able to destroy the bandit, and allow you to gain wealth and honor from the Son of Heaven'" 將出門, 顧其父曰: 慎無戚, 必能滅賊, 使大人取富貴於天子. These words direct us to interpret her subsequent scheming as an act of loyalty to the Tang (and also to her natal family), and her solicitous behavior toward Li Xilie and his sons as a pretense assumed to gain those greater ends. Du Mu writes:

> [Through] this [i.e., her actions] it is clear that she truly understood how to comport herself, as well as the subtle patterns of opposition and obedience, of insignificance and importance. Being able to get the better of Xilie was judiciousness; taking Xianqi's wife as her [adoptive] elder sister was wisdom; and in the end being able to destroy the bandits, without a thought for herself, was zeal. Multitudes of full-grown men with salaries and positions associated with Xilie when he rebelled. How could this have been because their talents or strength were insufficient [to oppose him]? Undoubtedly, if principle and [appropriate] order are achieved, then even a woman may accomplish something through them.
>
> 此誠知所去所就, 逆順輕重之理, 明也. 能得希烈, 權也; 娣先奇妻, 智也; 終能滅賊不顧其私, 烈也. 六尺男子有祿位者, 當希烈叛, 與之上下者眾矣. 此豈才力不足耶. 蓋義理苟至, 雖一女子, 可以有成.

Du Mu suggests that rather than being expedient, Guiniang's actions were tactical: she feigned wifely devotion to Li Xilie to work toward his downfall. Again, male behavior is the explicit standard of comparison, and Guiniang succeeds in acting with principle while "multitudes" of men, by aligning themselves with a rebel, betray the trust reposed in them when they were awarded positions in the empire's bureaucracy. Her skill in assessing what is truly important in turn allows her to demonstrate the virtues of judiciousness, wisdom, and zeal and in the end to accomplish what many men do not.

Both of these accounts show us women impelled to extraordinary deeds by extraordinary circumstances. Li Ao and Du Mu tell their stories well, crafting narratives that compel our attention and cast their protagonists as heroines deserving sympathy and acclaim. Each writer justifies the woman's unorthodox actions by comparing her favorably to others who failed to meet the same standards in their own behavior. That Miss Yang went too far for some later readers can be seen from the fact that when Li Ao's account was abridged for inclusion in the *New Tang History* (*Xin Tang shu* 新唐書) chapter on "exemplary women" (*lienü* 列女) in the eleventh century, the editors shifted the speeches urging the townspeople to fight and promising them rewards from her voice to her husband Li Kan's; she privately exhorts him to lead the defense, and cooks for those fighting, but does not take on a public role.[9] (Miss Dou is omitted from the "exemplary women" chapter altogether, though her deeds are briefly recounted at the end of Li Xilie's biography there.[10]) The lengthy evaluative discussions with which Li Ao and Du Mu conclude their accounts recognizes the unusual scope of each woman's actions and argue that her deeds are praiseworthy and worth remembering.

The third account of a remarkable woman I consider is unlike my first two examples in both its choice of heroine and the actions for which she is celebrated. Bai Xingjian's "Li Wa zhuan" is a tale of desire, betrayal, and redemption that unfolds on the private stage of a young man's relations with the courtesan Li Wa and with his family. But it too is a story about a woman who makes unexpected choices and earns her commemorator's admiration as a result. The terms in which Bai Xingjian evaluates his heroine's deeds place the tale squarely in the tradition of accounts of remarkable women.

First, some of the undeniable contrasts between "Li Wa" and the accounts of Miss Yang and Miss Dou: Li Wa is a courtesan, not a woman of the elite; her story is not tied to a particular historical moment; and

9. Ouyang Xiu and Song Qi, et al., *Xin Tang shu*, 205.5825–26.
10. Ouyang Xiu and Song Qi, et al., *Xin Tang shu*, 225B.6440–41.

the young man she ensnares remains anonymous throughout.[11] Instead of being centered on her laudable deeds, two-thirds of "Li Wa" recounts her less savory accomplishments: her roiling of the young man's heart, which leads him to abandon his career ambitions, his friends, and his family to move in with her and her "mother"; her role in the ruse through which she and her mother abandon him once his money is gone; and the depths to which the young man consequently sinks, beaten nearly to death by his father for dishonoring their family. This "practically inhuman behavior" 殆非人行, as Li Wa herself later describes it, is not the stuff of an account of exemplary female behavior.

The private sphere in which "Li Wa" unfolds also allows the reader a more intimate look at the chief actors and the dynamics of their interactions. The young man is arguably the chief protagonist in the first half of the tale, where we are granted glimpses into his feelings: how he "lingered, unable to leave" 徘徊不能去 at first sight of Li Wa; his preoccupation with her afterward, "his thoughts unsettled" 意若有失 until he ventures to return to her house; and much later, his fury and bewilderment after he realizes he has been duped. Li Wa, like Miss Yang and Miss Dou, is portrayed largely through her words and actions; juxtaposed with our insight into the young man's shifting emotional states, her inscrutability adds to her mystique. The private nature of the events recounted, the drama of the feckless young man's fall and his surprising redemption, the ambiguity of Li Wa's motivations throughout, and the access given the reader to the young man's inner feelings all contribute to produce an intricately structured story that remains engrossing twelve centuries after it was written, and all contribute to "Li Wa's" later identification as a *chuanqi*.

Yet in other respects, Li Wa's story is not so different from Miss Yang's and Miss Dou's. Indeed, her two principal deeds parallel theirs, although they are performed in different contexts. Like Miss Dou, she deceives her man, cultivating his affection while plotting to forsake him; he just happens to be a young man intended for a bureaucratic career rather than a rebelling general. Later, evidently regretting her treatment of him, she takes him in when he is begging on the streets; like Miss Yang, she forces him to do his duty (in this case, to study for the civil service exams and

---

11. Glen Dudbridge argues that the tale likely made composite reference to three brothers in the Zheng 鄭 clan in *Tale of Li Wa*, 43–52.

take up an official's career) when he lacks the backbone to do it by himself. Bai Xingjian's account allots more space to Li Wa's deceptions and their effects—emotional, social, professional, and economic—on the young man, but the final third is devoted to her efforts to restore him to his former status and the approbation she garners as a result. The young man's father's insistence that his son formally marry her is itself a mark of her transformation from object of opprobrium to object of praise. Thereafter she is an exemplary wife and daughter-in-law, lauded as "most excellent in wifely behavior" 婦道甚修 and "beloved and esteemed" 眷尚 by her husband's parents. Vis-à-vis the young man's family, her later efforts to further their ambitions for him and her exemplary devotion to the family once she marries into it make full amends for her earlier derailment of his trajectory.

To this description of the approval Li Wa wins from her marital family, Bai Xingjian adds his own praise, exclaiming, "Ah! That a fickle courtesan should have such integrity! Even the principled women of old cannot surpass her. Who could fail to heave a sigh!" 嗟乎, 倡蕩之姬, 節行如是, 雖古先烈女不能踰也, 焉得不爲之歎息哉. His evaluation is shorter than those that Li Ao and Du Mu include in their accounts, perhaps because he is commending her "womanly" excellence and has no need to compare her favorably to men. But like both of them, he instructs us on how to interpret the deeds he has just recounted, in effect arguing that a woman whose doings might seem suspect is in fact worthy of acclaim. Bai Xingjian's remarks position his account within the rubric of other accounts commending extraordinary achievements, in particular those enacted by women.

The connections among these accounts of remarkable women are unmistakable, from their titling as "accounts," to their deft presentation of dramatic stories, to the evaluative comments on integrity or principle with which they close. All were written within a few decades of each other. But to my knowledge, these similarities have not been acknowledged elsewhere, and the narratives have been treated very differently in the centuries since they were written.[12] Today "Li Wa" is a *chuanqi*,

---

12. Scholarship that draws connections between *chuanqi* and other contemporaneous prose has focused on connections between *chuanqi* writers and the *guwen* 古文 (ancient prose) movement. See (for examples) the brief references in Li Jianguo, "Tang

The Long, Slow Rise of Tang "Chuanqi"   109

frequently reprinted in anthologies of classical Chinese tales and refer-
enced in histories of Chinese literature as one of several *chuanqi* that treat
the complexities of romance and marriage for elite young men and the
(often lower-class) women with whom they fall in love. Li Ao's and Du
Mu's accounts are not designated *chuanqi*, and, as far as I have been able
to discover, are largely forgotten as examples of literary prose, their sto-
ries of devotion to the public good generating less interest than Li Wa's
ruination and redemption of a young man of good family.[13]

To be sure, there are differences among them, not the least that "Li
Wa's" emphasis on inner passions and private moments and its elision of
the young man's name allowed Bai Xingjian more scope for imagination
in recording his story (or even conceivably for greater fidelity to events).
Indeed, it could be made up entirely. But we also have no proof of the
historical veracity of Li Ao's and Du Mu's claims for Miss Yang and Miss
Dou. In addition, "Li Wa's" plot draws on a formula common in the col-
lections of stories of the occult to which *chuanqi* are often filiated in re-
cent scholarship, namely, the accidental encounter with a woman who is
not what she seems to be; it is just that Li Wa is a human woman rather
than a ghost or an animal who has taken on human form.[14] But "Li Wa"
shares as much and perhaps more with Li Ao's and Du Mu's accounts as
with those occult tales.

My argument is not that "Li Wa" is no different from Li Ao's and
Du Mu's accounts of their heroines, but that we cannot understand it and
its place in Chinese literary history unless we see its connections to texts
beyond *chuanqi*. Moreover, those texts include more than just accounts
of remarkable women. In finding worthy subjects for commemoration
among ordinary people (i.e., not the educated elite), "Li Wa" is akin to
Liu Zongyuan's 柳宗元 (773–819) account of a pharmacist in "Account
of Song Qing" ("Song Qing zhuan" 宋清傳) or Han Yu's 韓愈 (768–824)

---

bai sikao lu (dai qianyan)," 13, 38, and 48, in Li Jianguo, *Tang Wudai zhiguai chuanqi
xulu*, vol. 1; and the more extended discussions in Liu Kairong, *Tangren xiaoshuo*, 18–
33; Wu Zhida, *Tangren chuanqi*, 24–25; and Tai Jingnong, *Zhongguo wenxue shi*,
2:368–71.

    13. Li Ao's account appears in only one modern anthology of Tang prose that I have
found, Sun Wang and Yu Xianhao's *Tangdai wenxuan*, in three volumes and over 2600
pages (on 2:1309–15); I have yet to find Du Mu's in a modern anthology.

    14. See S. Allen, *Shifting Stories*, 153–56.

reflections on a Chang'an laborer in "Account of the Plasterer Wang Chengfu" ("Wuzhe Wang Chengfu zhuan" 圬者王承福傳), to name two roughly contemporaneous examples, neither of which has been called *chuanqi*.[15] Bai Xingjian surely knew that his example of female integrity, his focus on private life, and the length to which he spun out his tale were unusual, and that he was doing something new with the account form. To reduce that to its difference from stories of the occult is to miss much about how it would have resonated in its own time.

The Invention of Tang Chuanqi

To understand why these works are regarded as they are today, we must examine the history of how they have been categorized and transmitted between the ninth and the twentieth centuries. I am less concerned with the fact of retrospective genre creation, which is not unique, than with the means by which this particular set of texts cohered into a widely accepted category of analysis. The process through which the *chuanqi* genre came into being was one in which a small set of texts were cordoned off from the larger field of contemporaneous narrative works. Modern scholarship differentiates *chuanqi* from the related genre of *zhiguai*, simpler stories about the occult and other anomalies gathered into collections. *Chuanqi* are envisioned as more sophisticated, complex tales that developed out of that older, more primitive tradition, although in distinction to *zhiguai*, a number of *chuanqi* unfold entirely in the human realm and contain no occult elements ("Li Wa" being a prime example). A further distinction is that many key *chuanqi* originated as individually-circulating works, whereas *zhiguai* by definition circulated as collections of narratives. In this vision of generic development, *chuanqi* and *zhiguai* together constitute the main forms of Tang dynasty *xiaoshuo* 小説, the word now used for fiction, though in the Tang it referred primarily to collected tidbits of gossip.[16]

---

15. Li Fang et al., *Wenyuan yinghua*, 794.4197a–97b and 793.4194b–95a.

16. For further discussion of the relationship between *chuanqi* and *zhiguai*, see Li Jianguo, "Tang bai sikao lu (dai qianyan)," 5–8, in Li Jianguo, *Tang Wudai zhiguai chuanqi xulu*, vol. 1.

The Long, Slow Rise of Tang "Chuanqi"

Neither *chuanqi* nor *zhiguai* was in use as a generic term when these works were written, however; nor is it clear that the works now so designated would have been regarded as *xiaoshuo* (a term whose meaning changes so much over time that we might simply set it aside; to accommodate its shifting referents over time, I leave it untranslated).[17] This in itself should arouse our curiosity as we attempt to understand this material's history: not because retrospective categorical determinations are automatically wrong, but because they tell us more about how later readers perceived a body of work than how it was regarded in its own time. To understand literary history, we need to understand both.

The lineage thus created is also predicated on the assumption, so deeply embedded in the modern understanding of this material that it is rarely articulated, that *chuanqi* are closer kin to *zhiguai* than to other narratives that fall outside the *xiaoshuo* category. I suspect that this assumption, too, postdates the writing of the most emblematic *chuanqi*, and it applies to some examples better than others.

The works now designated *chuanqi* and *zhiguai* represent only a fraction of the narrative texts produced and circulated in Tang China. Of particular relevance here are narratives titled "accounts," *zhuan* 傳, or "records," *ji* 記. These include biographical and autobiographical narratives, pseudo-biographies built of elaborate wordplay (such as Han Yu's famous account of a writing brush),[18] stories with pointed morals attached, celebrations of a place or of the daring, loyalty, talent, self-sacrifice, or uprightness of an individual, and other such varied topics. Like *chuanqi*, these accounts and records often focus on a particular remarkable event or deed. Beyond this, many *chuanqi* are designated account/*zhuan* or record/*ji* in their titles. These similarities in content and shared conventions in titling suggest an affinity as significant as that to *zhiguai*.

The privileging of a certain set of works as *chuanqi*, understood as tales that evolved from *zhiguai* but were written up with more attention to style and detail, has its own story in the history of how this material was

17. Judith T. Zeitlin gives an overview of the term's evolution in "*Xiaoshuo*," 249–61. On the May Fourth–era adoption of *xiaoshuo* to refer to fiction, see Dudbridge, "A Question of Classification," 156–57.

18. That is, "Account of Mao Ying ['Hair Point']" ("Mao Ying zhuan" 毛穎傳), in Li Fang et al., *Wenyuan yinghua*, 793.4195a–96a.

transmitted over the centuries to the early twentieth century when the modern narrative began to emerge. That history is the product of decisions, occurring over several centuries, that individually were far from inevitable but in aggregate led to the retrospective creation of *chuanqi*. We can identify three periods, prior to the twentieth century, as particularly significant: the late ninth, tenth, and sixteenth centuries. Choices made at these crucial junctures in the transmission of these texts paved the way for identifying a group of especially fine tales within the larger body of contemporaneous narrative and eventually, their designation as *chuanqi*.[19]

The process began sometime in the mid- to late ninth century, when a man named Chen Han 陳翰 (fl. 870s–880s?) gathered together a miscellaneous group of short narratives under the title *Collection of Peculiar Hearsay* (*Yiwen ji* 異聞集).[20] Chen Han did not write any of the narratives himself, instead selecting some forty-odd pieces recorded by nearly as many writers over the course of the previous two to three centuries, Bai Xingjian's "Li Wa" among them.[21] All (or nearly all) appear to have circulated as independent works prior to their inclusion in *Yiwen ji*. The contents of the tales make up something of a topical hodgepodge, concerning variously political intrigue, romance, gods, ghosts, dreams, prognostication, dragons, animals that take on human form, magical objects, and so forth. Some are relatively short—less than two pages in a modern printed edition; others are more than double that, at seven or eight printed pages. In style, too, they are varied, some sprinkled with poems and poetic phrasing, and others much plainer. What they share is a concern with events that are extraordinary in one way or another: the *yi* 異, "peculiar" or "marvelous" or "strange," of Chen Han's title.

19. Dudbridge briefly outlines this progression in "A Question of Classification" (155–57), though his focus is somewhat different from mine.

20. The sole known datable event in Chen Han's life occurred in 874; 840 is the latest date mentioned in the narratives he is known to have included in the collection. See S. Allen, *Shifting Stories*, 247–48.

21. As the vagueness of these numbers suggest, the precise contents of *Yiwen ji* and the authorship and dating of many of the included texts are unknown. Thirty-eight tales are widely accepted as having been included, with another six titles whose link to *Yiwen ji* is more dubious. For more detailed discussions of the contents, see Li Jianguo, *Tang Wudai zhiguai chuanqi xulu*, 2:1181–98; Cheng Yizhong, "*Yiwen ji* kao"; and S. Allen, *Shifting Stories*, 244–52.

Chen Han's anthology is significant for the later formation of *chuanqi* for three reasons. First, it incorporates into the category of "peculiar" events that transpire entirely in the human sphere (such as we see in "Li Wa"). Many narrative collections were in circulation in the ninth century, falling into two broad groups: those about the weird and occult now termed *zhiguai* and *chuanqi* collections, including religious miracle tales; and those collecting historical gossip, often specialized by era. The events recounted in many of the individual *Yiwen ji* narratives would easily fit into one or the other sort of collection, those on political intrigue and romance falling into the latter group and the remainder into the former. Chen Han, however, brought them together into a single collection; and his title, "Collection of Peculiar Hearsay," marks the collection as one devoted to the "strange," *yi* being found in the titles of several collections of the kind. In juxtaposing the two kinds of narratives under such a title, Chen Han cast them all—even those that do not focus on the protagonist's experience of the occult—as stories of the strange, thus expanding the scope of the strange to include marvels within human activities. The *chuanqi* canon is characterized by the same breadth.

Second, and closely related, as an anthology made up of works that had previously circulated as independent texts, *Yiwen ji* transforms those individual texts into a collection. Reading, or writing, a collection of narratives on similar themes is a different experience from reading or writing a single text such as "Li Wa," which easily stands on its own. Once "Li Wa" is put into a collection to be read side by side with other texts, and under the title *Yiwen ji*, it becomes part of a larger whole instead of a work unto itself.[22] *Yiwen ji* represents the earliest explicit association among these varied texts I have found.[23] This is especially significant for texts— again "Li Wa" is a prime example—which do not fit as easily into the strange tale rubric, by marking it as akin in form as well as in content to the sorts of narratives that appear in collections. The association also directs us toward a particular interpretation of the events recounted in

22. See also S. Allen, *Shifting Stories*, 267–70.

23. Around the same time that Chen Han assembled *Yiwen ji*, a few writers compiled collections of more elaborate and "*zhuan*-like" narratives, suggesting a trend toward viewing collections as potential vehicles for such accounts; but these collections maintained the focus on the weird/*guai* 怪 found in earlier collections.

SARAH M. ALLEN

the collection's narratives, namely, evidence of the anomalous. In the case of Li Wa, we marvel at the strangeness of Li Wa's story rather than considering how to evaluate her character.

Finally, several key *chuanqi* ("Li Wa" among them) may not have survived long enough to be designated *chuanqi*—and so to help shape the genre's conception—had they not been included in *Yiwen ji*, because it is through *Yiwen ji* that they were incorporated, roughly a century later, into a much vaster compendium, to which I turn next.[24] Without *Yiwen ji*, our picture of *chuanqi*, and of Tang narrative more broadly, would be quite different.

A second formative moment occurred some hundred years later with the compilation, at imperial direction, of two compendia: *Extensive Records from the Taiping Reign* (*Taiping guangji* 太平廣記, presented to the throne in 978) and *Flowers from the Garden of Literature* (*Wenyuan yinghua* 文苑英華, presented in 987). These two encyclopedic books divided up between them much of the literary inheritance from the previous several centuries. Belles-lettres, including *shi* 詩 poetry and many prose forms such as letters, prefaces, communications to and from the throne, and so forth, were placed in *Wenyuan yinghua*, where they were organized by genre. Narratives from collections of tales about the occult, religious figures, historical gossip, and other miscellaneous events were all put in *Taiping guangji*, where they were organized by topic. Individually circulating narratives that concerned the occult or focused on romance also ended up in *Taiping guangji*, but more "serious" narrative accounts—those containing pointed morals or allegorical reference, and autobiographical accounts (even if playful), for example—were incorporated into *Wenyuan yinghua*, which contains five scrolls devoted to accounts/*zhuan*

---

24. Some twenty texts survive exclusively in *Taiping guangji* with *Yiwen ji* cited as their source, or (in synoptic form) among the twelfth-century compendium *Leishuo*'s 類説 selections from *Yiwen ji*. Although not all of these are "representative *chuanqi*," several are, including "Li Wa"; Li Chaowei's 李朝威 "Miraculous Marriage at Dongting" ("Dongting lingyin zhuan" 洞庭靈姻傳), in Li Fang et al., *Taiping guangji*, 419.3410–17 (as "Liu Yi" 柳毅); and Li Gongzuo's 李公佐 "Governor of the Southern Branch" ("Nanke taishou zhuan" 南柯太守傳), in Li Fang et al., *Taiping guangji*, 475.3910–15 (as "Chunyu Fen" 淳于棼). The *Taiping guangji* figure includes attributions to *Yiwen ji* and to *Record of Strange Hearsay* (*Yiwen lu* 異聞錄; eight) and *Record of Strange Hearsay* (*Yiwen ji* 異聞記; one), both believed to be errors for *Yiwen ji* (these numbers omit likely misattributions).

and thirty-eight devoted to records/*ji*;[25] the primary criterion for determining whether a narrative should go into *Wenyuan yinghua* or *Taiping guangji* appears to have been content. Though a very small number of narratives (I count four) were included in both, the divisions made here had a profound influence on how later readers perceived the material within the compilations.

In particular, the contents of *Taiping guangji* came to define the scope of pre-Song *xiaoshuo* as it has been understood for the past few centuries. The earliest book catalogs to list *Taiping guangji* categorize it as an "encyclopedia" (*leishu* 類書; literally "categorized writings") because of its topical organization.[26] Later catalogs, however, designate *Taiping guangji* as *xiaoshuo*.[27] A parallel shift is seen in the classification of surviving collections and individual narratives of the sort that went into *Taiping guangji*, which had once been most often categorized as histories (*shi* 史) of some type and then, beginning in the tenth century, were also labeled *xiaoshuo*.[28] Though the vast majority of the narratives preserved in *Taiping guangji* have received little attention in the modern construction of *xiaoshuo* and its history (for example, the hundreds of religious miracle tales and hagiographic accounts that make up roughly the first quarter of the compilation), virtually all of the works that are accorded a place in that history are included in *Taiping guangji*.

Taiping guangji's topical organization further blurred the distinction between individually circulating accounts or records and narratives from collections, continuing the trajectory begun in *Yiwen ji*. The collections themselves were dissolved, with narratives selected for inclusion placed under an appropriate subject heading. *Taiping guangji* does cite a source for the majority of its thousands of entries—collection titles (but not authors/compilers) for items drawn from collections, and author names for some but not all items that had circulated individually—so the distinction is not completely invisible. But with narratives from all sorts of sources placed side by side, the differences between them are obscured, paving

25. Li Fang et al., *Wenyuan yinghua*, 792.4186a–796.4215a and 797.4216a–834.4402a.

26. Wang Yaochen, *Chongwen zongmu*, 3.174; Zheng Qiao, *Tongzhi*, 69.814–2. For *leishu*, see Nugent, chapter 3 in this volume.

27. For example, Tuotuo (Toghto), *Song shi*, 206.5230.

28. See the discussion in S. Allen, "Narrative Genres," 283–85.

the way for narratives from a varied range of origins to be collectively classed as *xiaoshuo*.

The sixteenth century represents a third decisive point in the formation of Tang *chuanqi*, when the publication of several new anthologies of or including Tang materials earmarked a subset of the narratives preserved in *Taiping guangji* as most worthy of attention. *Taiping guangji* itself was also reprinted, possibly for the first time since the tenth century, in the 1560s. Both types of publication made these Tang (and pre-Tang) narratives more widely available than they had been for centuries. The anthologies were especially influential in selecting from the much larger body of texts those narratives that have since become the modern *chuanqi* canon.

Lu Cai's 陸采 (1497–1537) *Yu Chu's Records* (*Yu Chu zhi* 虞初志), likely dating to around the 1510s or 1520s, may have been the first of these new anthologies and is representative of the renewed interest in earlier narrative material.[29] *Yu Chu zhi* is not an exclusively Tang anthology, but of the thirty-one titles it includes, all but one date to the Tang or shortly thereafter. One of the Tang titles is itself a collection, Xue Yongruo's 薛用弱 (fl. ca. 820s) *Record of Collected Peculiarities* (*Jiyi ji* 集異記).[30] The other Tang titles are all discrete narratives and bear titles identifying them as records (*ji* 記, *lu* 錄, or in one case *zhi* 志) or accounts (*zhuan* 傳). This mode of titling is significant because although the majority of these narratives had been independently circulating accounts or records, six had originated in collections, where they would likely not have borne titles or individual generic designations (as indeed the *Jiyi ji* tales included in *Yu Chu zhi* do not).[31] Thus where *Yiwen ji* made individual accounts and records into a collection, *Yu Chu zhi* makes items from collections into individual accounts. This effectively erases the difference between individual

29. On the dating of *Yu Chu zhi*, see Cheng Yizhong, "*Yu Chu zhi* de bianzhe," 40.

30. Sixteen tales from *Jiyi ji* are included, each given a short descriptive title, such as the name of the protagonist. Because in *Yu Chu zhi* they are subsumed under the *Jiyi ji* title, with an attribution to "Xue Yongruo of Hedong from the Tang" 唐河東薛用弱, I count them collectively as one title. The included items represent less than half of the narratives that constituted the full *Jiyi ji*. Li Jianguo counts an additional thirty-five preserved in *Taiping guangji* (*Tang Wudai zhiguai chuanqi xulu*, 1:648–53).

31. I say "originated" here because Lu Cai himself surely did not see these texts in that "original" state.

The Long, Slow Rise of Tang "Chuanqi"

narratives and those from collections, even more completely than had *Taiping guangji*, where the citation indicates an item's origins. The juxtaposition of tales that originated in collections with tales that had once stood on their own suggests that to Lu Cai—and thus perforce to his readers—there was no distinction between them.

Textual similarities (and the lack of other known contemporaneous sources) indicate that Lu Cai likely drew many (perhaps most) of his texts from *Taiping guangji*, and others from another early sixteenth-century publication, Gu Yuanqing's 顧元慶 (1487–1565) *Xiaoshuo from Gu's Library* (*Gushi wenfang xiaoshuo* 顧氏文房小説).[32] Lu Cai's selections are not representative of either of these sources, however: he chooses engaging tales on themes with persistent appeal. Nearly half of the Tang titles concern a romance (or a brief fling): some end happily, some tragically; some are between human men and women, and some between human men and nonhuman women, whether goddesses or fox- or dragon-women. Other narratives involve encounters with heroes, divinities, long-dead historical figures, and other intriguing individuals. Two are about the disastrous end of Tang Emperor Xuanzong's 唐玄宗 reign (712–756). Above all, these are good stories that remain accessible centuries after they were first written down.

Other anthologies followed. The second section of Lu Ji's 陸輯 (1515–1552) *Sea of Stories, Past and Present* (*Gujin shuohai* 古今説海), printed by 1544, gathers sixty-four "alternative accounts" (*biezhuan* 別傳), almost all from the Tang and drawn from *Taiping guangji*. Lu Ji's selection is entirely different from Lu Cai's (perhaps suggesting that Lu Ji knew of *Yu Chu zhi*), but like Lu Cai, he makes no distinction between individually circulating narratives and those originally from collections, which are the majority here. Like Lu Cai, Lu Ji chooses lively, entertaining stories. Subsequent anthologies expanded on this selection, drawing additional tales from *Taiping guangji*, but the tales included in *Yu Chu zhi* and *Gujin shuohai* remained the core of anthologies published from later in the sixteenth century into the Qing. The repackaging of a selection of material in anthologies winnowed the nearly seven thousand items preserved in

---

32. *Gushi wenfang xiaoshuo* reprints forty texts from the Gu family's library, a number of them based on Song editions, according to notes appended to the individual texts.

SARAH M. ALLEN

Taiping guangji down into smaller sets that made choice highlights much easier to access than they had been for centuries.

It is also around this time that the term *chuanqi* appears to have gained popularity as designations for a subset of material within the broader field of *xiaoshuo*. The phrase "*chuanqi* of men of the Tang" 唐人傳奇 is used by several sixteenth-century critics, indicating that the term *chuanqi* was associated specifically with Tang works.[33] Exactly which works these writers had in mind is not clear, however. Hu Yinglin 胡應麟 (1551–1602) uses both *zhiguai* and *chuanqi* explicitly to refer to different types of *xiaoshuo*, listing them first among six categories of *xiaoshuo*. Though Hu Yinglin did not define either term—and in fact notes that the boundary between *chuanqi* and *zhiguai* is porous—he gives examples for each that demonstrate the differences between them. His four *zhiguai* examples are all collections of primarily brief narratives focused on the occult (two pre-Tang and two Tang), while the four *chuanqi* are all longer, originated as individually circulating narratives, and focus on human affairs and romance in particular.[34] Though his discussion suggests that Hu Yinglin may have conceived of *chuanqi* more narrowly (i.e., as stories of romance) than the term is used now, his comments are frequently cited today in support of the prevailing understanding of *xiaoshuo* as consisting of these two major categories of *chuanqi* and *zhiguai*. Elsewhere Hu Yinglin draws a contrast between simpler records of strange events from the pre-Tang period and a "purposeful pursuit of novelty" 作意好奇 found in Tang texts, reflecting a perception of change over time (though he does not use the terms *chuanqi* or *zhiguai* in this context).[35]

This centuries-long process through which a body of texts was identified and a vocabulary to describe them was developed paved the way for *chuanqi* to become widely recognized as a key stage in the history of Chinese narrative and Chinese fiction. Lu Xun 魯迅 (1881–1936) included three chapters on *chuanqi* from the Tang in his influential *Zhongguo xiaoshuo*

---

33. Both *zhiguai* and *chuanqi* occasionally appear in earlier texts, but the terms—*chuanqi* especially—seem to have gained recognition as generic designations only in the sixteenth century; see Li Jianguo, "Tang bai sikao lu (dai qianyan)," 8–12, in Li Jianguo, *Tang Wudai zhiguai chuanqi xulu*, vol. 1.

34. Hu Yinglin, *Xinjiao Shaoshi shanfang bicong*, 29.374.

35. Hu Yinglin, *Xinjiao Shaoshi shanfang bicong*, 37.486.

shilüe 中國小説史略 (*Brief History of Chinese* Xiaoshuo/*Fiction*; preface dated 1923), in which he made explicit the understanding that had taken shape in the anthologies and scattered critical comments of the sixteenth century.[36] He includes both tales that had originated as individual works and those from collections, reflecting the selections made in sixteenth-century anthologies, and his discussion highlights fine writing and an interest in "the marvelous" (*qi* 奇). His suggestion that these tales developed out of earlier, simpler antecedents, which he elsewhere labels *zhiguai*, and his subsumption of both into the broader category of *xiaoshuo*, draw on Hu Yinglin's observations on types of *xiaoshuo*. Lu Xun also echoes Hu's comments on the "purposeful pursuit of novelty" in Tang texts when he describes *chuanqi* as the result of a deliberate creation, a claim that resonated with the new understanding of *xiaoshuo* as "fiction" that had become increasingly popular in the late nineteenth and early twentieth centuries. Most of the works Lu Xun discusses in his chapters on *chuanqi* also appear within one or more of the sixteenth-century anthologies. It is the appearance of these works during the Tang that gives the dynasty its prominent place in the larger history of *xiaoshuo* as a stepping stone between the *zhiguai* collections of earlier centuries and the vernacular fiction of the late imperial period.

Lu Xun also compiled an anthology of his own. His *Anthology of Tang and Song Chuanqi* (*Tang Song chuanqi ji* 唐宋傳奇集, preface dated 1927) selects tales that had originally circulated independently (i.e., as *zhuan* or *ji*). Twenty-five of the thirty-two Tang titles included overlap with texts found in the two Ming anthologies *Yu Chu zhi* and *Gujin shuohai*. Around the same time, Wang Pijiang 汪辟疆 (1887–1966) published *Xiaoshuo by Men of the Tang* (*Tangren xiaoshuo* 唐人小説, preface dated 1929), including both individually circulating narratives and selections from collections (grouped together under the collection's title). Though the proportion of

---

36. Lu Xun, *Zhongguo xiaoshuo shilüe*, 59–82; the description of his characterization of *chuanqi* given here is drawn chiefly from his introductory remarks on 59. Lu Xun's interest in this work is in tracing the development of fiction in China; at the same time, he was clearly aware that many texts historically categorized as *xiaoshuo* were not fiction and that other works that he identified as part of Chinese fiction's lineage had not historically been considered *xiaoshuo* (issues he address in the first chapter of *Zhongguo xiaoshuo shilüe*). To mirror the polysemy and ambiguity of the term in Chinese, I have continued to use *xiaoshuo* even in translating twentieth-century texts in which "fiction" is likely the author's intended meaning.

titles overlapping these two Ming anthologies is lower (due to Wang Pi-jiang's inclusion of several tales from each of several collections), the topical scope of his chosen tales is very similar. Neither Lu Xun nor Wang Pijiang drew their tales directly from the Ming anthologies, instead going back to earlier sources—chiefly *Taiping guangji*—where possible.[37] Despite working largely from *Taiping guangji*, both take pains to reassert the distinction between tales from collections and independent tales. But their visions of "Tang *chuanqi*" or "Tang *xiaoshuo*" as tales about romance, or about ghosts, heroes, were-beasts, and the like, closely parallels that in the sixteenth-century anthologies.[38] The tales in these anthologies in turn form the basis of many subsequent anthologies, as well as of scholarship on Tang material.

In the decades since, several detailed histories of Tang *xiaoshuo* have added depth and nuance to the account Lu Xun gives in his three chapters on Tang *chuanqi*, incorporating more works and refining our picture of these works as literary texts and as historical artifacts.[39] Recent scholarship has increasingly taken note of the messiness of the subdivisions within the broader *xiaoshuo* corpus, as literary historians attempt to find a place for works that do not fit straightforwardly into either the *chuanqi* or *zhiguai* containers. But the broad outline sketched in Lu Xun's account—the kinship assertion between *chuanqi* and *zhiguai* as subsets of *xiaoshuo*, and the *chuanqi* canon established in these anthologies from the 1920s—remains largely intact.

We can thus trace over the course of these eleven centuries, from the ninth through the twentieth, the emergence of a body of texts—and an

---

37. Lu Xun's and Wang Pijiang's prefatory notes and their source notes for individual items indicate that they relied primarily on *Taiping guangji* but also referenced other sources such as Li Fang's *Wenyuan yinghua*, Gu Yuanqing's *Gushi wenfang xiaoshuo*, and Tao Zongyi's 陶宗儀 (1329–1410) compendium *Shuofu* 説郛 (Lu Xun, "Xuli" 序例, 2, in Lu Xun, *Tang Song chuanqi ji*, and *Tang Song chuanqi ji*, passim; Wang Pijiang, "Xuli" 序例, 1, in *Tangren xiaoshuo*, and *Tangren xiaoshuo*, passim).

38. Both anthologies also show overlap with the contents of Chen Han's much earlier *Yiwen ji*, but the resemblance is not as complete. Of the thirty-eight tales commonly accepted as being in *Yiwen ji*, twenty are in both anthologies, three are in one of them, and fifteen are in neither.[41]

39. Examples include Li Jianguo, *Tang Wudai zhiguai chuanqi xulu*, and Cheng Yizhong, *Tangdai xiaoshuo shi*.

idea about a type of text—that came to be known as *chuanqi*. The first step in this process, reflected in the compilation of *Yiwen ji* and then *Taiping guangji*, was the delineation of a body of narrative texts about remarkable events of many kinds, that—regardless of whether they originated as accounts/*zhuan* or records/*ji*, or in a collection—became a category unto themselves, separate from belles-lettres proper. Over time, this substantial body of narratives came increasingly to be referred to as *xiaoshuo*. The second step, seen in the sixteenth-century anthologies and the adoption of the term *chuanqi*, was the identification of a subset of tales most worth reading within that larger body of *xiaoshuo*. These developments laid the groundwork for the now-dominant understanding of *chuanqi* and their place in Chinese literary history in the twentieth century.

Conclusions

Chuanqi and the story of their emergence from *zhiguai* as the cream of the Tang *xiaoshuo* crop are mainstays of the prevailing understanding of Tang narrative and its significance in the broader history of Chinese literature. There are good reasons for this. The filiation of *chuanqi* to *zhiguai* recognizes genuine formal and thematic affinities among narratives from collections and narratives that once circulated independently as *zhuan* or *ji*, exemplified by the structural parallels between "Li Wa" and the stories of men who fall in with a woman who is not what she seems found in many *zhiguai* collections. More fundamentally, narratives from both types of sources express the same impulse to preserve a record of some extra-ordinary event.

Beyond this, in its attention to the throes of infatuation experienced by its unnamed protagonist, its fine delineation of his exchanges with Li Wa, and the complex balances that structure its plot, "Li Wa" *is* different from the accounts about Miss Yang and Miss Dou, vivid as the two latter are (as it is different from *zhiguai* as well). Thanks to these intricacies, "Li Wa" continues to reward reading and rereading, even if its appeal to today's readers is different from its appeal to readers of five hundred or a thousand years ago. It is no surprise that when Lu Xun, caught up in the

122   Sarah M. Allen

intellectual currents of his time, sought the roots of "fiction" in examples
of imaginative, compelling narratives from China's literary past in his
Zhongguo xiaoshuo shilüe, he granted "Li Wa" and other similar accounts
a central place.[40] Moreover, in locating Tang *chuanqi* within a teleologi-
cal account whose implicit goal is *xiaoshuo*'s later developments, he pro-
vides an argument about *why* they are important.

The difficulty is that once the *chuanqi* category is established, it needs
to be populated: historians and anthologists need to figure out which works
count and which do not. The fact that they have turned to *Taiping guangji*
to do so, and to *Yu Chu zhi* and *Gujin shuohai*, and not to *Wenyuan yinghua*
or to miscellaneous prose preserved in writers' individual literary collec-
tions, means that the boundary between "Li Wa" and accounts like those
about the Misses Yang and Dou is reified yet again. Meanwhile many other
Tang accounts, which could help illuminate the textual milieu in which
these works were produced, receive scant attention.

Histories can only be written in retrospect, if for no other reason than
whether or not a given event (or literary work) has any lasting impact can
only be revealed by the passage of time. But for that very reason, by the
time a given moment can be distilled into its history, the priorities and
interests of the historians will already be different from those being de-
scribed in the history. In the case of Tang narratives such as "Li Wa," it
was not until over a thousand years later that anyone thought to write
their history, and the history so written is the product of centuries of shift-
ing categorizations and values that reveal as much about the interests of
later readers as about these works' place in their own time. By this mea-
sure, Lu Xun and subsequent historians of Tang literature are right to
highlight the works they do, because these are the works that have mat-
tered most to later readers.

Examining another rich ninth-century narrative, one that has typically
not been accorded *chuanqi* status, Glen Dudbridge argued that "[t]o do
justice to these interesting works we should let them stand alone, not
pack them into pigeon holes."[41] My appeal here is motivated by similar

---

40. For a brief discussion of late nineteenth- and early twentieth-century Western-
influenced literary histories of Chinese and Japanese literature, and the importance of
fiction within them, see Denecke, chapter 8 in this volume.

41. Dudbridge, "A Question of Classification," 170.

concerns but draws a somewhat different conclusion. We can often appreciate much of the complexity of an individual text by "let[ting it] stand alone." But to understand history, we need context (though not pigeonholes). For all their interest, Miss Yang's and Miss Dou's stories are neither as gripping nor as accessible across many centuries as "Li Wa," and it is not surprising that they have fallen out of memory while "Li Wa" is still read. Thinking about "Li Wa" alongside these other two accounts is only one small step toward recognizing the interconnections among this broader textual field. But it is when we relocate "Li Wa" in the context of these and other explorations of human actions and of what makes for noteworthy behavior, that we can understand why Bai Xingjian concludes by exclaiming over Li Wa's "integrity." Texts exist in a matrix of other texts, and recognizing those relationships is crucial to writing history, which is always a story about change and hence of the differences among texts.

The conclusion to be drawn is less that the *chuanqi* story is wrong, than that it is not the whole story. The choices that literary historians since Lu Xun have made are conditioned by the choices that earlier readers have made about what to preserve, and where to preserve it. Such a history-by-milestones obscures the context that shows how those milestones came into being in the first place. Freeing "Li Wa" and other texts from the *chuanqi* label allows us to see their connections to a much broader range of works and to recognize contexts that would have been transparent to contemporaneous audiences. In the case of "Li Wa," this means seeing that Bai Xingjian participates in an ongoing exploration, traceable across other accounts from his own time and other historical periods, of how women might and should negotiate morally ambiguous choices. Li Ao and Du Mu, like Bai Xingjian, were skilled writers who clearly took pleasure in writing up accounts of people and events that caught their attention, whether to entertain their friends, to leave an edifying record for posterity, or both. "Li Wa," with its unusual heroine and elaborate plot, surely entertained as much as it edified. But viewed within the larger context of early ninth-century narrative, the differences between them are in degree rather than in kind.

In the circumstances that produced *chuanqi* we can see a neat reversal in what sorts of prose counted as "literature" over the course of the millennium between the late tenth and the early twentieth centuries. The inclusion of Miss Yang's and Miss Dou's stories in *Wenyuan yinghua* signals their status as belles-lettres—the *wen* 文 in *Wenyuan yinghua*—for the imperial servants charged with assembling the compilation. "Li Wa," in contrast, was relegated to *Taiping guangji* with other accounts preserved more for the information they contained on a certain topic than for their literary qualities (notwithstanding that "Li Wa" itself was assigned to the *za zhuanji* 雜傳記 or "miscellaneous accounts and records" section). By the early twentieth century, when Lu Xun wrote his *Zhongguo xiaoshuo shilüe*, the situation was neatly reversed: *xiaoshuo* as fiction had recently become a category within the new field of *wenxue* 文學, "literature," and "Li Wa" stood out as a prime example. As our ideas about what works are worth reading and preserving—and why—have changed, so too have our visions of those works' importance within a retrospective survey of China's literary past.

CHAPTER 5

The Case for Outsiders

TINA LU

A student of mine, a brilliant young scientist, asked me recently what the major breakthroughs of my field in the last generation had been. I was genuinely flummoxed. But the question set me to thinking about how our field—literary history of the Chinese-speaking world as performed outside of it—has morphed over the last half century or so, highly vulnerable and sensitive to changes in geopolitics. Even relatively late in the twentieth century, when Chinese universities were still emerging from the wake of the Cultural Revolution, one could imagine—and this is admittedly a crude reduction of contexts as diverse as Taiwan and Australia—the mission of universities outside the People's Republic of China as that of preserving texts and modes of reading, of doing what could not be done in China. But what now, in an era of far more generously supported Chinese universities and a more culturally hegemonic China?

Some of us have focused on our role as translators and mediators, not simply between languages but also between different parts of the North American academy, between different sets of theoretical concerns and literary histories, and between academic institutions of multiple languages. That role presupposes that whatever audience we have is in the English-speaking world (where scholars of Chinese are permanently secondary, playing a supporting role to the "real work" in North American and European humanistic studies, that is to say, the study of "their own" traditions and their claim to the global). What of our importance (if any) to the Chinese-speaking world? As far as it goes, are we a historical relic of a particular Cold War moment or a specific postcolonial condition, doomed to fade away?

It is easy to argue that the best literary histories are produced by those whose cultural and historical distance from their objects of study is the least: that way, they are in full mastery of the details and languages the rest of us find so daunting. Those of us who come to the field of premodern literature as adults find ourselves perpetually in a state of catch up, hampered and even defined by our gaps and absences. The argument that those who are closest know best approximates the argument for expertise, the currency of the academic realm. Surrounded by peers and students whose knowledge of *kunqu* 崑曲 (*kun*-style opera, linked to performance styles in Kunshan, and for centuries a form of singing of tremendous cultural cachet) is that not just of the connoisseur but the practitioner, I—who know so little of its stagecraft, who can never understand anything of what is being sung, who can barely match supertitles with what is taking place on stage—constantly fight the feeling that what I have to say is at best marginal and maybe even simply untenable. Perhaps if you are reading this, you share something of this fear.

Nonetheless, minimizing cultural distance between us and the premoderns we study comes at a cost. The same few decades that mark the growth of Chinese universities have clearly revealed some of the insidious and innocent ways that studying the past overlaps with laying claim to it. The larger pattern predates Confucius Institutes by two millennia or so. The means by which "the tradition" has been constituted and the impetus for creating such a tradition in the rearview mirror have both been inextricably linked to the Chinese state since a Chinese state can be said to have existed. Three thousand years ago, when the Zhou orthodoxy first coalesced, its foundational rhetorical moves were to appeal to the past. As an outsider, it is sometimes an enormous relief to stand outside of that.

I want to explore that space of outside in this essay: first, in examining very briefly the four-centuries-old study of *chuanqi* 傳奇 drama and second, in engaging with a single play in this form, *Predestined Love* (*Yizhongyuan* 意中緣; 1655) by Li Yu 李漁 (1610–1680).[1] In the study

---

1. *Chuanqi*, literally "account of the strange," refers both to the classical-language tale of the Tang dynasty and to the long plays of the Ming and Qing dynasties; on the former, see Allen, chapter 4 in this volume.

of the genre and its rules as a whole, neither premodern critics nor modern scholars point out the themes that are right at the surface. Similarly, in a particular text from the seventeenth century, I see things that I have no evidence of any other critic finding. Far from fatally undermining my observations, the silence of other critics and scholars—so many of them far more brilliant and most of them vastly more learned than I—constitutes a phenomenon that in itself demands some explication. In what might be a particularly intrusive and selfish form of literary criticism, I want to defend the outsider, with a recognition that my choice of genre is at least partially the product of chance, since it is what I happen to study; I suspect other forms also reveal different aspects to outsiders.

The libretti sung for the performance of a set of related Southern forms of drama, *chuanqi* were elevated and born as a modern genre in the 1570s, when many came to be sung in a new style, *kunqu*, in a collaboration between celebrated musician Wei Liangfu 魏良輔 (1522–1573) and Liang Chenyu 梁辰魚 (1519–1593), a playwright of elite social status. Some genres emerge without notice, but *chuanqi*'s golden age was highly self-conscious. With only a murky line demarcating practitioners from critics in the genre's first generations, southern drama writers concerned themselves with matters such as the relationship between stagecraft and written texts, how to resolve competing prosodic rules, and the differences between northern and southern rhymes and meter.

Some of these critical interests have persisted. (I beg the reader's forgiveness for the terse description that follows, which does not allow me to do justice to how much I am indebted to their work.) Consider, for example, literary historian Dai Bufan's 戴不凡 work dating mostly from the 1950s and 1960s, which also includes an introduction to the *chuanqi*, in which he covers topics such as the different regional forms of southern drama; how they were elevated by Wei Liangfu so that *kunqu* became the most culturally dominant among them; the distinctive characteristics of the *chuanqi* (among them, length; the fact that all characters can sing; and an introduction by a *mo* 末, a supporting male character); the plays' treatment of contemporary high politics (featuring Ming political figures like Yan Song 嚴嵩 [1480–1567] and Wei Zhongxian 魏忠賢 [1568–1627], for example); and finally brief cursory treatments of some of the most celebrated playwrights, with special pride of place assigned to

Tang Xianzu 湯顯祖 (1550–1616) and Kong Shangren 孔尚任 (1648–1718).[2] In their broadest outlines, these are also the main critical concerns of Wang Yongjian 王永健 and Guo Yingde 郭英德, working in the last few generations, in many articles, but also in volumes that survey the history of the form, the rise of *kun* style, the form's sources, its changing relationship to music, and its standing in elite culture.[3]

Some of this scholarly work is evidently invested in the power structures of the Chinese state and impossible to decouple from that state. For example, take a persistent target of inquiry in dramatic history: the role local styles played in late Ming performance. *Chuanqi* were the libretti for different regional styles, associated with different locations, with four or five major representatives, each named after a Jiangnan locality: Wenzhou style 溫州腔, Haiyan style 海盐腔, Yuyao style 余姚腔, Yiyang style 弋阳腔, and what became the dominant form to the elite, Kunshan style 昆山腔. These different performance styles left traces in the written libretti, and scholars have sought to categorize plays according to these local styles, even though the plays frequently carry traits of several styles at once. The enterprise's guiding concept—that diversity can be disciplined into a single dominant ancestral form, in itself pure—is genealogical or at least genealogically adjacent, and it is not much of a stretch to regard this work as doing to plays and playwrights what the state apparatus has done to humans: categorizing them according to patrilineages and ancestral places. The same research could serve to imagine a far more fluid and fundamentally heterogeneous genre in which these regional styles cross-pollinated and the drama itself was always the collaborative product of playwrights of elite education and performing artists of low status who were sometimes even owned and traded by the elites.

Moreover, the focus of the Chinese-language scholarship belies how little specialized learning is necessary to read them, how clever the plotting in many of them, and finally how immensely pleasurable reading them is. One need not be able to write or sing to enjoy the plays, any more than Shakespeare scholars have to be able to compose in iambs. These formal concerns—and perhaps more specifically a posture of learned appreciation, of being an aficionado, of being a hobbyist singer—represent a continuity

2. Dai Bufan, *Dai Bufan xiqu*.
3. Wang Yongjian, *Zhongguo xiju wenxue*; Guo Yingde, *Ming Qing chuanqi*.

from late Ming times, which should invite us to explore how they assumed a position of dominance and how it came to be that modern scholarship on the *chuanqi* should echo the interests of premodern elites.

To be clear, it is impossible to assume a position of neutrality in imagining oneself into the seventeenth century. For example, take the place of the *jiaban* 家班, the privately owned troupe of the sort possessed by the family of the celebrated belle-lettrist Zhang Dai 張岱 (1597–1684) and the playwright and official Ruan Dacheng 阮大鋮 (1587–1646), among many other wealthy connoisseurs of the time. The family owned not just the troupe but its members, as enslaved artists. Like the early modern garden, the *jiaban* combined artistic refinement and conspicuous consumption and the very limits of what it means when a few control the labor of many. When we as historians imagine the *jiaban*, we are forced to side with one position or the other over the ownership of humans. Scholarly work that matter-of-factly describes the growth of the family troupe over time or calmly associates it with *chuanqi*'s increasingly ensemble nature attests to our field's implicit identification with the owners.

It isn't just scholars of the Chinese-speaking world who routinely imagine themselves as the sort of men who owned other people. When a journalist asked him to imagine himself in the past, the late historian Jonathan Spence described the villa he would have owned in Hangzhou in the late Ming: "on the west side of the lake in the hills, looking down on what was then a totally unpolluted lake, and what was a kind of large and prosperous rural pleasure resort." In this imaginary sixteenth-century life, he retained his current-day wife, but imagined the two of them engaged in the refined pleasures that characterized the age. He assuaged any concerns the reader might have about Ming society with these reassurances: "People read very widely. It's a magnificent period in painting. The food is magnificent. It is not a slave society."[4] Can someone who imagines their place in Ming society as the owner of a Hangzhou villa reliably assess whether it was a slave society? (To be blunt: who was cooking the magnificent food? Or cleaning the villa? How would he have acquired his wife?)

Spence's fantasies make clear that insider status has nothing to do with being Chinese or possessing refined literary skills (part of what he yearned

---

4. Baker, "Best Time to Be Alive."

for was the ability to engage in "elegant poetry games, acrostic games, word games that the Chinese have always loved to play"). In our own day, some boundaries between outside and inside feel increasingly fluid: my classes are filled with native speakers of Chinese, whose national identity eludes parsing; English-language scholarship finds greater readership in Chinese translation than it does in the United States. And of course many Chinese intellectuals find themselves cast in the role of outsiders, whether because of political beliefs, gender, or class. Nonetheless, Spence spoke to a desire—not bound by nationality—to imagine early modern China from the perspective of the slaveowner and to funnel literary pleasure into elite cosplay.

Chuanqi were the performances most prized by the refined world Spence describes, and its cultural pleasures cannot be separated from a broader political economy in which some men own villas and others have their labor owned. When we examine the literary culture, it engages with and creates the hierarchies out of which it emerged. *Chuanqi* in particular constitute an ideological vocabulary—an observation so painfully obvious that in pointing it out I almost feel like the child pointing to the emperor's new clothes. But I look in vain for a scholarly community in any language that makes this argument. Every single one of these southern dramas, as I have pointed out elsewhere, includes an empire-shaking political event and some kind of domestic drama: the end ties together both plots, showing how these two conflicts are ultimately one. In a time when constant military action was necessary to secure borders, *chuanqi* demand that action takes place across a broad swathe of territory, sometimes as far as modern-day Burma or the Ryukyu islands; but what happens far away is shown to be necessary for fulfilling a love story between a boy and a girl. This is the imperial ethos written into drama, and because some foreground the political drama while others highlight the domestic narrative, the balance turns into an act of ideology, an implicit argument about which of the two spheres is primary.

Stagecraft also engages with the political. As with all Chinese drama, the characters are categorized according to role types grounded in social and biological identities. In *chuanqi*, in addition to the *mo* I mentioned already, these include *dan* 旦 (leading female), *sheng* 生 (leading male), *jing* 淨 (villain), *chou* 丑 (clown), *laodan* 老旦 (elderly female), *xiaodan* 小旦 (secondary female, usually a maidservant)—gender categories but also class and hierarchy categories, with the lead characters (the *sheng* and *dan*) always of elite status. Terms like *benfen* 本分 (one's "natural status") and *shoufen* 守分 ("keeping to one's station") are fraught and contested in early modern prose language sources, but they are baked into the very structure of much of the dramatic literature, with characters' social status essentialized and inviolable. A *chou* (clown) is a *chou* because of nature and rank, so this way of dividing up all people (villains and heroes, clowns and leads, the ruling and the ruled recognizable at a glance) naturalizes and fixes the hierarchies at the heart of the ruling orthodoxy. Even if the plots frequently involve disguise with the characters assuming a gender or social status not their own, the play's resolution demands a return to true status and then a confirmation that the character's role type represents their essentialized identity, so the play's social and political conflict can ultimately be healed.

One source of the ongoing appeal of *chuanqi* is the way plots return characters to their true status (their *benfen*) while stitching together otherwise thorny social problems. In other words, it isn't simply individuals whose essentialized identities are reaffirmed, but the relations that bind them together, an ideology known as *wulun* 五倫, or "the five normative relations" (which other than the last are notably hierarchical: liege to vassal, father to son, husband to wife, elder brother to younger brother, friend to friend). One might understand the plays as demonstrating the *wulun* to be fully adequate for representing a society, or rather, relationships are either revealed to be fully in alignment with the *wulun* or are eliminated over the course of the play. In attempting to resolve individual agency with the *wulun*, perhaps the single most common social problem *chuanqi* plays treat is the compatibility of romantic love with marriage. In other words, most are social romances.

Even if the play's conclusion echoes state ideology on the ultimate unity of private domestic life and public political life, the core of the play gives just as much time to the conflicts that lead to that resolution. The generic elements I have mentioned are often deployed in the service of political positions that are otherwise impossible to find in a premodern context that mostly obscures real political debate. As historian Eugene D. Genovese has said, often the historian is not studying a confrontation between classes so much as "a process by which a given ruling class successfully avoided such confrontations."[5] In the case of premodern China, the textual

---

5. Genovese, "A Question of Morals," 369.

traces we study include not just the mechanism for avoiding confrontation but also how the ruling classes talked about the avoidance or fretted about the collapse of that avoidant mechanism. But in drama of all sorts, exhilaratingly, that very confrontation is staged. Plays are rife with all manner of conflict: international, political, and domestic. In *chuanqi*, it is commonplace, even the norm, for servants to talk back to or scheme against their superiors (just as it is also the case that underlings willingly sacrifice themselves for their masters). Deployed over many individual plays, these generic characteristics function as a repertoire that is flexible and recursive, allowing for contradiction.

Let me demonstrate how this works in *Yizhongyuan*, a play about selling art that also addresses the relationship between the loftiest echelons of the elite and those who support them. Its author, Li Yu, was a pathbreaking commercial writer at a time when writing for money was incompatible with elite status. In other words, the play, whose impecunious lead female sells her elite-style paintings, engages with themes Li Yu must have confronted constantly in everyday life. Set around the year 1600, most of the characters are real-life historical figures, including two figures of such fame that their names approach the status of cultural brands: the male lead (*sheng*) is elite painter and calligrapher Dong Qichang 董其昌 (1555–1636), and one of the supporting roles (*mo*), Dong's real-life best friend Chen Jiru 陳繼儒 (1558–1639), known especially for his essays and calligraphy. (All references to Dong Qichang in this essay are to the play's character and not the real artistic giant.)

But the character with the most lines and stage time is the female lead (*dan*) who, though also a real-life figure, is of a social status that sharply contrasts with Dong Qichang's. The daughter of an impoverished *xiucai* (a scholar who has passed the lowest tier of the examination system), Yang Yunyou 楊雲友 is a forger of Dong Qichang's paintings who ends up marrying Dong, still forging his paintings but now with his blessing. At the beginning of the play, the two famous men long for permanent ghostwriters who will do their work. Ultimately each acquires one by entering into a match with a woman who is not a social equal: in the case of Chen Jiru, the courtesan Lin Tiansu 林天素 (again a real-life figure), and in the case of Dong Qichang, Yang Yunyou. In this spin on celebrity, loosely based on the past but largely fictitious, the titular "destiny" (*yuan* 緣) that the play describes and that connects each famous man to the woman he will marry is not just romantic but also professional and even commercial.

In the third act, the audience is introduced to a number of the play's most important characters: Yang Yunyou, her father, and the villainous monk Shikong 是空. One of *chuanqi*'s central generic characteristics is that characters of different social status sing together, so the thematic unfolding of social cohesion cannot be separated from the staging of musical ensemble. Although singing together is usually deployed to depict harmony, in act three, the same dramatic convention expresses conflict, which is musical and social discordance.

This act concatenates three separate, tonally divergent actions: first, the introduction of the villainous monk Shikong; second, the introduction of Yang Yunyou, which involves her producing a painting in Dong Qichang's style as an act of lyric self-expression; and third, a debt collector's storming into the house Yunyou shares with her father. Each part involves characters from different spheres (father and daughter, poor people of elite cultural accomplishment; Shikong, the fake monk, who is an ex-con and antique dealer; and finally the debt collector, from an even lower rung of society), who interact in a cacophony of different cultural discourses. But it isn't simply that characters speak and sing in different linguistic registers; the perspective of each differs as well. The play provides the standpoints of both debt collector and debtor, with a difference in perspective impossible to disaggregate from different cultural languages, whether the lyric self-expression of the girl painter, the decorous language of social nicety of her father (which may or may not be evasive), or the brutal economics of the debt collector. Act three combines allusive poetry, calculations of the interest rate on a fifty-tael loan (three taels, to be paid monthly), and language as blunt and vernacular as "my child, the debt collector is here again" 我兒, 討債的又來了.[6]

Drama does not erase conflict, even as it imposes a coherence on differing languages, actions, and characters, first and primarily through song but without smoothing out the attendant conflict. Sometimes in one song, a single character explains competing values, such as when the debt collector argues to the father that it is morally worse to shirk one's debts

---

6. Li Yu, *Yizhongyuan*, 400. Subsequently page numbers of the citations from this play will be marked in parenthesis in the text.

than to prostitute one's daughter: "Let me do your accounting for you: you'd be better off to welcome clients and be a turtle who stretches out its neck than to hide from debtors and be a turtle who shrinks its head into its shell" 我代伊籌, 倒不如開門接客龜伸頸, 也強如躲債逢人鱉縮頭 (400). Even if the debt collector is wrong, the absolutism of elite sexual mores has been decentered by a competing way to frame the situation. In transforming reneging on one's debts and whoring one's daughter into semantic equivalents, the song's parallelism produces moral relativism.

This part of act three revolves around a single song ("Bushiliu" 不是路), with characters taking turns and expressing opposing positions in the context of ensemble music making. Once again, when mutually exclusive positions are stanzas of the same song in the same rhyme scheme, the song does the work of relativizing, making it impossible to sympathize wholly with a single perspective. Take this example: returning home after a day in which he has tried and failed to earn money, Yunyou's father sings, "Returning home on a boat under the moon; the water is frozen, and I went fishing in vain" 戴月歸舟, 水凍無魚枉下鉤 (399). What initially looks like an aestheticized description of poverty comes off as an evasion of the truth when a debt collector barges into their house and, in the same meter and to the same tune and even the same rhyme, sings, "I mock your vain attempts to be a scholarly sort, with that square headdress [marking the special status of the *xiucai*] incapable of covering your shame" 我笑你空做儒流, 頭上方巾不蓋羞 (400). These men stake out positions that are mutually exclusive: either Yang Yunyou's father is an elite man down on his luck, whose poverty can even be a refined choice, or he is a hypocrite willing to use airs and graces to hide his moral cowardice.

In this act, the logic of song, in which repetition with difference allows for opposed perspectives, reappears in the prose dialogue, where certain words used recurrently—in conflicting ways—are rendered problematic. Shikong uses the word *siwen* 斯文 ("civilized" or "respectable") twice in the space of a few lines to describe Yunyou's father, but the two uses reveal the slipperiness not just of the speaker but also of the word itself.[7] In the first instance, Shikong appeases the debt collector: "You can't be

---

7. A highly loaded binome that originates in the *Analects* itself, *siwen* implies positionality. Bryan Van Norden's translation of the relevant passage: "Now that King Wen is gone, is not culture now invested here in me? If Heaven intended *this culture* to

The Case for Outsiders

blamed for collecting the interest; but in light of how 'respectable' he is, you should not have scolded him" 將本求利, 難怪你取討, 只是看斯文面上, 不該破口罵他 (400). In the second, he sides with the poor scholar against the debt collector: "He's nothing but a miser. How could he understand deference and 'respectability'?" 他是個守錢虜, 那裡曉得敬重斯文 (400). The same binome generates two opposing perspectives: the debt collector as a brusque businessman within his rights or the same figure as a crude, uncouth miser.

Repeated and reframed, other words also are transformed into an arena for social conflict. The debt collector enters and says, "That scholar is a bad sort; he takes on debt and plans to avoid payment. He's not afraid of going to court, just of losing decorum (*timian*)" 秀才心不善, 借債圖誆騙. 不怕打官司, 只怕壞體面 (400). After the debt collector barges into the house, the scholar protests using the same binome: "How can you come into the inner quarters [i.e., where Yunyou is]? That violates decorum (*timian*). Get out!" 怎麼走進內室裡來? 不成體面, 快些出去! (400). Using *timian*, the debt collector and father disagree as to whether the scholar is protecting the virtue of his daughter or using that as an excuse not to pay his debts. But they also disagree as to what *timian* itself means: whether as a moral end in itself or as a hypocritical vehicle that enables elite people to default on their debts.

Another term, *ruliu* 儒流 ("a scholarly sort")—also foundational to the cultural legitimacy and hegemony of the ruling class—undergoes the same treatment. The debt collector sings, "I mock your vain attempts to be a scholarly sort" 我笑你空做儒流 (400), while *ruliu* reappears in Shikong's promise to make a good match for Yang Yunyou. Shikong brags that his circle of acquaintances is rich with the right sort: "The people with whom I associate are noblemen; I do my trading in the most refined circles! Could I lack any scholars [*ruliu*] or officials?" 我結交的是三公五侯, 貿易的是藝林才藪, 少甚麼儒流官流 (400). The debt collector and Shikong regard *ruliu* as instrumental, but one disavows it while the other claims it.

Repetitions take place across larger semantic units as well, and here too they allow for the framing of social conflict. When Yang Yunyou's

---

perish, it would not have given it to those of us who live after King Wen's death" (9.5, emphasis added). In Ivanhoe and Van Norden, *Readings in Classical Chinese Philosophy*, 25.

father says he cannot pay, the debt collector voices what everyone in seventeenth-century China *knew* but never said: "With such a pretty daughter at home, you can't be afraid that you won't have silver to pay back a debt!" 你有這樣一個標致女兒在家，怕沒有銀子還債! (400). Yang Yunyou's father is appalled and turns the prospect down immediately: "I am a gentleman. How dare you accuse me of being a pimp?" 我做相公的人，烏龜是你罵的? (400). A few lines later, Shikong makes exactly the same proposition as the debt collector, that the father should sell his daughter and pay off his debts, but this time using the decorous language of marriage:

> Why not find a suitable match for your daughter? Your daughter is talented, with special abilities, and it wouldn't be extreme for her to command a larger bride-price. Then at that point you can pay back your debts and even pay for your wife's funeral.
>
> 何不尋個門當户對的人家送他出閣? 令愛有那樣高才，又有這般絕技，就多接些聘金也不爲過. 那時節，債也可以還，喪也可以舉了. (400)

The father's response to this proposal is not horror but concern over his reputation:

> I've had that idea all along too. It's just that as a person *of decorum* [timian again], how can I sell my daughter to pay back my debts, accepting a bride price to have my wife buried? But now unable to contend with my hunger I'll probably have to take that path. You travel in cultured circles. If you find someone suitable, I'd like you to be a matchmaker.
>
> 老夫一向也有此意，只是一個做體面的人，怎好賣女還債，受聘葬妻? 如今這口餓氣也爭不來了，將來畢竟要上這條路. 老師父在翰墨中走動，往來的都是富室官家，若有門當户對的，就求老師父作伐. (400)

The father protests too much; he says he cannot sell his daughter, but in fact proposes precisely that. The juxtaposition of these two moments— self-righteous horror at the prospect of selling his daughter, followed up with a request for some contacts to cut an advantageous deal in transacting her—hint that the difference between marriage and the sex trade is nothing but a hypocritical pose.

What about the father identifying himself as a person concerned with *timian* (decorum)? Other writings of the time refer to *timian* without irony, but the repetition—first by debt collector, then by cultured debtor as he pushes the debt collector out, and then again in the same cultured man's self-justification—sets *timian* into question, as if it might always be sanctimonious. *Timian* is directly implicated in the sale of his daughter: it is either that which prevents him from securing the best price he can for his daughter or that through which Shikong will find a good match who will pay him handsomely. Repetition poses a question of *timian*, whether it represents a single concept to one and all or is one thing according to the ruling class and quite another according to those ruled. Perhaps what looks to elite standards like a single set of standards (just better performed by the more cultured) looks to those at the bottom of the totem pole like an instrument to keep them down.

The effect is not confined to single binomes like *timian*, *ruliu*, or *siwen*. A concept like poverty is refracted multiply, seen differently by different characters, foregrounding social conflict and linguistic register. A father's account of his failure to find work, a debt collector's explanation of interest accrual, and finally the girl's composition of a poem in classical Chinese—all articulate poverty in different languages, each with no deeper claim to our belief than the others. Perhaps poverty can be tamed by aesthetics:

貧閨風透壁全無，　The wind pierces this poor boudoir, the walls broken up;
吹得詩腸別樣枯.　they blow my poetic soul even more dried up.
呵凍自傳蓬戶影，　Warming my cold hand with my breath, I paint myself
　　　　　　　　　　an image of my poor hovel,
也堪補入鄭公圖　it's all worth adding to a picture of Lord Zheng.(399).[8]

Or perhaps it is an impersonal product of math, where compound interest on a debt leads inexorably to the sale of a daughter.

The basic formal technique of repetition structures the play even at a larger scale. Shikong and Dong Qichang—in the space of about twenty

8. "The picture of Lord Zheng" refers to a painting of the poor by the official Zheng Xia 鄭俠 (1041–1119) that is said to have moved Song Emperor Shenzong 宋神宗 (r. 1067–1085) so much that he changed social policy. See Tuotuo (Toghto), *Song shi*, 321.10436.

138 Tina Lu

lines that cross two different acts—long not for a lover but for someone to do their work for them. Act two ends with Dong Qichang's desire to find someone to do all his painting for him. He says to Chen Jiru,

> If we each have a forger with us, then we only have to participate in those social interactions we absolutely have to, and all others we can kind of fob off and ask the forger to ghostwrite—that is the only long-term solution.
> 只除非各得一個捉刀人帶在身邊, 萬不得已的自己應酬, 可以將就打發的, 就教他代筆, 這才是個長久之計. (396)

Immediately thereafter, act three begins with Shikong's same desire: "I can rely on her pen to support me for my whole life" 只消靠他那管筆, 就可以受用一生了 (398). Along this axis, the men competing to marry Yang Yunyou are identical, both seeking someone to do their work for them. So much of the late imperial canon exerts itself to inform us of how unbridgeable and expansive the chasm is between people like Shikong and Dong Qichang. In the play, though, each is understood through the prism of the other. Their shared intentions, echoing each other so closely, blur the line between a shady antique dealer with a criminal record in the capital and perhaps the most famous elite artist of the Ming.

These layered uses of language—handing off different lines with the same rhymes to different speakers, the reappearance of certain keywords in different voices, the reappearance of the proposal to sell the daughter, the different ways of describing what it means to be poor—have the effect of undercutting any single speaker's perspective. In this polyvocal genre, no statement and no speaker possess the authority of lyric expression or expository prose. In fact, the audience member or the reader hears as much dissonance as harmony, with the potential (especially in plays where villains are not buffoons) of radically decentering the orthodoxy. Interrogating the very heart of early modern society, this particular three-page act is only unusual in how succinctly these challenges to elite hegemony unfold.

When I am asked what proof I have that mine is a legitimate reading of a seventeenth-century play, what I am really being asked for is confirmation in a contemporaneous, classical-language genre. Certain critiques were impossible to voice in genres that were too statist or too proximate to the lyric. In contrast, the many ventriloquized voices in a play are allowed to contradict one another, and drama's freedom from the ideological constraints of lyric forms is one of its great charms. Another kind of "proof" lies in how texts relate to one another. What I have been calling repetition, visible at the level of word and rhyme and plot, is actually intertextuality of the sort that reaches beyond the scope of this particular act and this play, creating a network of meaning to a reader who knows many texts. If the act is composed of words that echo one another, of speakers who echo one another, and of actions that echo one another, the play itself demands to be read intertextually, echoing and repeating other texts.

Most strikingly, a girl who paints a portrait on stage in a *chuanqi* play can never stand alone. A sensitive, educated girl reaching out to send a message in the medium of portraiture to someone she could never contact otherwise, in a scene where she describes what she paints as she paints, demands comparison to a far more famous girl painter, Du Liniang 杜麗娘, the romantic heroine of Tang Xianzu's *Peony Pavilion* (*Mudanting* 牡丹亭; 1598). In that play, one of the romantic pinnacles of traditional Chinese literature, the self-portrait is imbued with the power to fulfill her romantic yearnings and protect her chastity, so that she can both die of passion and marry her true love.

Yang Yunyou's onstage actions and songs turn the "female portraitist" into a field to be contested just as much as the use of the repeated word *timian*, and here as well *Yizhongyuan* radically destabilizes the unspoken hegemony of elite concerns. The daughter of a high official, Du Liniang's concerns as she paints in *Mudanting* are emotional and aesthetic. In Du Liniang's place stands Yang Yunyou, whose motivations for painting are nakedly financial:

The worst thing is, our family circumstances are dire, and we have no plan for making a living. And moreover, for years we have sunk into more and more grievous debt, with interest piling up and getting bigger by the day. Fortunately, I know something about the brush and ink and something about paint, but even if I earn a little to help our needs, ultimately we have so many gaps, how can I plug them?

所苦者，家計凋零，治生無策，又兼屢年欠下積補，子母相生，日重一日，還喜得奴家粗通翰墨，略曉丹青，雖然得些潤筆之資，以助薪水，究竟這千瘡百孔，那裡補救得來？(399)

The painting in *Mudanting* resurrects its painter from the dead; its counterpart in act three of *Yizhongyuan* performs a more quotidian life-saving function. Shikong has paid the month's interest, but the father makes a show of refusing the money until it is regarded as the price of the painting: "Those three taels—if they are a fee for my daughter's brush then I have a pretext for accepting it" 方才那三兩，或者當做小女的潤筆，還受之有名 (401). The magical painting of *Mudanting* has a counterpart in *Yizhongyuan* worth precisely three taels of silver.

This way of considering every word, every action, every song in a *chuanqi*—as always slightly unstable on its own, as best understood as one voice among many, as always demanding that we triangulate with its counterparts, whether those are other rhymes, other uses of the same word, other versions of the same action—goes some way toward suggesting what is at stake in act three's deliberate violation of the Aristotelian unity of action. The act jambs together literati-style painting and a debt collector's home invasion because there is no other way to play out its main theme, which is to question the relationship between financial need and aesthetic norms or that between elite culture and the people who actually do the work of producing it, and to ask whether the relationship is symbiotic or oppositional.

The basic relationship between elites and labor is conceived of in *Yizhongyuan* as twofold, at once emerging out of commercial ties and constituted by the *wulun*. In most other *chuanqi* (in *Mudanting*, for example), the relationship that lies outside the normative and needs to be recategorized according to it is romantic, an illicit love affair that is transformed into marriage; but in *Yizhongyuan* the transformation is from commercial to familial. The forger turns into a wife. In the beginning, the characters' motivations are commercial: she needs to sell the work she passes off as that by Dong Qichang while her father needs to pay his debts by selling his daughter. The action of the play transforms those impulses and relations into familial ones, so that by play's end, the debtor has been taken in by Dong Qichang as a father-in-law. As his wife, Yunyou can make good on her father's debts and serve him with filiality. The commercial world

The Case for Outsiders

is fully subsumed by the familial one, every messy transactional relation reclassified as one of the *wulun*.

Traces of that commercial relationship remain. *Dan* and *sheng* barely allude to romantic love; the two do not meet until the final act, and the play repeatedly dances around the likelihood that the distinguished, middle-aged Dong Qichang is not handsome like a normal romantic lead. If most *chuanqi* end by promising that *dan* and *sheng* can be lovers *and* husband and wife, the idea here is that the leads can be employer and employee *and* husband and wife. That Yunyou ends up as Dong Qichang's wife (and not the evil Shikong's) has to do with Dong Qichang's willingness to take care of her father and his official status. But what Dong Qichang and Shikong see in her is identical: less like a romantic ideal and much more like management's ideal of labor, that it should do what management demands and should have no negotiating power. In the finale, Dong Qichang celebrates his marriage this way:

> Half my life has been spent busy, suffering at the expense of pen and ink. Now I have your daughter, all those social obligations having to do with my calligraphy and painting, I won't be afraid that I'll lack a ghostwriter! To be a man of leisure for the second half of my life—I'll be able to have some success with that.
>
> 下官做了半世忙人, 總爲筆墨所苦. 如今得了令愛, 那些書畫應酬, 不怕沒人代筆! 這下半世的閑人, 有幾分做得成了. (472)

Lest we misunderstand what he really means, he sings: "From now on I won't be personally grasping that jade pen! I'm handing that over to this heroine" 從今玉管不親操, 都交付女英豪 (472). In chorus, everyone sings, "You'll be a pair of lazy husband and hard-working wife growing old together" 做一對懶夫勤婦同偕老! (472). For Dong Qichang, marriage is the legitimate acquisition of a laborer who does not need to be paid.

The same problem appears again and again in the play: under what circumstances can one person own another person's labor? Crucially, when does that ownership of labor involve ownership of the person? The important distinction is between two forms of labor: one of which is à la carte, where each act of labor is separately contracted and compensated, and the other of which entails a permanent relationship, whether normative (spousal, familial) or something like enslavement. Yang Yunyou begins as a contract worker who earns three taels for her painting in act three and in her later travels sells individual paintings for far more, but as Dong Qichang's wife, she ends up doing the same work in the context of a permanent relationship.

Make no mistake about it; art is explicitly treated as labor. Dong Qichang and Chen Jiru connect art neither with inspiration nor self-expression but with grinding work that can be done by them and others. They will manage a workforce, because the labor itself is alienated: "As long as it's an approximation, even if it's not 100% correct, you and I can offer direction and fix things up, and it will do" 只要畫得有幾分相似, 就不十分到家, 我和你指點一指點, 改正一改正, 就可以充得去了 (396). This play about artists is notably unconcerned with art itself except as the external manifestation of work (which is not, needless to say, one of the predominant positions in seventeenth-century poetics and art theory). Art's place in *Yizhongyuan* prefigures Karl Marx in his description of commodity fetishism: "It is nothing but the definite social relation between men themselves which assumes here, for them, the fantastic form of a relation between things."[9] The play recognizes that each work of art is nothing more or less than a momentarily crystallized set of social relations among people.

To claim Yunyou for himself, Shikong (who cannot marry her until his tonsure grows out) hires a dissolute, impotent elite man, Huang Tianjian 黃天監, to impersonate Dong Qichang; they deceive both Yang Yunyou and her father into believing that a real marriage is taking place, but in fact Yunyou is kidnapped and taken by boat to the capital. En route, Yunyou bands together with Shikong's slave, Miaoxiang, and the two of them kill Shikong. The three proceed onward to the capital, where Yunyou earns several thousand taels of silver doing what she did earlier for her father and will do later for Dong Qichang without pay: "A few fans or folios, it'll go up to fifty or sixty taels, and even at the cheapest, it'll be twenty-four taels" 不過畫幾柄扇頭, 或是幾幅單條册頁, 多的五六十金, 極寒傖的也是二十四兩畫帕 (448).

Act twenty-one stages a number of actions that most seventeenth-century writing on art does its best to obscure, that is, all the steps involved in the purchase of art: a price negotiation (in which Yunyou forces the buyer to increase his offer from twenty taels to forty), the subsequent

9. Marx, *Capital*, 165.

The Case for Outsiders

work of painting, and the actual act of payment. Afterward, the customer thanks her personally, and she rebuffs him, succinctly explaining that contract work is business, not a relationship:

No! I just spontaneously painted—I was not aware at all that it was for you. Even if I do see you with my eyes, I'm just seeing you off. There's no intent.

我隨手抽來就畫，那裡知道是你的？就把眼睛瞧你，也不過是看人打發的意思，有甚麼私心. (449)

We know that she has come to the capital to find a husband; or rather, she exposes herself on the open market precisely to find a life tenure outside of the market that is permanent, matches a normative relation, and does not pay her for her labor. But recall how every word and every action is layered in the play. The patterns of repetition work negatively as well; the logic that ties Yunyou to her father and Dong Qichang is contrasted here with her response to the bidder. The former are relationships, and the latter, contract work, but in the aggregate they create an unspoken category that is something like "labor."

Art is one form of labor among many that can be commanded and purchased, and the play presents a spectrum of the ways one person can claim the labor of another. Like all *chuanqi*, this play contains characters of different class status, although even by *chuanqi* standards the breadth of the social divide that separates Dong Qichang from the play's underlings is striking. After she is kidnapped, Yunyou meets two people who are both at Shikong's full disposal: Miaoxiang and Huang Tianjian. Miaoxiang belongs to the role type *laodan* (old female), but she is a girl Yunyou's age, imprisoned for years in a cellar to work as Shikong's sex slave. His other employee is Huang Tianjian, a comic figure whose genitalia rotted off because of venereal disease, rendering him a "natural eunuch" (*tianjian* 天監) and thus a safe figure to substitute for Shikong.

Note that these two use the same language to explain why they must do Shikong's bidding, despite not wanting to. Miaoxiang says: "I eat his food. I wear his clothes. I have no choice but to do what he says" 我既吃他的飯, 穿他的衣, 沒奈何只得隨他使喚 (420). Huang Tianjian uses much the same language in explaining his obedience to Shikong: "Now I eat his food. I wear his clothes. I ride in his boat" 我如今吃他的飯，穿他的衣，坐他的船 (422). Later still, after Yunyou has discovered the ruse and knows the identity of her true kidnapper, Shikong explains how he got Huang Tianjian to submit and why he no longer has any need of his services: "I wanted to use him, that's why I gave him wine and food to eat, and clothes to wear, a boat for him to ride in, but now I'm going to be the groom, so what further use do I have for him?" 當初我要用著他，所以把酒飯與他吃，衣服與他穿，大船與他坐，如今新郎是自己做了，還要他做甚麼 (440). What all three describe is how one can sell personal agency, not for profit or money but for food, clothes, and transportation, the means to keep on living. Note how the perspective of Shikong, the employer, differs from Huang Tianjian's. The words that Shikong uses to convey Huang Tianjian's dispensability become the logic through which Huang Tianjian expresses his absolute dependence on Shikong even as neither party understands their connections as a relationship, only as a longer set of transactions. Once the services have been rendered, no more food or drink or clothes.

In the course of the play, Yang Yunyou has been rewarded for her labors in two ways: first, as a free agent (selling her paintings in the capital), and second, subcontracted to a man for whom she is a permanent worker (her father and then Dong Qichang). Further down the social food chain, Miaoxiang and Huang Tianjian reside in a nightmarish portmanteau of the two models of compensation: on one hand, their labor is mapped onto the model of pay-as-you-go (for your work you will receive food and clothes), and on the other hand, since that payment makes possible bare survival (food and clothes), in practice they are Shikong's chattel, but with no obligation on Shikong's part.

When Shikong repeats the line "wine and food to eat, and clothes to wear," he does so in a darkly humorous scene in which Shikong and Huang Tianjian are negotiating his new terms now that he is no longer needed to impersonate Dong Qichang as a bridegroom. Like Yang Yunyou, Huang Tianjian moves between models of compensation, from contract worker to permanent staff. After Shikong strips Huang Tianjian of all his clothes (which he does not own) and threatens to abandon him naked on the riverbank, Huang Tianjian begs him for the chance to sell himself for money. Huang Tianjian plans to transfer ownership of himself to Shikong in exchange for ten taels of silver—in other words, sell himself into slavery. Shikong demands a performative gesture, an onstage kow-

The Case for Outsiders 145

tow: "Now that you have signed the deed of your body, we have to go through the ritual of master and slave. Come here and kowtow!" 既寫了身契, 就要行個主僕之禮. 過來磕頭! (441). In an aside to the audience (*bei* 背), Huang Tianjian says, "If I want his silver, then I have to pay him respect by picking up the yellow gold that fell by his knees. I need to bend my head to pick it up. So it's hard to say I'm too tired!" 既要他的銀子, 也説不得, 只得要拜施黃金落在膝頭邊, 只當低頭去拾難辭倦! (441). The aside suggests that Huang Tianjian thinks he is getting a better deal than Shikong; for the price of a mere gesture of obeisance, he will get ten taels of silver! But the real reason Huang Tianjian speaks in an aside has to do with *timian*, or decorum. The kowtow seals the relationship of master and slave, which in turn imagines their bond as something more akin to vassal and liege than employee and employer, and it violates decorum to acknowledge ritual actions as part of a network of transaction.

But then Shikong refuses to hand over the silver, referring again to the cost of food, drink, and transportation: "All the way from Hangzhou to here, the cost of your food on the road, the cost of your wine, the cost of the boat, the sedan chair, if you add it all up, it's much more than ten taels! It's enough that I should not be demanding it of you, but you want money from me for buying you?! What a presumptuous slave!" 你從杭州跟到這里. 一路上的飯錢酒錢船錢轎錢, 算來豈止十兩! 不要你找出來也夠了, 還問我要身價! 好放肆的奴才! (441). Matthew H. Sommer describes eighteenth-century cases that involve self-selling, some of them far more gruesome than the play's, but at least adhering to a certain consistent financial logic.[10] Huang Tianjian originally sold his labor as an impersonator in return for food, clothing, and transportation. Now that his value as an impersonator has fallen to nothing, his earnings can be backdated and called back.

In transforming messy, unclassifiable relationships into those that are to be categorized as one of the *wulun*, *chuanqi* plays often include stage rituals (for example, staged wedding ceremonies), but Huang Tianjian's kowtow is irredeemably heterodox. The servant regards it as transactional, while the master has exacted subjugation only through trickery. Moreover, the action—like the binomes I discussed earlier—forms part of *Yizhongyuan's* internal vocabulary: the transfer of money, the switch from employee

10. Sommer, *Polyandry and Wife-Selling*, 304–6.

to normative role. In neither Shikong's nor Huang Tianjian's eyes is their relation actually special. Although they use the language and forms of the liege-vassal (*zhupu* 主仆) relation, they continue to behave transactionally. One cannot imagine room for a feeling like loyalty. This perverted liege-vassal relationship must tint our understanding of the conclusion's marriage, in which Dong Qichang gains all the benefits of Yang Yunyou's labor by acquiring her as his wife. The precedent created by this kowtow leaves open the question of whether Huang Tianjian and Shikong's *zhupu* relationship is the demonic form of Yang Yunyou and Dong Qichang's marriage or instead simply one whose pure transactionality is rendered more clearly.

We moderns can only guess how this repetition was understood by seventeenth-century audiences, but I suspect scholars have long underestimated how varied responses to performance must have been, especially when we consider how important choices made by individual performers must have been and the diversity of the audience. Part of amplifying outsider voices involves allowing for their spaces among premoderns as well. Perhaps when that kowtow took place on stage, some felt a ripple of disjuncture between the ancient gesture of obeisance and its onstage execution as a transactional joke. But others must have brought experience and knowledge that a kowtow is always the way someone stronger exerts power over someone weaker. I see traces of that diversity of response being recouped in several essays in this volume; in an early period, it assumes the form of readers' and reciters' power over text, which David Schaberg describes among early rhetors as "the delight of citation and allusion [lying] simultaneously in the connection with past language in the marked repurposing for present aims."[11] This kind of dispersal of control over text and over performance is also something silenced by identification with the premodern elite.

Chuanqi are replete with fakes and doubles, but in *Yizhongyuan*, it isn't metatheatricality or romantic farce that demands their presence. Instead, among their other functions, doubles and fakes are commodified fragments of people. For example, consider the central conceit of the play, in which forgery decouples artistic work from a specific individual and commodifies the forger. Hence, Shikong and Dong Qichang seek "a talent" to save labor or earn money. In other cases, a person's identity can

---

11. See Schaberg, chapter 1 in this volume.

be broken into components whose value on the market can be known experientially through the play's plot. The play gives us characters who are identical except for one trait that is different; their differential outcomes reflect not on them but on everything around them, in what is perhaps a social critique, perhaps a cosmic one, and their shared identities are turned into abstractions that can be theorized and interrogated. These fragmented identities, these mirrored selves, are a means to theorize gender and an implicit critique of gender and power. Consequently, it is not just the modern reader who understands Yunyou's ability to forge Dong Qichang's work as speaking to a basic structural unfairness, but Dong Qichang himself. When he recognizes Yunyou's painting in his own style as emerging from a talent equal to his own, but out of the hand of a woman, Dong Qichang sighs: "The forged pen allows real feeling to emerge. Could it be that I, a male, am secondary to a female? The same talent, and I enjoy riches and glory, while she suffers poverty and hardship. How tragic!" 假筆眞情現, 難道我男子效蛾眉? 同是一般的技藝, 我享這樣的榮華, 他受那般的貧困, 豈不可憐! (406).

Yunyou's other double is not one of the most distinguished men of the Ming dynasty, but Miaoxiang, entrapped in sex slavery by the evil monk: "Trapped in a cellar, for years on end, I never see the sun" 藏在一個地窖之中, 成年不見天日 (420). She is a mirror version of the heroine, but if Dong Qichang is Yang Yunyou as a man, Miaoxiang is Yunyou as a lower-status woman, sold into domestic servitude after her parents' deaths, and then sold again to Shikong, who drugs and rapes her. Every reference to Miaoxiang's status makes it clear that she is a less fortunate version of Yunyou, but it is Yunyou who points out most clearly how alike they are: "Miaoxiang, you too were of a good family, and like me you were ensnared by an evildoer. Afterwards, the credit for taking vengeance on him was all yours. Even though the two of us have separate roles as mistress and maidservant, there is no real distinction in the meanness or not of our status" 妙香, 你當初也是好人家兒女, 與我同落奸人之計, 後來報此大仇, 也全虧了你. 我們兩個雖有主婢之分, 實無良賤之異 (454). She means literally that they are both properly *liangmin* 良民 (a commoner), though Miaoxiang has been sold and treated as *jianmin* 賤民 (of hereditary servile status). If we read Dong Qichang's comments and Yunyou's comments together, we emerge with a set of questions that tie the most privileged to the least, in overlapping dyads of doubles. What makes Dong Qichang noble and rich and Yang Yunyou not? What makes Yang Yunyou the mistress and Miaoxiang the slave? *They are the same.* Why does one person have power and the other not? Why does one group of people have power and others not? Outside of *chuanqi*'s particular generic, literary framework of layered repetitions, of mirrored selves, of a society in miniature, in the 1650s these essential political questions had no form through which they could be posed.

Yizhongyuan is a particularly rich play, but not singularly so, nor even singularly fascinated with a kind of politics that the rest of the political discourse largely either avoids or cannot articulate. I have chosen to write about *Yizhongyuan* in this essay because I love it. Readings of dozens of other plays could be just as politically engaged. Instead, that the Chinese-language field of theater studies largely ignores these problems, which are not only manifest at the level of genre but also at every level of language, in favor of the formal and technical issues, does not have to do with anything specific to this particular play.

I resist steering this discussion to Li Yu's biography, despite clues that attest to his outsider status when it came to ruling-class culture, especially his frankness about making money and his profound lack of attachment to the Ming dynasty. It may be obvious that my intent is not to judge a seventeenth-century life according to twenty-first-century standards (no seventeenth-century male life passes twenty-first-century muster). Instead, my point is simply that what he "thought" only comes to us through the prism of genre; no seventeenth-century writer could have so interrogated the world around them in this particular fashion in their own voice, nor even by ventriloquizing the voices of others. Instead, the ideas I have been writing about emerge through hearing multiple ventriloquized voices in tandem.

I propose a musicological metaphor, according to which *chuanqi* is a genre in which the harmonic line is particularly evident: minor characters get their own arias to sing or sing stanzas that mirror in meter and rhyme but not in content those of lead characters. These minor characters are nonelite people, in whose absence the plot fails to cohere and who persistently decenter the perspective of the elite figures. Prose dialogue is far more important than its counterpart in northern drama and further undercuts the lyric logic of the arias. What otherwise is barely audible in the written tradition of Chinese literature is rendered highly audible, but with the harmony always evident as part of a melodic line. To return that metaphor to these plays and to this play in particular: these nonelites will always end up subordinate figures. The play will conclude with a perfect couplet, imposing order out of potential dissonance. Yang Yunyou will continue to paint, but as a wife and filial daughter, not growing rich on her own. She cannot run off to the capital in search of fortune. The subterranean harmonies retreat underground, but only their presence makes the music feel symphonic.

It is not so much that the play takes sides but that it renders visible the usual seams of power. Yes, even as I implicitly accuse others of ideological blindness, it is obvious why the rendering of the invisible visible shouts itself out to me, to us, in the 2020s, into natural disaster whose heart is political and through which our political system unveils itself again and again. We, like Li Yu, are living through (to quote Gramsci, via Stuart Hall) "'the crisis of authority, which is nothing but 'the crisis of hegemony or general crisis of the state.'"[12]

I know my own period best, but I suspect those harmonies are to be heard in other genres, in other periods—but perhaps not so easily by everyone. *Chuanqi* are filled with characters who are like me: sometimes buffoons, sometimes foreigners, sometimes unlettered, always outsiders. Yet all too frequently in the plays, these characters demand at least a momentary sympathy. Can anyone who reads *Yizhongyuan* and instinctively identifies with Dong Qichang but not Miaoxiang pick out the harmonies as instinctively as I do? In doing so, there is a place for us, a whole crew of outsiders—whether it is because we stand outside of the Chinese-speaking world, because we are excluded from the national universities, or because we have no place inside the structures of Chinese states and their authority. Perhaps that is the way to understand literary history, as always in the process of making; Li Yu could not have imagined me, three and a half centuries later, a woman, an American, writing in scholarly forms and a language unknown to him. Those aspects of my outsider status allow me to amplify what has remained otherwise silenced.

12. Hall, "Gramsci and Us," 168.

CHAPTER 6

Theoretical Reflections on Literary History and Middle Period Chinese Poetry

Michael A. Fuller

René Wellek, reflecting grimly on a lifetime of work, concluded that in fact there is no "literary history" because there are no solutions to the enduring problems central to literary creativity:

> I discovered, by experience, that there is no evolution in the history of critical argument, that the history of criticism is rather a series of debates on recurrent topics, on "essentially contested concepts," on permanent problems in the sense that they are with us even today. Possibly, a similar conclusion is required for the history of poetry itself. "Art," said Schopenhauer, "has always reached its goals." Croce and Ker are right. There is no progress, no development, no history of art except a history of writers, institutions, and techniques. This is, at least for me, the end of an illusion, the fall of literary history.[1]

Yet Wellek, in focusing on the internal development of critical debates, was perhaps looking in the wrong places for historical change. Maurice

---

This essay brings together arguments about Middle Period literary history that I have developed since about 2000 in writings on Tang and Song dynasty poetry. As an overview of the role of the literary in the large arc of transformations of elite culture during this period, it draws significantly on my previous work: "Zai jiushiji sixiang," "'Renwen,'" "'Juan ye,'" "Moral Intuitions and Aesthetic Judgments," *Drifting among Rivers and Lakes*, and "Aesthetics and Meaning in Experience."

1. Wellek, *The Attack on Literature*, 77. See my discussion of this passage and the broader issue of the nature of literary history in *Drifting among Rivers and Lakes*, 7–10.

Theoretical Reflections

Mandelbaum offers the phrase "special histories" to describe inquiries such as social, political, military, economic, intellectual, and literary histories that "will seek to establish how a particular form of human activity, such as art, or religion, or science, has developed over time," but explains that the "historian is not dealing with materials which have no connections with other aspects of societal life. Consequently, he will often have to draw upon a wide variety of facts in order to account for the changes which occurred in that strand of human activity whose course he seeks to follow."[2] As Mandelbaum emphasizes, these forms of activity center on—and are defined by—permanent problems in human society. For example, one can describe political history as "the study of the organisation and operation of power in past societies."[3] The challenge of effectively and stably organizing the coercive power of the state never goes away, and there is only a relatively small range of possible solutions (theocracy, aristocracy, monarchy, oligarchy, democracy, and so on) that can be realized in progressively more complex ways as a society develops new technologies for production, communications, and so on. Although Mandelbaum lists "literary history" as one of these "special histories," his framework can be extended beyond social or political histories of literature to help define the methods and purpose of a distinctively *literary* history. To begin with, what is the permanent problem in human society around which we are to structure literary history?

There is perhaps some irony that a specifically *literary* history of literature cannot be a strictly internal history of genres, writers, readers, and texts. Literary experience—that which makes literary texts literary—participates, and serves a distinctive role in, the broader patterns of human experience. The processes of literary history are a trace of the negotiations—worked out through shifting genres and modes of writing—that shape the role of literary experience in a culture as it transforms. In this essay, I set out what I believe are the basic features of literary experience and how they variously relate to cultural change and then sketch out a literary history of *shi* poetry in China during the long period of epistemic change from the An Lushan rebellion of 755 to the end of the Song dynasty (960–1279). It is a story of the slow shift of meaning throughout this

2. Mandelbaum, "The History of Ideas," 45.
3. Hutton, "What Is Political History?" 21.

152   MICHAEL A. FULLER

period from the immanent patterns of the phenomenal realm—the world of lived experience—to an inwardness of moral structure and of the ways the rethinking of poetry and poetics participated in this transformation.

The Nature of Aesthetic Experience

Let me begin by expansively proposing that "literary experience" be defined simply as any aesthetic engagement with language.[4] In thinking about literary experience—in premodern China and more broadly—the framework of Kant's analysis of aesthetic judgments can provide the link between the literary and the larger structures of human meaning that is required for developing a properly literary history. My approach to modeling the literary here is not theory-driven; instead, I draw on Kant to develop an account that best fits the data as I have encountered them. These data include not just literary texts but also historical data that allow us to understand the role of aesthetic experience and of the place of literary texts in premodern China.

Kant turned to the question of aesthetic experience in the *Critique of Judgment* to address a problem as yet unresolved in his critical theory: even if the transcendental subject grounding our experience of the world ineluctably imposes large-scale structures on our modes of experience (most notably, causality and the dualities of subject/object and time/space), there is still no reason we should encounter order in the particular objects and events of experience, since the phenomenal realm is a play of appearances cut off from access to objects in themselves. How is it, then, that we apprehend order in the phenomenal realm, since we clearly do, and what are we to make of that order? Kant's proposed answer was to point to the role of aesthetic judgments. A judgment, for Kant, was simply when one regarded two "things" as belonging together under a higher-order concept. Most judgments are determinative, where one knows the more universal category under which one is placing the particulars. For reflective judgments, in contrast, there is a more universal concept linking

---

4. For an extended discussion of my approach to the literary, see Fuller, *Drifting among Rivers and Lakes*, 10–18.

Theoretical Reflections 153

the particulars, but this higher-order category is not known. In an aesthetic judgment, one—at least for a moment—does not seek the postulated concept but simply enjoys the fact that "the imagination (the power of a priori intuitions) [is in] harmony with understanding (the power of concepts)" in the act of apprehension.[5] In my use of Kant's framework, I consider an aesthetic judgment to be just one moment—a moment of aesthetic experience—in the totality of one's engagement with the particulars of experience. Yet this initial moment that intuits the presence of order in the flow of phenomena is utterly vital for our understanding of the world and reveals the basis on which we build our knowledge of the experiential realm. As Kant argues, "In a critique of judgment, the part that deals with aesthetic judgment belongs to it essentially. For this power alone contains a principle that judgment lays completely a priori at the basis of its reflection on nature: the principle of a formal purposiveness of nature, in terms of its particular (empirical) laws, for our cognitive power, without which principle the understanding could not find its way about in nature."[6] For Kant, a "purpose" is the concept by which an object has been made or come into existence, and purposiveness is the quality of having (or appearing to have) a purpose. He proposes in this passage a "transcendental" postulate that is required to ground any particular act of judgment: that Nature as a whole has a conceptual order that accounts for its existence. That is, intuitions of order among the particulars of experience must draw on this a priori belief that the phenomenal realm as a whole has some sort of coherence, and all empirical knowledge of the world grows from aesthetic judgments, which give form to and enact this guiding belief. This account of aesthetic experience as a moment of intuition of coherence among phenomena that grounds our understanding of the world strikes me as profoundly right, powerful, and liberating. It reframes how we think about literature and its history and compellingly reconnects them to the broader currents of experience.

Although the formal purposiveness of the phenomenal realm taken as a totality may serve as a grounding transcendental postulate, the particular ways cultures conceive of this formal coherence differ from society to society and over time as societies evolve. The conceptual structures (along with material embodiments) that at any time articulate a culture's

5. Kant, *Critique of Judgment*, 29–30.
6. Kant, *Critique of Judgment*, 33–34.

MICHAEL A. FULLER

understanding of the coherence of the manifold of experience in turn shape the materials out of which aesthetic experiences are created. Moreover, because aesthetic experience ultimately grounds the forms of coherence a culture discovers in the phenomenal realm, the possibilities for aesthetic experience explored in that culture in turn articulate new formations as the culture evolves. The modes of aesthetic production in the evolving structures of coherence for a culture trace the specifically *aesthetic* history of the arts.

Language and the Literary

Literature is the art of the aesthetic structuring of language. Language, however, is a challenging medium for intuitions of coherence since its connection to the world of experience is complex and unstable. The Chinese tradition from the beginning was aware of the problems of what and how words mean. Zhuang Zhou 莊周 (ca. 369–ca. 286 BCE), in a withering attack on reference in the relationship of words to things, argued, "The Way has never had borders, saying has never had norms. It is by a 'That's it' which deems that a boundary is marked" 夫道未始有封, 言未始有常, 為是而有畛也.[7] Much as in the "natural kinds" debates of modern philosophy, Zhuang Zhou asserted that the distinctions that humans single out through words are not in the world itself but of human origin.

The early Confucian philosopher Xun Kuang 荀況 (ca. 310–235 BCE) granted Zhuang Zhou's point but countered that Zhuang failed to understand that words were human institutions and had to be judged by how well they served human ends. For Xun Kuang, it fell to the kings to ensure the right use of language: "Therefore in the establishing of names by the one who is king, when the name is fixed and the substance discriminated, the Way is put into practice, and his intentions are communicated: thus he takes great care to lead the populace and be consistent and unified" 故王者之制名, 名定而實辨, 道行而志通, 則慎率民而一焉.[8]

---

7. Guo Qingfan, *Zhuangzi jishi*, 1:83. Translation in Angus C. Graham, *Chuang-tzŭ*, 57.

8. Xun Kuang, "On the Rectification of Names" ("Zhengming pian" 正名篇), in *Xunzi jijie*, 16.275. Compare with Knoblock, *Xunzi*, 3:128, which includes Knoblock's translation of Xun's full argument.

Theoretical Reflections

For Xun Kuang, the point of words was to distinguish and convey intentions, but the question remained of how one got one's intentions toward the world right. Xun Kuang insisted not only that human intentions served human ends but also, crucially, that humans have the faculties to adequately judge the appropriateness of the distinctions that realize intentions.

> On what does one rely to make distinctions? One relies on Heaven-given senses. When things are of the same category and same responsive characteristics, the disposition (*yi*) of [their] Heaven-given senses toward the phenomenon also is the same. . . . Articulated form and patterns of appearance are differentiated by the eye; the striking *sounds* in the notes and tunings are differentiated by the ear; the striking *flavors* among the sweet, bitter, salty, bland, hot, and sour are differentiated by the mouth; the striking odors among the fragrant, foul, grassy, florid, rotten, and putrid smells are differentiated by the nose. The painful, itchy, cool, hot, smooth, rough, light and heavy are differentiated by the body. The desires arising from joy, anger, sorrow, delight, love and hate are differentiated by the heart. In the heart there is a verifying faculty. This verifying faculty relies on the ears and then knowledge of sound is possible; it relies on the eyes for knowledge of forms to be possible. However, this verifying faculty must wait for the Heaven-given senses to register the category, and only then can it work.

> 然則何緣而以同異? 曰: 緣天官. 凡同類同情者, 其天官之意物也同. 故比方之疑似而通, 是所以共其約名以相期也. 形體、色理以目異; 聲音清濁、調竽、奇聲以耳異; 甘、苦、鹹、淡、辛、酸、奇味以口異; 香、臭、芬、鬱、腥、臊、漏庮、奇臭以鼻異; 疾、癢、凔、熱、滑、鈹、輕、重以形體異; 說、故、喜、怒、哀、樂、愛、惡、欲以心異. 心有徵知. 徵知, 則緣耳而知聲可也, 緣目而知形可也. 然而徵知必將待天官之當簿其類, 然後可也. 五官簿之而不知, 心徵知而無說, 則人莫不然謂之不知. 此所緣而以同異也.[9]

The embodied, phenomenal character of Xun Kuang's epistemology and theory of language proved crucial in shaping the Chinese literary tradition. The realm of the literary in early China was the crafting of language to question, explore, and articulate the ordering of the world of

---

9. Xun Kuang, "Zhengming pian," in *Xunzi jijie*, 16.415–18.

experience encountered through the Heaven-granted senses and mind. A literary history of the early Chinese textual traditions, then, traces the shifting modes of ordering language in its capacity to capture the intuitions of coherence that grounded premodern Chinese culture's evolving understanding of the world and the place of human society in it.

The Medieval World

Xun Kuang's embodied model of knowledge and language grounded in an ultimately unknowable Heaven proved powerfully enduring.[10] Although his minimalist Confucian model acquired accretions that supported the imperial enterprise and provided a firm place for humanity in the larger ordering of the universe in the early imperial period from the Han (206 BCE–220 CE) to the Sui (581–618) dynasties, the elaborate structures of correlative cosmology did not so much displace Xun Kuang's account as fill it in with more particular systems of connections between humans and the cosmos. In both models, humans were at home in a world filled with meaning: people, the objects of the phenomenal realm, and therefore the human relationship with those objects all participated in an order grounded in Heaven.

In the early imperial episteme, the myriad objects of the phenomenal realm shared a givenness with the human that grounded their connection with the human.[11] As discussed already, Xun Kuang argued carefully but somewhat abstractly that "When things are of the same category and same responsive characteristics, the disposition of [their] Heaven-given senses toward the phenomenon also is the same." In more common usage, "things of the same category respond to one another" 同類相感. This model

10. Xun Kuang: "Only the sage does not seek to know Heaven" 唯聖人爲不求知天. From "Discourse on Heaven" ("Tian lun" 天論篇), in *Xunzi jijie*, 11.309.

11. I borrow the term "episteme" from Foucault by way of Thomas Kuhn because I find it useful, but I also find Foucault's usage—shaped by particular ideological concerns—to be too constraining for my purposes. For me, "episteme" refers to the overall structure of "objective mind"—from Wilhelm Dilthey's hermeneutic framework—through which a society understands the world as encountered. See Dilthey, "Draft for a Critique of Historical Reason," 155.

Theoretical Reflections

of connection grounded the poetics of the "Great Preface to the Mao Recension of the *Classic of Poetry*." It also undergirded the model of literary encounter epitomized in the "Spirit Thought" ("Shensi" 神思) and "Sensuous Appearance of Things" ("Wuse" 物色) chapters of Liu Xie's 劉勰 (ca. 460s–ca. 520s) *Literary Mind and the Carving of Dragons* (*Wenxin diaolong* 文心雕龍).[12] Liu Xie in "Spirit Thought" argues:

> Thus wherein the immanent patterns of thought are subtle is the spirit as it wanders with things [*wu* 物, phenomenal objects]. The spirit resides in the breast, and resolve and *qi* control the gate. Things flow through the ears and eyes, and appropriate wording controls the hinge and trigger.
>
> 故思理爲妙, 神與物遊. 神居胸臆, 而志氣統其關鍵. 物沿耳目, 而辭令管其樞機.[13]

For Liu Xie, the literary imagination engages the objects of the phenomenal world, which in turn provide the human capacity for response with its material. In the "Sensuous Appearance of Things," he explains:

> The emotions are moved by things (*wu*), and wording comes forth from the emotions. A single leaf may at times meet with our disposition (*yi*), and in the sounds of insects there is that which is adequate to draw forth the mind. . . . Through this, for a poet moved by things, the association of categories is inexhaustible.
>
> 情以物遷, 辭以情發. 一葉且或迎意, 蟲聲有足引心 . . . 是以詩人感物, 聯類不窮.

In the process of writing, Liu Xie finds that "mountain forests and the marshy banks of rivers are indeed the secret treasure houses of [thoughts for] literary composition" 若乃山林皋壤, 實文思之奧府.[14]

---

12. See Stephen Owen's translation and discussion of "Spirit Thought" and "The Sensuous Colors of Physical Things," in *Readings in Chinese Literary Thought*, 201–10, 277–86.

13. Liu Xie, *Wenxin diaolong*, 26.493. Compare with Owen, "Spirit Thought," in *Readings in Chinese Literary Thought*, 202.

14. Liu Xie, *Wenxin diaolong*, 46.694–95. Since the focus of this essay is on developments after 800 CE, I regrettably cannot give the complexity and diversity of the

MICHAEL A. FULLER

At its most powerful, poetry in the early classical Chinese tradition drew on the poet's engagement with the landscape to situate moments of human experience in the larger patterns of the phenomenal realm.[15] No poet of this period drew on the patterns of the world more powerfully than did Du Fu 杜甫 (712–770), the great Tang dynasty poet who wrote at the end of the medieval literary tradition. His poetry presents the culmination of the medieval poetics of response, described in Liu Xie's observation that "the emotions are moved by things (*wu*), and wording comes forth from the emotions. A single leaf may at times meet with our disposition (*yi*), and in the sounds of insects there is that which is adequate to draw forth the mind." Du Fu's "Weary Night" ("Juan ye" 倦夜) is a crystalline example of this dynamic of response in which the objects he encounters engage his intentions but preserve their own substantial reality rather than serving as mere symbols of inwardness:[16]

竹涼侵臥內	Bamboo coolness invades the bedroom;
野月滿庭隅	the outland moon fills a corner of the courtyard.
重露成涓滴	The heavy dew forms water drops that fall;
稀星乍有無	the sparse stars flicker, now there, now gone.
暗飛螢自照	Fireflies gleam in their own light as they fly in the dark;
水宿鳥相呼	the birds stopping for the night on the water call out to one another.
萬事干戈裏	Ten thousand affairs all hemmed in with weapons:
空悲清夜徂	in vain I sorrow that the pure night passes.

Du Fu and his family had fled to Sichuan to avoid the chaos of the An Lushan rebellion in 760. He wrote "Weary Night" late in the summer of 764 as a meditation on the complex patterns flowing through the quiet nightscape. He, the fireflies, and the migrating geese all participate

---

transformations of literature—and poetry in particular—from the Han dynasty to the early Tang the attention they deserve in the telling of this larger story.

15. For important explorations of the relationship of this early imperial worldview to the poetry and poetics of medieval China, see Owen, *Traditional Chinese Poetry and Poetics,* and Pauline Yu, *The Reading of Imagery.*

16. Du Fu, *Du Shi xiangzhu,* 3:1176–77. For an extended discussion, see Fuller, "'Juan ye,'" 119–37.

Theoretical Reflections 159

in—and are moved by—the processes of autumnal transformation, and he, like them, sings out as he restlessly composes the poem.

The formal features of regulated verse (*lüshi* 律詩) as a genre—the parallelism of the middle couplets in particular—are central to crafting the experiential categories of correspondence that shape Du Fu's vision of the order of the world he encounters and his place in that world. Envisioned patterns pervade the poem, and Du Fu is only one participant in this vast shifting order. In the poem's long, restless night, "outside" elements transform Du Fu's small, quiet space. In the first couplet, a welcome evening coolness that partakes of the qualities of the bamboo through which it arrives formally and semantically parallels a bright moon that—shining unseen on the vast stretch of outlands surrounding Du Fu's cottage—brings that outlandish brilliance into his bedroom courtyard. The evening coolness in the courtyard creates dew as small glistening points, visible in the moonlight, that form and drop. Above and outside, the stars are small points, dimmed by the moonlight, that flicker in the damp, dense night air. Although "The moon is bright; the stars are sparse" surely draws on Cao Cao's 曹操 (155–220) "Short Song" ("Duange xing" 短歌行), the couplet is not coded allegory; instead, it presents a quiet world seemingly static yet shifting in the night. The third couplet continues the motif of small sensory elements appearing and disappearing in the courtyard and beyond, but now Du Fu, as the restless writer awake in the night, is directly drawn into the pattern along with the soon-to-die fireflies and migrating geese. At the end of the poem, Du Fu, having surveyed the correspondences among the elements of the scene that drew his attention, presents a complex mood. He has been brooding on the "wars and rumors of war" and brings the scene into those larger human patterns while at the same time putting this disturbing "season of man" into a yet larger pattern of transformation to which he stands as witness. Du Fu's subtle, complex, and powerful poetic articulation of how he sees his participation in a moment of time in "Weary Night" coincides with the end of an old world already shifting.

This model of a literature that draws its power from, and articulates, the human resonances with the world and its patterns was grounded in and gave voice to Xun Kuang's long-enduring Heaven-based phenomenology. In the end, however, the medieval episteme whose institutions, social order, and cultural practices were built on this model of the human place in the cosmos wavered and finally collapsed during the long period of transition from the mid-Tang to the end of the Song dynasty (960–1279). Phenomenologies are unstable by definition, with epistemological uncertainty as part of their basic structure. For those in early China, as for Kant, one knew the world only as one could encounter it, and one could know neither objects in themselves nor the self that did the knowing. At the beginning of the tradition, Xun Kuang warned against seeking to know Heaven—the grounding of our capacity for experience—and accepted the constraints imposed by Zhuang Zhou. Later, the Buddhist tradition, which arrived in China and became part of the culture during the medieval period, offered a phenomenology in which there was no self to know (i.e., *anātman*) and in which the objects of perception had no self-being (*svabhāva*). As a practical matter, these theoretical limits to knowing had little effect on life in early imperial China, from the governing of the realm to religious practices to writing poetry. But the failures of the imperial lineage and the great clans during the An Lushan rebellion revealed all too clearly the hollowness of the more comfortable Tang dynasty version of correlative cosmology in which those in authority in the medieval social hierarchy not only earned their positions based on the model of Heaven and Earth but also had Heaven-granted qualities appropriate to their preeminent social roles and received Heaven's support in the maintenance of a "natural" hierarchy.[17]

Rethinking the Way in Ninth-Century China

In the generation of Mid-Tang writers that emerged after the catastrophe of the An Lushan rebellion, central figures sought to formulate a chastened, human-centered account of knowledge and values that derived from early Confucianism.[18] In this model, the Way for humans was analogous

---

17. Peter K. Bol explores the transition from early Tang ways of thinking about culture and society to the models developed by literati writers in the ninth century and in the Northern Song dynasty in *"This Culture of Ours."*

18. I discuss these writers and their arguments in detail in "'Renwen,'" 195–222, as well as in "Zai jiushiji sixiang."

Theoretical Reflections

to those for Heaven and Earth but not modeled on them. Li Ao 李翱 (774–836) makes a representative argument:

> The sun, moon, stars, and constellations in ordered array in the sky are the patterns of Heaven. Mountains, rivers, grasses, and trees spread out on the Earth are the patterns of the Earth. Resolve, *qi*, language, and speech expressed by people are the human patterns.
>
> 日月星辰經乎天, 天之文也. 山川草木羅乎地, 地之文也. 志氣言語發乎人, 人之文也.[19]

The mid-Tang models for human action and organization in the human Way were grounded in an understanding of human nature revealed in the texts of the Confucian sages but also accessible through inquiry into the contemporary human condition. This continuity with the sage texts was grounded in Xun Kuang's basic position that humans, made of *qi*, were endowed with qualities that sages understood and that persisted as the foundation for the human Way. Bai Juyi 白居易 (772–846), for example, stressed both points about the continuity of sage norms:

> Now *wen* is far-reaching. The Three Materials each have their patterns. Among the patterns of Heaven, the Three Luminaries come first. Among the patterns of the Earth, the five elements come first.[20] Among human patterns, the Six Canons come first. Speaking of the Six Canons, the *Poetry* comes first. Why? The sage moved people's hearts and the realm was peaceful and harmonious. Among things that move people's hearts, nothing comes before the feelings; nothing is prior to speech, nothing more apt than music, and nothing deeper than the right. Poetry is rooted in the feelings, sprouts through speech, blossoms with music, and bears fruit in the right. From the sage and worthy above to the foolish and dull-witted below, from those as humble as pigs and fish to those as recondite as ghosts and spirits, *the groupings are diverse but the* qi *is the same; the forms*

---

19. Li Ao, "Miscellaneous Explanations, part one" ("Zashuo shang" 雜説上), in Dong Gao et al., *Quan Tang wen*, 637.6427.

20. The Three Luminaries are the sun, the moon, and the stars, or in a more specific reading, the sun, moon and Five "Stars" (which are in fact the planets Jupiter, Mars, Saturn, Venus, and Mercury). The Five Elements are metal, wood, water, fire, and earth.

differ, but the feelings are one: for they always responded when the sound entered and were moved when the feeling had been conveyed. [Emphasis added]

夫文尚矣, 三才各有文, 天之文三光首之, 地之文五材首之, 人之文六經首之. 就六經言, 詩又首之. 何者? 聖人感人心而天下和平. 感人心者莫先乎情, 莫始乎言, 莫切乎聲, 莫深乎義. 詩者根情苗言, 華聲實義. 上自聖賢, 下至愚騃, 微及豚魚, 幽及鬼神, 群分而氣同, 形異而情一, 未有聲入而不應, 情交而不感者.[21]

The human Way and human patterns are centered on human moral norms, which ground meaning in experience, while the patterns of the world of phenomena correspondingly withdraw in significance. As seen in Li Ao's and Bai Juyi's comments, the broad ninth-century discussion of *wen* (文, "pattern"), including the relation of "human pattern" (*renwen* 人文) to the patterns of Heaven and Earth and the nature of written *wen* (*wenzhang* 文章) that derived from the more abstract concept of *renwen*, reflected the new burden put on *wen* and those who wrote *wenzhang*.[22] The innovations in prose and poetry during this period also reflect the challenge for writers of developing forms to capture the shifting ground of aesthetic intuitions embodied in the *wenzhang* through which they explored and articulated how humans endowed the phenomenal realm with the meanings they discovered.

For the major mid-Tang writers, Du Fu's vision of being "of the same category" (*tonglei* 同類) with the creatures of the phenomenal realm gave way to a more self-reflective stance in writings that thematized the processes of making comparisons between the human community and the patterns of Heaven and Earth. I am not arguing here that suddenly in 800 all elite writers in China began to write mid-Tang poetry. Most authors continued to write "normal poetry," usually social verse in the style

21. Bai Juyi, "Letter to Yuan Nine" ("Yu Yuan jiu shu" 與元九書), in *Bai Juyi ji*, 5:2790. I discuss this passage in greater detail in "'Renwen.'"

22. There is no satisfactory translation for *wenzhang* in English. The term "literature" as it has been used for the past two centuries is too narrow, since *wenzhang* includes many types of official documents that writers included in their *wenji* 文集 (collected writings) as well as a range of more philosophical discussions. It is important to stress this point because there were long debates among Middle Period Chinese literati about the proper role of *wen* 文, "aesthetic mediation," in writing, reading, and the representation and apprehension of the truths most central to understanding the Way.

of the Dali reign period (766–780) writers. Instead, I suggest that the relation between such "normal poetry" and the range of innovations emerging at the time parallels the relationship that Thomas Kuhn in *The Structure of Scientific Revolutions* explores between the "normal science" that continues to articulate current paradigms and those researchers and thinkers who begin to develop paradigm-shifting models. Among the poets of the mid-Tang, some were more acutely aware of the fractures in the models for coherence in experience that they had inherited and thus explored aesthetic intuitions of a new form of coherence that would transform the failing models. The mid-Tang authors who reflected on the failures of the old model sought ways of writing *wen* that articulated new possibilities. They explored how an order based on the coherence of human nature might shape specific forms of aesthetic intuitions of meaning in the experiential realm. This shared project shaped the literary historical developments of ninth-century poetry, even though the approaches of the important writers of the time were by no means consistent: Han Yu 韓愈 (768–824), Meng Jiao 孟郊 (751–814), and their circle of friends wrote very different poetry from that of Bai Juyi, Yuan Zhen 元稹 (779–831), and Liu Yuxi 劉禹錫 (772–842). In the end, the imaginative intuitions of connection to the world of experience that they construct in their poetry all center on human terms and explore the central problem of how humans find their place among things.

Han Yu, for example, found many innovative ways in his poetry to stress the inward, human-centered processes of finding meaning. He had significant range, but at his most emphatic, he wrote wild old-style verse imposing imaginative forms on the landscape. In the more meditative eighth poem of "Autumn Thoughts" ("Qiuhuai" 秋懷), he begins with failed intimations of meaning in the autumn scene.[23] The resolution of the poem comes with Han Yu hearing the voices of men of long ago given voice through his son. Bai Juyi's poetry, seemingly more at home in the world, still foregrounds the movement of the human mind in creating categories. The approach to composition called "bitter chanting" (*kuyin* 苦吟) associated with the late Tang style refers precisely to the labor of crafting categories in the process of writing parallel couplets. Nonetheless,

---

23. Han Yu, *Han Yu quanji*, 1:366.

164 MICHAEL A. FULLER

brilliantly successful couplets in the late Tang style by poets like Jia Dao 賈島 (779–843), Du Mu 杜牧 (803–852), and Yao He 姚合 (ca. 779–ca. 855) are not mere artifice but articulate moments of human sensibility as it shapes perception. However, the ninth-century literary explorations of the role of sensibility in mediating one's encounter with the world also included a probing of the darker implications of this mediation as mid- and late Tang poets explored how intense sensibilities distort perspective. Meng Jiao's anguished old-style poetry sequences, such as "Cold Creek: Eight Poems" ("Han xi bashou" 寒溪八首), "Sadness of the Gorges: Ten Poems" ("Xia ai shishou" 峽哀十首), and "Apricots Die Young: Nine Poems" ("Xing shang jiushou" 杏殤九首) raise the problem, while Li He's 李賀 (790–816) verse takes a more finely crafted approach.[24] Li He's "The Grave of Little Su" ("Su Xiaoxiao mu" 蘇小小墓) draws the reader into the realm of the fantastic where one cannot be sure what is real and what is imagined.

幽蘭露	Dew drops on secluded orchids
如啼眼	are like weeping eyes.
無物結同心	There is nothing with which to bind a love-pledge:
煙花不堪剪	I cannot bear to cut the misty flowers.
草如茵	The grasses are like a mat;
松如蓋	the pine is like a canopy.
風爲裳	The breeze becomes a skirt;
水爲佩	the water becomes a pendant.
油壁車	The varnish-sided carriage,
夕相待	at dusk awaiting.
冷翠燭	The cold blue-glinting candle,
勞光彩	struggles to gleam.
西陵下	At the foot of West Mound,
風吹雨	wind blows the rain.[25]

24. See Meng Jiao, *Meng Jiao shiji*, 5.232–37 and 10.488–98.

25. Li He, *Li Changji geshi*, 1.46, in *Sanjia pingzhu*. Little Su was a famous Southern Dynasties singing girl. The persona in the poem obsessively constructs a scene based on a song attributed to her: "I ride a varnish-sided carriage, / you mount a blue-white horse. / Where shall we bind our hearts as one? / Under the pine and cypress of West Mound" 妾乘油壁車, 郎騎青驄馬. 何處結同心, 西陵松柏下. Lu Qinli, comp. *Xian Qin Han Wei*, 1481.

The similes, explicitly interjecting an active, interpreting sensibility, persistently assert an uncanny human presence in the landscape, but the very oddness of those similes casts doubt on the reliability of the informing sensibility. This doubt causes the final image of the blue-glinting candle—perhaps a real candle, perhaps a foxfire at a gravesite—to create a fantastic effect (following Todorov's account).

The poem's exploration of the mediation of a driven sensibility is an extension of pronouncements like Li Ao's "Resolve, *qi*, language, and speech expressed by people are the human patterns." If this assertion and many similar statements are true, and if meaning is to be found in these human patterns, how do these elements of resolve, *qi*, and language in fact interact in human experience? Li He leaves normative versions of resolve behind to focus instead on cases where an aberrant resolve is so great that the inner interpretative processes dominate the moment of encounter. The reader of the poem here finds it all but impossible to reconstruct the elements of the external world that are the supposed occasion for the responses out of which the poem grows. This, then, is poetry that is beginning to undo the claim of intelligibility that was part of the promise of adhering strictly to the human realm of meaning.

At the end of this period of intense experimentation, Li Shangyin 李商隱 (ca. 812–858), who wrote a short biography of Li He, continued to explore how subjectivity profoundly shaped our engagement with the world but pursued very different formal innovations. He developed a style in his untitled poems in particular that present narrative vignettes filled with urgency and longing, but in which the reader lacks the external references needed to anchor the interpretation of the poems.[26] Consider, for example, this poem "Untitled" ("Wuti" 無題):

相見時難別亦難	Seeing one another is hard; separation is also hard;
東風無力百花殘	the east wind is without force, the hundred flowers tattered.
春蠶到死絲方盡	The spring silkworm's silk stops only with its death;
蠟炬成灰淚始乾	the tears of the wax torch begin to dry only when it has become ash.

26. See my discussion in Fuller, "Zai jiushiji sixiang." Also see Robert Ashmore's reading of another "Untitled" poem by Li Shangyin in "Recent-Style *Shi* Poetry," 193–95.

曉鏡但愁雲鬢改	At the dawn mirror, [she] only grieves
	at the change in her cloud-like forelocks;
夜吟應覺月光寒	chanting at night, [she] surely is aware
	that the moon's gleam is cold.
蓬山此去無多路	Mount Penglai is not far from here:
青鳥殷勤爲探看	bluebird, try your best to spy [her out] for me.[27]

Two people with elegant sensibilities have had an affair: one partner desires the other; they are close by but cannot meet. It seems best to conclude that the speaker of the poem is a man, but this is just a conjecture. Over the centuries, commentaries on the poem have sought to fill in the story. I believe that such efforts miss the point in that these readings insist that the poems are interpretable only if their objective correlatives are known. Instead, the poems "Without Title" intensely explore feelings that offer a more radically conceived inner ground for coherence in experience. In these poems, Li Shangyin constructed moments of aesthetic experience that pushed the central elements of the shared cultural matrix of writing to the breaking point. While the wide range of innovations in poetry during the mid- and late Tang provided models for the construction of meaning in the phenomenal realm, at times the constraints imposed by human subjectivity that were revealed in the poetry of Meng Jiao, Li He, and Li Shangyin also threatened to sever human meaning from an experiential realm viewed as increasingly inaccessible.

Confucian Humanism and the Literary in the Northern Song Dynasty

The threat of the alienation of human meaning from a highly mediated world of experience was an enduring and real problem that shadowed the mid-Tang intellectual shift away from direct linkage of the human realm to that of Heaven and Earth. Still, for the next two hundred years, through the tumultuous period of the collapse of the Tang dynasty, the Five

---

27. Li Shangyin, *Li Shangyin shige*, 4:1461–67.

Theoretical Reflections

Dynasties (907–960) and into the early years of the Song dynasty, the revised Confucian model developed by mid-Tang writers served well enough in the project of reshaping the cultural institutions, including writing and governance, that define an episteme.

Ouyang Xiu 歐陽修 (1007–1072), the greatest writer and central cultural figure of the early Northern Song, viewed governance and writing in the framework of a Northern Song interpretation of the revived humanist Confucianism of the mid-Tang. In governance, he insisted on—and developed policies on—the principle that "the regulations of Yao, Shun, and the Three Kings necessarily were based on human feelings" 堯舜三王之治, 必本於人情.[28] His approach to writing in prose and poetry centered on this principle as well. In his commentary on the *Classic of Poetry*, for instance, he argued that the meaning of the early Zhou dynasty poems in the canon was still accessible because the modern reader could understand the intent of the poets and, through them, could come to grasp Confucius's central concerns, since Confucius shaped the collection by selecting these morally and aesthetically normative poems in particular. For Ouyang Xiu, as for the mid-Tang writers, proper understanding of the Confucian canon— made possible by a shared humanity—provided the norms for technique and imagination in writing. Given these commitments, Ouyang was less an innovator than a domesticator: his old-style poetry was often a sociable version of Han Yu's more radical experiments, while his old-style prose was skillful, well crafted, and fluent (in contrast to Shi Jie's 石介 [1005–1045] self-consciously "ancient" prose style).

However, a nexus of growing debates about the role of the state, the qualities that gave the literati elite its political and social authority, the grounds for moral action, and the proper reading of the foundational Confucian canon once again revealed the epistemological limits of Ouyang Xiu's human-centered Confucian phenomenology, with its origins in the mid-Tang rethinking of the Way. In the next generation, writers offered profoundly different solutions for apprehending the Way and the role of *wen* in that process.[29] Su Shi 蘇軾 (1037–1101), the most brilliant writer of the Song dynasty, was at one end of the continuum. He argued that indeed all one

---

28. Ouyang Xiu, "Discourse on Releasing Criminals" ("Zongqiu lun" 縱囚論), in *Ouyang Xiu shiwenji*, 1:563.

29. See the discussion in Bol, "*This Culture of Ours*," 254–99.

could know were the phenomena and not the metaphysical (*xing er shang* 形而上) entities like "Nature" (*xing* 性) behind them.[30] Still, for Su Shi, it is precisely *wen* that can represent and convey the human manner of participating in the phenomenal realm. *Wen*, in his account, captures a "marvelous" quality that is precisely an aesthetic intuition of order without a determinate concept. For Su Shi, the "inherent patterns of the myriad phenomena" provided the grounds for the coherence of human experience, and humans could capture—if not name—the particular structures of that realm through adequately supple writing. His account of his writing is remarkably almost Kantian in his delight in his capacity (without determinate rules) to accord with the patterns of what he encounters:

> My writing is like a spring of ten thousand gallons: it does not select the ground out of which it comes forth. On level land, it flows smoothly and quickly, and even a thousand *li* in a day is not hard. When it bends and breaks over mountain stones, it follows the object in taking its form and cannot be known. What can be known is that it always travels where it ought to travel and always stops where it cannot but stop. It is like this, and that is all. As for the rest, even I cannot know.
>
> 吾文如萬斛泉源, 不擇地皆可出. 在平地滔滔汨汨, 雖一日千里無難. 及其與山石曲折, 隨物賦形而不可知也. 所可知者, 常行於所當行, 常止於不可不止, 如是而已矣. 其他雖吾亦不能知也.[31]

Su Shi's *shi* poetry develops techniques to trace the human participation in the patterns of the phenomenal realm, a participation that includes the movement of the mind.

For example, Su Shi wrote "Aboard Boat, Rising at Night" ("Zhouzhong yeqi" 舟中夜起) in 1079 en route to taking up the post of magistrate in Huzhou:

微風蕭蕭吹菰蒲	A light breeze rustles, blowing the reeds;
開門看雨月滿湖	as I open the door to watch the rain, the moon fills the lake.

---

30. *Sushi Yi zhuan, juan 7*, in Su Xun, Su Shi, and Su Zhe, *San Su quanshu*, 1.351–55.

31. Su Shi, "Account of My Writings" ("Ziping wen" 自評文), in *Su Shi wenji* 蘇軾文集, 5:66.2069.

舟人水鳥兩同夢	The people on the boat and the water fowl both share the same dream;
大魚驚竄如奔狐	a large fish starts and scurries to hide like a fleeing fox.
夜深人物不相管	The night is late: people and phenomena do not involve one another;
我獨形影相嬉娛	alone I, my shape, and my shadow amuse ourselves.
暗潮生渚弔寒蚓	The hidden tide grows on the bank: I lament the cold earthworms;
落月掛柳看懸蛛	as the setting moon hangs amidst the willows, I watch the suspended spider.
此生忽忽憂患裏	In this life, so hurried amid sorrow and calamity,
清境過眼能須臾	can a pure scene passing before the eyes last more than a moment?
雞鳴鐘動百鳥散	The cock crows; the bell strikes; the many birds scatter:
船頭擊鼓還相呼	at the prow they beat the drum and call out to one another.[32]

This is a restless moonlit poem like Du Fu's "Weary Night," yet it differs significantly in its broader context, its form—"old style" verse rather than regulated verse—and its poetic sensibility. Su Shi frames the poem with a misreading: having slept only lightly and hearing the rustling of the reeds, he gets up to watch the rain only to discover a quiet moonlit scene. This contradiction of expectations creates a quality of wonder that at the same time introduces a slight estrangement that heightens Su Shi's careful engagement with the scene and persists until the final couplet. He creates connections in the poem not through the parallelism and formal structures of regulated verse but through shifts and juxtapositions in and between the couplets. As he observes the nightscape, most of the world is sleeping, drawing together the people and the birds. Somehow, the fish that intrudes into the scene reminds Su Shi of a fox; the connection is odd and points to his wayward nighttime mood. The poem then weaves together moments of abstract musing with acute observation of the scene. The reverie on the passage of time in the second-to-last couplet stands in for—and performs the mood of—the hours that have passed until dawn. In the final vision, men and birds join

---

32. Su Shi, *Su Shi shiji*, 17.891–92. I discuss this poem in greater detail in "In Praise of Alienation," 45–47.

again, with Su Shi among them, in a return to the diurnal cycles of life. The synthesis is complex and draws the inwardness of Su Shi as the persona in the poem into the unfolding patterns he discovers in the phenomenal realm.

Su Shi's poetics of encounter that revealed patterns immanent in the phenomenal realm met increasing resistance from a counterposition emerging in the transformations of late Northern Song elite culture. Cheng Yi 程頤 (1033–1107) in particular argued against Su Shi's aesthetic model for knowledge. In contrast to Su Shi's focus on the manifestation of the myriad patterns of the phenomenal realm, Cheng Yi argued that it was possible—and indeed, crucial—to know the metaphysical "Nature" and "Heavenly Principle" that alone could properly ground moral knowledge. Cheng Yi set aside contemporary debates about proper style for writing and rejected concern for style altogether. For him, any focus on the aesthetic ordering of language stood in the way of grasping moral knowledge:

> Someone asked, "Does composing artfully patterned texts (*zuowen*) harm the Way?" He said, "It does: in composing, if one does not focus one's intent, one will not be skillful. If one focuses one's intent, then one's resolve resides here, and how can it become as large as Heaven and Earth?"
>
> 問:"作文者害道者否?" 曰:"害也. 凡爲文, 不專意則不工, 若專意則志局於此, 又安能與天地同其大也."[33]

Cheng Yi and the other advocates of *Daoxue* in the Northern Song rejected the claims of phenomenal knowledge, or the knowledge of what can be seen and heard, and asserted a new approach to reading texts to grasp the mind of the sage.

The Role of the Literary in Epistemic Change

The last phase of the great Middle Period epistemic shift arose as the Southern Song (1127–1279) elite explored alternative modes of apprehending an order beyond the immediate givenness of the senses presented by

---

33. Cheng Hao and Cheng Yi, *Er Cheng yishu*, 188.

Su Shi and Cheng Yi. In this final phase, it is crucial to recall that an episteme is not just a philosophical system but an array of social institutions and practices, technologies, and a built environment (including cityscapes)—as well as corpora of texts—that embody philosophical commitments. In the early years of the Middle Period epistemic transition, the disappearance of the great clans in the Huang Chao rebellion of the 880s, the growth of a new meritocratic elite stratum to staff the bureaucracy after the founding of the Song dynasty, and the revised organs, policies, and ethos of government, along with the spread of woodblock printing, all contributed to shaping the transitional episteme of the Northern Song dynasty.[34] Similarly, the events surrounding the fall of the north and the founding of the Southern Song, the overproduction of students participating in an examination system that increasingly accepted the *Daoxue* interpretative framework, the rise of specifically local elite families who grounded their social and moral authority in traditions of learning given specific form in their acceptance of Confucian duties, and the greater flourishing of printing all contributed to the specific forms the emerging late imperial episteme took as it evolved on the basis of the new *Daoxue* culture of the Southern Song.[35]

Yang Wanli 楊萬里 (1127–1206) and Lu You 陸游 (1125–1210), the two greatest poets of the early Southern Song, grew to prominence while Zhu Xi 朱熹 (1130–1200) was shaping his new *Daoxue* synthesis in debates with Zhang Shi 張栻 (1133–1180), Lü Zuqian 呂祖謙 (1137–1181), and Lu Jiuyuan 陸九淵 (1139–1192). Although Yang Wanli and Lu You started out as "technical" poets concerned with crafting, they ended their careers supporting Su Shi's position that poets in particular had the power

34. For the decline of the Great Clans, see Tackett, *The Destruction of the Medieval Chinese Aristocracy*. Hugh Clark has written a series of three essays in *Journal of Song-Yuan Studies* with the title "Why Does the Tang-Song Interregnum Matter?" that explains the complex transformations of Chinese culture during the Five Dynasties period, and Peter K. Bol in *"This Culture of Ours"* has described the intersection of culture and governance in the Northern Song.

35. I explore the role of these societal developments in shaping Southern Song literature in Fuller and Lin, "North and South: The Twelfth and Thirteenth Centuries." I return to the topics in *Drifting among Rivers and Lakes*.

MICHAEL A. FULLER

through *wen* to capture patterns immanent in the world. Yang Wanli argued that,

> I at first have no intent to write this particular poem, but this thing, this event happens to strike me. My intention also happens to be moved by this thing or this event. The encounter is first, the response follows, and this poem comes out. How is it my creation? It is Heaven's. This is called inspiration.
>
> 我初無意於作是詩, 而是物是事適然觸乎我. 我之意亦適然感乎是物是事. 觸先焉, 感隨焉, 而是詩出焉. 我何與哉. 天也. 斯之謂興.[36]

Much of Yang Wanli's poetry in his distinctive "Chengzhai style" ("Chengzhai ti" 誠齋體, Chengzhai being Yang's studio name) captures moments of inspired encounter with the world, such as in this quatrain, the second of "Afternoon Wind in a Cold Grove: Two Poems" ("Wanfeng hanlin ershou" 晚風寒林二首):

樹無一葉萬梢枯	The trees are without a single leaf, ten thousand branches sere:
活底秋江水墨圖	a living ink painting of an autumn river.
幸自寒林俱淡筆	Initially the cold grove is all pale brushstrokes,
却將濃墨點栖烏	but they use dark ink to dot the roosting crows.[37]

What is striking in the scene is notable to an interpreting human sensibility, yet the scene is real, and Yang Wanli captures it brilliantly. The monochromatic pale light and, in the middle distance, a grove of dark, bare trees lining the riverbank are indeed effects that Song dynasty landscape painters sought to convey precisely because the images capture the lonely, sere beauty of an autumn evening. Yang Wanli notes that nature has provided the finishing touches to this "painting"—as he imagines an artist might do—by adding the final dark dots as the crows gather to roost for the evening. The impressionistic technique of the poem reflects an in-

---

36. Yang Wanli, "Answering the letter of Xu Da, Military Commander of the Arsenal at Jiankang Superior Prefecture" ("Da Jiankang fu dajunku junmen Xu Da shu" 答建康府大軍庫軍門徐達書), in *Yang Wanli ji jian jiao*, 6:67.2841.

37. Yang Wanli, *Yang Wanli ji jian jiao*, 2:10.555.

Theoretical Reflections

wardness of vision, but the poem still embodies a way that compelling patterns of the world draw forth the powerful human response that Yang Wanli identifies as "inspiration" at the core of poetic composition.

Much like Yang Wanli, Lu You also underscored the need to be adequately adroit in capturing what the world presents. He famously asserted:

| 天機雲錦用在我 | The loom of Heaven and its cloud brocades were for my use: |
| 剪裁妙處非刀尺 | But the marvelous part of the cutting was not in the knife and ruler.[38] |

Still, while stressing the role of the aesthetic dimension in the revelation of patterns in the world, Lu You and Yang Wanli also affirmed the moral significance of those patterns to address the increasingly pressing need in elite cultural discourse to foreground that moral dimension. Lu You particularly acknowledged the importance of crafting in poetry but cautioned about its dangers:

> On the whole, in poetry one wants skill, but skill is not the ultimate. Long refining [poetry] causes it to lose its basic import. Intense crafting harms its upright fervor (qi).
>
> 大抵詩欲工, 而工亦非詩之極也. 鍛煉之久, 乃失本指, 斷削之甚, 反傷正氣.[39]

Zhu Xi, expanding Cheng Yi's philosophical arguments, challenged Lu You's and Yang Wanli's foundational claim that the transformations of the phenomenal realm that were the material of their literary composition possessed and—for the poet—revealed an immanent moral order.

---

38. "On the First Day of the Ninth Month, Reading My Draft Poetic Collection at Night, Being Moved, I Dash Off Lines to Compose a Song" ("Jiuyue yiri yedu shigao yougan zoubi zuoge" 九月一日夜讀詩稿有感走筆作歌), in Lu You, *Jiannan shigao jiaozhu* 劍南詩稿校注, 4:25.1802–3. In a later poem, "Composition" ("Wenzhang" 文章), Lu You similarly asserts: "Writings in origin are formed by Heaven: / the marvelous hand by chance attains them" 文章本天成, 妙手偶得之. *Jiannan shigao jiaozhu*, 8:83.4469.

39. Lu You, "Funerary Memorial for Master He [He Dai 何逮 (1153–1203)]" ("Hejun mubiao" 何君墓表), in *Lu Fangweng quanji*, 1:245.

Zhu Xi argued instead that truly normative *wen* of the ancient sages derived from their inner substance as a form of pure externalization:

> Now the *wen* of the sages and worthies of old can be called flourishing. However, from the beginning, how could they have had the intent to learn to compose patterned texts like this? There was this substance within, so there must have been this patterning without. It is like Heaven having this *qi*: there must be the brilliance of the sun, moon, stars, and constellations. The earth having this shape, there must be the arrays of mountains and rivers, plants and trees. Since the minds of the sages and worthies had a pure, refined, luminous substance that expansively filled all within, then its manifestation on the outside must spontaneously have been ordered, distinct, and brilliant, and could not be hidden.
>
> 夫古之聖賢, 其文可謂盛矣. 然初豈有意學爲如是之文哉. 有是實於中, 則必有是文於外. 如天有是氣, 則必有日月星辰之光耀. 地有是形, 則必有山川草木之行列. 聖賢之心既有精明純粹之實以旁薄充塞乎其内, 則其著見於外者, 亦必自然條理分明, 光輝發越而不可揜.[40]

Still, Zhu Xi's students could not understand how a metaphysical Heavenly Principle—and the human moral nature that was identical to it—could inhere in the world if they were outside of the transformations of the experiential realm. Over and over they asked Zhu Xi about the relation of material substance (*qi* 氣) and Heavenly Principle. In such a framework, aesthetic experience could no longer give one the intuitions of order in the phenomenal world through which to begin grasping moral principle as humans can know it.

In the late Southern Song, writers like Liu Kezhuang 劉克莊 (1187–1269) struggled with the problem of the role of aesthetic form in *Daoxue*'s moral order. He never developed a satisfactory answer or a poetry that could give shape to compelling aesthetic intuitions about the immanence of the *Daoxue* moral order in the world. Yet his efforts did help the *Daoxue* scholars develop, at the end of this period, a new relationship between aesthetic experience and moral order. As Zhen Dexiu 眞德秀 (1178–1235), one of the major *Daoxue* advocates of the late Southern Song,

---

40. Zhu Xi, "Reading the 'Treatise' [on Rites and Music] in the [*New*] *Tang History*" ("Du Tang zhi" 讀唐志), in *Zhu Xi ji*, 6:70.3653–54.

Theoretical Reflections

explains, "The rhetorical forms of the poets revealed the mysteries of the moral principle of the sages and worthies" 詩人比興之體, 發聖賢理義之秘.[41] They acknowledge that sustainable structures of meaning required— could not survive without—the complement of representations crafted through the sensuous intuitions of literary form. The Way, they learned, needed *wen*.

* * *

Literary history traces the forces that shape the possibilities for aesthetic experience in writing and the patterns of experiments through which writers devise formal approaches to structuring aesthetic intuitions of meaning in the phenomenal realm. Yet such experiments are not merely reactive: they probe emerging fractures in meaning while they offer new solutions in a complex dialogue in a larger culture. The literary history of Middle Period Chinese poetry reveals the complexity of the dynamics of reshaping literary practice in an era of epistemic shift. That literary history, sketched so briefly here, points to the historically shifting nature of literary meaning and the embeddedness of literary meaning in a larger world of human experience.

41. Zhen Dexiu, "Preface to *Poems on the Past*" ("Yonggu shi xu" 詠古詩序), in *Quan Song wen*, 313:7169.149–50.

CHAPTER 7

Poetic Omens and Poetic History

Lucas Rambo Bender

This chapter explores the usefulness to literary history of topics that may seem to lie on the margins of literature. One of the difficulties of writing "literary history" at the temporal and cultural remove from premodern China at which we currently find ourselves lies in the fact that the concept of "literature" represents neither a native nor a neutral description of the phenomena we treat under this heading. While it is true, therefore, that even the most focused literary history will "often have to draw upon a wide variety of facts in order to account for the changes which occurred in that strand of human activity whose course [it] seeks to follow"—to recall the words of Maurice Mandelbaum cited by Michael A. Fuller in the preceding chapter's discussion of literature as a "special history"—it is ultimately "the [special] historian's conception of his subject matter that, in the first instance, dictates the principles of inclusion of certain materials in his work and governs the exclusion of others."[1] As a result, literary history is always in danger of creating its own object by isolating a static, preconceived, etic vision of "literature" out from the emic matrices into which its materials might originally have fit. To forestall this possibility, therefore, and to better understand those emic matrices and the ways they may have changed over time, it can be useful every now and then to turn our attention away from the core of what we recognize as literature and toward its entanglements with other domains.

---

1. Mandelbaum, "The History of Ideas," 45, and *The Anatomy of Historical Knowledge*, 34.

Poetic Omens and Poetic History   177

My case study here is the relationship between poetry and omens. Even though omens appear in poetic forms from the Han all the way through the Qing—whether sung by children in their villages, written by religious adepts, or produced unawares by literati poets—modern scholars have generally assumed, and sometimes explicitly argued, that properly "literary" poetry never had much to do with them. Pauline Yu, for example, took issue with the subtitle of Stephen Owen's *Traditional Chinese Poetry and Poetics: Omen of the World*, arguing that it cast "a more mystifying glow on the whole [poetic] process than seems appropriate," rendering the Chinese lyric not "an historical document" (as she believes it was) but "a kind of a sign" whose "true significance may lie on another order of experience from that of daily life," an order that may be "religious or even transcendent."[2] Certainly it is true, as Yu suggests, that most Chinese readers in the premodern era would not have considered most poems to be omens. Yet when we examine the poems they did treat as omens and the ways that treatment changed over time, it becomes apparent that these oppositions—between "history" and "religion," "transcendence" and "daily life"—should not be thought of as given or fixed. Instead, tracing the history of the relationship between poetry and omens can help us better understand in which periods and in what ways premodern Chinese poetry might have been suffused with a "mystifying glow" and where Yu's cautions might be more justified.

The key finding of this chapter is that, when we survey surviving materials that speak to these questions, we find significant heterogeneity over time—heterogeneity that is, moreover, of two different sorts. On the one hand, the relationship of poetry and omens develops from the Han dynasty to the Song along a linear trajectory, with poetic omens becoming increasingly domesticated to the contours of literati life. On the other hand, however, the changing status of omens in literary theoretical discourse suggests sharp discontinuities from period to period in emic understandings of the poetic art. After outlining these two historical narratives, the chapter concludes with a discussion of the apparent contradiction between them. This contradiction, I suggest, may help us better understand what it was in the nature of "literature" in the premodern

---

2. Yu, Review of *Traditional Chinese Poetry and Poetics*, 352. Note that Owen disavows these implications in the book, writing that "These omens are not prophecies (though one who knows the world's cycles may be able to read something of the future in them)"; see Owen, *Traditional Chinese Poetry and Poetics*, 44.

Varieties of Poetic Omens and Their Evolution over Time

There is not space in this short essay to give anything like a detailed introduction to the premodern Chinese omenscape in general or even to the topic of poetic omens specifically, which has a surprisingly complex history.[3] Like "literature," "poetic omens" is an etic term grouping together materials that might not have made a natural category in the periods under consideration. Indeed, these materials are discussed under several different headings in surviving premodern texts, all of which imply slight but significant shifts in how these phenomena were understood. In official histories that follow the model established in Ban Gu's 班固 (32–92) *History of the Han* (*Han shu* 漢書), for instance, poetic omens are generally collected under the title *shiyao* 詩妖 (poetic prodigies); in various Song dynasty anecdote collections (broadly, *biji* 筆記), they are discussed under the heading of *shichen* 詩讖 (poetic prophecies); in the fourteenth-century compendium *Comprehensive Examination of Documents* (*Wenxian tongkao* 文獻通考), they are labeled *shiyi* 詩異 (poetic anomalies); in the Qing encyclopedia *Complete Collection of Illustrations and Writings from Antiquity to the Present* (*Gujin tushu jicheng* 古今圖書集成), they are collected as *yaochen* 謠讖 (folk-ditty prophecies); and in the Qing-compiled *Complete Tang Poems* (*Quan Tang shi* 全唐詩), they are separated into *yao* 謠 (folk ditties) and *chenji* 讖記 (records of prophecies). To further complicate matters, many of these categories contain omens that are not in what we would recognize as poetic forms—most

---

3. Here the most in-depth study is Sun Rongrong, *Chenwei yu wenxue yanjiu*, though it contains only one chapter on poetic omens. For a review of Chinese scholarship on the topic, see Wang Xian and Xiao Jing, "Jin shiwunian shichen." Although this article is now somewhat dated, it is largely the same scholars surveyed here who have continued to publish in the field. In Western languages, the best resource is Zongli Lu's *Power of the Words*, which gives extensive examples of poetic omens from the Han through the Six Dynasties. Despite its title and its useful discussion of related phenomena, Michel Strickmann's *Chinese Poetry and Prophecy* does not deal with these materials in any detail.

Poetic Omens and Poetic History 179

notably the official histories' *shiyao* sections, which also include linguistic omens of several other sorts.

Recognizing the difficulties presented by the many different premodern terms used for these materials, modern Chinese scholars who have worked on poetic omens have often simplified them into two categories: *yaochen* and *shichen*.[4] *Yaochen*, as they use the term, are predominantly oral, produced by the folk (*min* 民), and concerned with the governance of the empire. *Shichen*, by contrast, are predominantly written by literati (*shi* 士) and mostly concern the author's fate or that of people close to them. According to the commonly accepted narrative, *yaochen* make up the vast majority of poetic omens from the pre-Qin period through the Tang, while *shichen* originate in the Six Dynasties (220–589), appear occasionally in the Tang, and preponderate in the Song and late imperial period.

For the sake of convenience, I sometimes use the designations *yaochen* and *shichen* in what follows. But I would like to suggest that this distinction does not provide a fully adequate map of the materials in question. Instead, if we draw our categories more finely, as I do in the following two tables—Table 1 analyzes the *shiyao* collected in the eponymous sections of the official histories and Table 2 considers the *yaochen* compiled in the great *Gujin tushu jicheng*—we can begin to recognize somewhat more clearly the process by which this shift from a predominance of *yaochen* to a large percentage of *shichen* might have occurred.

These tables must be read with caution. Not only are the data far from robust—no doubt vastly more poetic omens were produced and lost over the centuries, especially in earlier periods from which so little survives—but by definition, the sources that preserve these poetic omens are always more recent (sometimes by centuries) than the omens are purported to be.[5] Although there is no reason I know of to suspect that the survival of

4. Wu Chengxue may have established this convention his 1996 article "Lun yaochen yu shichen." This article is expanded and republished in his *Zhongguo gudai wenti xingtai yanjiu*. See also Shu Daqing, "Zhongguo gudai zhengzhi tongyao."

5. When it comes to the standard histories at least, the date of their compilation can tell us more or less how far our texts are from the events they claim to record, but with *Gujin tushu jicheng*, the chronological difficulties are more pronounced. For example, I have not differentiated those poetic omens that derive from the Tang and are preserved in authentic Tang sources from those that supposedly derive from the Tang but are preserved in (sometimes quite late) Song *biji*, since it is generally impossible to know for certain whether the authors of those Song *biji* may have had access to earlier materials

Table 1
Poetic Omens in the Standard Histories

Title of History	Han shu	Hou Han shu	Song shu	Nan Qi shu	Sui shu	Jin shu
Date of history (CE)	82	445	488	537	636	648
Total page count[a]	4,273	3,682	2,470	1,036	1,904	3,306
Total entries[b]	6	12	48	16	19	41
By children[c]	6	11	23	4	10	20
By the folk	—	1	20	7	2	17
By special individuals[d]	—	—	4	—	3	3
By imperial family	—	—	1 (not a poem)	4 (2 poems)	4	1 (not a poem)
By literati	—	—	—	1 (not a poem)	—	—
Discovered, no author	—	—	—	—	—	—

Note: Table only includes standard histories where there is a section devoted to omens; no omens have been collected from other sections of the histories.

[a]Page numbers are from the Zhonghua shuju standard printings. No total page counts are given for *Wudai shiji bukao* or *Qing shi gao* because these are not standard histories but were prepared more recently on the basis of surviving materials.

[b]The total number of entries may not always be equivalent to the number given in the breakdown, as I double-count certain examples where both elements are present.

[c]I only attribute specific omens to children when the histories are explicit; unattributed "ditties" 謠 are listed under "By the folk."

[d]"Special individuals" include madmen, women, Buddhists, Daoists, and deities. This category is drawn from the traditional bibliographical practice of separating the writings of these groups out at the end of each temporal period, beginning with the *Sui shu* (the first surviving bibliographical catalog to include literary writings by these classes of individuals) and continuing through the compilation of late imperial and even modern compendia such as the *Quan Tang shi* and Lu Qinli's 逯欽立 (1910–1973) *Xian Qin Han Wei Jin nanbeichao shi* 先秦漢魏晉南北朝詩. The history of this practice is complex, with different groups separated out in different collections and bibliographies; there are also collections and bibliographies that do not draw these distinctions. Nonetheless, the fact that these groups were routinely separated out in this way suggests that their writings could sometimes be thought of as existing on the margins of the core literati tradition. This line of the table is thus intended to represent, however roughly, a traditional emic category; it is not an assertion that we should in general think of the literary productions of these classes of individuals as separate from those of "the literati."

Continued on next page

Table I—*Continued*

Jiu Tang shu	*Xin Tang shu*	*Wudai shiji bukao*	*Jin shi*	*Song shi*	*Yuan shi*	*Ming shi*	*Qing shi gao*
945	1060	NA	1345	1345	1370	1739	NA
5,407	6,472	NA	2,906	14,262	4,678	8,642	NA
8	24	26	3	10	2	3	4
2	12	· 8	2	1	1	1	2
5	10	6	—	5	1	1	—
—	1	7	—	1	—	1	—
1 (not a poem)	—	5 (2 poems)	1 (not a poem)	—	—	—	—
1 (based on folk song)	1	—	—	1?	—	—	—
—	—	—	—	2	—	—	2

Lucas Rambo Bender

Table 2
Poetic Omens in the *Gujin tushu jicheng*

	Qin-Han	Six Dynasties	Sui-Tang-Wudai	Song-Liao-Jin	Yuan-Ming
Years in span	441	369	379	319	365
Total selections (no. per decade)[a]	22 (0.5)	128 (3.5)	78 (2.1)	70 (2.2)	31 (0.8)
Children, omens of the state (% of total)	19 (86)	63 (49)	19 (24)	10 (14)	12 (39)
Folk or soldiers, omens of the state (% of total)	2 (9)	48 (38)	21 (27)	13 (19)	11 (35)
Madmen, omens of the state (% of total)	—	1 (1)	—	—	—
Women, omens of the state (% of total)	1 (5)	—	—	—	—
Buddhists or Daoists, omens of the state (% of total)	—	7 (5)	7 (9)	2 (3)	2 (6)
Emperors or high officials, omens of self/state (% of total)	—	4 (3)	15 (19)	3 (4)	2 (6)
Literati, omens of the state (% of total)	—	3 (2)	5 (6)	3 (4)	—
Literati, omens of the self (% of total)	—	2 (2)	11 (14)	32 (45)	4 (13)
Literati, omens of others (% of total)	—	—	—	7 (10)	—

Note: This table only collects truly *poetic* omens, rather than the other sorts of linguistic omens that sometimes go under the title of *shiyao* in the histories.

[a] Since the *Gujin tushu jicheng* takes material (mostly) verbatim from heterogeneous sources, in some cases it can be difficult to determine what defines a "single" entry. These numbers are thus approximate, useful only for pointing out trends. I omit discovered omens, even when they are "poetic" in the sense of rhythmic and rhymed. I also exclude omens presented as faked.

our sources shows any particular bias against one type of poetic omen versus another, we should nonetheless bear in mind the possibility that dynamics of transmission are shaping what we can perceive in ways we cannot. These considerations suggest that there would only be marginal

---

that are now lost. As a result, omens attributed to the Tang in *Gujin tushu jicheng* may sometimes tell us more about the Song than they do about the Tang.

utility in incrementing these statistics through other sources, which still would not allow us to localize developments in the history of poetic omens with any real precision. Even the limited data given here can, I hope to suggest, illustrate something of the momentum characterizing the epochal shift from *yaochen* to *shichen*.

The most obvious trend discernible in these tables concerns the bourgeoning and decline of poetic omens in the standard histories and in the sources surveyed by *Gujin tushu jicheng*. Poetic omens are relatively rare in the early period up to the Eastern Han; proliferate in and around the Six Dynasties, Tang, and Song; and become less frequent from the Yuan dynasty onward. The phenomenon does not disappear in these later dynasties—as readers of Chinese fiction will know—but the dwindling numbers in these sources are striking given the relatively large volume of textual materials that we have, especially from the Ming. The analysis below may suggest one explanation for this drop-off: that the mundanity of poetic omens in Song dynasty materials began to vitiate the interest of at least the *shichen* variety as anything other than a useful narrative device. But I leave it to other scholars with greater expertise in the late imperial period to confirm or disconfirm this suspicion and to offer other reasons this diminution might have occurred. Here I focus on those eras when poetic omens appear to have been a relatively prominent topic in literati culture.

A second trendline in these data traces an expansion over time in the types of subjects who can create poetic omens. Every one of the *shiyao* recorded in *Han shu* is a children's ditty (*tong yao* 童謠), sung by the presumably illiterate children of pre-Qin and Han villages.[6] *History of the Latter Han* (*Hou Han shu* 後漢書), however, introduces the possibility that omens might be produced by adult members of the folk as well,[7] and *History of the Song* (*Song shu* 宋書), compiled on the basis of fifth-century documents, for the first time includes poetic omens produced by madmen, Buddhists, and Daoists.[8] In histories compiled in the sixth and seventh centuries, emperors and members of the imperial family also prove capable of producing poetic omens,[9] and in *New History of the Tang* (*Xin*

---

6. See Ban Gu, *Han shu*, 27.2.1393–96.

7. Fan Ye, *Hou Han shu*, 13.3284.

8. Shen Yue, *Song shu*, 31.914, 919–20.

9. See, for instance, Xiao Zixian, *Nan Qi shu*, 19.382, and Wei Zheng et al., *Sui shu*, 22.636.

Tang shu 新唐書), we finally have a "poem" (*shi* 詩) apparently written by a literatus cited as an omen of the state.[10] One might say that the capacity for creating poetic omens gradually approached the literati from the margins of what they might have considered their familiar community. Children, the original producers of all such portents, are perhaps more distant—more difficult to understand, more capable of saying something strange and uncanny—than adult members of the folk;[11] Buddhists and Daoists, despite the arcana of their religions, increasingly frequented literati circles over the course of the Six Dynasties; and by the end of this period, even if members of the imperial family were invested with an aura that kept them distinct from the literati at large, they often strove to present themselves as exemplary members of that class. Each step along this path thus would have made it more conceivable that the literati responsible for transmitting these poetic omens might have produced some themselves.

This same narrative is also evident in the materials collected in *Gujin tushu jicheng*. But because this compendium (unlike the histories) includes materials that are not directly concerned with the fortunes of the state, it tells another story as well. Not only do we see in these materials that the proportion of children's ditties decreases in each period from the Six Dynasties through the Song, while the proportion produced by literate adults increases—that in the Han, 95 percent of poetic omens derive from the folk, whereas in the Song nearly 50 percent are produced by literati. Equally important, we see that omens predicting the fate of the poem's author, his family, or his friends become more common with each passing era. In the Han, again, all surviving poetic omens concern the state; by the Song, such omens make up less than half the total number. As the capacity to produce poetic omens gradually drew closer to the literati, so did the futures those omens portended.

To some degree, this second narrative may reflect the changing character of elite literary production, which over the course of the Tang and Song became decreasingly centered on the court and increasingly focused on the lives of the literati. Yet if there is in fact a connection here, then

---

10. Ouyang Xiu and Song Qi et al., *Xin Tang shu*, 35.920.

11. The most "uncanny" of all poetic omens, of course, are those that are not produced by any known agent but are instead discovered on rocks or other materials. For simplicity, I am leaving such discovered omens out of the discussion here.

Poetic Omens and Poetic History

poetic omens by this time must have been sufficiently linked to elite literature to have been influenced by its transformations. As we will see in the next section, that had not always been the case.

Changing Frameworks of Interpretation

Phenomena that we might be tempted to identify as poetic omens, or at least their precursors, appear in a number of early texts. In the *Zuo Tradition* (*Zuo zhuan* 左傳), for example, the Wu noble Jizha 季札 proves capable of recognizing the fate of various historical polities through the performance of their music and their poems.[12] Similar ideas are also found in other early texts, including *Xunzi* 荀子, the "Record of Music" ("Yue ji" 樂記) in *Records of Ritual* (*Li ji* 禮記), and the "Great Preface to the Mao Recension of the *Classic of Poetry*" ("Mao Shi daxu" 毛詩大序), which goes so far as to suggest that adepts could perceive the "impending doom of a state" (*wang guo* 亡國) from observing its poetry and music.[13] To some degree, these adepts are characterized by what we might reasonably call mantic abilities, and for this reason, these texts' visions of poetry's portentous significance might easily strike us as continuous with the poetic omens collected in the official histories and in encyclopedic compendiums like *Gujin tushu jicheng*.

Early writers, however, seem generally to have drawn a distinction between this latter sort of "poetic prodigies" and canonical poetry of the *Classic of Poetry* (*Shi jing* 詩經) type. Although *Han shu*, for example, cites two "children's ditties" from *Zuo zhuan* in its section on *Shiyao* 詩妖, it does not discuss the concert for Jizha or the *Classic of Poetry* in the same context. The distinction may have had to do with the greater orthodoxy of the *Shi jing* versus such prodigies. According to Han exegesis, the majority of the poetry in that classic derived from and documented the good governance of the ancient sages. By contrast, Han authors of surviving discourses on poetic anomalies discuss them only as deriving from and manifesting bad governance, which they understand as causing abnormal perturbations in

---

12. *Chunqiu Zuo zhuan zhushu*, 39.667b–73a.
13. See *Xunzi jishi*, 20.469; *Li ji zhushu*, 19.663b; and *Mao Shi zhengyi*, 1.14a.

186   LUCAS RAMBO BENDER

the five phases (*wuxing* 五行) of cosmic *qi* 氣. Fu Sheng's 伏胜 (fl. ca. 200 BCE) *Great Commentary on the* Classic of Documents (*Shang shu dazhuan* 尚書大傳), for instance, lists poetic omens as one of five anomalies that occur as a result of "wood [*qi*] disturbing metal [*qi*]" 木沴金.[14] *Han shu*, likewise, offers a commentary on this passage as part of its "Wuxing zhi" 五行志 ("Treatise on the Five Phases"), explaining that "When a ruler is overwhelmingly *yang*, violent and oppressive, and his subjects fear punishment and thus block up their mouths, then *qi* of resentment and slander is expressed in children's ditties" 君炕陽而暴虐, 臣畏刑而柑口, 則怨謗之氣發於童謠.[15] Wang Chong 王充 (d. ca. 100 CE) similarly suggests that "Children's ditties are produced by the influence of the Sparkling Deluder [Mars]" 童謠熒惑使之, since "the Sparkling Deluder is a star of fire" 熒惑火星—that is, of "overwhelming *yang*." According to Wang, boys are associated with *yang qi*, and so is the mouth and hence speech. An overabundance of *yang* thus naturally produces anomalies related to boys and their words.[16]

Although this correlative quasi-physics never disappears from the tradition, the Six Dynasties and Tang witnessed the development of new explanations of poetic omens more in line with the philosophical and religious tendencies of the medieval period. One of these tendencies was the personalization of what, in the Han, had often been attributed to something more like mechanism. Whereas Wang Chong had credited children's ditties to the influence of Mars's "overwhelming *yang qi*," for instance, a number of Six Dynasties and Tang texts, from Gan Bao's 干寶 (d. 336) *In Search of the Supernatural* (*Soushen ji* 搜神記) to Pan Yan's 潘炎 (fl. 708) "Rhapsody on the Children's Ditty" ("Tongyao fu" 童謠賦), describe the Sparkling Deluder Star—now an immortal in the Daoist pantheon—taking the form of a child, "coming down to earth to create a children's ditty in order to communicate to the ruler" 降爲童謠 分告聖君.[17] Such poetic omens were now personalized, religious revelations

---

14. For this text, and the problems in reconstructing it, see Vankeerberghen and Lin, "*Shangshu dazhuan* de chengshu."

15. Ban Gu, *Han shu*, 27a.1377.

16. Wang Chong, *Lunheng jiaoshi*, 22.943–44 and 23.958.

17. Gan Bao, *Xinjiao Soushen ji*, 8.69; Pan Yan, "Tongyao fu," in Dong Gao et al., *Quan Tang wen*, 442.4508b.

Poetic Omens and Poetic History

delivered, in the words of Zhang Yue 張説 (663–730), by "messengers from Heaven" 天使.[18]

This development in the understanding of poetic omens can be seen as representing a step toward the literati, and it may have further paved the way for another: the appropriation of poetic prognostication by members of the religious orders that flourished in the Six Dynasties and Tang. In an early instance of this trend, *Song shu* records a children's ditty that had been started by the Eastern Jin Buddhist monk Zhu Tanlin 竺曇林, predicting (once its riddles were decoded) that Liu Yu 劉裕 (363–422) would defeat Huan Xuan 桓玄 (369–404) and overthrow the Jin dynasty.[19] *History of the Sui* (*Sui shu* 隋書), compiled a little more than a century later, similarly attributes to the Daoist patriarch Tao Hongjing 陶弘景 (456–536) a "pentasyllabic verse" (*wuyan shi* 五言詩) that predicted Hou Jing's 侯景 (503–552) rebellion against the Liang at least thirty years in advance.[20] Over the course of the Tang, anecdotes of this sort became so common that they account for the preponderance of Tang dynasty poetic omens preserved from recognizably Tang sources. Poetic omens of this kind even seem to have played a role in legitimizing the dynasty at important points in its history, as according to Wen Daya's 溫大雅 (d. 629) eyewitness account of the Tang founding, Li Yuan 李淵 (566–635) was not persuaded to ascend the throne until he heard that his accession had been predicted in "songs" 歌謠 composed by the "spirit person" 神人 Huihua Ni 慧化尼 (unknown elsewhere, but from her appellation here, a Buddhist nun) and in a "poetic prognostication" 詩讖 written by the Daoist Wei Yuansong 衛元嵩 (fl. 570).[21]

That such religious orders still remained at a certain mystifying remove from the literati who recorded their poetic omens may be suggested by the fact that all pre-Tang sources are silent on the question of exactly how they came up with their prognostications. Tang texts, however, do occasionally offer humanizing insight into the process. Sometimes these adepts are depicted as themselves taken by surprise by their own ability, as in a story

---

18. Zhang Yue, "Huangdi zai Luzhou xiangrui song" 皇帝在潞州祥瑞頌, in Dong Gao et al., *Quan Tang wen*, 221.2230a.

19. Shen Yue, *Song shu*, 31.919.

20. Wei Zheng et al., *Sui shu*, 22.637.

21. See Bingham, "The Rise of Li in a Ballad Prophecy"; and Bokenkamp, "Time after Time."

about the Daoist Li Xiazhou 李遐周, whose "techniques of the *dao*" (*daoshu* 道術) enabled him to write poems predicting the An Lushan rebellion but apparently did not allow him to understand that prediction until it came true.[22] Elsewhere, poetic prophecy seems to be an offshoot of the admirable insight such adepts possessed into darker layers of reality. When in the Tianbao period (742–756), for example, Gao Shi 高適 (d. 765) memorialized to the court a poetic omen that had supposedly foretold the empire's flourishing, he described the composition in the following terms:

The arising of auspicious portents truly derives from the governance of a [righteous] king; the emergence of poetry derives at base from the mores of the state (*guo feng*). Humbly I observe that the mother of a certain Mr. Lu of Fanyang, *née* Wang, of Langya, had a nature that matched with the mysterious and faint and a substance that matched with the still and silent; she was refined and subtle with the root of the *dao* and sped to the gate of the mysterious. She thoroughly connected with the mind of heaven and earth and so in advance recorded a flourishing of excellent portents. Back in the second year of the Jinglong reign (708), she wrote a palindrome poem on "The Heavenly Treasure," in 812 words. It has a set number to its cycling, just as cold and hot alternate in due course; and its responsive transformations are inexhaustible, so it can be said to be unfathomed by *yin* and *yang* [like the *dao* itself]. She thus advised her son, saying: "After I die, you should put this down in a secret record. You will meet with a period wherein the court follows the great *dao* and will encounter an exceptional ruler. When this happens, present the immortal chart [i.e., the palindrome poem, which would have visually resembled a diagram] I have made to him."

符瑞之興, 實由王政; 歌詩之作, 本自國風. 伏見范陽盧某母瑯琊王氏, 性合希夷, 體於靜默, 精微道本, 馳騖元關, 旁通天地之心, 豫紀休徵之盛. 去景龍二載, 撰天寶迴文詩, 凡八百一十二字. 循環有數, 若寒暑之遞遷; 應變無窮, 謂陰陽之莫測. 誡其子曰: 吾沒之後, 爾密記之. 當逢大道之朝, 必遇非常之主. 則眞圖之製, 便可上言.[23]

22. This is how the story is presented in Lu Gui's 盧瓌 (fl. early tenth century) now-lost *Shu qing shi* 抒情詩 (which gives the name as Li Jinzhou 李進周); see Li Fang et al., *Taiping guangji*, 163.1184–85. Zheng Chuhui's 鄭處誨 (*jinshi* 834) account has it that others did not understand his poems (Zheng Chuhui, *Minghuang zalu*, 2.33).

23. Gao Shi, "Wei Dongping Xue Taishou jin Wangshi ruishi biao" 爲東平薛太守進王氏瑞詩表, in Gao Shi, *Gao Shi ji jiaozhu*, 305–6.

Poetic Omens and Poetic History 189

Here Ms. Wang's capacity to produce portents apparently derives from her access to the mysterious *dao*, which underlies the world's changes and thus allows her to predict them.

Some of the language Gao uses here is clearly Daoist in inclination. But it also echoes the Xuanxue/"obscure learning"–inflected thought of contemporary Classical study and thus signals how sharp distinctions that had previously been drawn between the Classics and poetic prodigies had by this point begun to break down.[24] Gao's claim that Ms. Wang's poem matches the *dao* in being "unfathomed by *yin* and *yang*," for example, directly recalls the official Tang interpretation of the *Classic of Changes* (*Yi jing* 易經), wherein we read that the *dao* "is what *yin* and *yang* do not fathom" 陰陽不測—an idea that provides a stark contrast to the mechanisms of *qi* by which Han writers understood poetic omens to be produced.[25] Equally important, Gao attempts in the first sentence of his memorial to link Ms. Wang's omen to the *Guo feng* 國風 ("Airs [or Mores] of the States") section of the *Shi jing*. In making this connection, Gao might have been drawing on the authority of the Tang subcommentary on that classic, *The Corrected Interpretations of Mao's Recension of the Classic of Poetry* (*Mao Shi zhengyi* 毛詩正義), since its introduction depicts the *Shi jing* as full of poetic omens.

> The arising of sadness and happiness is mysteriously one with what is so-of-itself (*ziran*); the beginnings of joy and anger are not within human control. Therefore, swallows and sparrows express their feelings in their chirping, and simurghs and phoenixes dance and sing. Thus, the antecedents of poetry's logic are at one with the creation of the universe, and the use of poetry's traces changes according to its cycles.
>
> 若夫哀樂之起, 冥於自然; 喜怒之端, 非由人事. 故燕雀表啁噍之感, 鸞鳳有歌舞之容, 然則詩理之先, 同夫開闢; 詩迹所用, 隨運而移.[26]

In context, the primary problem the editors of this commentary are trying to solve in this quote is the fact that—unlike the rest of the Classics,

---

24. For Xuanxue-inflected Classicism in the Tang, see Bender, "*The Corrected Interpretations of the Five Classics.*"

25. *Zhou Yi zhushu*, 7.149a.

26. *Mao Shi zhengyi*, "*Mao Shi zhengyi* xu," 3a.

which were originally produced by sages—many of the poems in the *Shi jing* derive from the nonsagely folk, who lack the authority to ground a classic. The subcommentary's solution is to suggest that the folk are a conduit for omens: their production of poetry is as spontaneous (*ziran*) and thus as revelatory of the deeper workings of the world as was the portentous appearance of the phoenix in response to the virtue of King Wen of Zhou. By linking Ms. Wang's palindrome poem with this tradition, Gao Shi assures the court there is nothing heterodox about her prognostications and that, in fact, they merely affirm the continuities between the current emperor and the ancient sages.

Similar connections between poetic omens and the Classics can also be found elsewhere in surviving Tang dynasty materials.[27] If *Mao Shi zhengyi* derives from the beginning of the dynasty, for instance, a similar account of the *Classic of Poetry* can be found near the end, in the preface to Gu Tao's 顧陶 (fl. 856) *Selections of Tang Poetry Arranged by Category* (*Tangshi leixuan* 唐詩類選), which argues that in the time of the ancient sages, "By getting [poetry] from reapers and wood-gatherers and presenting it to the court, they recognized in advance the sprouting of order and disorder: thus the importance of poetry is vast and far-reaching" 得芻蕘而上達, 萌治亂而先覺. 詩之義也, 大矣遠矣.[28] Tang readers would not have missed the echo of the *Yi jing*'s "its importance is vast" 義大矣, a phrase that is cited more than a dozen times in surviving Tang discussions of literature—including several official productions of the court—to the effect that the ancient sages "observed the patterns of heaven [i.e., astral signs] to know the changing times, and observed human patterns [i.e., literature] to complete the empire's moral transformation" 觀乎天文以察時變, 觀乎人文以化成天下.[29] In each invocation of this phrase, a connection is drawn between literature and the portents that court astrologers observed

---

27. An example very close to Gao Shi's can also be found in Kāśyapa Zhizhong's 迦葉志忠 708 memorial presenting mantic folksongs to Empress Wei (d. 710) by saying that they manifest "the virtue of the Queen Consort" 后妃之德, a phrase from the Mao "Great Preface" to the *Shi jing*. See Liu Xu et al., *Jiu Tang shu*, 51.2173.

28. Li Fang et al., *Wenyuan yinghua* 文苑英華, 714.3686b.

29. The idea that *wen*'s "timely importance is vast" 時義大矣 is found in several places in the *Yi jing*; see *Zhou Yi zhushu*, 2.48b and 3.62b. For citations of this phrasing used with reference to contemporary literature, see Yang Jiong 楊炯 (ca. 650–ca. 693), *Yang Jiong ji*, 3.34; Xiao Yingshi 蕭穎士 (717–768), "Wei Chen Zhengqing jin *Xu shangshu* biao" 爲陳正卿

Poetic Omens and Poetic History 191

in the heavens, a connection that Tang intellectuals thus grounded, in stark contrast to their Han predecessors, in the *Classics*.

All these ideas appear in texts surviving from the early years of the Song as well, perhaps indicating the degree to which the nascent Song court, which quite explicitly set out to imitate the Tang, took this vision as characteristic of Tang ideology. The court-sponsored 1013 compendium, *Primal Tortoise of the Bureau of Bamboo-Strips* (*Cefu yuangui* 冊府元龜), for example, cites the above *Yi jing* passage prominently in the preface to its section on "Loving Literature" ("Hao wen" 好文) and invokes the idea that the poems of the *Shi jing* were poetic omens in the preface to its section on "Popular Ditties" ("Yaoyan" 謠言).[30] Beginning around the 1020s, however, interest in the connection between the Classics and state-oriented *yaochen* seems to have begun to diminish. What we find instead are an increasing number of discussions linking the canonical poetics of the *Classic of Poetry* to the burgeoning phenomenon of *shichen*: poetic omens by and about the literati.

This shift significantly changes the nature of the connection. In the case of *yaochen*, what had to be explained was the mechanism by which a particular sort of individual could predict events on such a large scale as the state. When it comes to *shichen*, by contrast, the author merely has to predict (generally inadvertently) what will happen to himself or his family. As a result, writers such as Wu Chuhou 吳處厚 (fl. 1087) turned to other aspects of *Shi jing* lore.

Poetry articulates intent, and through words we know things: this is true and not deception. Li Gou [1009–1059] of the Jiangnan region was learned in the Classics and skilled at writing, and when he took the official exams, he claimed first place in a face-to-face test with the emperor. However, he once wrote a poem that went:

People say that where the sun sets is the edge of heaven,
but as I gaze toward heaven's edge, I do not see my home.
I truly regret that green mountains block my view with their shining,
and that now, even the green mountains have been blocked by clouds.

進續尚書表, in Dong Gao et al., *Quan Tang wen*, 322.3267a; and Lü Wen 呂溫 (772–811), "Renwen huacheng lun" 人文化成論, in Dong Gao et al., *Quan Tang wen*, 628.6342b.

30. Wang Qingruo et al., *Cefu yuangui*, 40.457a and 894.10576a.

Someone of understanding said, "Observing the meaning of this piece, it has many layers of obstruction; thus I fear that Mr. Li will not be successful in his career." In the end, it was as he said.

Similarly, before Lord Chen Wenhui [Chen Yaozuo 陳堯佐, 963–1044] had met with success, he once wrote a poem that went:

> Over ten-thousand leagues of fine mountains, the clouds suddenly withdraw;
> on this lone tower, the moonlight is bright as the rain begins to clear.

Observing this poem's meaning, we can see that it is different from Li Gou's. Is it not appropriate that Wenhui should have become prime minister and lived to over eighty years of age?

詩以言志, 言以知物, 信不誣矣. 江南李覯, 通經術, 有文章, 應大科, 召試第一. 嘗作詩曰: 人言日落是天涯, 望極天涯不見家. 堪恨碧山相掩映, 碧山還被暮雲遮. 識者曰: 觀此詩意, 此有重重障礙, 李君恐時命不偶. 後竟如其言. 又陳文惠公未逢時, 嘗作詩曰: 千里好山雲乍斂, 一樓明月雨初晴. 觀此意, 與李君異矣. 然則文惠致位宰相, 壽餘八十, 不亦宜乎?[31]

In these stories, Wu appeals not to the legendary practice of collecting the poetry from among the folk but rather to the claim, made paradigmatically in the "Great Preface," that poetry "articulates intent" 言志, perfectly externalizing poets' internal dispositions.[32] Both the poems of the *Shi jing* and Song-dynasty *shichen*, he implies, are manifestations of the character of the poet—and character, as the saying goes, is destiny.

This explanation of the relationship between poetry and omens might seem more rational, less "mystifying," than the accounts of *yaochen* discussed above. In some cases, we do find the apparently reasonable idea that poetry is an expression of a writer's complement of *qi*, and that that *qi* will also determine whether they are healthy or frail, energetic or retiring.[33] Elsewhere, however, we find more mysterious processes at work in *shichen* as well. The 1169 collection *Matters Ancient and Modern, Divided by Category* (*Fenmen gujin leishi* 分門古今類事), for instance, attributes *shichen* to the workings of fate.[34] The preface explains that the collection

---

31. Wu Chuhou, *Qingxiang zaji*, 7.3a–b.
32. *Mao Shi zhengyi* 1.13a.
33. See Weixinzi, *Xinbian Fenmen gujin leishi*, 13.200.
34. See Weixinzi, *Xinbian Fenmen gujin leishi*, 14.215–16.

Poetic Omens and Poetic History

records without exception [all anecdotes that show that] flourishing and decay, failure and success, nobility and baseness, poverty and wealth, death and life, longevity and early death, along with every motion and stillness, every word and every silence, every drink we take and bite we eat—our fate [in all of these things] is determined beforehand, and is given shape in dreams, portended in divination, and seen in physiognomy, and manifests correspondences between omens and what is experienced.

凡前定興衰、窮達、貴賤、貧富、死生、壽夭, 與夫一動一靜、一語一默、一飲一啄, 分已定於前, 而形於夢, 兆於卜, 見於相, 見應於識驗者, 莫不錄之.[35]

Clearly, the idea that poetic omens (which make up one of the categories of materials collected in this text) might manifest more mysterious facets of reality—that they might be "determined," as the *Fenmen gujin leishu* puts it elsewhere in this preface, "in the darkness" 定於幽冥—had not disappeared. Instead, passages like this one suggest that these mysterious levels of reality had merely become more accessible and more germane to the daily life of the literati in Song accounts of *shichen* than they generally appeared to be in Six Dynasties and Tang accounts of *yaochen*. In contrast with these earlier texts, it is in the Song no longer merely religious adepts, madmen, children, or the uncanny folk who have access to these mysteries. Ordinary literati have it as well, in their dreams, in their poetry, and—as Wang Mao 王楙 (1151–1213) explains in his account of poetic omens—in their minds, the quintessentially mantic organ.[36]

Various other mechanisms that might account for *shichen* are also explored in Song texts, including the common idea that one might effectively curse oneself or others by writing inauspicious verse.[37] At this

35. "Shuben *Fenmen gujin leishi* xu" 蜀本分門古今類事序, in Weixinzi, comp., *Xinbian Fenmen gujin leishi*, 1.

36. Wang Mao, *Yeke congshu*, 19.183.

37. See the common attitude criticized in Huihong's 惠洪 (1071–1128) *Lengzhai yehua*, 4.37: "When you're rich you should not be talking about poverty; when young and hale you should not be talking about decline and old age; and when healthy and strong you should not be talking about sickness or death. When someone breaks these rules, people call that a *shichen*" 富貴中不得言貧賤事, 少壯中不得言衰老事, 康強中不得言疾病事死亡事, 脫或犯之, 人謂之詩讖. The same attitude is also criticized in Hong Mai's 洪邁 (1123–1202) *Rongzhai suibi*, 1.14.

point, however, further discussion of these ideas would largely reaffirm the narrative traced in this section and the last regarding the gradual migration of poetic omens to the provinces of the literati. Instead of belaboring that point, I turn now to consider how a recognition of this trend might contribute to understanding better the history of the supposedly nonmantic mainstream of poetry in middle-period China.

Poetic Omens and Poetic Thought

On this question, there are obvious limitations to what we can say with confidence. For most periods of Chinese history, there are relatively few surviving sources that explicitly link mainstream poetics with poetic omens, and the sources that do generally do so only glancingly. In some cases, however, a sensitivity to what sorts of omens were recognized at a given time can highlight previously overlooked facets of contemporary poetic discourse. This is true even when it comes to famous texts that have otherwise been well mined for their poetic thought.

I can find little evidence suggesting a strong connection between poetic omens and elite literary thought in the Han or the Six Dynasties. Instead, as I have already indicated, the few explicit discussions of poetic omens that survive tend to draw a clear distinction between the ditties of village children and the literary culture to which elites were supposed to aspire. Wang Chong, for instance, argues pointedly that the sort of intelligence that can be discerned in folk chants is fundamentally different from the knowledge of sages and worthies, which is achieved by learning. Children's ditties, he maintains, are an "aberration" or "prodigy" (*yao* 妖) of a sort more similar to a shaman (*wu* 巫) channeling the words of a spirit (*shen* 神).[38] And although the distinction between such mediumism and elite culture might be seen as breaking down in such famous early medieval works of literary theory as Lu Ji's 陸機 (261–303) "Poetic Exposition on Literature" ("Wen fu" 文賦) or Liu Xie's 劉勰 (ca. 460s–520s) *The Literary Mind and the Carving of Dragons* (*Wenxin diaolong* 文心雕龍)—both of which discuss literary creativity in

---

38. Wang Chong, *Lunheng jiaoshi*, 26.1082.

Poetic Omens and Poetic History

images drawn from shamanic spirit journeys—neither of these texts discuss poetic omens.[39]

In focusing attention on some of the more "mysterious" aspects of literary composition, however, texts such as *Wen fu* and *Wenxin diaolong* may have prepared the way for the eventual incorporation of poetic omens into Tang criticism. As is well known, the eighth and ninth centuries witnessed a proliferation of poetic discourse that suggests excellent lines come from "searching in the dark" (*mingsou* 冥搜), are inspired by the "aid of the spirits" (*shenzhu* 神助), draw on unaccountable "visions" (*jing* 境), and require that an author "pluck the remarkable from beyond images . . . and inscribe thought of the darkest mysteries" 采奇於象外 . . . 寫冥奧之思.[40] Tang sources also preserve numerous statements suggesting that the arcane practices of Buddhists and Daoists might aid in the production of verse that is nonetheless often indistinguishable from literati writings.[41] This effacement of clear boundaries between the mechanisms responsible for the production of elite poetry, on the one hand, and poetic prodigies, on the other, may have allowed the latter to become in this period a possible paradigm for understanding the former.

The earliest text I have found that directly invokes poetic omens in its discussion of mainstream verse is the early eighth-century Wuchen 五臣 ("Five Officials") commentary to the great medieval anthology *Selections of Refined Literature* (*Wen xuan* 文選). In a memorial introducing this commentary, Lü Yanzuo 呂延祚 (fl. ca. 718) depicts *Wen xuan* as a collection of omens produced by adepts possessed of mysterious insight into recondite realms of significance:

> Since the time of the [*Classic of*] *Poetry*, nothing is greater than [*Wen xuan*].
> It preserves words impassioned and intense, and when we assessed the

---

39. Liu Xie comes closest in the "Yuefu" 樂府 and "Shixu" 時序 chapters of *Wenxin diaolong*, where he brings up the *Shi jing* mythology that adept interpreters could recognize the fate of a kingdom from its music. See Liu Xie, *Zengding Wenxin*, 7.82 and 45.539.

40. The final quote derives from Jiaoran's 皎然 (ca. 720–ca. 798) *Shiyi* 詩議; see Zhang Bowei, *Quan Tang Wudai shige*, 108. These discourses have been discussed in Owen, *The End of the Chinese "Middle Ages,"* 107–29.

41. On this topic, see Owen, "How Did Buddhism Matter in Tang Poetry?"; Mazanec, "How Poetry Became Meditation in Ninth Century China"; and Bender, "Against the Monist Model."

matters they spoke of, [we could tell that their authors] lodged their minds in the hidden and subtle, darkening its omens, and that they adorned things to subtly criticize, borrowing other eras to tether their feelings [about their own]. If one does not have mysterious understanding, one cannot penetrate [the text's] meaning.

風雅其來, 不之能尚. 則有遺詞激切, 揆度其事, 宅心隱微, 晦滅其兆, 飾物反諷, 假時維情, 非夫幽識, 莫能洞究.[42]

Explicitly mantic language of the sort found in this preface does not appear commonly in the commentary itself, and as far as I know, scholars have never considered the possibility that Lü was serious in suggesting that the authors collected in *Wen xuan* produced "darkened omens." Instead, the Wuchen annotators' propensity to tie the poetry in *Wen xuan* to "the affairs of the writers' times" has usually been understood as following in the tradition of the Mao-Zheng commentaries on the *Shi jing*.[43] Here, however, our recognition of the common Tang dynasty connection between the *Shi jing* and poetic omens—seen once again in Lü Yanzuo's memorial—may offer a new angle on Tang interpretative practice.

Chinese poetic omens are never clear: whether *yaochen* or *shichen*, all depend on reading the poem as saying something radically different from what it seems to be saying. Sometimes the meaning of such omens is only disclosed retrospectively by the events they turn out to predict; at other times, it can be understood in advance by acute interpreters. An example of this sort of interpretation can be found in an anecdote recorded in *History of the Jin* (*Jin shu* 晉書):

When Wang Gong [d. 398] was defending Jingkou, he raised troops to punish Wang Guobao [d. 397]. A folk ditty went:

In past years you ate white rice;
this year you eat barley husks.
The lord of heaven is punishing you,
making it stick in your throat. . . .

42. Lü Yanzuo, "Jin jizhu *Wen xuan* biao" 進集注文選表, in Dong Gao et al., *Quan Tang wen*, 300.3042b.

43. For instance, see Zheng Tingyin, Wen xuan *wuchen zhushi*, which analyzes the Wuchen commentary in terms of techniques derived from *Shi jing*.

Poetic Omens and Poetic History

Someone of understanding said, "'In past years you ate white rice': this speaks of [Wang Gong] attaining his ambition. 'This year you eat barley husks': husks are coarse and foul, and the essence of the barley is gone; this indicates that he will be defeated. This is the lord of heaven punishing him. To have it 'stick in your throat' means that air won't get through. This is an omen of death. . . ." Wang Gong soon died.

王恭鎮京口，舉兵誅王國寶. 百姓謠云: "昔年食白飯, 今年食麥麰. 天公誅謫汝, 教汝捥喉嚨. . . ." 識者曰: "昔年食白飯, 言得志也. 今年食麥麰, 麰粗穢, 其精已去, 明將敗也. 天公將加譴謫而誅之也. 捥喉嚨, 氣不通, 死之祥也. . . ." 恭尋死.[44]

In terms of its interpretative leaps, the reading offered in this passage by "someone of understanding" is relatively tame: poetic omens often use more elaborate sorts of indirection, involving puns, the rebus-like composition of single characters out of sequential characters in a line, and five-phase correspondence.[45] Yet even in this anecdote, we can discern in the "someone of understanding" an ostentatious interpretative virtuosity that resembles that evinced by the Wuchen commentators in their readings of *Wen xuan*. Consider, for example, the opening lines of their commentary to Cao Zhi's 曹植 (192–232) "To Ding Yi" ("Zeng Ding Yi" 贈丁儀), in which details that apparently pertain to the poet's immediate experience are taken as omens of the state:[46]

> At the beginning of autumn, the cold air comes;
> the trees of the courtyard subtly wither and let fall.
>
> [Commentary:] This refers to the *dao* of petty people growing; it begins from subtlety.

---

44. Fang Xuanling et al., *Jin shu*, 28.848.

45. These techniques have been cataloged in several places, including Bolianzi, *Gudai yuyan quanshu*, 190–256, which provides useful examples of each. For a less systematic but usefully illustrated account of such techniques, see Z. Lu, *Power of the Words*, 116–41.

46. In particular, they take the poem as a whole as criticizing "Emperor Wen's having enough furs and cloaks for himself and not thinking of people below him" 文帝衣裘自足而不念下人之無衣也. If the use of the title "Emperor Wen" is supposed to denote that Cao Pi 曹丕 (187–226) was emperor at the time this poem was written, the interpretation is impossible, since one of Cao Pi's first acts as emperor was the execution of Ding Yi (d. 220) and his family. For the interpretation to be even remotely plausible, the poem would have had to have been written after 217, when Cao Pi was created crown prince, but before his accession in 220.

Congealing frost lies on the jade stairs;
a cool breeze buffets the soaring pavilions.

> [Commentary:] [Cao and Ding] are treading on congealing frost that will ultimately turn to hard ice: this refers to secret plots achieving success. "A cool breeze buffets the soaring pavilions" hints that orders are coming from below to those above.

"初秋涼氣發, 庭樹微銷落": 喻小人道長, 從微起也. "凝霜依玉除, 清風飄飛閣": 履凝霜至於堅冰, 謂陰謀漸長也. "清風飄飛閣" 喻教令自下而上也.[47]

Although this interpretation has obvious roots in the Mao commentary concepts of stimulus-image (*xing* 興) and comparison (*bi* 比) as well as in the development of those concepts in Wang Yi's 王逸 (ca. 89–158) commentary to the *Verses of Chu* (*Chu ci* 楚辭), it is more flamboyantly interpretative than either. Comparison with Li Shan's 李善 (d. 689) commentary on the same poem suggests that the connections between these images and their ostensible political import were not so conventional as to be assumed by Tang readers; instead, the Wuchen commentators, who are critical of Li's interpretative reticence, are clearly offering a hermeneutical coup in divining the coming of governmental disorder in what might seem to be mere observations of autumn weather.[48] By emphasizing that their commentary derives from "mysterious understanding" (*you shi* 幽識), in other words, the Wuchen commentators position themselves in roughly the role of the "someone of understanding" (*shizhe* 識者) who appears so regularly in anecdotes concerning poetic omens. In this respect, their work is more distinct from earlier hermeneutics than has often been claimed. Their rebus-like reconstructions of the historical contexts behind poems should be seen as a phenomenon proper to the Tang, when poetic omens with political implications had begun being ascribed to literati.

Further development along these lines can be discerned in the "Poetry Standards" (*shige* 詩格, brief treatises containing poetic pedagogy and exemplary criticism) of the late eighth through tenth centuries, at least a few of which implicitly or explicitly compare poetry to omens. The clear-

---

47. Xiao Tong, *Xinjiaoding Liujia zhu Wen xuan*, 3:24.1493.

48. For their criticism of Li Shan, see Lü Yanzuo, "Jin jizhu *Wen xuan* biao," in Dong Gao et al., *Quan Tang wen*, 300.3042b.

Poetic Omens and Poetic History

est example can be found in *The Secret Meanings of the* Classic of Poetry (*Ernan mizhi* 二南密旨), a ninth-century *shige* attributed to Jia Dao 賈島 (779–843).[49] This text—whose title, incidentally, offers further evidence of the Tang connection between the *Shi jing* and poetic omens—provides its readers a long list of poetic images and topics that can serve as "omens" (*zhao* 兆) of state situations. "Late autumn," for example, "is an omen that the ruler is getting more benighted" 殘秋君加昏亂之兆也, whereas "late winter is an omen that cruelty is coming to an end and enlightenment beginning" 殘冬酷虐欲消向明之兆也.[50] This language of omens also features in its readings of individual poems.

> A poem by Li Duan [d. ca. 784] goes: "From circling in the clouds, a pair of cranes descends; / across the water, a single cicada cries." This is an omen that the careers of worthy people will advance.
>
> 李端詩: "盤雲雙鶴下, 隔水一蟬鳴." 此賢人趨進兆也.[51]

As in the Wuchen commentary, this comment should probably be understood as an ostentatious interpretative leap, revealing the "secret meanings" of poetry that will not be accessible to any but the most adept "people of understanding." Other *shige* make this feature of their interpretative practice even clearer. As *Shiping* 詩評 (*Poems Evaluated*) puts it, "If you had all those throughout the world who do not understand poetry look at a poem until the end of time, they would only see its words, not its meaning: this is poetry's wondrousness" 使天下人不知詩者, 視至灰劫, 但見其言, 不見其意, 斯爲妙也.[52] Going a step further, *Essential Standards of the Airs and Sao* (*Fengsao yaoshi* 風騷要式), a tenth-century *shige* that shows the influence of the *Ernan mizhi*, suggests that many of the meanings its interpretations uncover were probably not intended by the poets. Instead, poets "often criticize the state spontaneously, without

---

49. The attribution has been questioned, but since the poetry discussed in the text is largely from the poets of the Dali 大曆 reign (766–779), it is thought to have been put together during or shortly after Jia's time. See Zhang Bowei, *Quan Tang Wudai shige*, 371.

50. Zhang Bowei, *Quan Tang Wudai shige*, 378.

51. Zhang Bowei, *Quan Tang Wudai shige*, 381.

52. Zhang Bowei, *Quan Tang Wudai shige*, 501.

realizing it" 往往自諷自刺而不能覺.[53] This statement cannot help but remind us of those Tang *yaochen* that were obscure even to their authors.

Over the course of the eleventh and twelfth centuries, the *shige* genre declined and was replaced by more discursive forms of poetry criticism, such as "poetry chats" (*shihua* 詩話) and *biji*. These genres represent the main venues for the preservation of *shichen* anecdotes, a fact that rather changes the nature of the relationship between poetic omens and poetic thought. If we previously had to be sensitive to instances wherein criticism of elite poetry drew more or less subtly on contemporary ideas about poetic omens, by the Song, poetic omens have become normalized as explicit instances of such criticism. Instead of asking, therefore, whether and how an awareness of poetic omens might help us better understand the poetics that prevailed in this period, we might better ask what aspects of those paradigms are crystalized in *shichen* anecdotes.[54] In the space that remains, I want to point out two such aspects.

The first has to do with the increasing domestication of the futures foretold by poetic omens. Previously, poetic omens had dealt almost exclusively with affairs of state, the dignity and importance of which might have made them seem a realm more propitious to the eruption of the darker strata of reality than were the vicissitudes of literati experience. In their form, however, *shichen* anecdotes suggest that the personal histories of the literati are no less tied to these darker strata than are the grander vistas of state history. In this context, it is worth noting that the Song rise of *shichen* was roughly contemporaneous with the invention of new critical genres like the year-chart (*nianpu* 年譜) and the chronologically organized (*biannian* 編年) collection, which also work to ground poetry in narratives of poets' individual experiences rather than those state-level processes to which it was primarily tied by Tang works like the Wuchen

---

53. Zhang Bowei, *Quan Tang Wudai shige*, 451.

54. This question has been discussed by several scholars. See Zou Zhiyong, *Songdai biji shixue*, 44–73; and Wang Dianyin, "Shichen, you yiwei." These discussions are too complicated to fully summarize here, but both are particularly useful in linking the phenomenon of *shichen* to what they consider a general predilection of premodern Chinese readers to take the biographical and historical lives of poets as inextricably central to their poems. As should be clear, I think this predilection was more historically variable than it is often assumed to have been.

Poetic Omens and Poetic History 201

commentary and the "Poetry Standards."[55] Rather than suggesting, therefore, that poetry was "not historical" and that its "true significance may lie on another order of experience from that of daily life"—as Pauline Yu worried—we might speculate that the increasing incorporation of poetic omens into elite literary discourse in the Song was part of the process by which poetry became understood as properly focused on the literati's daily lives and by which their daily lives attained to the level of history.

This elevation of literati lives was, however, only an equivocal gain, as can be seen in the second way *shichen* crystallize larger tendencies of Song dynasty poetic culture. Late Tang and Song *shichen* anecdotes suggest that as poetic omens became less alien to the literati, their own poetry sometimes took on the uncanniness that had previously been characteristic only of the poetry of the folk and religious adepts. We find, for instance, numerous stories in these periods of writers who were horrified by the mantic significance of the poems they produced. In the ninth-century *New Accounts of the Great Tang* (*Da Tang xinyu* 大唐新語), we read of Liu Xiyi 劉希夷 (651?–680?) revising a line he recognizes as inauspicious, only to produce an even more obvious omen of his impending death.[56] A later anecdote from the *Fenmen gujin leishi* similarly describes the last ruler of the Southern Tang, Li Yu 李煜 (ca. 937–978), devastated to find that during a night of blackout drinking he had written a poem portending his and his polity's demise.[57] It was also possible in some cases for literati to write poems that inadvertently cursed their audience. Pang Yuanying's 龐元英 (fl. 1082) *Collection of Chats* (*Tansou* 談藪), for example, records a story of a man doomed by the unintended resonances of his friend's poem about a puppet, and Zhou Zizhi's 周紫芝 (1082–1155) *Poetry Chats from Bamboo Slope* (*Zhupo shihua* 竹坡詩話) tells of a poet whose ill-considered verse, ostensibly in the voice of the sort of imaginary abandoned woman commonly found in pre-Tang and Tang ballads, condemned his host's wife to death a few days later.[58] *Zhupo shihua* also records another case in

---

55. For a useful discussion of these topics, see Asami Yōji, *Chūgoku no shigaku ninshiki*, 385–459. For *shichen* as a species of historical contextualization, see Asami, *Chūgoku no shigaku ninshiki*, 460–82.

56. See Liu Su, *Da Tang xinyu*, 8.128.

57. Weixinzi, *Xinbian Fenmen gujin leishi*, 13.198.

58. See Pang Yuanying, *Tansou*, 200; and Zhou Zizhi, *Zhupo shihua*, 16a–b.

which it was not so much the content of the poem that was inauspicious as its quality. In this anecdote, the poet Guo Xiangzheng 郭祥正 (1035–1113) recognized he was soon to die because a couplet better than any he had ever written before came to him in a dream.[59] In all such instances, poetry became a space wherein literati increasingly had to worry about saying the wrong thing (or sometimes even the right thing). If Song poetry, therefore, tends toward the cheerful and bland in comparison with the more marked extremes of Tang verse, *shichen* anecdotes suggest that this may sometimes have been a cheeriness under compulsion.[60]

Conclusion

To summarize, the history of poetic omens tracks two shifts in literary thought: first, the development, in the late Six Dynasties and Tang, of what we might call an esoteric account of poetic production, and second, the dissolution of this esotericism in the Song and late imperial periods. In the Han, only the folk could access those obscure mechanisms of the cosmos that foretold the future, and then only inadvertently; literati were supposed to speak to politics through a more secular form of learning. In the Six Dynasties, however, peripheral members of the literati class began to draw on these mysteries to produce versified prophecy, and in the Tang, not only did it become a commonplace notion that the general poetic mores of the literati offered omens of dynastic fortune, but individual literati poems began to be interpreted as drawing arcane political lessons from mysterious insight. Finally, the Song witnessed the devaluation of this sort of insight as the sources of omens became so broadly accessible to literati poets that self-cursing became an occupational hazard and as the content of the portents they produced ceased to apply primarily to

---

59. Zhou Zizhi, *Zhupo shihua*, 16b.

60. This point is well illustrated by Song attitudes toward the Tang poet Meng Jiao 孟郊 (751–814). After he was mocked by Su Shi 蘇軾 (1037–1101), criticism of what was perceived as Meng Jiao's overwrought poetry became a veritable Song pastime. For a discussion of Meng Jiao's dramatic overreactions to failing (and later passing) the official examination as *shichen* foretelling his failure as an official, see Jiang Shaoyu 江少虞 (*jinshi* 1118), *Songchao shishi leiyuan*, 46.613.

Poetic Omens and Poetic History   203

state-level history. By this point, poetic omens no longer represented the sort of aspirational paradigm they had in the Tang but became instead a mark of the literati's increasingly inescapable historical consciousness.

One of the suggestions of this chapter is that these shifts in literary thought can be understood in more than one way. In previous work, I have seen them as epistemic ruptures (to use the Foucauldian terminology invoked by Fuller in the preceding chapter), fundamental reorientations of the models a culture uses to conceptualize itself and its world.[61] Though this chapter partly supports those arguments, it has also endeavored to provide an alternate account of this history, by which the development of poetic omens can be seen as largely continuous, with the steadily increasing propinquity of literati poetry and poetic omens over the course of a millennium contributing to the production of new and apparently opposed poetic paradigms. Several conclusions might be drawn from the fact that both perspectives offer a degree of insight. We might, for instance, question whether continuity and rupture, as models of literary history, are quite as mutually exclusive as some have recently suggested.[62] More to the point here, however, is the possibility that apparently vertiginous epistemic changes in some particular domain, such as medieval Chinese "literature," may in some cases result partly from the concatenation of more comprehensible cultural trajectories that are exiled beyond the margins of the subject by their treatment in special histories.

If the story traced here illustrates a theoretical point about literary history, in other words, it is that the core matter of the field will often fail to manifest a self-contained developmental logic, especially when it comes to cultures historically distant from the present scholarly culture that defines what "literary history" includes and excludes. In such historically distant cultures, phenomena that seem to lie on or beyond the borderlands of what we consider the "literary" may sometimes become

---

61. See Bender, *Du Fu Transforms*, and "Against the Monist Model."

62. For recent scholarship that draws a sharp division between literary histories that emphasize rupture and those that emphasize continuity, see Underwood, *Why Literary Periods Mattered*. Underwood's survey of the historical development of periodization in English literary studies does, however, provide useful insights into why different eras and academic cultures might incline to one model or the other, insights that might be applicable, mutatis mutandis, to Chinese literary studies as well.

part of its emic understanding, indexing and explaining epistemic shifts whose profundity would be alternately masked or inexplicable were we to look only at literature per se. For this reason, "the [special] historian's conception of his subject matter" cannot continue indefinitely dictating the inclusion and exclusion of materials in the literary history of such a historically distant cultural world. Instead, we must allow ourselves to be surprised by the diversity over time of the cultural formations that fit, nowadays, under the heading of "literature."

CHAPTER 8

Tuning Literary Histories to World Time

Wiebke Denecke

After a "genuine crisis in literary historiography" that David Perkins diagnosed in his memorably titled book *Is Literary History Possible?*[1] literary historiography is having a remarkable resurgence in the early twenty-first century. A major concern for Perkins was epistemological: how can we know and represent the historical development of literatures? What can we do about the inevitable teleologies that warp this genre, be they the fate of a nation, the succession of zeitgeists, the grand line-up of genius writers, or ideologies of modernity and avantgarde progressivism? Perkins acknowledged the social and cultural importance of literary historiography but believed that "we cannot write literary history with intellectual conviction, but we must read it. The irony and paradox of this argument are themselves typical of our present moment in history."[2]

Although national literary historiography is obviously a modern genre, any textual culture of some historical depth will develop genealogies or even genres of structuring its past, often for current ideological or aesthetic purposes. In East Asia we can trace this phenomenon back to the ancient period, to texts like the "Great Preface to the Mao Recension of the *Classic of Poetry*" ("Mao Shi daxu" 毛詩大序). It tells of the moral decline of the Way of the former kings, the "changed" poems that were written as a result, and the rise of a new form of poetry that criticized the

---

1. Perkins, *Is Literary History Possible?* 60.
2. Perkins, *Is Literary History Possible?* 17.

powerful and their lack of virtue. In the early medieval period, with the Six Dynasties, literary genealogies became a more systematic pursuit and a form of cultural self-reflection in the wake of the dramatic changes that came with the fall of the Han empire. The preface to Xiao Tong's 蕭統 (501–531) *Wen xuan* 文選 (*Selections of Refined Literature*) became a highly influential genealogical model in East Asia, and Japan's earliest anthologies in Literary Chinese, *Kaifūsō* 懷風藻 (*Florilegium of Cherished Airs*, 751) and the three imperial anthologies compiled under Emperors Saga and Junna in the early ninth century make clever use of Chinese models to write their own—emerging—"literary history" and that of their reference culture, China.[3]

The focus in this essay is on literary historiography that emerged with the nation-state in nineteenth-century Europe and spread around the world as a model for national literature pedagogy. This modern, Western-style global genre has at its core the idea that a nation is a monolingual, monoethnic community defined by a "people" unified by a "national language" and "national spirit," expressed in a "national literature." Today, in the wake of the fierce critiques of nation-state ideology and its not just faulty but dangerous conflation of ethnicity, language, and literature, one of the greatest challenges for literary historians is how to write from our world of modern nation-states about literary traditions before the nation. How do we face the fact that, however astutely we pitch our academic critiques of the nation-state ideology, literary historiography has a deep connection to the pedagogy of mass education in the "national literature" of any country, and the fact that nation-states and their ideologies and educational institutions are stronger than ever today? They are here to stay for now, as we try to think beyond them.

As we face the tension between political realities and academic values and ambitions, how can we take literary historiography along and beyond the nation-state, the genre's most tenacious teleology? How can we tune literary historiography to world time to reflect our ever more global experience of the world and do more justice to premodern literary traditions? This essay takes a phenomenological and critical approach. Rather than striving for a theoretical solution to the epistemological problem of

---

3. Denecke, "Writing History in the Face of the Other"; and Denecke, *Classical World Literatures*, chaps. 2 and 3, 62–119.

literary historiography, which, I agree with Perkins, is impossible, I look at the pragmatic uses of the genre and critically evaluate the motivations and agendas that have driven the work of literary historians. I explore this through two cases studies. First, I strategically survey recent English-language histories of major European-language literatures and non-Western or "minor" literatures that gain global recognition through the medium of Anglophone literary histories. What deeper motivations can we uncover from the diversity of new approaches to literary historiography? What are their implications and consequences, and how can we make the best use of challenges and opportunities inherent in this moment of new enthusiasm for literary historiography? I pursue these questions through the typology of new logics, new ethics, and new epistemology apparent in literary histories today.

Second, I showcase how modern Western-style literary historiography emerged outside the West in regions with millennia-old literary traditions to be adapted into this new genre. The earliest Western-style literary histories in East Asia were written in the 1880s in Japan, but on China, which at the time had been Japan's reference culture for about one and a half millennia. With Japan rapidly Westernizing and becoming the premier colonialist power in the region, Japanese reform politicians and scholars pioneered this genre in East Asia before the Chinese and long before the Koreans. Literary historiography was both a product and tool of this process, enabling Japan to put itself on par with Western civilizations and above the venerable civilization of China. Research on the emergence of modern literary historiography in China, Japan, and Korea has overwhelmingly focused on telling a single-nation story for Sinologists, Japanologists, and Koreanists. But this is a complex East Asian story, unfolding during a transformational moment of regional power balance that needs to be researched in regional context and comparison. I introduce distinctions between "idiographic," "heterographic," and "xenographic" literary histories, written, respectively, on the author's own, a neighboring and culturally deeply connected, or a completely foreign literary tradition. This allows us to understand to which local purposes this Western-style genre could be put in colonial and semi-colonial contexts. It provides us with a critical starting point from which to detect and overcome the lingering legacy of these earliest literary histories in today's literary historiography of East Asian literatures.

Both of these phenomenological case studies serve the larger point of this essay: that it is time to systematically historicize the practice of literary historiography. Where and when have people (and what kind of people?) written literary histories, with what agenda and to what effect? How can we, based on this understanding, write *critical* literary histories that are mindful of the shifting scope, functions, and terminologies of "literature" through the ages and the literary historian's vantage point from her particular historical moment—in short, histories that avoid as much as possible grossly anachronistic ideological frameworks, such as the national literature paradigm, that severely distort our understanding of the past and say more about our present than the narrated past? I argue that such critical literary histories, which are already beginning to be written, will help us tune literary historiography to a more equal and diverse "world time," taking into account all of the world's textual traditions from the past five millennia of recorded human history and their distinctive practices of literary historiography.

Anglophone Literary Historiography Now: A Typology of New Uses

One of the most exciting things about the revival of literary historiography in the early twenty-first century is the diversity of its new forms and concerns. Perkins's epistemological worry over the inevitability of distorting teleologies has found no philosophical solution, but literary historians no longer seem to consider them to be paralyzing obstacles. Quite the contrary, many explicitly embrace them to put literary historiography to new uses: for a new logics, a new ethics, and a new epistemology of the genre.

NEW LOGICS OF LITERARY HISTORIOGRAPHY: THE NATION BEYOND MONO- AND MULTILINGUAL

By now we are fully aware of the flaws of nineteenth-century colonial-era national literary historiography. National literary historiography is strongest at telling the story of modern literatures, the period of its own genesis. When projected back beyond the nineteenth century, lingering modernist biases unduly prioritize the vernacular and "nationalizable" over the historically far more important cosmopolitan, macro-regional dynamics of premodern literary cultures.

Downplaying the importance of transregional cosmopolitan languages—for example, Latin for medieval and early modern Europe, or Literary Chinese/Sinitic for premodern East Asia—reduces and limits the historical veracity of national literary histories and makes them intrinsically anachronistic. The modern vernacular language movements of the nineteenth and twentieth centuries that reformers in many countries around the world spearheaded in the process of modern state building and national liberation were based on an ideology of vernacular triumphalism, the idea that a nation is a monolingual, monoethnic community. Vernacular triumphalism is the most typical master narrative in textbooks of "national language education," which in our current world of strong nation-states is a formidable force that will keep the national literature paradigm in power, never mind academic critiques. David Damrosch has emphasized that the nation retains real value—as a national market and a national culture framed in international contexts—and that we should not consider it the flawed opposite of our cosmopolitan concepts of the "world,"[4] noting that this is particularly true for small, newly founded countries like Slovenia. We may say that the same holds for national literary historiography. In its worst incarnation in schoolbooks in totalitarian regimes, it can serve as a propagandistic tool to propagate nationalistic ideology, but in its best incarnation, it can present a national literary tradition as a diverse and often multilingual historical accretion process, in broader regional or world contexts.

Thus, "nation" and "world" are by no means opposites, and recent literary histories relate them in productive ways to claim a place for "minor" or marginalized literatures; rewrite the national literary histories of major European languages into global, postcolonial histories; or write beyond the monoethnic nation by showcasing the multilingual dynamics of particular literary cultures. These new uses of literary historiography work directly or indirectly through the logic of the nation-state.

4. Cheah and Damrosch, "What Is a World (Literature)?," 318.

The most obvious candidates for new national literary histories are those of "minor" literatures of newly established nation-states in the post-1989 world. Consider the Republic of Macedonia, a successor state of Yugoslavia. In the preface to the English translation of works by the scholar Dimitri Mitrev (1919–1976), *The Code of Macedonian Literary History*, Katica Kulavkova remarks: "This selection of Mitrev's works was made in order to serve as a prolegomena and apologia of Macedonian ethnic and cultural identity, read primarily through the texture of nineteenth and twentieth century Macedonian literature."[5] The Baltic state of Latvia is a comparable case: Pauls Daija's *Literary History and Popular Enlightenment in Latvian Culture* traces the emergence of Latvian literary culture in the eighteenth century under tsarist Russia. He shows how Baltic German elites launched an enlightenment movement geared toward educating the peasant population. Pastors such as Gotthard Friedrich Stender wrote didactic secular "edification" literature (Erbauungsliteratur).[6] Thus, here, the "national enlightenment" narrative is intertwined with German-language writing, complicating this new Latvian literary history.

There are also new national literary histories of major colonial European literatures. While newly "instated" national literatures have asserted their identity by starting to write literary histories, often in English so they may be noticed on a global stage, literary histories of major languages and nations have been rewritten to acknowledge and expand into their colonial past. *French Global: A New Approach to Literary History*, edited by Christie McDonald and Susan Suleiman, did just that: rewriting French literary history from the Middle Ages to the present as a history of the literary interactions in Francophone communities across the world, most of them created in the process of colonization and migration. Here we have a history based on a national language that implicitly celebrates its unifying power alongside the ethnic and cultural diversity of its colonial and postcolonial locales.

Choosing contemporary transnational political formations to write a "multicultural" regional literary history is more problematic. Maarten De Pourcq and Sophie Levie's edited volume *European Literary History: An Introduction* is welcome at a time when the European Union and European

---

5. Katica Kulavkova, preface, in Mitrev, *Code of Macedonian Literary History*, 10–11.
6. Daija, *Literary History and Popular Enlightenment*, 59, 73.

identity are under attack by independence movements. But it is clearly a volume shaped in the image of the current moment. The introduction calls literature one of the "international affairs" that binds Europeans.[7] It positions itself explicitly as a textbook for introductory courses in cultural studies, media/literary studies, and "European studies," all recently instituted fields that have emerged over the past few decades in Europe. The cover's collage of European cityscapes—the Colosseum, the Eiffel Tower, a Dutch windmill—confirms the reader's impression that we have a metonymic "EU anthology." It features essays matching themes (such as "desiring," "exploring new worlds," "defining the nation") with literary masterpieces from EU member states, arranged along a timeline from the Middle Ages into the modern period. So here we have a literary history that looks multicultural and multilingual but relies on a conventional notion of national literatures and a few of their greatest literary works. The volume models literary history on a contemporary political and economic order that is deeply anachronistic to the literatures it features.

Some of the most interesting literary histories today are works that focus on the multilingual dynamics of certain politically or culturally bounded regions. In "How to Do Multilingual Literary History? Lessons from Fifteenth and Sixteenth-Century North India," Francesca Orsini speaks out against the distorting effect of single-language histories and urges us to take the multilingual reality of literary cultures seriously. She criticizes Sheldon Pollock's model of the gradual vernacularization during the second millennium CE of the "Sanskrit cosmopolis" that had thrived throughout South Asia in the first millennium. According to Pollock, during that time "vernacular cosmopolitan" languages emerge that take the transregional role of the old venerable language of Sanskrit. Orsini finds that for North India's highly multilingual and multilocational literary cultures, "diglossia," a hierarchical symbiosis between a "higher" cosmopolitan and "lower" local idioms, is not fitting, since a hierarchical relationship only really existed vis-à-vis the elevated Sanskrit, but not quite so between for example Persian and Hindavi. Orsini therefore prefers non-hierarchical terms like "bilingualism," "multilingualism," or "heteroglossia."[8] Overall she underscores the importance of uncovering "emic" categories that were used by historical

7. De Pourcq, "General Introduction," 2.
8. Orsini, "How to Do Multilingual Literary History?" 231.

actors during the period under discussion, asking how fifteenth- and sixteenth-century writers from various areas in North India talked about and conceptualized their language repertoire. She calls for new tools to analyze the peculiarities of multilingual literary cultures, including a greater attention to the material practices of writing, as well as oral performance and circulation.[9] Orsini's intervention is particularly important for understanding that we need to develop models of multiliterate cultures based on non-Western regions with radically different political, social, and literary institutions that do not fit a "diglossia" model, which was developed (and largely sufficient) for describing the case of Western European Christian Latinity and its modern aftermath.

There are also literary histories now that focus on the cognitive aspects of multilingual practices in writing and reading. With *Multiliterate Ireland: Literary Manifestations of a Multilingual History*, Tina Bennett-Kastor writes a postcolonial multilingual literary history of sorts, giving attention to Celtic and Gaelic languages, Latin, and Anglo-Norman French. Along the way, she reflects on cognitive linguistic phenomena of cultural encounters such as "code switching," the quick alternation between languages in speech; "congruent lexicalization," where speakers stich phrases in two different but related languages together; or "macaronic texts" that rely on mixing codes and linguistic registers, often resulting in "kitchen vulgarity." More typically researched by cognitive scientists and linguists who focus on the example of contemporary languages, these fundamental patterns of linguistic processes and the creative possibilities they bring have affected most writers in world history and have so far received far too little attention in literary historiography. Bennett-Kastor's volume will hopefully serve as a model for cognitively oriented multilingual and multiliterate histories to come.

Multilingual and multiliterate historiography has also recently discovered "translation literatures," literatures that started with or even mainly consist of translations from other languages. Regarding antiquity and the medieval world, Denis Feeney has argued for early Latin literature as a "translation literature" and explores the implications of this exceptional case in the ancient Mediterranean in *Beyond Greek: The*

---

9. Orsini, "How to Do Multilingual Literary History?" 242.

Beginnings of Latin Literature. Daringly, Stuart Gillespie's *English Translation and Classical Reception: Towards a New Literary History* shows how the issue of translation can be brought to bear on English literary studies and "make the Classics belong," as he puts it. He also shows how, between the sixteenth and eighteenth centuries, the neoclassical modeling of English on Latin texts created a "translation literature-period" in English literary history where translation was not just one particular part of literary culture but in some ways the very creative force driving the development of English literature.[10] In *Translation's Forgotten History: Russian Literature, Japanese Mediation, and the Formation of Modern Korean Literature,* Heekyoung Cho shows a comparable process in the radically different context of colonial Korea. The large-scale adoption and translation of Western knowledge and literature in Japan at the turn of the twentieth century led to a situation where Russian literature, for example, drove literary innovation and shaped the emergence of modern Korean literature through intermediary Japanese translations circulating in colonial Korea under Japanese imperialist rule. Literary histories of "translation literatures" (or periods) are in this way most radical in their focus on multilinguality. The common idea of translation as a form of ultimately inferior mimesis, as distinct from the "real" literary tradition, disappears into a constellation where processes of translation become the literary tradition.

Looking over the great diversity of approaches to relating languages, people, and today's nation-states, we can only conclude that the nation can be a legitimate and productive driving factor in certain types of literary historiography.

THE NEW ETHICS OF LITERARY HISTORIOGRAPHY:
FROM *ANCILLA NATIONIS* TO *ANCILLA RECONCILIATIONIS*

One of the most strident voices against national literary historiography in the late nineteenth century was Hugó Meltzl (1846–1908), a scholar born to a German-speaking family in the multiethnic world of Transylvania

---

10. Gillespie, *English Translation*, chap. 1, esp. 13, 19.

under the Habsburg monarchy. In 1877, in the inaugural issue of the first journal of the emerging discipline of comparative literature, he saw literary history as "deplorable" and "useless" and castigates it as an *ancilla nationis* or *ancilla philologiae*, a handmaiden of the nation-state and positivistic philology.[11] Reflecting the diverse world of its origins, the journal had the cosmopolitan Latin name of *Acta Comparationis Litterarum Universarum*, along with Hungarian, German, and French titulations. For Meltzl and his colleagues, who functioned in a multiethnic and multilingual environment, it was natural that national literary historiography felt particularly untrue and uncomfortable. Recently scholars have retooled literary historiography for this region, plagued by an unresolved aftermath of a history of violence and wars, into an ethical instrument: an *ancilla reconciliationis*, a handmaiden to reconciliation and renegotiation of collective memory. Marcel Cornis-Pope and John Neubauer, the editors of the multivolume *History of the Literary Cultures of East-Central Europe*, proclaim an "ethical imperative" at the heart of their task: "The primary inspiration for our project is thus an ethical imperative rather than an epistemological longing. For us, pace Perkins, the crucial question is not whether literary histories based on consensus are *possible*, but whether a history can be instrumental in moving a transnational public toward morally and politically desirable consensus."[12] Eastern Europe was once covered under the umbrella of grand multiethnic empires such as the Ottoman and the Austro-Hungarian empires. They fell apart in the twentieth century and have further partitioned into strong-willed, even belligerent nation-states, making the region rife with ethnic tensions and unresolved territorial conflicts. Here we indeed need an *ancilla reconciliationis*, dramatically more so than in Western Europe where the EU might be struggling but the postwar reconciliation processes among previously embittered war enemies has created a shared transnational identity of sorts.

East Asia is another region in sore need of an *ancilla reconciliationis*. The "history wars" over the aftermath of Japanese imperialism has become ever more heated around the comfort women issue, territorial disputes, and clashes over proper ways to honor the war dead and the representation in schoolbooks of the history of twentieth-century conflict, colonization,

11. Meltzl, "Vorläufige Aufgaben."
12. Cornis-Pope and Neubauer, "General Introduction," 15.

and war. The national movements of the early twentieth century, which divided the formerly shared literary world of East Asia's "Sinographic sphere" into modern nation-states and national, vernacular languages and literatures, certainly did not encourage the development of a regional identity with a shared "East Asian" cultural heritage. The unresolved and divisive aftermath of Japanese imperialism in the second half of the twentieth century, when neither acceptable apologies and productive dialogue nor strategies for reconciliation were achieved, has led to escalating political alienation and economic competition in the region. These are some of the reasons, despite the existence of Chinese, Japanese, and Korean literary historiography for more than a century, that regional literary historiography of East Asia is only recently emerging, with a new generation of scholars pushing for regional approaches to East Asian cultural history and East Asian studies as a whole.

The first attempt of a comparative history of East Asian literatures in any language is the third volume of *Nihon "bun" gakushi* 日本「文」学史 (*A New History of Japanese "Letterature"*). Titled *"Bun" kara "bungaku" e: Higashi Ajia no bungaku o minaosu* 「文」から「文学」へ：東アジアの文学を見直す (*The Path from "Letters" to "Literature": A Comparative History of East Asian Literatures*), it was conceived by Kōno Kimiko and myself; written with a team of mostly Japanese, Korean, and Chinese scholars; published in Japanese; and will soon appear in Chinese and Korean. We were convinced that the ethical imperative of this volume could only come fully to fruition through personal encounters and dialogues, and thus we invited all authors to an editorial workshop at Waseda University that allowed us to discuss one another's essays—it was a balancing act of scholarly diplomacy. It is all the more heartening that a book review published in *Hankook Ilbo* 한국일보, a South Korean newspaper, praised the volume for fostering reconciliatory scholarly dialogue in the midst of the fierce political tensions between the South Korean and Japanese governments.

More than any other genre of literary studies, literary histories typically serve a pedagogical purpose and reach beyond the more properly scholarly pursuits of our profession. These are examples of transnationally collaborative literary histories in regions with fraught histories that can have tremendous effect on collective identity formation and society as a whole, especially if they serve as reading materials and reference works in school and college education.

NEW EPISTEMOLOGIES OF LITERARY
HISTORIOGRAPHY: CULTURAL CHRONOLOGIES
AND CONCEPTUAL HISTORIES

Other types of recent literary histories have developed innovative approaches to epistemological issues, such as Perkins's worry about the distorting effect of teleologies. "Cultural chronologies" dissolve the linearity of literary histories driven by a dominant master narrative into a more complex rhizomatic structure and open the literary to its cultural historical context. "Conceptual histories" historicize and thus disarm teleologies by taking into account the changing definition of the literary through the ages, thereby reducing the dangers of imposing modernist anachronistic concepts and frameworks.

Over the past few decades, Harvard University Press has published "new" literary histories, encyclopedic cultural chronologies of sorts. Denis Hollier's *A New History of French Literature*, David E. Wellbery and Judith Ryan's *A New History of German Literature*, Greil Marcus and Werner Sollors's *A New Literary History of America*, and David Der-wei Wang's *A New Literary History of Modern China* sidestep the dominant master narratives focused on periodization and great authors, works, and genres. They entice the reader with surprising anecdotes and micro-facts that pinpoint moments of cultural change in snap-shot fashion; they include figures and phenomena of larger and lesser canonical status (rather than only the "great authors" and their worlds) and emphasize historical contexts and the social functions of literary phenomena (rather than focusing on genres); and they make for thought-provoking and absorbing reading and excel at surprise appearances.

Perkins saw Hollier's new history of French literature and considered this postmodern format parasitical: "There must be a positive construction of literary history before there can be the deconstruction that characterizes the next stage in historical sophistication."[13] Put differently, he believed that these "new" literary histories could only be meaningfully read if readers were already familiar with a conventional narrative of major authors, works, and genres and could appreciate the innovative form and topics against this backdrop. It is undeniable that a reader socialized

---

13. Perkins, *Is Literary History Possible?* 58.

Tuning Literary Histories

in Western cultural history and with no background knowledge of Chinese history and culture will have a harder time reading the new literary history of modern China than reading the American, French, or German one. But in the modern period at least, Western and Chinese history have become so entangled with one other that a literary history of modern China will stand on more familiar ground than a history covering the three millennia of classical Chinese literature before the global entanglements of modernity. The change in our cognitive mindset and habits that the digital revolution has catalyzed over the past decades is making us ever better readers (and writers) of complex rhizomatic structures and processes. We are more than grateful, even thirsty, for the enhanced degree of thought-provoking complexity, diversity, and nuance that the cultural chronologies have introduced into the arena of literary historiography.

Another type of literary historiography that disarms the epistemological problem of distorting teleologies are what I call "conceptual literary histories." They take seriously the fundamental realization that literature is a concept whose reference and significance has shifted over time and space and make the moving target of these changes into a self-reflective red thread in their table of contents. What was called literature in various corners of fifteenth- or eighteenth-century Europe is all rather different, and again different from what literature means today (not to mention the many different words and associated concepts for literature in other European languages and their parallel and divergent developments over the past centuries). The same holds for each macro-region of the world. This approach requires the diachronic tracking of semantic change and pragmatic reference in a given language and culture, considered in a broader transregional context. Things get even more complex if we talk about "literature" during China's Qing dynasty (1644–1912) or the South Asian Mughal empire (sixteenth to nineteenth centuries). These vast multilingual empires were home to diverse literary cultures—in literary and vernacular forms of in one instance Chinese, Manchu, Mongolian, Tibetan, and, in the other Persian, Urdu, and Arabic, to name just the most important ones. To understand what "literature" means as concept and practice, we need to trace the most comparable phenomena in these traditions and their historical semantics and understand their sociopolitical functions and linguistic interactions through time. In addition, because at the beginning of the twenty-first century we inevitably look at them through the globalized lens of Western cultural history, we have to confront the question of how the history of these concepts and practices of literature are even comparable to—or precisely partially untranslatable into—the trajectory of relevant concepts and practices in European cultural history.

Although everyone would agree that any concept and practice of literature (and literary history) has changed dramatically across time and space, this point has yet to make its systematic mark on literary historiography, even for the major European literatures. Take the example of *historiae literariae*, a practically forgotten genre of literary histories popular in seventeenth- and eighteenth-century Europe before the advent of national literary historiography in the nineteenth century. These *historiae literariae* were encyclopedic repositories of all scholarly knowledge at the time, and they had a strong connection with the emerging field of bibliography, the compilation of various types of book lists on given subjects.[14] They were inspired by Francis Bacon, among others, who envisioned their subject matter as "nothing other than the recollection from all history of the disciplines and arts and of the periods and areas of the world in which they flourished. Their origins, development, and vicissitudes throughout the various parts of the world (for the sciences and man travel together), their decline, disappearance, and restoration are recounted. . . . Outstanding authors should be noted, the more famous books, schools, traditions, academies, societies, associations, orders, finally all that pertains to the world of letters."[15] They became most popular in Germany, where they were a central part of college curricula during the seventeenth and eighteenth centuries, developed by people like Peter Lambeck (*Prodromus historiae literariae*, 1659), Hermann Conring (at the University of Helmstedt), or, later also in German instead of Latin, by Jacob Friderich Reimmann (*Versuch einer Einleitung in die Historiam Literariam derer Teutschen*, 1708–1713). This world of "letters" in the broadest sense has today virtually disappeared from our consciousness (unlike our idea of a "republic of letters," which survives as its shadow, alive and well).[16] More problematically, the oblivion of this

---

14. Blum, *Bibliographia*, 35–49.

15. Bacon, *De dignitate et augmentis scientiarum*, II.4.502. Translation from Blum, *Bibliographia*, 39–40.

16. Grunert and Vollhardt's edited volume *Historia Literaria* is one of the few publications on this major genre.

important genre is part of a systematic set of distortions of the past caused by modern prejudice—here in particular, national literary historiography. Herbert Jaumann puts this problem most cogently and urges us to "compile a topology of typical distortions and misunderstandings that have taken root since the so-called early enlightenment period."[17] Unfortunately, this call has gone unheeded so far, and there are currently few signs that literary historians would direct a self-reflective gaze to the history of the changing definitions of literature and of their discipline, grasp its importance for understanding Europe's literary cultures before the eighteenth century, and incorporate this awareness into their literary histories.

A conceptual historical approach is even more needed when writing on non-Western literary traditions—in European languages or actually almost any language, as the translation and nativization of European concepts in particular over the past two centuries of accelerating Westernization has thoroughly transformed just about any language and the literary and intellectual worlds produced in it. Kōno Kimiko and I conceived the abovementioned revisionary literary history of Japan in an East Asian context. *Nihon "bun" gakushi: A New History of Japanese "Letterature"* problematizes the concept of *bungaku* 文学, which in the late nineteenth century was coined as a neologism for the Western concept of "literature" at the time (in particular national literature and the novel) and sketches the changing contours of the traditional world of *bun* 文 ("letters," Ch. *wen*) from its beginnings through its transformational reshaping as Western-inspired "literature" (or "letterature" 「文」学, as we have called it) from the late nineteenth century to the present. With a core meaning of "pattern" on animal or human skin, the associations of *bun* extend to the "human pattern" of "writing," to "texts," "civilization," "the civil (versus the martial)" and, not least, the Confucian values of virtue and self-cultivation embodied in King Wen ("civil") and King Wu ("martial"), the founders of the Zhou dynasty (1046–256 BCE). In short, the broad range of its meaning across human civilization and the humanities, as we call them today, is not unlike the broad scope of "letters" as the perimeter of learning and knowledge in pre-nineteenth-century Europe. The suppression of this prehistory of a respective broader world of "letters" in modern literary histories of European and

---

17. Jaumann, "Historia literaria und Formen gelehrter Sammlungen," 111.

East Asian literatures are similarly comparable. This project is inspired by German forms of conceptual history (*Begriffsgeschichte*), in particular by Hans Blumenberg's metaphorology,[18] but it is not a chronological analysis of the successive usages of the word *bun*, as practiced by the more positivistic philological varieties of *Begriffsgeschichte*. Rather, to summarily sketch the larger arch of the structure and argument of the three (actually rather different) volumes, the project probes the practices and conceptualizations that formed around *bun* in political life, court culture, material culture, knowledge transmission and education, devotional practices and beliefs; in interactions between various social classes and the sexes; and in the diverse spectrum of inscription ranging from orthodox literary Sinitic to vernacular Japanese practices and genres.

Our task as literary historians becomes much more complicated when we write literary histories that are self-reflexive, namely, histories that historicize themselves in their own longer tradition of evolving concepts and practices of "literature" and "literary historiography." But it is particularly vital to write self-reflexive histories of non-Western literatures with rich century- or millennia-old textual archives, which predate the (also conceptual) onslaught of Western colonization and imperialism and can only be appropriately captured when liberated from the anachronistic straitjacket of the nineteenth-century European national literature model. The attention to historical change and cultural difference that such self-reflexive literary histories can produce brings them in many ways much closer to the historical periods and places they describe, because they are mindful of the changing definitions and practices of literature and thus manage to reduce anachronistic distortions.

Idiographic, Heterographic, and Xenographic Histories of East Asian Literatures

Let me extend the phenomenological and critical approach to literary historiography beyond the current moment and into the history of a non-Western macro-region home to one of the richest and most continuous

---

18. Müller and Schmieder, *Begriffsgeschichte*; Denecke, "'Bun' no gainen o tōshite."

literary traditions today: East Asia. When, to what purpose, and with which agenda did people come to write Western-style literary histories? East Asia is a premier case for showing how crucial it is to ask these critical questions if we want to understand why and how the European genre of national literary historiography became so popular so rapidly. National "literary historiography" (*bungakushi* 文學史) started in Japan with the 1880s, quickly resulting in dozens of works with that label in Japan and China, often textbooks for the newly established Western-style schools and universities. Educational reforms in response to the encroachment of Western imperialist powers and Japan's rise to a Western-style imperialist power were the most central catalysts of this genre, which came to flourish particularly after the startling reversal of the traditional East Asian power balance that came with Japan's victory over China in the First Sino-Japanese War (1894–1895). Professors—a novel social class of modern "intellectuals"—needed textbooks fitted to newly developed academic programs and curricula on both Western and native knowledge. There is an interesting paradox here: for traditional literati and emerging intellectuals in East Asia the newly coined Western-style concept of literature (Ch. *wenxue*; J. *bungaku* 文學) was hard to grasp, because Europe's late nineteenth-century national literature paradigm did not map well onto the traditional East Asian world of letters and literary composition. Many of these early literary histories start off with attempts to attach a "definition" to this new concept of literature. In contrast, the concept of literary history seemed less problematic. At least it was enthusiastically reiterated and reproduced on book covers, with little explicit struggle to comprehend its meaning. Part of the problem of reading this large and varied corpus of early literary histories from the tumultuous and formative two decades around the turn of the twentieth century is that the popularity of that generic label covered up vast differences in what the writers of such literary histories actually understood as literature.

Research on these early literary histories focuses almost exclusively on single national traditions, with Sinologists, for example, keenly interested in pinpointing who wrote the first *real* literary history of China—proposing Chinese authors such as Lin Chuanjia 林傳甲 (1877–1922) and Huang Ren 黃人 (1866–1913) and largely neglecting several decades of previous such histories written by Japanese to whom these Chinese authors were indebted.[19] Such pursuit of linear national(istic) origin stories obscures the nature and function of this genre and the historical forces behind its meteoric rise in East Asia. Instead, the emergence of modern Western-style literary historiography in China, Japan, and Korea is an East Asian story embedded in the intense cultural competition that unfolded alongside Japan's political grasp for military and economic supremacy in East Asia at the time. Only Korean scholar Cho Tong-il 趙東一, with the intuitively cosmopolitan gaze of a smaller nation and a critical eye for Japan's imperialist ambitions, has traced the origins of modern national literary historiography in East Asia comparatively.[20] To critically historicize the emergence of this genre in the late nineteenth century, I propose to typologize literary histories into "idiographic," "heterographic," and "xenographic" ones, written, respectively, on the writer's own, a culturally related, or completely foreign literary tradition. Once we do so, powerful regional patterns emerge that reveal systemic biases that we need to take into account when evaluating these early literary histories. We tend to read these histories too much at face value, proceeding intuitively from the anachronistic question of how modern their content looks by today's standards. This triadic scheme forces us to historicize early literary histories and ask how the cultural background, agenda, and mindset of their authors systematically affected the content.

It comes as no surprise that the earliest literary histories were devoted to China—a natural consequence of China's traditional status as venerable reference culture in the region—although they were written by Japanese reformist politicians and Sinologists, and are thus heterographic.[21] They were hardly foreigners to Chinese literature, but stood in a Japanese Sinological tradition that reached back a dozen centuries, while also looking toward a future of Japanese hegemonic ascent in the region. Many of them regarded Chinese literature with ambivalent eyes. These heterographic histories start with Suematsu Kenchō's 末松謙澄 (1855–1920) *A Short History of China's Ancient Literature* (*Shina kobungaku ryakushi* 支那古文学略史).

---

19. See Doleželová-Velingerová, "Literary Historiography in Early Twentieth-Century China"; Chan, "*Wen* and the 'First History(-ies) of Chinese Literature"; P. Chen, "The Story of Literary History."

20. Cho Tong-il, *Higashi Ajia bungakushi hikakuron.*

21. Denecke, *Classical World Literatures,* 1–10.

Tuning Literary Histories

Written by Suematsu while he was studying law at Cambridge University and published in 1882, this seems to be the earliest work published under the label of "literary history" in East Asia. It offers a vivid picture of what devising a literary history for a Japanese student in 1880s England entailed. Born in the 1850s, Viscount Suematsu, eventually a highly decorated politician, diplomat, and writer, was trained in a private academy of Classical (Chinese) studies. After earning his law degree at Cambridge, he went on to become a member of Japan's first Diet in 1890 and held several ministerial posts. It is remarkable that he embraced the new label of literary history, a genre he must have encountered during his studies in Cambridge. Second, Suematsu's work is a macrohistorical analogy, a cross-application to East Asian civilization of "classical (Greco-Roman) studies," whose curricular and cultural centrality he also witnessed at Cambridge.

The canon of texts he discusses is still part of the traditional world of letters: he presents a line-up of titles broadly organized by the four bibliographical categories, starting with the *Classic of Documents* and quickly moving to the "Masters," and later to "Literary Collections" and "Histories." But the frame and some of his choices belie a man from a new era: in the opening he justifies the study of China's ancient literature (*Shina kobungaku* 支那古文学) by saying that it is just as important for the study of "Oriental literatures" (*Tōyō bungaku* 東洋文学) as the study of Greek and Latin literatures for "Occidental literatures" (*Seiyō bungaku* 西洋文学).[22] Even the title and opening phrase of his work are sparkling with fresh words and concepts: an (abridged) "history" of the ancient "literature" of "*Shina*" (China) as part of "Oriental literatures" that is a new *comparandum* to the variety of national "Occidental literatures." Among these, *Shina* (and "literature") was probably the most fateful new concept. Originally a phonetic loan from Sanskrit that had been used to denote China since the medieval period, it acquired a new meaning and tone in the late nineteenth century, when the Japanese started to use it to put themselves on equal footing with their formerly hegemonic regional superpower. This was not explicitly derogatory, but with the foundation of the Republic, intellectuals and politicians promoted *Zhongguo* 中國 as the official toponym for China. Because the foundation of modern sinology

---

22. Suematsu, *Shina kobungaku ryakushi*, 1.1A.

as *Shinagaku* in particular by the so-called Kyoto school of sinology (in contrast to Japan's traditional sinology, *kangaku* 漢学) unfolded during the high tide of Japanese colonialism since the 1920s, the Chinese increasingly protested against the term. In 1946 the Japanese government agreed to erase it from official use.[23] Despite its premodern roots, the sudden pervasive use of *Shina* by Suematsu and his contemporaries clearly marked a new relationship with China. *Shina* boldly forced on the venerable ancient Middle Kingdom a kind of neutral equality that flew in the face of traditional power relations in the region. That Suematsu cared about political power, economic wealth, and military strength is evident from the fact that he gives much space and prime place in the first volume to the masters text *Guanzi* 管子.[24] He gets into issues of "economic theory" (*keizairon* 経済論) and praises *Guanzi's* "secret art" of enriching the people. Shang Yang 商鞅 (ca. 390–338 BCE), the legalist architect of Qin's military power, gets special attention for his role of "enriching" and "strengthening" the state of Qin, terms that resonate with Suematsu's time.[25]

While colonialist undertones vis-à-vis China only enter literary historiography in the later 1990s, Suematsu set an important example for retrojecting China into antiquity, his focus on China as a "classical civilization" with an "ancient literature" implying its contemporary decline. In strong contrast to literary histories of Japan, which emerged as comprehensive surveys from the earliest to the contemporary period and from canonical works to popular genres previously not considered serious literature, many Japanese authors of literary histories of China into the 1900s focused heavily on the canonical works of China's ancient and medieval period—up to the Song dynasty (960–1279). China was stuck in the earlier period as an ancient "high civilization" with a problematic (or at least silent) present and future. They refrained from associating China with modernity and the European notion of literature as epitomized by the novel, instead emphasizing how Japan measured up to this standard in the eleventh century with Murasaki Shikibu's 紫式部 (d. ca. 1014) *Tale of Genji* (*Genji monogatari* 源氏物語).

---

23. See Fogel, "New Thoughts on an Old Controversy"; and Guex, "Le Shinagaku."

24. Suematsu, *Shina kobungaku ryakushi*, 1.8A–12B.

25. Suematsu, *Shina kobungaku ryakushi*, 2.5B–6B.

Kojō Teikichi's 古城眞吉 (1866–1949) *Literary History of China* (*Shina bungakushi* 支那文学史) of 1897 was the first chronologically comprehensive history. He was a largely self-taught Sinologist who lived in China between 1897 and 1901. A few years after his return, he became a professor at the recently founded academic institution that became Tōyō University. His history is admirable in its systematic approach. He orders the material by dynastic periods, treads a broad swath of textual (not just narrowly "literary") genres, and prefaces each section with a brief summary introduction. Two prominent voices of his time contributed prefaces to Kojō's history: intellectual historian and philosopher Inoue Tetsujirō 井上哲次郎 (1855–1944) and Taguchi Ukichi 田口卯吉 (1855–1905), a statesman, economic thinker, and cultural historian who two decades earlier had published a highly successful sister project of sorts, *A Short History of Japanese Civilization* (*Nihon kaika shōshi* 日本開化小史), which situated Japanese letters and literature in the broader frame of the history of civilizations (*bunmeishi* 文明史). Both celebrate Kojō's work as the first ever literary history of China, omitting any reference to Suematsu's work. Instead, Inoue mentions the existence of earlier histories of Japanese literature, which had appeared since 1890, and thus seems to trace its genealogy through previous Japanese literary histories written by Japanese scholars. Taguchi and Inoue propose different reasons for the absence of literary histories of China and the need for the Japanese to start writing them. Inoue castigates the ineptness of the contemporary Chinese to curate their own literary tradition and pins his hopes on Japanese scholars to take on this job. He says that the Chinese innately lack the cognitive ability to synthesize, accuses them of not understanding modern academic research and the importance of writing literary histories, and concludes that for these reasons (plus the fact that Chinese literature was still a new research object for Western scholars at the time), it is the Japanese who are compelled to fill the gap and write literary histories of China.[26] In Inoue's arguments, the heterographic literary historiography of China by Japanese writers took on explicitly imperialist tones in the wake of Japan's victory over China in the First Sino-Japanese War. Although Kōjo's literary history has been considered a turning point in

---

26. Inoue, "Preface," in Kōjo, *Shina bungakushi*, 23.

Japanese Sinology—its continuing value confirmed for example by Yoshi-kawa Kōjiro in the 1960s[27]—in one point it looks radically different from today's Chinese literary histories or even those that were published shortly thereafter. Kōjo's still very Confucian conception of "letterature" made him highlight Confucian studies through various periods and virtually exclude popular literature, namely, the novel and drama.

In 1897 Sasagawa Rinpū 笹川臨風 (1870–1949), a practicing haiku poet inclined toward popular literature, published a history of Chinese novels and drama. But even Sasagawa felt compelled, in his *Literary History of China* (*Shina bungakushi* 支那文学史) published the following year, to justify the inclusion of drama and novels in a comprehensive survey history of Chinese literature, for example, by claiming a distinguished lineage for these genres in China's "southern" culture and *Zhuangzi*'s 莊子 parables. He attributes China's reticence in producing fiction instead to the strong influence of "northern" Confucian culture and the political function of literature (*bunshō keikoku* 文章経国), putting Japan on the right (Western side) of history and emphasizing that unlike in China, novels and drama flourished in Europe and Japan.[28]

In a next step, two decades after Suematsu's history, xenographic histories in European languages appear: Herbert Giles's (1845–1933) *A History of Chinese Literature* of 1901, followed in 1902 by Wilhelm Grube's (1855–1908) *Geschichte der chinesischen Litteratur* in German.[29]

Only after the heterographic and xenographic histories did the first idiographic literary histories of China, written by Chinese academics, appear, starting with Lin Chuanjia's—a whole generation after the earliest

27. Mizobe Yoshie, "Meijiki no Nihon ni okeru Chūgoku shōsetsushi kenkyū ni tsuite," 116.

28. Sasagawa, *Shina bungakushi*, 259–61. The question of the rapidly changing status of fiction and its effect on literary historiography is particularly important, because Japanese intellectuals picked up on the high reputation novels had in Europe at the time. William Hedberg has shown how the Meiji and Taishō period reception of Chinese premodern vernacular novels, such as *Water Margin*, influenced the earliest histories of Chinese literature written by Japanese scholars. See Hedberg, *The Japanese Discovery of Chinese Fiction*, 95–144.

29. Let us leave aside here Vasily Vasilyev's (1818–1900) Очерк истории китайской литературы (*Abridged History of Chinese Literature*) of 1880, which preceded Suematsu's work. See Denecke, "The Politics of (Dis)similarity."

Tuning Literary Histories

Japanese literary histories of China. As a newly appointed instructor at the recently founded Jingshi University (later Beijing University) who had passed the provincial examinations two years earlier, Lin hastily compiled lecture notes over the summer months of 1904. In 1910 they were published under the title *Literary History of China* (*Zhongguo wenxueshi* 中國文學史). Lin had to fit his hastily compiled lecture manual for the new literature program to the new university regulations of 1903. The sixteen chapters in *Literary History of China* exactly match the first sixteen clauses of the regulations on "research and the substance of literature," while dispensing with the last twenty-five.[30] His lectures were very popular, reprinted in many forms until 2005,[31] and although he explicitly mentions Sasagawa Rinpū's *Shina bungakushi*, Lin's work is clearly a Chinese approach to China's literary heritage and served very different purposes. Many of its features did not fit well with the new modernist literary ideology in the wake of the May Fourth movement of 1919 but give us a fascinating glimpse of early twentieth-century Chinese literary culture in transformation. First, it is a textbook for learning the tools of traditional philology (including script and calligraphic styles, rhyme books, and etymology) and forms of textual analysis (such as rhetorical devices and argumentation). Second, it introduces novices to the arts of literary composition (chapter 6). Third, even when Lin goes into a seemingly chronological mode (chapters 7–14), he does so through the screen of traditional bibliographical categories and genres, starting with Classics, Histories, and Masters. Fourth, he not only omits novels and drama but rails about how base and despicable these genres are—not to be considered a part of venerable letterature but at best a part of a history of popular manners. Lin's notes appeared just as Liang Qichao 梁啓超 (1873–1929) was launching his call for reform of the national novel and proclaiming its great future.[32] However much criticized by post–May Fourth scholars as messy or not even a "real literary history," his work presents a unified vision. We see a glimpse of a waning world in which students were equipped with a mixture of traditional philology, textual composition, and training in the historical

---

30. P. Chen, "The Story of Literary History," 6.

31. Fu Xiangxi, *Ershi shiji qianqi Zhongguo wenxueshi,* 118–19.

32. On this, see further comments in Fu Xiangxi, *Ershi shiji qianqi Zhongguo wenxueshi,* 120–21.

lineages of various central genres. Rather different from Japan, "Chinese literary history" in China had not yet turned into a modern academic subject, a form of idiographic Sinology, but was in part still a tool to enable students to participate in China's living, late Qing textual culture. Classical literature, especially poetry, continued to play a prominent role in literary education and culture in twentieth-century China.

Literary histories of Japan appear about a decade after the earliest Japanese histories of Chinese literature, but they are, in strong contrast to those of China, off to an idiographic start. Recent graduates of the new literature curriculum at what was later Tokyo University, Mikami Sanji 三上参次 (1865–1939) and Takatsu Kuwasaburō 高津鍬三郎 (1864–1921), published their *Literary History of Japan* (*Nihon bungakushi* 日本文学史) in 1890. They undertook a systematic full-scale application of European models to their own literary heritage, making this the earliest literary history on any East Asian tradition to basically bear all features of the "national literature paradigm," as it later emerged in China since the 1920s and Korea since the 1950s and 1960s. They programmatically excluded Japan's literature in Literary Sinitic and upgraded the development of vernacular, popular literature to the master narrative of their history, promoting premodern tales as the equivalent of the European "novel." Thus, unlike China, which Japanese literary historians initially arrested in the timeframe of venerable antiquity, Japan emerges proudly as a modern nation in this first literary history, with a fully fledged vernacular literary tradition on par with Europe. This was certainly not a disinterested move, but a strategy to assert Japan's legitimate claim to modernity—and China's backwardness and loss of authority in the present.

Not surprisingly, xenographic literary histories of Japan by avid European observers of Japan's rise on the global stage appear, in relative chronology, a decade more quickly than those of China: William George Aston's (1841–1911) *A History of Japanese Literature* of 1899 and Karl Florenz's (1865–1939) *Geschichte der japanischen Literatur* (*History of Japanese Literature*) of 1906. Unlike for China, heterographic literary histories for Japan trailed far behind. The Japanese literary history by Chinese scholar and translator Xie Liuyi 謝六逸 (1898–1945) was published in 1927/1929 in Shanghai—almost forty years into the history of Japanese literary historiography in Japanese. So the order of the triadic scheme for Japan is diametrically opposed to the Chinese case: a paradigmatic idiographic

Tuning Literary Histories

beginning, with a quick appearance of xenographic literary histories, and few, much later heterographic samples.

Literary histories of Korea first appear forty years—two generations—after the genre made its appearance in Japan for Chinese literature: An Hwak's 安廓 (1886–1946) *Chosŏn munhaksa* 朝鮮文學史 (*Literary History of Chosŏn*) of 1922. Not only do we have to wait for the liberation from Japanese colonialism in 1945 to see idiographic literary historiography of Korea properly emerge—soon to be divided into those written in the North and the South. Revealingly, even xenographic Korean literary histories only appear in the second half of the twentieth century, such as Andre Eckardt's (1884–1974) *Geschichte der koreanischen Literatur* (*History of Korean Literature*) in 1968. Thus, for Korea the triadic scheme is different still, starting with a single idiographic literary history and only coming into its own after the colonial period, when heterographic and xenographic literary histories slowly start appearing, mostly written by Koreans and Korean diaspora scholars or Westerners who happened to have lived in Korea for a long time. The Korean case almost explodes the triadic scheme, making most enterprises of Korean literary historiography "idiographic" of sorts.[33]

In sum, as the authoritative reference culture in the region, China received earliest attention as a subject for new literary histories. Japanese Sinologists performed that service for their venerable reference culture, with an ambivalent mixture of age-old admiration and increasingly imperialist pride in the successes of Japan's speedy modernization and Westernization. This pride also fueled the first idiographic literary histories that the Japanese started writing about their own tradition. Westerners could ignore neither the past greatness of China nor the ascending power of the Japanese empire and thus set quickly to write literary histories of China and Japan for their respective European audiences. In the region, the Chinese were still traditionally disdainful of their little neighbor Japan; for Koreans, writing Japanese literary histories became a highly ambivalent task at best. This regional disinterest (even distaste) toward Japan stands in stark contrast to the ascent of Japanese literature studies in the

---

33. For a more extensive comparative treatment of early East Asian literary historiography, in particular also xenographic literary histories, see Denecke, "The Politics of (Dis)similarity."

West. Almost no one, regionally or internationally, had interest in chronicling the literary legacy of Korea[34]—until Koreans took this task upon themselves with the stirrings of anticolonial activism in the 1920s and after liberation with the establishment of Korean literary studies in the 1950s and 1960s.

Outlook: Tuning Literary Historiography to World Time

The power dynamics underlying the early development of literary historiography on China, Japan, and Korea in East Asia makes us painfully aware of the political agonism, ideological inequalities, and systematic asynchronicities of this process. Once we typologize them into idiographic, heterographic, and xenographic literary histories, the systemic patterns in the different order and timing of their development for China, Japan, and Korea suddenly become apparent. This East Asian story is what we need to take into account, even if we want to understand the story of any one of these national traditions—such as the origins of the modern literary historiography of China. The scheme has general value for other literatures: it makes us self-reflective and mindful as we study and write literary histories—be it of literatures that we feel we own as a whole, or partially, or only distantly, academically. It helps us uncover and avoid (as much as possible) the accidental ideological exigencies of our own historical moment. This is certainly a very tall order. Hardly any other area and genre of today's literary studies demands such an effort of self-transcendence, of overcoming our own historical constraints in large and small ways.

The critical phenomenological assessment of Anglophone literary historiography today revealed new logical (narrative), ethical, and epistemological concerns. We saw how forms of national literary historiography

---

34. Note that in 1927, Canadian missionary James Scarth Gale (1863–1937) published a *History of the Korean People* that contained references to and translations of songs, poems, and other literary works, but it is not framed as a literary history. See Rutt, *James Scarth Gale*.

are legitimate and much needed today (rather than considering them simply passé after all the critiques of nation-state ideology). Literary histories are also written to heal conflict regions or force foe nations into cultural dialogue between collaborating scholars, messengers of peace and dialogue—in a world where our politicians increasingly fail or openly refuse to foster constructive transnational dialogue. I showcased how crucial it is to write self-reflective, critical literary histories that account for the shifting scope and practices of literature and are thus most successful in avoiding anachronistic presentism.

If anything, we will find that we are moving ever further away from debates about a singular notion of literary historiography defined by only a handful of parameters and debatable issues proposed by scholars of Western literatures at North American or European universities, as was the case during the second half of the twentieth century—be it an Erich Auerbach, a René Wellek and an Austin Warren, a Hans Robert Jauss, or a David Perkins. Instead, literary historians are now identifying and probing a variety of new roles for literary historiography in our rapidly changing world, where the very meaning and clear disciplinary definition of "history" and "literature" is fading. This is the most exciting part of our current moment, as our academic disciplines undergo transformational changes and develop into more globalized, comparative, and holistic forms of humanistic research, beyond the older ineffectual buzzword of "interdisciplinarity." One thing is clear: now more than ever we need literary historiographies that can better serve us in a world challenged by nationalisms, inequality, scarcity of resources, and the massive demographic displacements and new strength of migrant communities. As the most pedagogical-*cum*-academic genre of literary studies, literary histories can put many stakes into our shaky ground.

CHAPTER 9

When Literary Relations End—and Begin Again

JING TSU

A controversial valuation of modern Chinese literature from the 1990s—against the idea of world literature—remains memorable. It was a legendary showdown between two leading figures at the height of American academy's cultural wars in the 1990s. Non-Western representation was on the rise, area studies was rebelling against its Cold War cartography, and any attempt to protect the hierarchical structure of literary and national identities, with the West on top, was under assault.[1] Revisiting the controversy over his treatment of Misty School poet Bei Dao 北島 (b. 1949) thirteen years later—in which he was criticized for condescending toward the Chinese poet's attempt to garner a world audience through translation at the sacrifice of quality poetry—Stephen Owen remained steadfast in 2003, this time with an unapologetic analogy: "For a young Korean poet to be translated into Tagalog and acclaimed in Manila is, no doubt, a matter of satisfaction; but it has less cachet than to be translated into English or French and invited to New York or Paris. It is unfair, but it is a fact."[2]

By now many would agree with that valuation. It has only become more incontrovertible in recent discussions of world literature, where the influence of the geopolitical and institutional landscape—from what gets

---

An earlier version of this essay was published in *Journal of World Literature* 5, no. 2 (2020): 287–97.

1. Owen, "What Is World Poetry?" 28–32; Chow, *Writing Diaspora*, 1–26, esp. 1–2; Yeh, "Chayi de youlü," 94–96.

2. Owen, "Stepping Forward and Back," 533.

When Literary Relations End

translated and backstage skirmishes of literary awards to the self-perpetuating academic establishment that canonizes them—has been exposed, revealing the many biases that promote them and hidden favoritism that results from them.

But that has only confirmed the importance of the literary market. To have a spot in the international marketplace, to invoke Goethe, is assumed to be a true measure for a writer's success. No matter how much one disputes and challenges definitions of the world, world stature is a goal that writers ultimately seek. In this view, writers are seen as oriented toward the world stage in the way that, as Owen suggested, cosmopolitan Paris—along with French—is ultimately more attractive than the new Asian urban milieu of Manila and Tagalog. No one seems to dispute that the international structure of value and its commodification is as real as the Swedes who hand out the Nobel Prize every year. Owen was challenged on where he placed that value, not the consensus that endorses the underlying economy.[3] It is also true that the challenge was issued to him because of the authoritative position he occupied structurally in the chain of academic valuation. Some observers have suggested that his position was what made him a target, but that seems to be a convenient way of not examining how everyone in this marketplace contributes to the question of literary values in flux. For scholars of modern literature, who engage with and partake in that process in real time, literary history is not an artifact but is necessarily incomplete.

It has since been acknowledged that the literary world—including the academy—encompasses different alternatives and standards of value. At the same time, disengaging from the international marketplace is not an option, because to be world literature at all, a minimal condition must be met: the writer has to desire an audience. A writer, and their text, wants to be read by as many readers as possible, leaving only the question of how a particular writer can strategically move themself along that chain in securing the appropriate audience and reception. World literature, in

---

3. As Rey Chow put it, "what is absent . . . is an account of the institutional investments that shape his own enunciation. The *absence* constitutes a definite form of power by not drawing attention to itself and thus not subjecting itself to the harsh judgment of 'self-interest.'" The same, however, could be said of her own speaking position, as far as the circulatory movement of power goes. See Chow, *Writing Diaspora*, 1.

234   JING TSU

short, takes the world as its end goal. It was not until the early twenty-first century, with the most recent revitalization of world literary studies on a wide scale, that this goal came under explicit scrutiny—where the "unfair" factor was problematized as the very condition for generating literary distinctions at all.

Valuations of Insignificance

For a volume of essays that mostly addresses the well-established field of premodern Chinese literary studies, I venture to resituate the orientation toward a "field" in a contemporary, ever-volatile context of the "world." Much of the critical reflection on literary history, as outlined in Xiaofei Tian's introduction to this volume, has to do with pulling at the seams of an already made literary history. Premodern studies allows for this advantage. An obvious revisionist approach is to tug at received narratives and show that what came after was in truth selectively remembered or "repressed."[4] Modern or contemporary literature, by virtue of coming in later, cannot avail itself of the advantage of seniority. It cannot use "repression" as a way of containing what comes after—because you cannot repress a past that has not yet come to pass. Modern literature, however made to submit to the tradition and innovations that came before, has aspirations of its own that differ from scholarly priorities in conceptualizing literary history. An important reason to leave room for this consideration, in my view, is that unlike premodern writers, modern writers can and do speak for themselves. They change their styles and aesthetics even as scholars try to frame and peg down their value, sometimes precisely in adaptation or response to the latter's opinions. For these writers, budding or well known, literary history can be a specialized, privileged, and distant concept that has little relevance to why and how they write.[5] Scholars of modern literature may find themselves carrying out the more

---

4. See Tian, introduction in this volume.

5. For an example of literary history retaining relevance in the present (albeit a present that is now long past), see Nugent, chapter 3 in this volume.

When Literary Relations End 235

necessary, humble task of documenting writers' voices rather than putting themselves first as authorized interpreters or spokespeople. Contemporary literature, especially, lives in an incomplete mode, in the way that modernity—as Leo Ou-fan Lee once observed in the earlier cosmopolitan context of republican Shanghai—was experienced as an incomplete project. In this respect, the current volume's internal reflections on the premodern field can perhaps benefit from a counterbalance of turning outward for incongruous comparisons, found in living examples that do not stay fixed at the edge or center, yet are committed to a place in literary history. Here, theorizing about a world context shows its own challenges.

Of the approaches to world literature, Pascale Casanova's contribution remains the most relevant to the contemporary world. This is so not because her theorization is infallible—many, in fact, have picked at her shortcomings—but because her framework has been the most reflexive in grasping the core vulnerability in the study of world literature. This reflection was built into her 2005 essay, "Literature as a World," her first English-language publication after the translation of *La République mondiale des lettres* into English the year before.[6] Contrary to the success of her debut, it did not express the confidence of a new manifesto. The essay began with a series of questions that expressed more doubt than would be expected of a programmatic statement.

Other proposed world literary studies from around the same time were more recognizably literary than Casanova's sociological theoretical approach. David Damrosch's reconsideration of world literature extended the traditional scope of literature outward, while Franco Moretti was drawing on comparative morphology to build a quantitative model for mapping literary evolution and, later, inspiring algorithm-based experiments with long-distance reading.[7] Casanova was also going up against, while being inspired by, the frameworks of three of the most influential social theorists of the twentieth century—Pierre Bourdieu, Fernand Braudel, and Immanuel Wallerstein. Her tentativeness bespoke caution,

6. Casanova, "Literature as a World," 71–90, and *The World Republic of Letters*.
7. Damrosch, *What Is World Literature?*; Moretti, *Graphs, Maps, Trees*. Also see the work of the Stanford Literary Lab at https://litlab.stanford.edu/.

236   JING TSU

so much so that she formulated her set of three questions, carefully, not once but twice:

> Is it possible to re-establish the lost bond between literature, history and the world, while still maintaining a full sense of the irreducible singularity of literary texts? Second, can literature itself be conceived as a world? And if so, might an exploration of its territory help us to answer question number one? Put differently: is it possible to find the conceptual means with which to oppose the central postulate of internal, text-based literary criticism—the total rupture between text and world? Can we propose any theoretical and practical tools that could combat the governing principle of the autonomy of the text, or the alleged independence of the linguistic sphere?[8]

Casanova was undecided when faced with the choice between the text's sufficiency as a world unto itself, hence affirming the text's integrity in generating internally motivated criticism, and the world that makes the text dependent on it. In this opening paragraph, Casanova was working against certain assumptions that may be reconstructed as follows. First, it had not been possible to restore the historical and world context of literature and keep the irreducible meaning of the text intact and qualify as irreducibly singular; a text has to be explained by literature's conventions, like style, genre, period, and aesthetic standards. Second, on its own literature has not been enough to claim a world, because of the assumptions made in the first statement, by which literature relies critically on a historical and social context to construe its relevance and value; reading text for its own sake denies that linkage to the world. One idea is to have it both ways, which is what Casanova pushed for so that we need not choose. Two decades after her initial foray, world literature, it turned out, is not a neutral conceptual amalgamation that can bring all the literatures together like a benign host. Always coming from somewhere and motivated by the vantage point of a specific place, the provincialism of world literature is not always convincing in persuading the world. It must compete with others for this title. It is quite unthinkable these days to equate French-language literature, Casanova's literary universe—or even

---

8. Casanova, "Literature as a World," 71.

Western literature, for that matter—with the world (Owen's invocation of Paris no longer signals an assured advantage). The third assumption that Casanova was working against is that since literature cannot be a world in and for itself, its spatiality can only be abstract and unfixed. It cannot take for granted a national audience or community that comes with national territoriality.

There seems to be really only one question for Casanova: what can the relationship between literature and the social look like such that, together, they can account for a world space? That is the desire at the heart of the valuation—to restore that social bond while maintaining the uniqueness of the literary text. One might consider that this is where Owen might find true reconciliation: where a national or provincial writer can become a world writer without having to compromise, exchange, or sell his or her social origin.

The desire for the literary to be aesthetically sufficient in itself and—with the larger social power of world representation—outside itself became a cornerstone and justification of the study of world literature. It hypothesizes, on one hand, the wish to canonize world texts writ large, and to include, on the other hand, the lesser, smaller, more distant traditions along the way. The smaller, less distinguished examples provide the canvas on which the former stands out (literary history shares a similar problem of erecting a pyramid of values). Texts aligned with the "Greenwich Meridian" solidify their influence or popularity through translation or oral transmission, while the rest of world literature, writ small, constitute the masses—or literary humanity—that adapt, pass along, or transform these known world texts.

Herein lies a problem: more locally bound texts move into the foreground only when they are considered relevant to understanding, augmenting, or disputing the promoted texts. Although it is true that in some cases major texts fall out of favor until they are rediscovered in a new context, once they do, they tend to overshadow their local translations, which end up augmenting the influence of the already known. At present it is still Shakespeare, Ibsen, Cao Xueqin, or Lu Xun who gets pegged to a world value and translated into Arabic, Japanese, and other languages. Locally and regionally revered writers like twentieth-century Indonesian Chinese writer Huang Dongping 黄東平 (1923–2014) are implicitly understood as the influenced—rather than the influencers.

This deep unfairness generates the literary map in which the marginalized also became accustomed to seeing themselves. When mainland Chinese writer Yu Dafu 郁達夫 (1896–1945) moved to Southeast Asia during the Japanese occupation in China in 1938, he was maligned for trying to upset that balance. He urged local writers to lift themselves up by writing about where they were rather than slavishly follow the examples of the mainland Chinese writers—much like Bei Dao was urged to resist the temptation of "world literature."[9] Unappreciated at the time was the depth of Yu Dafu's insight. He grasped something that was ahead of his time: the fact that while second- and third-tier writers do not generally break into the national or world circuit of recognition, there would be no global circuit to speak of without them, as they constitute the local pieces of the world picture; they *are* its literary humanity. This is the kind of clash that results from the potential conflict between the priorities of different literary histories—Chinese versus Southeast Asian, in this case. So when world literature stakes its reputation on the principle of diversification and accommodation, it erects this distinction on the condition of asymmetry.

Departing from Owen and Casanova, one might ask what happens when a text or author does not care to be received by the world or buy into the idea of world literature. Can one say "no" to world literature?

Smaller literary artifacts and writers, in fact, constitute the majority of literary humanity that stays largely undifferentiated in the backdrop of world literary space. They are the ones who cannot afford to divorce themselves from history or local reality. Tightly bound to their space of history and time, they seldom rise so high into the aesthetic stratosphere as to start theorizing or speculating about themselves as a threshold to the world. A widely known vernacular text like *Romance of the Three Kingdoms* (*Sanguo zhi yanyi* 三國志演義), a fourteenth-century historical novel based on the political events of second- to third-century China, can be happily transmitted and reworked in Korean, Thai, Malay, Javanese, Vietnamese, Mongol, Makassarese, and Cambodian for more than two centuries without ever having the blessing of world literature.[10] It has been perfectly well enriched by the different local contexts in Asia that

9. Yu Dafu, "Jige wenti" 幾個問題, "Nanyang wenhua de qiantu" 南洋文化的前途, in Yu Dafu, *Yu Dafu haiwai wenji*, 480–85.

10. Salmon, "Introduction," 29–31.

re-create and riff on its characters and narration, fortifying a shared regional cultural repertoire that continues to generate interest.

An influential life away from the world spotlight is even truer of writers who do not expect their texts to circulate or leave a permanent mark on the world. The small output of twentieth-century Macanese literature—written in Chinese and Macau Portuguese by writers of mixed Portuguese and Chinese descent—can share and persist in a pathos of insignificance without being disabled or preempted by precarity.[11] Macau has been the least globally visible link in the often invoked geopolitical tripartite, Taiwan–Hong Kong–Macau, partly because of the distant past of the Portuguese empire. Poets like Yiling 懿靈 (b. 1964) openly revel in Macau's trivial status as a faded former colony that sits on the periphery of mainland China's periphery. What motivates Macanese writing, as Agnes Lam (b. 1972) put it, is the fact that "On a world map, Macau is like a dot made by the tip of a hair strand dipped in ink—it is only so big."[12]

Smallness raises anxiety; yet being small enough can turn a sense of precarity into a motivation for local literary ecologies that do not aspire to be canonized in literary history. That may be more than what world literature can ever do for them. Being insignificant can matter much more than being elevated to the pantheon of world literature—and being embraced by a world audience.

Instead of being recognized on their own terms, however, small literatures are often drawn into world literature, whether or not they want it, as points of comparison. The contrast between local, reality-bound texts and universalist aesthetics-driven literature, in this way, makes the two-tiered distinction clear: one for local color, the other for philosophical and aesthetic insight. Kim Chew Ng, contemporary Malaysian Chinese writer based in Taiwan and champion of modernist writing, for instance, went so far as to reject the realist, local strain of Malaysian Chinese literature that took root in Malaysia. Realism, he charged, held back modernist techniques from breaking new aesthetic ground in Chinese-language literature, thereby keeping it from becoming global. The dearth of original literary innovations in Chinese-language literature, on his count,

---

11. Tsu, "Weak Links, Literary Spaces, and Comparative Taiwan," 123–44; Tsu, "Comparative Taiwan Literature," 173–95; de Almeida, *Writing the Margin*, 126–84.

12. De Almeida, *Writing the Margin*, 130; Lam, "Wu ziwo yishi de chengshi."

was due to the unquestioned fetishism of bearing witness to reality as history.[13]

Such debates flare up in the Chinese-language literary world because for the majority of writers in that space the link, or yoke, to the world was, importantly, never lost such that the linkage can be redesired as a union. For them, history matters more than literary history. Recovering the "lost bond" might have provided the raison d'être for Casanova's project, but it remains a tentative one for others. World literary space, one might modestly speculate, may be simply the socially lived space— combative, inspirational, and multifaceted—with no particular privilege, valuation, or exceptional status accorded to the literary. In this sense, rethinking literature under unconventional rubrics by tracing its different trajectories—short, long, or unintended—may provide useful counterpoints testing the limits of accommodation.

Here, the undoing of world literature becomes a real proposition. It is instructive to probe this central vulnerability that Casanova left us. What happens when we start (rather than end) with the conclusion that the literary is not driven by the prospect of resolving the loss of that social union with the world or of gaining value? Writing across space and time, in other words, may fulfill different purposes: to be a great aesthetic masterpiece, a private memory, national canon, personal testimony, or a show of resistance and complicity. Some of these literary results can serve a short-term purpose and hence may never—nor wish to—intersect with the kind of world literary space critics offer.

If the idea of world literature is mainly proffered for academic consumption, then certainly Casanova had reasons to fear that literary criticism would inevitably lose touch with the world context to which it refers. Following this logic, how do we account for writers in this world picture of moving parts who do not wish to grow greater—more encompassing, more famous, more sophisticated—but to settle into a niche with acceptable constraints? Does one have to desire—and desire only—becoming part of the world picture?

I raise these questions at a time when the world model, as it has been laid out by Casanova and others, is changing faster than literary history

---

13. Ng, "Minor Sinophone Literature," 15–28. See Fang Xiu, *Notes on the History of Malayan Chinese New Literature.*

can record or absorb. World affairs at the present are increasingly pulled toward a non-Western rather than Western "Greenwich Meridian," prompting new reactions and accommodations. What is emerging, though, is not simply new competition to replace the old standard but a vast field of potential for one to see texts and genres in new ways—literary artifacts from the past that were never intended to be accessed by a world public, enlivened and subsumed under existing topographies of area and local writings, and new literary experiments that are still in progress. The study of modern Chinese literature, as with other established literary fields, continues to stick to genres like fiction and, to a much lesser extent, poetry and drama. The world context—in the sense that Casanova meant as a space forged jointly by history, the social, and the cultural—may be better served by other vantage points.

This is where national literary history ought to be taken more seriously in its presentist moment, not just subsumed under past precedents where "nation" had not yet been invented.[14] As contemporary China redefines its relation to the world differently and reorganizes its internal cultural space in more tightly controlled ways, two observations can be made to this end. First, what scholars have analyzed in the past as diasporic literature in obvious settings like Taiwan, Hong Kong, or North America no longer encompasses all the different pathways that diasporic writing takes. Second, a closer cooperation between the space of literature and the space of rule inside China also makes it difficult to parse literature in the terms Casanova gave us, because the link between the world and the text, far from being lost, has only grown more complex.

A similar kind of geopolitical sea change prompted Goethe in 1827 to speculate on the world literary marketplace in the hope of accounting for all literary motions. A similar opening in scale from the regional to the national, or the national to the global, shook up China's sense of its place in the world in 1898 when diplomat Chen Jitong 陳季同 (1851–1907) first brought the idea of "world literature" (*shijie wenxue* 世界文學) to Shanghai, just as the Qing empire was at the beginning of its demise.[15]

"World literature," I suggest, is due for another transformation—much like the concept of literary history—this time oriented toward

14. See Chen, chapter 2 in this volume.
15. Tsu, *Sound and Script in Chinese Diaspora*, 123–24.

restructuring the framework of literary value as we know it. The new spaces that may emerge from this process are not merely diasporic, Sinophone, overseas, Chinese—or any of the familiar working rubrics—but created in tandem with China's global motion. Some of these movements had been there all along but remained unseen, like private letters sent across continents. Other groups coexist within the cultural, social, state, and foreign space of others, inside and outside of China. It is worth attempting a pivot away from the mainstream modern Chinese literary studies by redirecting attention to how to evaluate world literature when the perspective taken does not seek to give value. To this end, I identify three figurative spaces for analysis: (1) the syncretic, (2) the rebel, and (3) the governed. These are not intended to be topological or exhaustive categories but incomplete projects that fell between world spaces and literary histories.

The Syncretic

In a nineteenth-century Catholic church in Havana, known as Iglesia Nuestra Señora de La Caridad, visitors throng almost daily to the altar of Ochún. They adorn it with sunflowers, and no one seems to mind that Ochún is a local variant of the Virgin Mary—one of the many ways West African deities mixed with Catholic saints via enslaved Africans. In a side chamber next to the main altar at the front of the church, however, a more curious syncretism is on display. Hanging on the wall adjacent to the centerpiece—a statue of Christ on the crucifix—is a portrait of Guanyin, the female Bodhisattva. With an accentuated halo around her head, she is receiving three male visitors in the presence of a lamb. This peculiar rendering of the nativity scene was produced by the St. Joseph's Deaf and Dumb Artists Association in Tsim Sha Tsui in Hong Kong. The association was last listed in 1965 as located on the eleventh floor of El Mirador Mansion.[16] The drawing was a gift—though for whom, when, and for what purpose is not known.

That the two artifacts of syncretism could be displayed together at the church in the Caribbean compels us to see the Chinese element through

---

16. Gellhorn, *McKay's Guide to the Far East and Hawaii*, 103.

When Literary Relations End   243

a different lens. Here it is not at all strange to see Guanyin decontextualized, because the context for seeing that decontextualization was equally taken out of context and reblended into a new landscape. The link from southern China to Cuba has long been there, however. Since 1847, with the arrival of 571 Chinese laborers to work on the sugarcane plantations and railroads on the island, at least 125,000 Chinese peasants, mostly men from the southern provinces of Guangdong, Macau, and Fujian, had come to Cuba by 1874.[17] Some were retransported from California, where they had joined the Gold Rush and helped build the transcontinental railway, despite the Exclusion Acts that limited their entry from 1872 to 1943.[18] The history of Chinese laborers, particularly in California, helped to shape US immigration laws and prompted the Chinese to struggle for their permanent rights. The Chinese laborers in Cuba, in contrast, never rose above slavery. An 1874 report, commissioned by the Chinese government to investigate the horrors of widespread abuse, detailed the desperate conditions and extreme measures for survival.[19]

Chinese who migrated to Cuba brought with them the dialects and folk religious practices of their home villages and prefectures. These included Mazu, a folk deity widely observed among seafaring communities in Fujian, and Buddhist practices, hence the figure of Guanyin that became part of the local religious landscape. They intermarried with local women, and their Chinese dialects survived by mixing with creole and Spanish. Some of the expressions of the late nineteenth-century Chinese are still evident today, such as referring to the United States as "patterned flag country" or referring to the Chinese not as Zhongguoren 中國人 or Huaren 華人 but as Tangren 唐人—an older designation evoking the Tang dynasty.[20] Linguistic assimilation was too matter-of-fact and practical to be called concerted strategies.

Under these circumstances, a new literary channel opened up. A few letters were sent home, following by remittances, which the Chinese clan

17. See Hu-DeHart, "Chinese Coolie Labour in Cuba," 67–86; López, *Chinese Cubans*; Meagher, *The Coolie Trade*.

18. See Salyer, *Laws Harsh as Tigers*, chaps. 2–4.

19. See *The Cuba Commission Report*.

20. Lei Jingxuan, *Yuanzai Guba*, 41. See also the collected memoirs in Lei Jingxuan, *Molu yimin*.

244   JING TSU

associations helped set up and deliver with the correspondence. These personal writings maintained the norms and conventions of Chinese writing, despite being part of a syncretic landscape. In one such letter written to his wife in July 1961, a Chinese man in Cuba tried to assure his wife of his emotional fidelity with style and eloquence:

> As I continued to read your letter, I can't help but pace back and forth. You accused me of lingering in this foreign land, being too absorbed in pleasure to think of returning, and having taken on a new love. How you've wronged me! Yet I can't blame you for complaining out of hardship, so now I will tell you the truth. A man is no grass or wood, and should he on occasion seek out flowers and pay visit to willows, it is but to be expected of the life of an overseas guest in a foreign land. As for taking on a new wife, the thought never crossed my mind. Please believe me, I am not a heartless bloke or a faithless man. There is not a moment when I don't think about my wife and children. I only regret that I have yet to make good on my ambitions and that I have disappointed you, putting you and the family through this hardship and destitution. This is my fault, and I hope you can forgive everything that I've done.[21]

Familiar literary expressions made this short letter stand out. To "seek out flowers and pay visit to willows" was a common reference to illicit sexual pleasures, a euphemism already common in Tang dynasty vernacular writings and with a poetic etymology that can be traced back to the songwriter Liu Yong 柳永 (987–1053), who mastered the art of circumspection by famously recounting his amorous encounters in the pleasure quarters with synecdochal suggestiveness. "Man is neither grass nor wood" is the perfect moral complement to illicit pleasures. The phrase was common vernacular usage in late Ming fiction. The idea that humans were susceptible to feelings became almost a platitude in popular works like *Water Margin* (*Shuihu zhuan* 水滸傳). The phrase usually invited a follow-up reflection on human sentience and the desire to do right. Here, though, it is turned into the husband's justification for having been led astray. Without the stylistic dressing and literary conventions to elevate its content, his letter would have been a rather uninspiring piece of con-

---

21. Lei Jingxuan, *Yuanzai Guba*, 28–29.

When Literary Relations End

fession. With no wife around, a failing business, gambling addiction, and plenty of native women to mix with, he had little to offer his loyal wife at home if not poetic consolation.

These expressions were neither uniquely literary nor used in an original way. That was not their role. In a syncretic space, literary conventions are invoked to enliven a familiar cultural repertoire—not to innovate it. He wrote it for the sake of his wife back home, where such platitudes had meaning and signified something familiar.

Writing home opened the unofficial channels that extended this cultural pathway from a place of syncretism. The authors were deliberate in their use of known expressions so that their experiences and choices abroad were easily recognizable across distance, translatable at home. Cast in legible conventions, the husband's confession to dalliance was thereby not adulterous but made human, almost deserving of sympathy. High literary aesthetics, as an alternative, would not have served the need to reinforce the social bonds or make them durable in the world space. The syncretic helped literary conventions mix and signal a commonality.

Epistolary writings create a form of syncretized literary space that by definition travel a distance, that is, to be sent, to be read, to arrive somewhere else. Letters are a spatializing form of writing, yet they have long been overlooked in the world literary space because they were assumed to be private. Just as one allows for texts to be translated and read in unintended linguistic contexts, though, there is reason to give private writings the same consideration.

One reason epistolary writings have not been recognized as an important form of diasporic writing is that the implicit preference in world literature bends toward the novel form. Novelistic reconstructions of the indentured labor experiences—and in English, the currency language of world literature—have better spoken for that history.[22] Scholars have long

---

22. Cuban-born American novelist Cristina García's *Monkey Hunting* (2003) interposes the experiences of five generations of African Cuban Chinese with those of a black creole Cuban woman. Ruthanne Lum McCunn draws on historical documents to create a fictional account, *God of Luck* (2007), of the Chinese laborers in Peru, a common stopover on the way to Cuba, thereby fusing genres to retell the story. In Patricia Powell's *The Pagoda* (1998), set in Jamaica, mixing and fusion take a literal, physical form: the female protagonist Lau A-Yin, who was raised and dressed as a boy in China, finds her gender-crossed clothes fused with her skin upon arriving at the island.

been habituated to seeing diasporic literature as outside of canonical literature, rather than as a medium that carries it to other parts of the world. Letters by Chinese emigrants around the world have only recently garnered attention.[23] The Chinese were trafficked to Southeast Asia, Africa, the Americas, Australia, and the Caribbean. Their literary space—attached to host places and never quite singularly Chinese—is where the conversion between syncretism and nativism can take place.

That kind of fused spatiality has been much sought after as of late. In recent times, different Chinese writings—American Cuban, Hong Konger, Jamaican, mainland Chinese, Fujianese, Brazilian Chinese, and so on—seek to recast diasporic syncretism as their own particular, claimed experience.[24] This letter from the Chinese man in Cuba to his wife, for example, has been kept in a private family archive. It was published by his grandson, Lei Jingxuan 雷竞璇, as part of a personal quest to reconnect to that overseas history.[25]

Yet this attempted recovery and preservation can only be accomplished by believing that that link had been lost. Apart from individuals' recuperated memory, these syncretic spaces are also being reoccupied in China's current national narrative. Since the 1990s, China has taken a greater interest in the writings of Chinese migrants. Scholarly conferences and state TV series have been produced to document and recover that history in accordance with a narrative of China's rise, explicitly linking it to a form of people power.[26] China's global vision includes overturning a history of neglect toward its overseas people to inspire a kind of global nationalism. What prompted the Chinese to write home and the literary space those writings built, in other words, is being reabsorbed into a new syncretism between writing, state power, and reworlding. The letter, as an example, testifies to how this fusion can separate itself out as well as recombine into new configurations.

23. Benton and Liu, *Dear China: Emigrant Letters*.

24. Yuan Yiping, *Tixiao jia Baxi*; Young, *Pao*; Lee-DiStefano, *Three Asian-Hispanic Writers*; López-Calvo, *Dragons in the Land of the Condor*.

25. Lei Jingxuan, *Yuanzai Guba* and *Molu yimin*.

26. A number of articles and discussions appear on the state's official website for the Belt and Road Initiative. See, for instance, Chen Yiping, "Huaqiao Huaren." Critics worry that these policies aim to blur the distinction between the Chinese in China and those outside of China. See Sun Xi, "Dajia tan Zhongguo"; Lou Yu, "Zhongguo dui Lamei."

Not all forms of shared space can blend or adapt, however. A different case has to be made for insisting on standing out, or being left behind, as though to freeze the motion of diaspora in a single frame. Writers who acquired a regional or local following tend to be poignantly aware of the next step up on the scale of literature. They rebel against the limits of their marginality by insisting on honoring a greater contract between what they write about and the language in which they write. Without available recourse to ready-made national literary history, they struggle for their niche in a different way.

The Rebel

The rebel is a figure of nostalgia in the Chinese world literary space. In China's modern history, the rebels against the Qing rule, after the non-Chinese Manchus from the northeast overran the Ming empire in 1644, are still commemorated as the true die-hard loyalists to the last Chinese-run empire. Dissident literature and poetry after 1949, especially after 1989, claim a similar position of conscientious patriotism, often holding the status quo up to a better version of itself. The Nationalists, in this way, held themselves as the true bearers of the proper Chinese cultural lineage, whereas the Red Guards—through the same trope—assume themselves to be the vanguards of revolution. In other words, the rebel is first and foremost a figure of opposition, a separatist stance that allows it to be externalized as the object of nostalgia.

For lack of a better word, though, "nostalgia" has come to encompass a whole range of complex affects in relation to one's homeland. There have been ample scholarly arguments against nostalgia as a binding experience in Chinese diaspora because of its subservience to the ideal of return. Sauling Wong argued that the rerooting experience in the migratory context is what gives overseas Chinese a second life, while Shu-mei Shih has outright rejected diaspora in fear of any echo that might support mainland Chinese chauvinism.[27]

27. Wong, "Global Vision and Locatedness," 35–46; and Shih, "Against Diaspora," 80–110.

248 JING TSU

Still, such arguments do not do justice to the varied world space that the Chinese writers have long inhabited and written in. What distinguishes a nostalgic from a rebel is dependent on the side he or she takes with respect to the lost status quo. An outlaw in the eyes of the Qing might be a loyal subject to the Ming; a temporary sojourner or traitor from a nationalistic perspective is a permanent guest settler in the host context; a communist sympathizer in Taiwan can be branded as a friend or traitor to the leftist ideology; a dissident from the inside is a person who speaks truth to power on the outside.[28]

For many overseas Chinese writers, their loyalties are put to the test as they move from guest to citizen or are forced to choose between this and that side of patriotism. While syncretism accounts for fusion and adaptation, the rebel has to maintain his or her opposition out of allegiance to a distant homeland that is largely maintained in a nostalgic imaginary; he has to write for the host context and local audience and preserve an inner allegiance to a different, idealized place of belonging. The rebel assimilates himself to where he is situated—not to fit in but to stand out by holding on to a different cause. This often plays out in the insistence with which he writes in Chinese, especially when it is prized not as a literary language but as a minority tongue.

In the 1950s, a pressing concern for Indonesian Chinese writer Huang Dongping was to find a way to publish in a mainland Chinese literary journal. It was the recognition that every writer writing in Chinese outside of China coveted. The cross-straits politics that would come to define the fraught relationship between Taiwan and mainland China had not yet solidified, and overseas loyalties were not nearly as divided. The closest Huang Dongping could manage at the time was Hong Kong. He recalled hand copying his own manuscript.[29] Each stroke of the character had to be heavily imprinted to press through layers of carbon paper. The editors in Hong Kong did not always understand his lexical usage, which showed time and distance from standard Chinese. They misarranged his

---

28. See Tsai, *A Passage to China*:; Chen Yingzhen 陳映真 (1937–2016), "'Guiyingzi zhishi fenzi' he 'zhuanxiang zhenghouqun'" 鬼影子知識分子和轉向症候群, in Chen Yingzhen, *Chen Yingzhen wenxuan*, 489.

29. Huang Dongping, *Duanpian erji*, 70–75, 266–90, 296–305; *Huang Dongping quanji*.

text in the process of typesetting and put some of the characters in the wrong order, which Huang had to correct by repeating the painstaking process all over again.

Reaching a mainland Chinese readership was difficult for many writers, but it was still the ultimate affirmation of one's achievement as a Chinese-language writer outside of China. Huang Dongping had made his fame among the Chinese in Indonesia with his trilogy, *Songs of Sojourn* (*Qiaoge sanqu* 僑歌三曲), a three-part epic that documents the plight of the Chinese in Indonesia through the volatile political, social, and ethnic landscape in the region. In a faithfully realist style, the trilogy reads like reportage but with strong subjective pathos. Huang wanted the story of overseas Chinese to be heard back home, emotionally unfiltered.

To many contemporary critics in the Chinese-speaking world, this was too much realism—too raw for aesthetic digestion, too distant to be a core part of Chinese literary history. The home audience Huang Dongping had imagined was one that would feel the urgency of the overseas Chinese experience as much as he did, but Huang was not much discussed beyond his coterie of regional readers and fans. He remains a rather underacknowledged figure even under the capacious tent of Sinophone studies, which has shown a strong preference for modernist writers in its selection of marginality. The exclusion is fitting in some ways, as Huang was never a self-professed writer, let alone a world writer. His loyalty and concern were grounded in the local, and writing always meant scribbling things down in one's private time while making ends meet with other jobs. His literary writings were out of sync with the aesthetic concerns of the mainstream Chinese literary space into which he sought to reintegrate.

Huang Dongping was born in East Kalimatan in 1923. His family came from the tiny speck of an island Quemoy off the coast of Taiwan, which was significant for his later local canonization. Quemoy was strategically important during the Cold War as a first line of defense against any potential takeover from the mainland. His father took the family back there in 1932, when Huang was twelve. After the island fell to Japanese control during the Pacific War, they took refuge in Hong Kong, only returning to Southeast Asia in 1941.

Chinese-language books were available, and Huang immersed himself in them and avidly read the literary supplement in Chinese-language newspapers. It was a popular (perhaps the only) circulated platform for Chinese writing. Huang did not continue any formal education after returning to Indonesia. He secured a job working as an accounts keeper in a dry goods store that sold dried fish paste. It was his job for the next several decades. Between taking inventories, he read Lu Xun 魯迅 (1881–1936).

In a country where the Chinese language has to exist alongside Dutch, Japanese, English, and Indonesian (established as the national language in 1945), Huang had to teach himself how to be a writer. Writers like Lu Xun and Yu Dafu were looked to as the giants of modern Chinese literature. But the Chinese language was not easy to acquire as a minority language in Southeast Asia, a subject Huang delved into in his shorter works, such as "An Orphan Seeks Education" ("Gu'er qiuxue ji" 孤兒求學記) and "A Teacher's Experience" ("Yige jiaoshi de jingyu" 一個教師的境遇). In Indonesia and Malaysia, Chinese-language schools were mostly privately funded by Chinese businesspeople, with no formal instruction available in the public school system. The language was banned at several points due to ethnic and political tensions. The Nationalists and communists of China competed in Southeast Asia to win over the hearts and minds of overseas Chinese by sending language textbooks and embedding messages of patriotism in language teaching.

Huang acculturated himself to writerly Chinese by hand-copying the works of established mainland modern Chinese writers; he tried internalizing their style. He reminisced about how he had to set up an oasis for himself in the storage area in the back of the store, where the heavy stench and wet debris of sugar-salt curing mixtures soaked the cement floor. Next to where Huang put his books, other employees lined up their toothbrushes, rinse cups, and dishes of soap in a jagged row. Huang worked on his notes and collected newspaper clippings for possible storylines in between tasks. In this unlikely setting for creativity, he passed a decade trying to improve his written Chinese.

It paid off, and he was prolific. Sustained by the tumultuous political periods in Southeast Asia, he lived through the end of Dutch colonialism, Japanese occupation, Indonesia's struggle for nationalism, and their rippling and often conflicting effect on the ethnic Chinese communities. The Chinese, for instance, were made scapegoats during the massacre under Sukarno in 1955–1956 and were again the targeted ethnic group in the riots of May 1998. These events exposed the long-standing economic and social tensions between Chinese and their host communities:

> To think: hundreds of millions of my fellow countrymen, over generations, left their homes and livelihood to travel far across oceans and disperse to such expansive, foreign corners of the earth. On the soil that belonged to other peoples, what kind of life did they lead? . . . It is radically different from the life lived in one's own country, because it is a life of forced exiles: a life that depends on self-reliance amidst other clans, a life eked out under the oppression and killings of the colonizers. . . . As an overseas Chinese who was raised abroad, what can I do for the overseas Chinese community? That is the question I always ask myself. I immersed myself in the lives of the vastly different types of Chinese—their life, thoughts, emotions, and needs, before I gradually realized that recording their lives is the only work someone like me can do—without a motive for profit and only for the sake of tinkering with the pen.[30]

Huang's loyalty to the history of overseas Chinese was self-ordained. No one else assigned him that task; no patriotism bound him to that duty. The choice to commemorate the hundreds of thousands of Chinese across generations—who were mostly voiceless and left no written records—was assumed by him as a witness's responsibility. In so doing, he wrote in a rebel space, insistently against the grain of the dominant society in Indonesia, but also out of step with what the actual Chinese audience at home would read and identify with. After all, an educated urban reader in Hong Kong may find it just as unfamiliar to read about the experience of a nineteenth-century Chinese laborer as a Muslim Indonesian would.

To introduce another layer of incongruency in the rebel space, Huang's reputation landed him in an unusual place in the recent reconfiguration of world literary space. Both Quemoy and Indonesia enshrined him as their writer. To Quemoy, Huang is one of their own by claims of origin; for the Chinese in Indonesia, he is part of the story of the country's independence. Since 2003, the Quemoy provincial government embarked on a project of publishing a "Quemoy literature series," which produced

---

30. Huang Dongping, *Duanpian erji*, 281–84.

thirty volumes of Quemoy works, including work by ten overseas writers. The same initiative drove the first publication of Huang's complete works in ten volumes in 2004.[31] The reason for this retroactive acknowledgment had to do with Quemoy's increasing local consciousness. Unwilling to be simply swept up in the political currents between the mainland and Taiwan, Quemoy seeks a role as a nodal point between mainland China and Taiwan in cross-straits relations. As the project's key architect, Yang Shuqing 楊樹清, explains, Quemoy's significance does not reside in its past but instead lies in its "cultural role as the 'intermediary'":[32]

> Apart from maintaining a mutually dependent relationship with mainland China . . . [Quemoy] serves as a conduit for the westward spread of the Central Plains [i.e., Chinese] culture, transmitting it to the Taiwan Straits to places like Penghu, Taiwan, and across the South China Seas. It carried the Min [i.e., southern Chinese topolect] influence southward by establishing a second home in the South Seas [i.e., Southeast Asia]. Be it Singapore, Malaysia, Indonesia, Brunei, the Philippines, Indochina, or North America—the Quemoy people are everywhere, along with their clan associations and cultural centers.

The literary space of the rebel is highly desirable for the process of institutionalization. Nothing erects a new literary center more effectively than performing a canonizing power that honors writers and, at the same time, enlists them under its registry. Because the rebel writer always writes from a place different from where he stands, he is particularly desirable as a potential recruit. Rebel writing persists in a nongoverned space, which makes it all the more valuable for different national traditions to claim this kind of outlier as theirs. It is no coincidence that Huang Dongping

---

31. Quemoy is not unique in this case. Other recent precedents include Macau literature, largely driven and canonized by the Macao Foundation (Aomen jijinhui) in an effort to build "cultural confidence" (*wenhua zixin* 文化自信); see http://www.xinhuanet.com/book/2017-01/04/c_129431516.htm. In building its own identity, Taiwan has fostered the production of Hakka literature to showcase its multiethnic literary humanity.

32. Yang Shuqing, "Jinmen zu yu Jinmen xue" 金門族與金門學, in Yang Shuqing, *Jinmen zuqun fazhan*, xxi–xx.

When Literary Relations End 253

is sought after by multiple traditions that happen to be also trying to reinvent their modern story. Quemoy is responding to the geopolitical priorities of Taiwan and mainland China in the region while Chinese Indonesia is also reacting and competing for influence. In this way, their shared interest in Huang's works provides a rare demonstration of how value is generated in the regional and world literary chain. The attention lavished on his works is double-edged, because it is not an accreditation of him having "made it" as a writer, but a way of co-opting the rebel as subject.

Both the syncretic and the rebel operate in ways that are ambiguous in rule, hybrid in their ethnoscape, and partly unclaimable. Their intended audiences, similarly, also change according to circumstance. Yet there remains the question of what happened to this process when the space of literature coincides with the space of rule—when there are no ambiguities or margins to exploit to one's advantage. Casanova had envisioned that the restored link between literature, history, and the world would also preserve the singularity, or integrity, of the literary text. But what if singularity becomes absorbed into a new scheme of worlding altogether? When world and text coincide and rejoin, what more is there to be desired of the literary space? These questions, finally, bring us to the last configuration to be discussed—the governed.

The Governed

For decades, literary scholars have used the term "singularity" to describe the irreducible experience of interacting with a literary text—the unique event that has been enshrined as the act of reading. Casanova's reliance on the transparency of the term affirms a long-held opposition between text as a singular event, on one hand, and text that stands in the world as a horizon of shared experience, on the other. In recent years, a different notion of singularity has overtaken the signification of that term. Singularity, for futurist Ray Kurzweil, is a coming technological state in which the velocity of change self-generates at an exponential, not incremental, rate. In the 2019 short story by contemporary science fiction writer Chen

Qiufan 陳楸帆 (b. 1981), "Fear Machine" ("Kongju jiqi" 恐懼機器), the two definitions collide.[33]

Chen Qiufan's futuristic tale is set on a new planet in the distant future, where the human genome is manipulated by machines. Under this condition, humans evolve through an artificially intensified process of natural selection. A breed of fearless young male warriors, known as Artificial Genome Units, is born. Their sex organs removed so as to maintain full aggression, they slaughter and demolish and are driven solely by the instinct for conquest. Yet an anomaly appears in their midst. Ah Gu 阿古, unlike the others, feels fear and is also paralyzed by it. He is rejected by the group as an imperfect specimen and a danger to the group's survival, so he is left alone to pursue his own quest to eradicate the cowardly sensation.

Along the way, he comes across sphinx-like figures who give him counsel and company but are ultimately unable to help him. Until, that is, he finally meets an entity, in the human form of a fisherman, called Fragment. Their doubling of one another is suggested by a symbiotic relationship whereby one is differentiated from the other like pearl and clam. Unbound by the laws of space and time, Fragment can be in several places at once. He helps Ah Gu come to the realization that the fear in him was an intended flaw. His fear was algorithmically programmed into the system to introduce randomness in reaction and decision making so that the engineered evolution does not proceed solely in one direction—that is, turning cloned young men into perfect killing machines—but absorbs new genetic material for diversification.

Fragment speaks with apparent profundity. His speech is philosophical while technical. In a rather enigmatic Socratic dialogue, he weighs Ah Gu's questions by providing topical information but never giving direct commentary. He is strikingly immune to any expressions of sympathy toward Ah Gu's plight, which the other interlocutors were at least moved to acknowledge. He is a straight interlocutor with no detectable ulterior motives or stakes of his own and is almost coldly clinical in his take on the situation. This all makes sense when we learn, in a footnote at the end of the story, that Fragment's part of the dialogue was generated by

---

33. Chen Qiufan, "Kongju jiqi," in Chen Qiufan, *Rensheng suanfa*.

an algorithm. It was modeled on Chen Qiufan's style of writing as interpreted and taught through machine learning.

That was the experiment at the core of the short story collection *The Algorithm for Life* (*Rensheng suanfa* 人生算法), in which "Fear Machine" was the final piece. Chen Qiufan worked for the Chinese tech giant and search engine company Baidu when he was working on becoming a science fiction writer, and his interest in artificial intelligence and cloning was prefigured in the obsession with mirroring, doubles, and automatons in his earlier writings. "Balin" 巴鱗, the eponymous short story about a half-human, half-beast character, centers on an extended physical duel between the young male protagonist and Balin. Balin mimics his physical gestures like an automaton trying to reproduce the behavior of the original.

The exploration in these stories of how to generate original, autonomous will in a constructed feedback loop poses the question of breaking control and introducing true singularity. In "Fear Machine," the singularity that ended up releasing spontaneous genetic evolution was a flaw; in "Balin" it was the counterpoint of the nonhuman. In both instances, without the spontaneity of agency, the uniqueness of the literary text is no longer an experience dependent on the human subject. The unexpected happens regardless of whether or not humans grasp it. Singularity now operates beyond and even independent of human agency.

Chinese science fiction has become a major platform for questioning human-dictated control—and human centrism. Skeptical of and even hostile to mainstream modern Chinese and intellectual humanism, it sets itself apart by rejecting the human as the measure of all things. It was Liu Cixin 劉慈欣 (b. 1963), author of *Three-Body Problem* (*Santi* 三體), who made the charge explicit:

> In my limited encounter with literature, it is as though there is always a nagging voice telling me that this speck of a planet, and this flicker of time that humans occupy is all that is worth putting into expression and feeling. The rest of the expanse of time and space is not worth a partial glance, because there is no human, therefore no humanity, because literature is humanity. . . . That is why the impression literature gave me is that it is an act of supreme narcissism.[34]

34. Liu Cixin, "Chaoyue zilian," 75–81.

The point, however, is not that all humanism is bad—only the variety that has been amply associated with conquest and Western-style colonialism. Liu Cixin and Chen Qiufan thematize that prominently in their works. Liu Cixin draws his theory of alien-human encounter from the model of the settlers' annihilation of the Native American peoples in North America (though notably not from China's own history of taming the southern frontier). By scaling up humanism to the cosmos—not just the world—writers like Liu and Chen are reaching for a new standard for humanity. As Ken Liu, Liu Cixin's translator and fellow sci fi writer, explains of writers' current perspective: "when you go into space, you become part of this overall collective called 'humanity.' You're no longer Chinese, American, Russian, or whatever. Your culture is left behind. You're now just 'humanity' with a capital H, in space."[35] The message here is that the new host leading this conversation about humans' fate in the cosmos is concerned with what it means to be, first and foremost, human. For science fiction writers, thinking about the fate of humanity rather than that of a single people is perfectly in keeping with its mission. Yet that futuristic vision cannot help but bring the geopolitics of the present to bear. A notable change in tone is that the Chinese are leading this conversation—once the provenance of Western invocations of humanity, where it required no "Western" qualifier. Via fiction written in Chinese, Liu's suggestion is that for sci fi writers this normalization should seem so matter-of-fact that no national qualifiers would be necessary; "Chinese" is the new universal.

Chinese science fiction has risen in recent years as a rare contemporary genre that enjoys the auspices of the state and its official channels. Few other countries have start-up companies that are devoted to growing science fiction—from identifying, training, and promoting writers to translating and marketing them abroad. These agencies are also in frequent collaboration with the space industry, artificial intelligence institutes, and other key areas of national defense research to introduce writers to contemporary topics that are of national interest. In August 2020, the National Film Bureau (part of the state entity that regulates ideology-related work) and the China Association for Science and Technology (a nongov-

35. Sonnad, "Inside the World of Chinese Science Fiction."

ernmental association of Chinese scientists and engineers) jointly published a directive, "Some views on promoting the development of science fiction films" ("Guanyu cujin kehuan dianying fazhan de ruogan yijian" 關於促進科幻電影發展的若干意見). It identifies film as the primary medium for propagating science fiction, although it is implicit that sci fi writers will continue to generate the storyline and content. It urges the industry to observe Xi Jinping's 習近平 (b. 1953) thought in following the "correct direction" and highlighting "Chinese values, inherit[ing] Chinese culture and aesthetics," and disseminating "scientific thought." The directive also emphasizes high-tech special visual effects in film, an area, it is urged, where Chinese sci fi cultural workers can shine. Science fiction once again shifts into a literary space that can be aligned with, and even complements, current state visions.

By virtue of its futuristic bent, science fiction converges with China's forward-looking design—and their explicit reliance on science and technology for governance—ever since the time of Deng Xiaoping 鄧小平 (1904–1997). Multiyear plans like 2025, 2035, 2049, and so on are not simply the vestiges of a Soviet-styled socialist planned economy but bids for the future. Science fiction happens to assist in promoting science and technology by providing an additional narrative alongside China's miraculous rise since the 1980s. The genre has not always coincided harmoniously with state directives, to be sure, having come under assault and censorship at several points in the twentieth century. It has certainly never reached the shores of high literature or intellectual culture prior to now; it rose from the bottom up.

Together with the syncretic and the rebel spaces, the governed has always been deeply embedded in the historical, the social, and the world. As the world space now responds to new influencers, new universalisms are being put forth, while the existing ones, stemming from a more familiar Western worldview, have every intention of keeping their place. The moment is rife for reconsidering whether world literature needs to be preserved as a heuristic label, historical artifact, or simply a common dissensus. With Casanova's world space, it was simpler. French hegemony was the historical given, leaving only its ramifications for critical examination. With the controversy over modern Chinese poetry in the world, it was also simple. World literature used to be a place of value; everyone recognizes and desires the same prize. Yet now, smaller ecologies exist, and they do not look to the same value chain. The question of just who is dominating or hosting the world space has become more important than the representation it supports.

* * *

When literary relations end, they cease in the terms in which they have been known, but not in their relations to the world. That obligation does not terminate. In the cases where writers opt out of world participation, their decision to sit on the sidelines or preference to be insignificant still speaks volumes as to why the world can never be uniform or fair. Only when the world literary space risks falling apart do these limitations become clear and, hopefully, instructive. Those broken relations we can mend and transform, only if world literature tries to extend beyond its academic and institutional purpose in renewing its own engagement with the world. Underlying all three cases I analyzed here is a modest proposal: the world space for literature is simply *the world*. Restoring lost links means renewing the ones that have always been there and acquiring new and adjacent fields of knowledge to illuminate how the world works. Rarely has literature been tasked with this kind of worldly responsibility and social commitment. The world now—where nothing has yet been set in stone and everything is in motion—demands at least a serious and extended reflection on literary value as made, not given, and on how it perhaps always serves the purpose of now rather than the future. After all, few relationships last forever, but they can always try a new beginning.

Works Cited

Allen, Joseph R. *In the Voice of Others: Chinese Music Bureau Poetry*. Ann Arbor: Center for Chinese Studies, University of Michigan, 1992.

Allen, Sarah M. "Narrative Genres." In *The Oxford Handbook of Classical Chinese Literature (1000 BCE–900 CE)*, edited by Wiebke Denecke, Wai-yee Li, and Xiaofei Tian, 273–87. Oxford: Oxford University Press, 2017.

————. *Shifting Stories: History, Gossip, and Lore in Narratives from Tang Dynasty China*. Cambridge, MA: Harvard University Asia Center, 2014.

An Hwak 安廓. *Chosŏn munhaksa* 朝鮮文學史. Seoul: Hanil Sŏjŏm, 1922.

Asami Yōji 浅見洋二. *Chūgoku no shigaku ninshiki: Chūsei kara kinsei e no tenkan* 中国の詩学認識: 中世から近世への転換. Tokyo: Sōbunsha, 2008.

Ashmore, Robert. "Recent-Style *Shi* Poetry: Heptasyllabic Regulated Verse (*Qiyan Lüshi*)." In *How to Read Chinese Poetry: A Guided Anthology*, edited by Zong-qi Cai, 181–98. New York: Columbia University Press, 2008.

Bacon, Francis. *De dignitate et augmentis scientiarum*, 1604. Turnhout: Brepols, 2010.

Bai Juyi 白居易. *Bai Juyi ji jianjiao* 白居易集箋校. Annotated by Zhu Jincheng 朱金城. 6 vols. Shanghai: Shanghai guji chubanshe, 1988.

Baker, Russell. "Best Time to Be Alive; No Time Like the Past." *New York Times Magazine*, April 18, 1999. https://www.nytimes.com/1999/04/18/magazine/best-time-to-be-alive-no-time-like-the-past.html.

Balsamo, Luigi. *Bibliography: History of a Tradition*. Berkeley, CA: Rosenthal, 1990.

Ban Gu 班固. *Han shu* 漢書. Annotated by Yan Shigu 顏師古. 12 vols. Beijing: Zhonghua shuju, 1962.

Bender, Lucas Rambo. "Against the Monist Model of Tang Poetics." *T'oung Pao* 107, nos. 5–6 (2021): 633–87.

————. "The Corrected Interpretations of the Five Classics (*Wujing zhengyi*) and the Tang Legacy of Obscure Learning (*Xuanxue*)." *T'oung Pao* 105, nos. 1–2 (2019): 76–127.

260   *Works Cited*

———. *Du Fu Transforms: Tradition and Ethics amid Societal Collapse*. Cambridge, MA: Harvard University Asia Center, 2021.

Benjamin, Walter. *Illuminations*. Edited by Hannah Arendt. Translated by Harry Zohn. New York: Harcourt, Brace, & World, 1968.

Bennett-Kastor, Tina L. *Multiliterate Ireland: Literary Manifestations of a Multilingual History*. Lanham, MD: Lexington Books, 2015.

Benton, Gregor, and Liu Hong. *Dear China: Emigrant Letters and Remittances, 1820–1980*. Berkeley: University of California Press, 2018.

Bingham, Woodbridge. "The Rise of Li in a Ballad Prophecy." *Journal of the American Oriental Society* 61, no. 4 (1941): 272–80.

Binski, Paul. *Medieval Death: Ritual and Representation*. Ithaca, NY: Cornell University Press, 1996.

Blanco, María del Pilar, and Esther Peeren, eds. *The Spectralities Reader: Ghosts and Haunting in Contemporary Cultural Theory*. London: Bloomsbury, 2013.

Blum, Rudolf. *Bibliographia: An Inquiry into Its Definitions and Designations*. Translated by Mathilde V. Rovelstad. Chicago: American Library Association, 1980.

Bokenkamp, Stephen. "Time after Time: Taoist Apocalyptic History and the Founding of the T'ang Dynasty." *Asia Major*, 3rd series, 7, no. 1 (1994): 59–88.

Bol, Peter K. *"This Culture of Ours": Intellectual Transitions in T'ang and Sung China*. Stanford, CA: Stanford University Press, 1992.

Bolianzi 柏蓮子. *Gudai yuyan quanshu: Zhongguo chenyao wenhua* 古代預言全書: 中國讖謠文化. Changchun: Shidai wenyi chubanshe, 1999.

Boyd, Brian. *Why Lyrics Last: Evolution, Cognition, and Shakespeare's Sonnets*. Cambridge, MA: Harvard University Press, 2012.

Brindley, Erica Fox. *Ancient China and the Yue: Perceptions and Identities on the Southern Frontier, c. 400 BCE–50 CE*. Cambridge: Cambridge University Press, 2015.

Broadwell, Peter, Jack W. Chen, and David Shepard. "Reading the *Quan Tang shi*: Literary History, Topic Modeling, Divergence Measures." *Digital Humanities Quarterly* 13, no. 4 (2019). http://www.digitalhumanities.org/dhq/vol/13/4/000434/000434.html.

Burke, Seán, ed. *Authorship: From Plato to the Postmodern: A Reader*. Edinburgh: Edinburgh University Press, 1995.

Cambridge History of English and American Literature, edited by A. W. Ward et al. New York: Bartleby.com, 2000 (digitized from print edition: New York: Putnam 1907–21).

Campany, Robert Ford. *The Chinese Dreamscape, 300 BCE–800 CE*. Cambridge, MA: Harvard University Asia Center, 2020.

———. "Ghosts Matter: The Culture of Ghosts in Six Dynasties *Zhiguai*." *Chinese Literature: Essays, Articles, Reviews* 13 (December 1991): 15–34.

Carruthers, Mary. *The Book of Memory: A Study of Memory in Medieval Culture*. Cambridge: Cambridge University Press, 1990.

Casanova, Pascale. "Literature as a World." *New Left Review* 31 (January–February 2005): 71–90.

———. *The World Republic of Letters*. Translated by M. B. DeBevoise. Cambridge, MA: Harvard University Press, 2004.

Works Cited

Cerquiglini, Bernard. *In Praise of the Variant: A Critical History of Philology*. Translated by Betsy Wing. Baltimore: Johns Hopkins University Press, 1999.

Chan, Kwok Kou Leonard. "*Wen* and the 'First History(-ies)' of Chinese Literature." In *A New Literary History of Modern China*, edited by David Der-wei Wang, 190–95. Cambridge, MA: Harvard University Press, 2017.

Cheah, Pheng, and David Damrosch. "What Is a World (Literature)? A Conversation." *Journal of World Literature* 4 (2019): 305–29.

Chen, Jack W. "On the Act and Representation of Reading in Medieval China." *Journal of the American Oriental Society* 129, no. 1 (January–March 2009): 57–71.

———. "Poetry, Ghosts, Mediation." *Qui Parle* 31, no. 1 (June 2022): 7–26.

Chen, Jack W., Anatoly Detwyler, Xiao Liu, Christopher M. B. Nugent, and Bruce Rusk, eds. *Literary Information in China: A History*. New York: Columbia University Press, 2021.

Chen, Pingyuan. "The Story of Literary History." In *The Oxford Handbook of Modern Chinese Literatures*, edited by Carlos Rojas and Andrea Bachner, 92–111. Oxford: Oxford University Press, 2016.

Chen Qiufan 陳楸帆. *Rensheng suanfa* 人生算法. Beijing: Zhongxin chubanshe, 2019.

Chen Qiyou 陳奇猷, ed. and annot. *Han Feizi jishi* 韓非子集釋. 2 vols. Shanghai: Shanghai renmin chubanshe, 1974.

Chen Yingzhen 陳映真. *Chen Yingzhen wenxuan* 陳映真文選. Beijing: Sanlian shudian, 2009.

Chen Yiping 陳奕平. "Huaqiao Huaren yu 'Yidai yilu' ruanshili jianshe" 華僑華人與一帶一路軟實力建設. https://www.ydylcn.com/zjgd/334718.shtml.

Cheng Hao 程顥 and Cheng Yi 程頤. *Er Cheng yishu* 二程遺書. Shanghai: Shanghai guji chubanshe, 1992.

Cheng Junying 程俊英 and Jiang Jianyuan 蔣見元. *Shi jing zhuxi* 詩經注析. 2 vols. Beijing: Zhonghua shuju, 1991.

Cheng Yizhong 程毅中. *Tangdai xiaoshuo shi* 唐代小説史. Beijing: Renmin wenxue chubanshe, 2003.

———. "*Yiwen ji* kao" 異聞集考. In *Gu xiaoshuo jianmu* 古小説簡目, 131–49. Beijing: Zhonghua shuju, 1981.

———. "*Yu Chu zhi* de bianzhe he banben" 虞初志的編者和版本. *Wenxian* 文獻 2 (1988): 39–42.

Childs-Johnson, Elizabeth. "The Ghost Head Mask and Metamorphic Shang Imagery." *Early China* 20 (1995): 79–92.

Cho, Heekyoung. *Translation's Forgotten History: Russian Literature, Japanese Mediation, and the Formation of Modern Korean Literature*. Cambridge, MA: Harvard University Asia Center, 2016.

Cho Tong-il 趙東一. *Higashi Ajia bungakushi hikakuron* 東アジア文学史比較論. Translated by Toyofuku Kenji 豊福健二. Tokyo: Hakuteisha, 2010.

Choo, Jessey J. C. "*Yiwen leiju*." In *Early Medieval Chinese Texts: A Bibliographic Guide*, edited by Cynthia L. Chennault, Keith N. Knapp, Alan J. Berkowitz, and Albert E. Dien, 454–64. Berkeley: Institute of East Asian Studies, 2015.

Chow, Rey. *Writing Diaspora: Tactics of Intervention in Contemporary Cultural Studies*. Bloomington: Indiana University Press, 1993.

Works Cited

Chunqiu Zuo zhuan zhushu 春秋左傳注疏. Annotated by Du Yu 杜預 and Kong Yingda 孔穎達. In Ruan Yuan 阮元, ed., *Chongkan Songben Shisanjing zhushu fu jiaokan ji* 重刊宋本十三經注疏附校勘記, vol. 6. Taipei: Yiwen yinshuguan, 1965.

Clark, Hugh. "Why Does the Tang-Song Interregnum Matter? A Focus on the Economies of the South." *Journal of Song-Yuan Studies* 46 (2016): 1–28.

———. "Why Does the Tang-Song Interregnum Matter? The Legacy of Division and the Holistic Empire." *Journal of Song-Yuan Studies* 49 (2020): 1–44.

———. "Why Does the Tang-Song Interregnum Matter? The Social and Cultural Initiatives of the South." *Journal of Song-Yuan Studies* 47 (2017–2018): 1–31.

Cornis-Pope, Marcel, and John Neubauer. "General Introduction." In *History of the Literary Cultures of East-Central Europe*, edited by Marcel Cornis-Pope and John Neubauer, 1–18. Amsterdam: John Benjamins, 2004.

———, eds. *History of the Literary Cultures of East-Central Europe*. 4 vols. Amsterdam: John Benjamins, 2004–2010.

Crespi, John. *Voices in Revolution: Poetry and the Auditory Imagination in Modern China*. Honolulu: University of Hawai'i Press, 2009.

Cuba Commission Report: A Hidden History of the Chinese in Cuba. Baltimore: Johns Hopkins University Press, 1993.

Dai Bufan 戴不凡. *Dai Bufan xiqu yanjiu lunwenji* 戴不凡戲曲研究論文集. Hangzhou: Zhejiang renmin chubanshe, 1982.

Daija, Pauls. *Literary History and Popular Enlightenment in Latvian Culture*. Newcastle upon Tyne, UK: Cambridge Scholars, 2017.

Damrosch, David. *What Is World Literature?* Princeton, NJ: Princeton University Press, 2003.

De Almeida, Rosa Vieira. "Writing the Margin: Sinophone Macau Literature of the Pre-Postcolonial Era, 1987–1999." Ph.D. diss., Yale University, 2018.

De Pourcq, Maarten. "General Introduction." In *European Literary History: An Introduction*, edited by Maarten De Pourcq and Sophie Levie, 1–12. New York: Routledge, 2018.

De Pourcq, Maarten, and Sophie Levie, eds. *European Literary History: An Introduction*. New York: Routledge, 2018.

Deleuze, Gilles, and Félix Guattari. *Kafka: Toward a Minor Literature*. Translated by Dana Polan. Minneapolis: University of Minnesota Press, 1986.

Denecke, Wiebke. "'Bun' no gainen wo tōshite Nihon 'bun' gakushi o hiraku" 「文」の概念を通して日本「文」学史を開く. In *"Bun" no kankyō: "bungaku" izen* 「文」の環境：「文学」以前, edited by Kōno Kimiko 河野貴美子, Wiebke Denecke, Shinkawa Tokio 新川登亀男, and Jinno Hidenori 陣野英則, 1–40. *Nihon "bun" gakushi* 日本「文」学史 = *A New History of Japanese "Letterature,"* vol. 1. Tokyo: Benseisha, 2015.

———. *Classical World Literatures: Sino-Japanese and Greco-Roman Comparisons*. Oxford: Oxford University Press, 2014.

———. "The Politics of (Dis)similarity: New Tools to Understand the Emergence of Modern Literary Historiography in East Asia." In *Ähnlichkeit in Lyrik und Poetik der Gegenwart / Similarity in Contemporary Poetics*, edited by Nikolas Immer, Frank Kraushaar and Henrieke Stahl. Neuere Lyrik: Interkulturelle und interdisziplinaere Studien, Vol. 14. Frankfurt a.M.: Peter Lang, 2022.

———. "Writing History in the Face of the Other: Early Japanese Anthologies and the Beginnings of Literature." *Bulletin of the Museum of Far Eastern Antiquities* 76 (2006): 71–114.

Derrida, Jacques. *Specters of Marx: The State of Debt, the Work of Mourning, and the New International.* Translated by Peggy Kamuf. London: Routledge, 1994.

Dilthey, Wilhelm. "Draft for a Critique of Historical Reason." In *The Hermeneutics Reader: Texts of the German Tradition from the Enlightenment to the Present,* edited by Kurt Mueller-Vollmer, 149–52. New York: Continuum Press, 1985.

Ditter, Alexei K. "*Chuxue ji.*" In *Early Medieval Chinese Texts: A Bibliographic Guide,* edited by Cynthia L. Chennault, Keith N. Knapp, Alan J. Berkowitz, and Albert E. Dien, 52–57. Berkeley, CA: Institute of East Asian Studies, 2015.

Doleželová-Velingerová, Milena. "Literary Historiography in Early Twentieth-Century China (1904–1928): Constructions of Cultural Memory." In *The Appropriation of Cultural Capital: China's May Fourth Project,* edited by Milena Doleželová-Velingerová, Oldřich Král, and Graham Sanders, 123–66. Cambridge, MA: Harvard University Asia Center, 2001.

Dong Gao 董誥 et al., comps. *Quan Tang wen* 全唐文. 12 vols. Beijing: Zhonghua shuju, 1987.

Du Fu 杜甫. *Du Shi xiangzhu* 杜詩詳注. Edited and annotated by Qiu Zhaoao 仇兆鰲. 5 vols. Beijing: Zhonghua shuju, 1979.

Du Mu 杜牧. *Fanchuan wenji jiaozhu* 樊川文集校注. Edited by He Xiguang 何錫光. 2 vols. Chengdu: Ba Shu shushe, 2007.

Dudbridge, Glen. "A Question of Classification in Tang Narrative: The Story of Ding Yue." In *India, Tibet, China: Genesis and Aspects of Traditional Narrative,* edited by Alfredo Cadonna, 151–80. Firenze: Leo S. Olschki Editore, 1999.

———. *The Tale of Li Wa: Study and Critical Edition of a Chinese Story from the Ninth Century.* London: Ithaca Press, 1983.

Durrant, Stephen, Wai-yee Li, and David Schaberg, trans. *Zuo Tradition/Zuozhuan* 左傳: *Commentary on the "Spring and Autumn Annals."* 3 vols. Seattle: University of Washington Press, 2016.

Eckardt, Andre. *Geschichte der koreanischen Literatur.* Stuttgart: Kohlhammer, 1968.

Engler, Balz. "Textualization." In *Literary Pragmatics,* edited by Roger D. Sell, 179–89. London: Routledge, 1991.

Fan, Jiayang. "Liu Cixin's War of the Worlds." *New Yorker,* June 24, 2019. https://www.newyorker.com/magazine/2019/06/24/liu-cixins-war-of-the-worlds.

Fan Ye 范曄, comp. *Hou Han shu* 後漢書. 12 vols. Beijing: Zhonghua shuju, 1965.

Fang Xiu. *Notes on the History of Malayan Chinese New Literature, 1920–1942.* Translated by Angus W. McDonald. Tokyo: Centre for East Asian Cultural Studies, 1977.

Fang Xuanling 房玄齡 et al., comps. *Jin shu* 晉書. 10 vols. Beijing: Zhonghua shuju, 1974.

Feeney, Denis. *Beyond Greek: The Beginnings of Latin Literature.* Cambridge, MA: Harvard University Press, 2016.

Fisher, Mark. "What Is Hauntology?" *Film Quarterly* 66, no. 1 (Fall 2012): 16–24.

Fogel, Joshua A. "New Thoughts on an Old Controversy: *Shina* as a Toponym for China." *Sino-Platonic Papers* 229 (2012): 1–25.

Works Cited

Fu Xiangxi 付祥喜. *Ershi shiji qianqi Zhongguo wenxueshi xiezuo biannian yanjiu* 20 世紀前期中國文學史寫作編年研究. Beijing: Beijing shifan daxue chubanshe, 2013.

Fuller, Michael A. "Aesthetics and Meaning in Experience: A Theoretical Perspective on Zhu Xi's Revision of Song Dynasty Views of Poetry." *Harvard Journal of Asiatic Studies* 65, no. 2 (December 2005): 311–55.

———. *Drifting among Rivers and Lakes: Southern Song Dynasty Poetry and the Problem of Literary History.* Cambridge, MA: Harvard University Asia Center, 2013.

———. "In Praise of Alienation: A Role for Theory in Reading Classical Chinese Poetry." In *Hsiang Lectures in Chinese Poetry.* Montreal: Center for East Asian Research, McGill University, 2019.

———. "'Juan ye': dui Zhongguo gudian chuantong zhong roushen shixue de fansi" 倦夜: 對中國古典傳統中肉身詩學的反思. Translated by Qiao Jiyan 喬吉燕. *Zhongguo xueshu* 中國學術 38 (2017): 119–37.

———. "Moral Intuitions and Aesthetic Judgments: The Interplay of Poetry and *Daoxue* in Southern Song China." In *Modern Chinese Religion I: Song-Liao-Jin-Yuan (960–1368 AD),* edited by John Lagerwey, vol. 1, 1307–77. Leiden: Brill, 2015.

———. "'Renwen': Zhong Tang shiqi shige he shenmei jingyan zhuanbian" 人文: 中唐時期詩歌和審美經驗轉變, translated by Liu Qian 劉倩. In *Chuanhe Kangsan jiaoshou rongxiu jinian wenji* 川合康三教授榮休紀念文集, edited by Lin Zongzheng 林宗正 and Jiang Yin 蔣寅, 195–222. Nanjing: Fenghuang chubanshe, 2017.

———. "Zai jiushiji sixiang yu meixue shanbian de yujing xia zaitan Li Shangyin shige" 在九世紀思想與美學嬗变的語境下再談李商隱詩歌. *Tangdai wenxue yanjiu* 唐代文學研究 18 (2019): 73–84.

Fuller, Michael A., and Shuen-fu Lin. "North and South: The Twelfth and Thirteenth Centuries." In *The Cambridge History of Chinese Literature,* edited by Kang-I Sun Chang and Stephen Owen, vol. 1: *To 1375,* 465–556. Cambridge: Cambridge University Press, 2010.

Gadamer, Hans-Georg. *Truth and Method.* 2nd rev. ed. Translation revised by Joel Weinsheimer and Donald G. Marshall. London: Continuum, 1988.

Gan Bao 干寶. *Xinjiao Soushen ji* 新校搜神記. Collated by Hu Huaichen 胡懷琛. Shanghai: Shangwu yinshuguan, 1957.

Gao Shi 高適. *Gao Shi ji jiaozhu* 高適集校注. Annotated by Sun Qinshan 孫欽善. Shanghai: Shanghai guji chubanshe, 1984.

García, Cristina. *Monkey Hunting.* New York: Knopf, 2003.

Gellhorn, Eleanor Cowles. *McKay's Guide to the Far East and Hawaii.* New York: D. McKay, 1965.

Genovese, Eugene D. "A Question of Morals." In *In Red and Black: Marxian Explorations in Southern and Afro-American History,* 368–73. New York: Pantheon Books, 1971.

Gillespie, Stuart. *English Translation and Classical Reception: Towards a New Literary History.* Malden, MA: Wiley-Blackwell, 2011.

Graff, Richard. "Prose versus Poetry in Early Greek Theories of Style." *Rhetorica: A Journal of the History of Rhetoric* 23, no. 4 (Autumn 2005): 303–35.

Graham, A. C., trans. *Chuang-Tzŭ: The Inner Chapters.* Indianapolis: Hackett, 2001.

Works Cited

Grunert, Frank, and Friedrich Vollhardt. *Historia Literaria: Neuordnung des Wissens im 17. und 18. Jahrhundert*. Berlin: Akademie, 2007.

Guex, Samuel. "Le Shinagaku et la modernisation de la sinologie japonaise." *ASIA* 68, no. 1 (2014): 65–82.

Gujin tushu jicheng 古今圖書集成. Compiled by Chen Menglei 陳夢雷, Jiang Tingxi 蔣廷錫, et al. 82 vols. Beijing: Zhonghua shuju, 1985.

Guo Maoqian 郭茂倩, comp. *Yuefu shiji* 樂府詩集. 4 vols. Beijing: Zhonghua shuju, 1979.

Guo Qingfan 郭慶藩, ed. *Zhuangzi jishi* 莊子集釋. 4 vols. Beijing: Zhonghua shuju, 1961.

Guo Yingde 郭英德. *Ming Qing chuanqi xiqu wenti yanjiu* 明清傳奇戲曲文體研究. Beijing: Shangwu yinshuguan, 2004.

Hall, Stuart. "Gramsci and Us." In *The Hard Road to Renewal: Thatcherism and the Crisis of the Left*, 161–73. London: Verso, 1988.

Han Yu 韓愈. *Han Yu quanji jiaozhu* 韓愈全集校注. Edited by Qu Shouyuan 屈守元 and Chang Sichun 常思春. 5 vols. Chengdu: Sichuan daxue chubanshe, 1996.

Hedberg, William C. *The Japanese Discovery of Chinese Fiction: The Water Margin and the Making of a National Canon*. New York: Columbia University Press, 2020.

Hesiod. *Theogony*. In *Hesiodi Theogonia, Opera et Dies, Scutum*. Edited by Friedrich Solmsen. In *Fragmenta Selecta*, edited by R. Merkelbach and M. L. West. Oxford: Oxford University Press, 1970.

Hollier, Denis, ed. *A New History of French Literature*. Cambridge, MA: Harvard University Press, 1989.

Hong Mai 洪邁. *Rongzhai suibi* 容齋隨筆. 2 vols. Shanghai: Shanghai guji chubanshe, 1978.

Hu, Baozhu. *Believing in Ghosts and Spirits: The Concept of Gui in Ancient China*. Abingdon, UK: Routledge, 2021.

Hu, Qiulei. "From Singing Ghosts to Docile Concubines: Elite Domestication of the Local in the Wu Songs." *Journal of the American Oriental Society* 139, no. 4 (October–December 2019): 843–58.

Hu Yinglin 胡應麟. *Xinjiao Shaoshi shanfang bicong* 新校少室山房筆叢. Edited by Zhou Ying 周嬰. 2 vols. Taipei: Shijie shuju, 2009.

Hu-DeHart, Evelyn. "Chinese Coolie Labour in Cuba in the Nineteenth Century: Free Labour or Neo-Slavery?" *Slavery and Abolition* 14, no. 1 (April 1993): 67–86.

Huang Dongping 黃東平. *Duanpian erji* 短篇二集. Singapore: Tow Yee Cultural Society, 1993.

———. *Huang Dongping quanji* 黃東平全集. 10 vols. Jinmen: Jinmenxian shejiao wenhua huodong jijinhui, 2004.

Huihong 惠洪. *Lengzhai yehua* 冷齋夜話. Punctuated and collated by Zhu Mou 朱牟 and Wu Hang 吳沆. Beijing: Zhonghua shuju, 1988.

Huters, Theodore D. "Literary Histories." In *Literary Information in China: A History*, edited by Jack W. Chen, Anatoly Detwyler, Christopher M. B. Nugent, Xiao Liu, and Bruce Rusk, 395–406. New York: Columbia University Press, 2021.

Hutton, Ronald. "What Is Political History?" In *What Is History Today . . . ?* edited by Juliet Gardiner, 21–23. Hampshire, UK: Macmillan Education, 1988.

Ivanhoe, Philip, and Bryan Van Norden, eds. *Readings in Classical Chinese Philosophy.* 2nd ed. Indianapolis: Hackett, 2005.

Jackson, Virginia. *Dickinson's Misery: A Theory of Lyric Reading.* Princeton, NJ: Princeton University Press, 2005.

Jaumann, Herbert. "Historia literaria und Formen gelehrter Sammlungen, diesseits und jenseits von Periodizität. Eine Reihe von Überlegungen." In *Historia Literaria: Neuordnung des Wissens im 17. und 18. Jahrhundert,* edited by Frank Grunert and Friedrich Vollhardt, 103–11. Berlin: Akademie, 2007.

Jiang Shaoyu 江少虞. *Songchao shishi leiyuan* 宋朝事實類苑. 2 vols. Shanghai: Shanghai guji chubanshe, 1981.

Jiang Xiumei 江秀梅. *Chuxue ji zhengyin jibu dianji kao* 初學記徵引集部典籍考. 2 vols. Yonghe, Taiwan: Hua Mulan wenhua chubanshe, 2006.

Jiao Xun 焦循, ed. *Mengzi zhengyi* 孟子正義. 2 vols. Beijing: Zhonghua shuju, 1987.

Kant, Immanuel. *Critique of Judgment.* Translated by Werner S. Pluhar. Indianapolis: Hackett, 1987.

Karlgren, Bernhard, trans. "The Book of Documents." *Bulletin of the Museum of Far Eastern Antiquities* 22 (1950): 1–81.

Kern, Martin. "Creating a Book and Performing It: The 'Yaolüe' Chapter of *Huainanzi* as a Western Han Fu." In *The Huainanzi and Textual Production in Early China,* edited by Sarah A. Queen and Michael Puett, 124–50. Leiden: Brill, 2014.

Kern, Martin, and Robert E. Hegel. "A History of Chinese Literature?" *Chinese Literature: Essays, Articles, Reviews* 26 (2004): 159–79.

Knechtges, David R., and Stephen Owen. "General Principles for a History of Chinese Literature." *Chinese Literature: Essays, Articles, Reviews* 1 (January 1979): 49–53.

Knoblock, John. *Xunzi: A Translation and Study of the Complete Works.* 3 vols. Stanford, CA: Stanford University Press, 1994.

Kojō Teikichi 古城貞吉. *Shina bungakushi* 支那文學史. Tokyo: Keizai sasshisha, 1897.

Kōno Kimiko 河野貴美子, Wiebke Denecke, Shinkawa Tokio 新川登亀男, and Jinno Hidenori 陣野英則, eds. *"Bun" kara "bungaku" e: Higashi Ajia no bungaku o minaosu*「文」から「文学」へ——東アジアの文学を見直す. *Nihon "bun" gakushi* 日本「文」学史 = *A New History of Japanese "Letterature,"* vol. 3. Tokyo: Benseisha: 2019.

Lam, Agnes. "Wu ziwo yishi de chengshi" 無自我意識的城市. *Macao Daily,* August 12, 2010.

Lambeck, Peter. *Prodromus historiae literariae.* Hamburg: Michael Piper, 1659.

Lebovitz, David. "Historical Poetry, Poetical History, and the Roots of Commentary: Rui Liangfu and the Formation of Early Chinese Texts." PhD diss., University of Chicago, 2019.

Lee-DiStefano, Debbie. *Three Asian-Hispanic Writers from Peru: Doris Moromisato, José Watanabe, Siu Kam Wen.* Lewiston, NY: Edwin Mellen Press, 2008.

Lei Jingxuan 雷竞璇. *Molu yimin: Guba Huaqiao fangtan lu* 末路遺民: 古巴華僑訪談錄. Hong Kong: Oxford University Press, 2017.

———. *Yuanzai Guba* 遠在古巴. Hong Kong: Oxford University Press, 2015.

Lewis, Mark Edward. *The Flood Myths of Early China*. Albany: State University of New York Press, 2006.

Li Fang 李昉 et al., comps. *Taiping guangji* 太平廣記. 10 vols. Beijing: Zhonghua shuju, 1961.

———. *Taiping yulan* 太平御覽. 4 vols. Beijing: Zhonghua shuju, 1960.

———. *Wenyuan yinghua* 文苑英華. 6 vols. Beijing: Zhonghua shuju, 1966.

Li He 李賀. *Sanjia pingzhu Li Changji geshi* 三家評註李長吉歌詩. Edited and annotated by Wang Qi 王琦 et al. Shanghai: Shanghai guji chubanshe, 1998.

Li ji zhushu 禮記注疏. Annotated by Zheng Xuan 鄭玄, Kong Yingda 孔穎達, et al. In Ruan Yuan 阮元, ed., *Chongkan Songben Shisanjing zhushu fu jiaokan ji* 重刊宋本十三經注疏附校勘記, vol. 5. Taipei: Yiwen yinshuguan, 1965.

Li Jianguo 李劍國. *Tang Wudai zhiguai chuanqi xulu* 唐五代志怪傳奇敍錄. Rev. ed. 3 vols. Beijing: Zhonghua shuju, 2017.

Li Shangyin 李商隱. *Li Shangyin shige jijie* 李商隱詩歌集解. Edited by Liu Xuekai 劉學鍇 and Yu Shucheng 余恕誠. 5 vols. Beijing: Zhonghua shuju, 1988.

Li, Wai-yee. "Concepts of Authorship." In *The Oxford Handbook of Classical Chinese Literature (1000 BCE–900 CE)*, edited by Wiebke Denecke, Wai-yee Li, and Xiaofei Tian, 360–76. Oxford: Oxford University Press, 2017.

Li Yu 李漁. *Yizhongyuan* 意中緣. In *Liweng chuanqi shizhong jiaozhu* 笠翁傳奇十種校注, 1:387–474. Tianjin: Tianjin guji chubanshe, 2009.

Lin Chuanjia 林傳甲. *Zhongguo wenxueshi* 中國文學史. Shanghai: Kexue shuju, 1910.

Linton, Anna. "Blithe Spirits: Voices from the Other Side in Early Modern German Lutheran Funeral Poetry." In *Early Modern Ghosts: Proceedings of the 'Early Modern Ghosts' Conference Held at St. John's College, Durham University on 24 March 2001*, edited by John Newton with Jo Bath, 18–32. Durham, UK: Centre for Seventeenth-Century Studies, Durham University, 2002.

Liu Baonan 劉寶楠, ed. *Lunyu zhengyi* 論語正義. Punctuated and collated by Gao Liushui 高流水. 2 vols. Beijing: Zhonghua shuju, 1990.

Liu Cixin 劉慈欣. "Chaoyue zilian: kehuan gei wenxue de jihui" 超越自戀: 科幻給文學的機會. *Shanxi wenxue* 7 (2009): 75–81.

Liu, James J. Y. "The Study of Chinese Literature in the West: Recent Developments, Current Trends, Future Prospects." *Journal of Asian Studies* 25, no. 1 (November 1975): 21–30.

Liu Kairong 劉開榮. *Tangdai xiaoshuo yanjiu* 唐代小說研究. Shanghai: Shangwu yinshuguan, 1955.

Liu Su 劉肅. *Da Tang xinyu* 大唐新語. Punctuated and collated by Xu Denan 許德楠 and Li Dingxia 李鼎霞. Beijing: Zhonghua shuju, 1984.

Liu Su 劉餗. *Sui Tang jiahua* 隋唐嘉話. In *Tang Wudai biji xiaoshuo daguan* 唐五代筆記小說大觀, vol. 1, 87–116. Shanghai: Shanghai guji chubanshe, 2000.

Liu Xie 劉勰. *Wenxin diaolong zhu* 文心雕龍註. Annotated by Fan Wenlan 范文瀾. Hong Kong: Shangwu yinshuguan, 1960.

———. *Zengding Wenxin diaolong jiaozhu* 增訂文心雕龍校注. Edited by Huang Shulin 黃叔琳 and Li Xiang 李詳. Beijing: Zhonghua shuju, 2000.

Liu Xu 劉昫 et al., comps. *Jiu Tang shu* 舊唐書. 16 vols. Beijing: Zhonghua shuju, 1975.

Lohmann, Roger Ivar. "The Night I Was Attacked by a Ghost." *Sapiens*, October 28, 2016. https://www.sapiens.org/culture/night-attacked-by-ghost/.

López, Kathleen M. *Chinese Cubans: A Transnational History*. Chapel Hill: University of North Carolina Press, 2013.

López-Calvo, Ignacio. *Dragons in the Land of the Condor: Writing Tusán in Peru*. Tucson: University of Arizona Press, 2014.

Lou Yu 樓宇. "Zhongguo dui Lamei de wenhua chuanbo: wenxue de shijiao" 中國對拉美的文化傳播: 文學的視角. *Lading Meizhou yanjiu* 拉丁美洲研究 39, no. 5 (October 2017): 31–44.

Lu Qinli 逯欽立, comp. *Xian Qin Han Wei Jin nanbeichao shi* 先秦漢魏晉南北朝詩. 3 vols. Beijing: Zhonghua shuju, 1983.

Lu Xun 魯迅. *Tang Song chuanqi ji* 唐宋傳奇集. Tianjin: Tianjin guji chubanshe, 2002.

———. *Zhongguo xiaoshuo shilüe* 中國小説史略. In *Lu Xun xiaoshuo shilun wenji* 魯迅小説史論文集. Taipei: Liren shuju, 1992.

Lu You 陸游. *Jiannan shigao jiaozhu* 劍南詩稿校注. Edited and annotated by Qian Zhonglian 錢仲聯. 8 vols. Shanghai: Shanghai guji chubanshe, 1985.

———. *Lu Fangweng quanji* 陸放翁全集. 3 vols. Beijing: Zhongguo shudian, 1986.

Lu, Zongli. *Power of the Words: Chen Prophecy in Chinese Politics, AD 265–618*. Bern: Peter Lang, 2003.

Luo Jiyong 羅積勇 and Zhang Pengfei 張鵬飛, eds. *Tangdai shilü shice jiaozhu* 唐代試律試策校注. Wuhan: Wuhan daxue chubanshe, 2009.

Ma Duanlin 馬端臨, comp. *Wenxian tongkao* 文獻通考. 2 vols. Taipei: Taiwan Shangwu yinshuguan, 1987.

Mandelbaum, Maurice. *The Anatomy of Historical Knowledge*. Baltimore: Johns Hopkins University Press, 1977.

———. "The History of Ideas, Intellectual History, and the History of Philosophy." *History and Theory* 5 (1965): 3–53.

Mao Shi zhengyi 毛詩正義. In Ruan Yuan 阮元, ed., *Chongkan Songben Shisanjing zhushu fu jiaokan ji* 重刊宋本十三經注疏附校勘記, vol. 2. Taipei: Yiwen yinshuguan, 1965.

Mao Shi zhuanjian tongshi 毛詩傳箋通釋. Edited by Ma Ruichen 馬瑞辰. Beijing: Zhonghua shuju, 1989.

Marcus, Greil, and Werner Sollors, eds. *A New Literary History of America*. Cambridge, MA: Harvard University Press, 2012.

Marx, Karl. *Capital*. Translated by Ben Fowkes. London: Penguin, 1990.

Mather, Richard B. *The Poet Shen Yüeh (441–513): The Reticent Marquis*. Princeton, NJ: Princeton University Press, 1988.

Mazanec, Thomas J. "How Poetry Became Meditation in Ninth Century China." *Asia Major*, 3rd series, 32, no. 2 (2019): 113–51.

McCunn, Ruthanne Lum. *God of Luck*. New York: Soho Press, 2007.

McDonald, Christie, and Susan Rubin Suleiman, eds. *French Global: A New Approach to Literary History*. New York: Columbia University Press, 2010.

McMullen, David. "Historical and Literary Theory in the Mid-Eighth Century." In *Perspectives on the T'ang*, edited by Arthur F. Wright and Denis C. Twitchett, 307–42. New Haven, CT: Yale University Press, 1973.

Meagher, Arnold J. *The Coolie Trade: The Traffic in Chinese Laborers to Latin America, 1847–1874*. Philadelphia: Xlibris, 2008.

Mei Dingzuo 梅鼎祚, comp. *Caigui ji* 才鬼記. In *Siku quanshu cunmu congshu* 四庫全書存目叢書, edited by Siku quanshu cunmu congshu bianzuan weiyuanhui 四庫全書存目叢書編纂委員會, vol. 249. Ji'nan: Qi Lu shushe, 1997.

Meltzl, Hugo. "Vorläufige Aufgaben der vergleichenden Litteratur." *Összehasonlító Irodalomtörténeti Lapok/Zeitschrift für vergleichende Litteratur/Journal de littérature comparée* 1, no. 9 (1877): 180–82.

Meng Jiao 孟郊. *Meng Jiao shiji jiaozhu* 孟郊詩集校注. Edited and annotated by Hua Chenzhi 華忱之 and Yu Xuecai 喻學才. Beijing: Renmin wenxue chubanshe, 1995.

Mikami Sanji 三上参次 and Takatsu Kuwasaburō 高津鍬三郎. *Nihon bungakushi* 日本文学史 Tokyo: Kinkōdō, 1890.

Mitrev, Dimitar. *The Code of Macedonian Literary History.* Translated by Nikolina Utkovska. Skopje: St. Clement of Ohrid, National and University Library, 2011.

Mizobe Yoshie 溝部良恵. "Meijiki no Nihon ni okeru Chūgoku shōsetsushi kenkyū ni tsuite: bungakushi ni okeru kijutsu o chūshin ni" 明治期の日本における中国小説史研究について：文学史における記述を中心に. *Chūgoku kenkyū* 中国研究 10 (2007): 109–44.

Moretti, Franco. *Graphs, Maps, Trees: Abstract Models for a Literary History.* London: Verso, 2007.

Müller, Ernst, and Falko Schmieder. *Begriffsgeschichte und historische Semantik: Ein kritisches Kompendium.* Berlin: Suhrkamp, 2016.

Ng, Kim Chew. "Minor Sinophone Literature: Diasporic Modernity's Incomplete Journey." In *Global Chinese Literature: Critical Essays*, edited by Jing Tsu and David Derwei Wang, 15–28. Leiden: Brill, 2010.

Nienhauser, William H. Jr. "Qing Feng, Duke Xian of Wey, and the *Shijing* in the Sixth Century B.C.: Some Preliminary Remarks on the *Shi* in the *Zuo zhuan*." *Oriens Extremus* 50 (2011): 75–98.

Ning Jiayu 寧稼雨. *Zhongguo wenyan xiaoshuo zongmu tiyao* 中國文言小説總目提要. Ji'nan: Qi Lu shushe, 1996.

Orsini, Francesca. "How to Do Multilingual Literary History? Lessons from Fifteenth and Sixteenth-Century North India." *Indian Economic and Social History Review* 49, no. 2 (2012): 225–46.

Ouyang Xiu 歐陽修. *Ouyang Xiu shiwenji jiaojian* 歐陽修詩文集校箋. Annotated by Hong Benjian 洪本健. 3 vols. Shanghai: Shanghai guji chubanshe, 2009.

Ouyang Xiu 歐陽修 and Song Qi 宋祁, et al., comps. *Xin Tang shu* 新唐書. 20 vols. Beijing: Zhonghua shuju, 1975.

Ouyang Xun 歐陽詢 et al., comps. *Yiwen leiju* 藝文類聚. 2 vols. Shanghai: Shanghai guji chubanshe, 2007.

Owen, Stephen. *The End of the Chinese "Middle Ages": Essays in Mid-Tang Literary Culture.* Stanford, CA: Stanford University Press, 1996.

———. "How Did Buddhism Matter in Tang Poetry?" *T'oung Pao* 103, nos. 4–5 (2017): 388–406.

———. *The Making of Early Chinese Classical Poetry.* Cambridge, MA: Harvard University Asia Center, 2006.

———. "Meaning the Words: The Genuine as a Value in the Tradition of the Song Lyric." In *Voices of the Song Lyric in China*, edited by Pauline Yu, 30–69. Berkeley: University of California Press, 1994.

———. *Readings in Chinese Literary Thought*. Cambridge, MA: Council on East Asian Studies, 1992.

———. "Reproduction in the *Shijing* (Classic of Poetry)." *Harvard Journal of Asiatic Studies* 61, no. 2 (December 2001): 287–315.

———. "The Self's Perfect Mirror: Poetry as Autobiography." In *The Vitality of the Lyric Voice: Shih Poetry from the Late Han to the T'ang*, edited by Shuen-fu Lin and Stephen Owen, 71–102. Princeton, NJ: Princeton University Press, 1986.

———[Yuwen Suoan 宇文所安]. "Shi zhong you shi (shang, xia)" 史中有史 (上、下). *Du shu* 讀書 5 (2008): 21–30; 6 (2008): 96–102. Translated, with some condensation, from "New Directions in Literary History," unpublished lecture.

———. "Stepping Forward and Back: Issues and Possibilities for 'World' Poetry." *Modern Philology* 100, no. 4 (May 2003): 532–48.

———. *Traditional Chinese Poetry and Poetics: Omen of the World*. Madison: University of Wisconsin Press, 1985.

———. "What Is World Poetry? The Anxiety of Global Influence." *New Republic* 203, no. 21 (November 19, 1990): 28–32.

Pan Jianguo 潘建國. *Zhongguo gudai xiaoshuo shumu yanjiu* 中國古代小説書目研究. Shanghai: Shanghai guji chubanshe, 2005.

Pang Yuanying 龐元英. *Tansou* 談藪. In *Quan Song biji* 全宋筆記, edited by Zhu Yi'an 朱易安 et al., 2nd series, vol. 4. Zhengzhou: Daxiang chubanshe, 2006.

Perkins, David. *Is Literary History Possible?* Baltimore: Johns Hopkins University Press, 1992.

Poo, Mu-chou. "The Concept of Ghost in Ancient Chinese Religion." In *Religion and Chinese Society*, edited by John Lagerwey, 173–87. Hong Kong: Chinese University of Hong Kong Press and École Française d'Extrême-Orient, 2004.

———. "The Culture of Ghosts in the Six Dynasties Period (c. 220–589 C.E.)" In *Rethinking Ghosts in World Religions*, edited by Mu-chou Poo, 237–68. Leiden: Brill, 2009.

Powell, Patricia. *The Pagoda*. San Diego: Harcourt Brace, 1998.

Pratt, Mary Louise. *Toward a Speech Act Theory of Literary Discourse*. Bloomington: Indiana University Press, 1977.

Qian Zhongshu 錢鍾書. *Guanzhui bian* 管錐編. 4 vols. Beijing: Zhonghua shuju, 1986.

Quan Song wen 全宋文. Edited by Zeng Zaozhuang 曾棗莊 and Liu Lin 劉琳. 360 vols. Shanghai: Shanghai cishu chubanshe, 2006.

Quan Tang shi 全唐詩. 25 vols. Beijing: Zhonghua shuju, 1985.

Reimmann, Jacob Friderich [Jacob Friedrich]. *Versuch einer Einleitung in die Historiam Literariam derer Teutschen*. Halle: Rengerische Buchhandlung, 1708–1713.

Rutt, Richard. *James Scarth Gale and His History of the Korean People*. Seoul: Royal Asiatic Society, Korea Branch & Taewon, 1972.

Works Cited

Salmon, Claudine. "Introduction." In *Literary Migrations: Traditional Chinese Fiction in Asia, 17th–20th Centuries*, edited by Claudine Salmon, 1–36. Singapore: ISEAS, 2013.

Salyer, Lucy E. *Laws Harsh as Tigers*. Chapel Hill: University of North Carolina Press, 1995.

Sanders, Graham. *Words Well Put: Visions of Poetic Competence in the Chinese Tradition*. Cambridge, MA: Harvard University Asia Center, 2006.

Sasagawa Rinpū 笹川臨風. *Shina bungakushi* 支那文学史. Tokyo: Hakubunkan, 1898.

Saussy, Haun. "Recent Chinese Literary Histories in English." *Harvard Journal of Asiatic Studies* 79, nos. 1–2 (2019): 231–48.

Schaberg, David. "Functionary Speech: On the Work of *Shi* 使 and *Shi* 史." In *Facing the Monarch: Modes of Advice in the Early Chinese Court*, edited by Garret P. S. Olberding, 19–41. Cambridge, MA: Harvard University Asia Center, 2013.

———. *A Patterned Past: Form and Thought in Early Chinese Historiography*. Cambridge, MA: Harvard University Asia Center, 2001.

———. "Song and the Historical Imagination in Early China." *Harvard Journal of Asiatic Studies* 59, no. 2 (December 1999): 305–61.

———. "Speaking of Documents: Shu Citations in Warring States Texts." In *Origins of Chinese Political Thought: Studies in the Composition and Thought of the* Shangshu *(Classic of Documents)*, edited by Martin Kern and Dirk Meyer, 320–59. Leiden: Brill, 2017.

Schuessler, Axel. *ABC Etymological Dictionary of Old Chinese*. Honolulu: University of Hawai'i Press, 2007.

Sell, Roger D. "Literary Pragmatics: An Introduction." In *Literary Pragmatics*, edited by Roger D. Sell, xi–xxiii. London: Routledge, 1991.

Shen Yue 沈約, comp. *Song shu* 宋書. 8 vols. Beijing: Zhonghua shuju, 1974.

Shih, Shu-mei. "Against Diaspora: The Sinophone as Places of Cultural Production." In *Global Chinese Literature: Critical Essays*, edited by Jing Tsu and David Der-wei Wang, 80–110. Leiden: Brill, 2010.

Shu Daqing 舒大清. "Zhongguo gudai zhengzhi tongyao yu chenwei, chenyu, shichen de duibi" 中國古代政治童謠與讖緯、讖語、詩讖的對比. *Qiusuo* 求索 11 (2008): 164–66.

Siku quanshu zongmu tiyao 四庫全書總目提要. Edited by Yongrong 永瑢 et al. Compiled by Ji Yun 紀昀 et al. 4 vols. Shanghai: Shangwu yinshuguan, 1933.

Sima Qian 司馬遷. *Shi ji* 史記. 10 vols. Beijing: Zhonghua shuju, 1982.

Sommer, Matthew H. *Polyandry and Wife-Selling in Qing Dynasty China: Survival Strategies and Judicial Interventions*. Berkeley: University of California Press, 2015.

Song Lian 宋濂 et al., comps. *Yuan shi* 元史. 15 vols. Beijing: Zhonghua shuju, 1976.

Sonnad, Nikhil. "Inside the World of Chinese Science Fiction, with *Three-Body Problem* Translator Ken Liu." *Quartz*, December 2, 2016. https://qz.com/847181/chinese -sci-fi-the-three-body-problem-and-invisible-planets-with-translator-ken-liu/.

Storck, Willy F. "Aspects of Death in English Art and Poetry—II. Catalogue Raisonné of Representations." *Burlington Magazine for Connoisseurs* 21, no. 114 (September 1912): 314–19.

Strickmann, Michel. *Chinese Poetry and Prophecy: The Written Oracle in East Asia*. Edited by Bernard Faure. Stanford, CA: Stanford University Press, 2005.

Su Shi 蘇軾. *Su Shi shiji* 蘇軾詩集. Edited and annotated by Wang Wen'gao 王文誥. Punctuated and collated by Kong Fanli 孔凡禮. 8 vols. Beijing: Zhonghua shuju, 1982.

Works Cited

———. *Su Shi wenji* 蘇軾文集. Punctuated and collated by Kong Fanli 孔凡禮. 6 vols. Beijing: Zhonghua shuju, 1986.

Su Xun 蘇洵, Su Shi 蘇軾, and Su Zhe 蘇轍. *San Su quanshu* 三蘇全書. Edited by Zeng Zaozhuang 曾棗莊 and Shu Dagang 舒大剛. 20 vols. Beijing: Yuwen chubanshe, 2001.

Suematsu Kenchō 末松謙澄. *Shina kobungaku ryakushi* 支那古文学略史. Tokyo: Bungakusha, 1882.

Sun Rongrong 孫蓉蓉. *Chenwei yu wenxue yanjiu* 讖緯與文學研究. Beijing: Zhonghua shuju, 2018.

Sun Wang 孫望 and Yu Xianhao 郁賢皓. *Tangdai wenxuan* 唐代文選. [Nanjing]: Jiangsu guji chubanshe, 1994.

Sun Xi 孫喜. "Dajia tan Zhongguo: Zhongguo qiaowu zhengce de 'xuqiuce' fansi" 大家談中國: 中國僑務政策的"需求側"反思. BBC China, March 7, 2016. https://www.bbc.com/zhongwen/simp/comments_on_china/2016/03/160307_coc_overseas_policy.

Sun Xidan 孫希旦, ed. *Li ji jijie* 禮記集解. Punctuated and collated by Shen Xiaohuan 沈嘯寰 and Wang Xingxian 王星賢. 3 vols. Beijing: Zhonghua shuju, 1989.

Sun Yirang 孫詒讓, ed. *Zhouli zhengyi* 周禮正義. Collated and punctuated by Wang Wenjin 王文錦 and Chen Yuxia 陳玉霞. 14 vols. Beijing: Zhonghua shuju, 1987.

Tackett, Nicolas. *The Destruction of the Medieval Chinese Aristocracy*. Cambridge, MA: Harvard University Asia Center, 2014.

Tai Jingnong 臺靜農. *Zhongguo wenxue shi* 中國文學史. Taipei: Guoli Taiwan daxue chubanshe, 2004.

Tam, Koo-yin. "The Use of Poetry in *Tso Chuan*: An Analysis of the 'Fu-shih' Practice." Ph.D. diss., University of Washington, 1975.

Tang Guangrong 唐光榮. *Tangdai leishu yu wenxue* 唐代類書與文學. Chengdu: Sichuan chuban jituan, Ba Shu shushe, 2008.

Teiser, Stephen F. *The Ghost Festival in Medieval China*. Princeton, NJ: Princeton University Press, 1988.

Tian, Xiaofei. *Beacon Fire and Shooting Star: The Literary Culture of the Liang (502–557)*. Cambridge, MA: Harvard University Asia Center, 2007.

———. "'Each Has Its Own Moment': Nie Gannu and Modern Chinese Poetry." *Frontiers of Literary Studies in China* 12, no. 3 (2018): 485–525.

———. "From the Eastern Jin through the Early Tang (317–649)." In *The Cambridge History of Chinese Literature*, edited by Kang-I Sun Chang and Stephen Owen, vol. 1: *To 1375*, 199–285. Cambridge: Cambridge University Press, 2010.

———. "Literary Learning: Encyclopedias and Epitomes." In *The Oxford Handbook of Classical Chinese Literature (1000 BCE–900 CE)*, edited by Wiebke Denecke, Wai-yee Li, and Xiaofei Tian, 132–46. Oxford: Oxford University Press, 2017.

———. "Muffled Dialect Spoken by Green Fruits: An Alternative History of Modern Chinese Poetry." *Modern Chinese Literature and Culture* 21, no. 1 (2009): 1–44.

Todd, H. A. "Apropos of the Trois Morts et Les Trois Vifs." *Modern Language Notes* 3, no. 3 (March 1888): 58–59.

Tsai, Chien-hsin. *A Passage to China: Literature, Loyalism, and Colonial Taiwan*. Cambridge, MA: Harvard University Asia Center, 2017.

Tsu, Jing. "Comparative Taiwan Literature." *boundary 2* 45, no. 3 (August 2018): 173–95.

Works Cited

———. *Sound and Script in Chinese Diaspora*. Cambridge, MA: Harvard University Press, 2010.

———. "Weak Links, Literary Spaces, and Comparative Taiwan." In *Comparatizing Taiwan*, edited by Shu-mei Shih and Ping-hui Liao, 123–44. New York: Routledge, 2014.

Tuotuo (Toghto) 脫脫, comp. *Jin shi* 金史. 8 vols. Beijing: Zhonghua shuju, 1975.

———. *Song shi* 宋史. 40 vols. Beijing: Zhonghua shuju, 1977.

Underwood, Ted. *Why Literary Periods Mattered: Historical Contrast and the Prestige of English Studies*. Stanford, CA: Stanford University Press, 2013.

Van Zoeren, Steven. *Poetry and Personality: Reading, Exegesis, and Hermeneutics in Traditional China*. Stanford, CA: Stanford University Press, 1991.

Vankeerberghen, Griet 方麗特 and Lin Fan 林凡. "*Shangshu dazhuan* de chengshu, liuchuan ji qi shehui lishi yiyi" 尚書大傳的成書、流傳及其社會歷史意義. In *Beijing daxue Zhongguo guwenxian yanjiu zhongxin jikan* 北京大學中國古文獻研究中心集刊, edited by Beijing daxue Zhongguo guwenxian yanjiu zhongxin 北京大學中國古文獻研究中心, vol. 11, 142–54. Beijing: Peking University Press, 2011.

Wan Weicheng 萬偉成. "Xiang shi xue: Zhongguo shige piping de yizhong teshu xingshi" 相詩學: 中國詩歌批評的一種特殊形式. *Foshan kexue jishu xueyuan xuebao* 佛山科學技術學院學報 26, no. 5 (2008): 18–22.

Wang Chong 王充. *Lunheng jiaoshi* 論衡校釋. Annotated by Huang Hui 黃暉. 4 vols. Beijing: Zhonghua shuju, 1990.

Wang, David Der-wei, ed. *A New Literary History of Modern China*. Cambridge, MA: Harvard University Press, 2017.

Wang Dianyin 王佃印. "Shichen, you yiwei de shixue piping yangshi" 詩讖, 有意味的詩學批評樣式. *Jinggangshan xueyuan xuebao* 井岡山學院學報 29, no. 1 (2008): 50–52.

Wang Li 王力. *Shi jing yundu; Chu ci yundu* 詩經韻讀; 楚辭韻讀. Beijing: Zhongguo renmin chubanshe, 2004.

Wang Li 王力, gen. ed. *Wang Li gu Hanyu zidian* 王力古漢語字典. Beijing: Zhonghua shuju, 2000.

Wang Mao 王楙. *Yeke congshu: fulu* 野客叢書: 附錄. 3 vols. Shanghai: Shangwu yinshuguan, 1939.

Wang Pijiang 汪辟疆. *Tangren xiaoshuo* 唐人小說. Reprinted as *Tangren chuanqi xiaoshuo* 唐人傳奇小說. Taipei: Wenshizhe chubanshe, 1999.

Wang Qinruo 王欽若, et al., comps. *Cefu yuangui* 冊府元龜. 12 vols. Beijing: Zhonghua shuju, 1994.

Wang Xian 王嫻 and Xiao Jing 蕭婧. "Jin shiwunian shichen yanjiu zongshu" 近十五年詩讖研究綜述. *Lanzhou jiaoyu xueyuan xuebao* 蘭州教育學院學報 26, no. 1 (2010): 48–51.

Wang Xianqian 王先謙, comp. *Shi sanjia yi jishu* 詩三家義集疏. Edited by Wu Ge 吳格. 2 vols. Beijing: Zhonghua shuju, 2009.

Wang Yaochen 王堯臣. *Chongwen zongmu: fu buyi* 崇文總目: 附補遺. Shanghai: Shangwu yinshuguan, 1937.

274   *Works Cited*

Wang Yongjian 王永健. *Zhongguo xiju wenxue de guibao: Ming Qing chuanqi* 中國戲劇文學的瑰寶: 明清傳奇. Nanjing: Jiangsu jiaoyu chubanshe, 1989.

Wang Yunxi 王運熙. "Jianlun Tang chuanqi he Han Wei Liuchao zazhuan de guanxi" 簡論唐傳奇和漢魏六朝雜傳的關係. In *Zhongxi xueshu* 中西學術, vol. 2, edited by Zhu Liyuan 朱立元 and Pei Gao 裴高, 1–10. Shanghai: Fudan daxue chubanshe, 1996.

Wei Zheng 魏徵 et al., comps. *Sui shu* 隋書. 6 vols. Beijing: Zhonghua shuju, 1973.

Weixinzi 委心子, comp. *Xinbian Fenmen gujin leishi* 新編分門古今類事. Annotated by Jin Xin 金心. Beijing: Zhonghua shuju, 1987.

Wellbery, David E., and Judith Ryan, eds. *A New History of German Literature.* Cambridge, MA: Harvard University Press, 2005.

Wellek, René. *The Attack on Literature and Other Essays.* Chapel Hill: University of North Carolina Press, 1982.

Wing, Yun-Kwok, Sharon Therese Lee, and Char-Nie Chen. "Sleep Paralysis in Chinese: Ghost Oppression Phenomenon in Hong Kong." *Sleep* 17, no. 7 (1994): 609–13.

Wong, Sauling. "Global Vision and Locatedness." In *Global Chinese Literature: Critical Essays,* edited by Jing Tsu and David Der-wei Wang, 35–46. Leiden: Brill, 2010.

Wu Chengxue 吳承學. "Lun yaochen yu shichen" 論謠讖與詩讖. *Wenxue pinglun* 文學評論, no. 2 (1996): 103–12.

———. *Zhongguo gudai wenti xingtai yanjiu* 中國古代文體形態研究. 3rd ed. Beijing: Beijing daxue chubanshe, 2013.

Wu Chuhou 吳處厚. *Qingxiang zaji* 青箱雜記. Shanghai: Shangwu yinshuguan, 1920.

Wu Zhida 吳志達. *Tangren chuanqi* 唐人傳奇. Taipei: Wanjuanlou tushu youxian gongsi, 1991.

Xiao Tong 蕭統, comp. *Wen xuan* 文選. 6 vols. Shanghai: Shanghai guji chubanshe, 1986.

———. *Wen xuan, or Selections of Refined Literature, Vol. I: Rhapsodies on Metropolises and Capitals.* Translated by David R. Knechtges. Princeton, NJ: Princeton University Press, 1982.

———. *Xinjiaoding Liujia zhu Wen xuan* 新校訂六家注文選. Annotated by Lü Yanji 呂延濟 et al. Edited by Yu Shaochu 俞紹初, Liu Qundong 劉群棟, and Wang Cuihong 王翠紅. 6 vols. Zhengzhou: Zhengzhou daxue chubanshe, 2013.

Xiao Yi 蕭繹. *Jinlouzi jiaojian* 金樓子校箋. Annotated by Xu Yimin 許逸民. 2 vols. Beijing: Zhonghua shuju, 2011.

Xiao Zixian 蕭子顯, comp. *Nan Qi shu* 南齊書. 3 vols. Beijing: Zhonghua shuju, 1972.

Xu Jian 徐堅 et al., comps. *Chuxue ji* 初學記. 2 vols. Beijing: Zhonghua shuju, 2010.

Xu Jiong 徐炯, comp. *Wudai shiji bukao* 五代史記補考. In *Wudai shishu huibian* 五代史書彙編, edited by Fu Xuancong 傅璇琮, Xu Hairong 徐海榮, and Xu Jijun 徐吉軍. 10 vols. Hangzhou: Hangzhou chubanshe, 2004.

Xu Shen 許慎. *Shuowen jiezi fu yinxu bihua jianzi* 説文解字附音序筆畫檢字. Edited by Xu Xuan 徐鉉. Beijing: Zhonghua shuju, 2013.

Xu Sinian 徐斯年. "Huang Moxi de *Zhongguo wenxueshi*" 黃摩西的中國文學史. In *Lu Xun yanjiu yuekan* 魯迅研究月刊 12 (2005): 24–32.

Xu Yuangao 徐元誥, comp. *Guo yu jijie* 國語集解, punctuated and collated by Wang Shumin 王樹民 and Shen Changyun 沈長雲. Beijing: Zhonghua shuju, 2002.

Works Cited

Xunzi jijie 荀子集解. Annotated by Wang Xianqian 王先謙. 2 vols. Beijing: Zhonghua shuju, 1997.

Xunzi jishi 荀子集釋. Annotated by Li Disheng 李滌生. Taipei: Taiwan xuesheng shuju, 1988.

Yan Zhitui 顏之推. *Yanshi jiaxun jijie zengbu ben* 顏氏家訓集解增補本. Edited by Wang Liqi 王利器. Beijing: Zhonghua shuju, 1993.

Yang Bojun 楊伯峻, annot. *Chunqiu Zuo zhuan zhu* 春秋左傳注. Rev. ed. 4 vols. Beijing: Zhonghua shuju, 1990.

Yang Jiong 楊炯. *Yang Jiong ji* 楊炯集. In *Yang Jiong ji Lu Zhaolin ji* 楊炯集盧照鄰集, edited by Xu Mingxia 徐明霞. Beijing: Zhonghua shuju, 1980.

Yang Shuqing 楊樹清. *Jinmen zuqun fazhan* 金門族群發展. Taipei: Daotian chuban youxian gongsi, 1996.

Yang Wanli. *Yang Wanli ji jianjiao* 楊萬里集箋校. Annotated by Xin Gengru 辛更儒. Beijing: Zhonghua shuju, 2007.

Yao Xuan 姚鉉. *Tang wencui* 唐文粹. N.p.: Jiangsu shuju, 1883 or 1884.

Yeh, Michelle. "Chayi de youlü: dui Yuwen Suoan de yige huixiang" 差異的憂慮: 對宇文所安的一個回響. *Jintian* 今天 1 (1991): 94–96.

Young, Kerry. *Pao*. London: Bloomsbury, 2011.

Yu, Anthony C. "'Rest, Rest, Perturbed Spirit!' Ghosts in Traditional Chinese Fiction." *Harvard Journal of Asiatic Studies* 47, no. 2 (December 1987): 397–434.

Yu Dafu 郁達夫. *Yu Dafu haiwai wenji* 郁達夫海外文集. Edited by Yu Feng 郁風. Beijing: Sanlian shudian, 1990.

Yu, Pauline. *The Reading of Imagery in the Chinese Poetic Tradition*. Princeton, NJ: Princeton University Press, 1987.

———. Review of *Traditional Chinese Poetry and Poetics: Omen of the World*, by Stephen Owen. *Harvard Journal of Asiatic Studies* 47, no. 1 (June 1987): 350–57.

Yuan Yiping 袁一平. *Tixiao jia Baxi* 啼笑嫁巴西. Tianjin: Baihua wenyi chubanshe, 2003.

Zeitlin, Judith T. *The Phantom Heroine: Ghosts and Gender in Seventeenth-Century Chinese Literature*. Honolulu: University of Hawai'i Press, 2007.

———. "Xiaoshuo." In *The Novel*, vol. 1: *History, Geography, and Culture*, edited by Franco Moretti, 249–61. Princeton, NJ: Princeton University Press, 2006.

Zhang Bowei 張伯偉, ed. *Quan Tang Wudai shige huikao* 全唐五代詩格彙考. Nanjing: Jiangsu guji chubanshe, 2002.

Zhang Tingyu 張廷玉 et al., comps. *Ming shi* 明史. 28 vols. Beijing: Zhonghua shuju, 1974.

Zhao Erxun 趙爾巽 et al., comps. *Qing shi gao* 清史稿. 20 vols. Taipei: Dingwen shuju, 1981.

Zheng Chuhui 鄭處誨. *Minghuang zalu* 明皇雜錄. In *Minghuang zalu, Dongguan zouji* 明皇雜錄、東觀奏記, punctuated and collated by Tian Tingzhu 田廷柱. Beijing: Zhonghua shuju, 1994.

Zheng Qiao 鄭樵, comp. *Tongzhi* 通志. 3 vols. Taipei: Taiwan Shangwu yinshuguan, 1987.

Zheng Tingyin 鄭婷尹. Wen xuan *wuchen zhushi zhi bixing siwei* 文選五臣注詩之比興思維. Taipei: Hua Mulan wenhua chubanshe, 2008.

Zhou Xinglu 周興陸. "Dou, Lin, Huang sanbu zaoqi Zhongguo wenxueshi bijiao" 竇, 林, 黄三部早期中國文學史比較. *Shehui kexue jikan* 社會科學輯刊 5 (2003): 135–41.

Zhou Yi zhushu 周易注疏. Annotated by Wang Bi 王弼, Kong Yingda 孔穎達, et al. In Ruan Yuan 阮元, ed., *Chongkan Songben Shisanjing zhushu fu jiaokan ji* 重刊宋本十三經注疏附校勘記, vol. 1. Taipei: Yiwen yinshuguan, 1965.

Zhou Zizhi 周紫芝. *Zhupo shihua* 竹坡詩話. In *Yingyin Wenyuange Siku quanshu* 影印文淵閣四庫全書, vol. 1480. Taipei: Taiwan shangwu yinshuguan, 1985.

Zhu Xi 朱熹. *Zhu Xi ji* 朱熹集. Punctuated and collated by Guo Qi 郭齊 and Yin Bo 尹波. 10 vols. Chengdu: Sichuan jiaoyu chubanshe, 1996.

———. ed. *Sishu zhangju jizhu* 四書章句集注. Beijing: Zhonghua shuju, 1983.

Zhu Ziqing 朱自清. *Lun yasu gongshang* 論雅俗共賞. Hong Kong: Gangqing chubanshe, 1979.

———. *Shiyanzhi bian* 詩言志辨. N.p.: Kaiming shudian, 1947.

———. *Zhu Ziqing quanji* 朱自清全集. 12 vols. Nanjing: Jiangsu jiaoyu chubanshe, 1988–98.

Zink, Michel. *The Invention of Literary Subjectivity*. Translated by David Sices. Baltimore: Johns Hopkins University Press, 1999.

Zou Zhiyong 鄒志勇. *Songdai biji shixue sixiang yanjiu* 宋代筆記詩學思想研究. Beijing: Zhongguo shehui kexue chubanshe, 2014.

Contributors

Sarah M. Allen is Associate Professor of Comparative Literature at Williams College. She is the author of *Shifting Stories: History, Gossip, and Lore in Narratives from Tang Dynasty China* (2014). She is a coeditor of *Tales from Tang Dynasty China: Selections from the* Taiping guangji (2017) and of *The Poetry of Li He* (2023).

Lucas Rambo Bender is Assistant Professor of Chinese Literature at Yale University. He is the author of *Du Fu Transforms: Tradition and Ethics amid Societal Collapse* (2021).

Jack W. Chen is Professor of Chinese Literature at the University of Virginia. He is the author of *The Poetics of Sovereignty: On Emperor Taizong of the Tang Dynasty* (2010), and *Anecdote, Network, Gossip, Performance: Essays on the* Shishuo xinyu (2021). He is a coeditor of *Idle Talk: Gossip and Anecdote in Traditional China* (2013) and *Literary Information in China: A History* (2021).

Wiebke Denecke is Professor of East Asian Literature at MIT. She is the author of *The Dynamics of Masters Literature: Early Chinese Thought from Confucius to Han Feizi* (2011) and *Classical World Literatures: Sino-Japanese and Greco-Roman Comparisons* (2014). She is a coeditor of *A New History of Japanese "Letterature"* (2015–2019) and the *Oxford Handbook of Classical Chinese Literature (1000 BCE–900 CE)* (2017), among others.

278 *List of Contributors*

Michael A. Fuller is Professor Emeritus of Chinese Literature at the University of California, Irvine. He is the author of *The Road to East Slope: The Development of Su Shi's Poetic Voice* (1990), *Drifting among Rivers and Lakes: Southern Song Dynasty Poetry and the Problem of Literary History* (2013), *An Introduction to Chinese Poetry: From the Canon of Poetry to the Lyrics of the Song Dynasty* (2017), and *An Introduction to Literary Chinese* (1999).

Tina Lu is Colonel John Trumbull Professor of East Asian Languages and Literatures at Yale University. She is the author of *Persons, Roles, and Minds: Identity in* Peony Pavilion *and* Peach Blossom Fan (2001) and *Accidental Incest, Filial Cannibalism, and Other Peculiar Encounters in Late Imperial Chinese Literature* (2009). She is a coeditor of *Approaches to Teaching* The Story of the Stone (2012).

Christopher M. B. Nugent is Professor of Chinese at Williams College. He is the author of *Manifest in Words, Written on Paper: Producing and Circulating Poetry in Tang Dynasty China* (2010). He is the editor of *The Poetry of Hanshan (Cold Mountain), Shide, and Fenggan* (2017) and *The Poetry and Prose of Wang Wei* (2020) and a coeditor of *Literary Information in China: A History* (2021) and *The Poetry of Li He* (2023).

David Schaberg is Professor of Asian Languages and Cultures and Dean of Humanities (2011–2022) at UCLA. He is the author of *A Patterned Past: Form and Thought in Early Chinese Historiography* (2005), and a cotranslator of *Zuo Tradition/Zuozhuan* 左傳: *Commentary on the "Spring and Autumn Annals"* (2016).

Xiaofei Tian is Professor of Chinese Literature at Harvard University. She is the author of *Tao Yuanming and Manuscript Culture: The Record of a Dusty Table* (2005), *Beacon Fire and Shooting Star: The Literary Culture of the Liang (502–557)* (2007), *Visionary Journeys: Travel Writings from Early Medieval and Nineteenth-Century China* (2011), *The Halberd at Red Cliff: Jian'an and the Three Kingdoms* (2018), and several books in Chinese, including *Qiushuitang lun* Jin Ping Mei (2003; revised ed., 2020) and *Yingzi yu Shuiwen: Qiushuitang zixuanji* (2020). She is the translator of *The World of a Tiny Insect: A Memoir of the Taiping Rebellion and Its Aftermath* (2014) and *Family Instructions for the Yan Clan and Other Works by Yan Zhitui (531–590s)* (2021). She is the editor of *Reading Du Fu: Nine Views* (2020) and *The Poetry of Ruan Ji* (2017) and a coeditor of the *Oxford*

Handbook of Classical Chinese Literature (1000 BCE–900 CE) (2017) and *The Poetry of Li He* (2023).

Jing Tsu is John M. Schiff Professor of East Asian Languages and Literatures and of Comparative Literature at Yale University. She is the author of *Failure, Nationalism, and Literature: The Making of Modern Chinese Identity, 1895–1937* (2005), *Sound and Script in Chinese Diaspora* (2011), and *Kingdom of Characters: The Language Revolution That Made China Modern* (2021). She is a coeditor of *Global Chinese Literature: Critical Essays* (2010) and *Science and Technology in Modern China, 1880s–1940s* (2014).

Index of Personal Names and
Titles of Works

An Hwak 安廓 (1886–1946), 229
Analects. See Confucius
Aston, William George (1841–1911), 228
Auerbach, Erich (1892–1957), 231

Bai Juyi 白居易 (772–846), 93, 161–62, 163;
 and "Yu Yuan jiu shu" 與元九書, 161–62
Bai Xingjian 白行簡 (776?–826). *See* "Li
 Wa zhuan" 李娃傳
Ban Gu 班固 (32–92), 36n37, 81, 178
Ban Jieyu 班婕妤 (Lady Ban, d. ca.
 6 BCE), 91
Bao Zhao 鮑照 (ca. 414–466), 88
Bei Dao 北島 (b. 1949), 232, 238
Benjamin, Walter (1892–1940), 44–46
Blumenberg, Hans (1920–1996), 220
Bourdieu, Pierre (1930–2002), 235
Braudel, Fernand (1902–1985), 235

Cai Yong 蔡邕 (132–192), 60
Caigui ji 才鬼記, 58–59, 68
*Cambridge History of Chinese Literature,
 The*, 3, 6, 18
*Cambridge History of English and Ameri-
 can Literature, The*, 15
Cao Cao 曹操 (155–220; Wei Emperor
 Wu 魏武帝), 95; and "Duange xing"
 短歌行, 159

Cao Pi 曹丕 (187–226), 197n46
Cao Zhi 曹植 (192–232), 85, 92; and
 "Gongyan shi" 公讌詩, 84–85, 89, 92,
 94–95; and "Zeng Ding Yi" 贈丁儀,
 197–98
Cefu yuangui 冊府元龜, 58, 191
Chen Han 陳翰 (fl. 870s–880s?). *See
 Yiwen ji* 異聞集
Chen Jitong 陳季同 (1851–1907), 241
Chen Qiufan 陳楸帆 (b. 1981), 253–56;
 and "Balin" 巴麟, 255; and "Kongju
 jiqi" 恐懼機器, 254–55; and *Rensheng
 suanfa* 人生算法, 255
Cheng Yi 程頤 (1033–1107), 170–71,
 173
Chosŏn munhaksa 朝鮮文學史. *See* An
 Hwak 安廓
Chu ci 楚辭, 83–84, 91, 92, 198
Chuxue ji 初學記, 73, 76–80, 82–97
Classic of Changes. See Yi jing 易經
Classic of Documents. See Shang shu 尚書
Classic of Poetry. See Shi jing 詩經
*Columbia History of Chinese Literature,
 The*, 2–3
Confucius, 34–36, 38n44, 44, 73–74, 167;
 and *Analects* (*Lunyu* 論語), 26, 31,
 35n33, 36, 38n41, 38n42, 134n7
Conring, Hermann (1606–1681), 218

282   *Index of Personal Names and Titles of Works*

Dai Bufan 戴不凡 (1922–1980), 127

Dai Song 戴嵩 or Dai Gao 戴嵩 (fl. early sixth century), 89; and "Yue chonglun xing" 月重輪行, 89–90, 91

Da Tang xinyu 大唐新語, 76, 201

Deleuze, Gilles (1925–1995), 54

Derrida, Jacques (1930–2004), 52–53

Dilthey, Wilhelm (1833–1911), 156n11

Du Fu 杜甫 (712–770), 158; and "Juan ye" 倦夜, 158–60, 169

Du Mu 杜牧 (803–853), 164; and "Dou lienü zhuan" 竇烈女傳, 103–6, 107–9, 121–24

Eckardt, Andre (1884–1974), 229

Fan Yun 范雲 (451–503), 1

Fengsao yaoshi 風騷要式, 199–200, 201

Fenmen gujin leishi 分門古今類事, 192–93

Florenz, Karl (1865–1939), 228

Foucault, Michel (1926–1984), 9, 60, 156n11

Fu Sheng 伏胜 (fl. ca. 200 BCE). See *Shang shu dazhuan* 尚書大傳

Gadamer, Hans-Georg (1900–2002), 43, 46

Gale, James Scarth (1863–1937), 230n34

Gan Bao 干寶 (d. 336). See *Soushen ji* 搜神記

Gao Shi 高適 (d. 765), 188–89

García, Cristina (b. 1958), 245n22

Genji monogatari 源氏物語, 224

Genovese, Eugene D. (1930–2012), 131

Geschichte der chinesischen Literatur. See Grube, Wilhelm

Geschichte der japanischen Literatur. See Florenz, Karl

Geschichte der koreanischen Literatur. See Eckardt, Andre

Giles, Herbert (1845–1935), 226

Goethe, Johann Wolfgang von (1749–1832), 233, 241

Gramsci, Antonio (1891–1937), 149

"Great Preface to the Mao Recension of the *Classic of Poetry.*" See "*Mao Shi daxu*" 毛詩大序

Grice, Paul (1913–1988), 43

Grube, Wilhelm (1855–1908), 226

Gu Tao 顧陶 (fl. 856). See *Tangshi leixuan* 唐詩類選

Gu Yuanqing 顧元慶 (1487–1565). See *Gushi wenfang xiaoshuo* 顧氏文房小說

Guanzi 管子, 224

Guattari, Félix (1930–1992), 54

Gujin shuohai 古今說海, 117

Gujin tushu jicheng 古今圖書集成, 178, 182, 183–84

Guo Maoqian 郭茂倩 (fl. twelfth century). See *Yuefu shiji* 樂府詩集

Guo Xiangzheng 郭祥正 (1035–1113), 202

Guo yu 國語, 31, 34n30

"Gushi shijiushou" 古詩十九首, 84–85

Gushi wenfang xiaoshuo 顧氏文房小說, 117

Hall, Stuart (1932–2014), 149

Han Yu 韓愈 (768–824), 24n5, 111, 163, 167; and "Wuzhe Wang Chengfu zhuan" 圬者王承福傳, 109–10

Han Feizi 韓非子, 37

Han shu 漢書, 81, 82, 178, 180, 183. *See also* Ban Gu 班固

He Da 何達 (1915–1994), 25

Hesiod (fl. 750 BCE), 41

History of Chinese Literature, A. See Giles, Herbert

History of Japanese Literature, A. See Aston, William George

Hou Han shu 後漢書, 180, 183

Hu Yinglin 胡應麟 (1551–1602), 118–19

Huainanzi 淮南子, 36n37, 80–81, 82, 83. *See also* Liu An 劉安

Huang Dongping 黄東平 (1923–2014), 237, 248–53; and *Qiaoge sanqu* 僑歌三曲, 249; and "Gu'er qiuxue ji" 孤兒求學記, 250; and "Yige jiaoshi de jingyu" 一個教師的境遇, 250

Huang Ren 黄人 (Huang Moxi 黄摩西, 1866–1913), 4, 221

Index of Personal Names and Titles of Works

Huihong 惠洪 (1071–1128), 193n37
Hun Liangfu 渾良夫 (fl. 480 BCE), 54–60, 68, 70

Inoue Tetsujirō 井上哲次郎 (1855–1944), 225

Jauss, Hans Robert (1921–1997), 43, 231
Jia Dao 賈島 (779–843), 164; and "Ernan mizhi" 二南密旨, 199
Jiao Xun 焦循 (1763–1820), 38n43
Jinlouzi 金樓子. *See* Xiao Yi 蕭繹
Jin shu 晉書, 196–97
Jiu Tang shu 舊唐書, 62, 65, 181
Jiyi ji 集異記, 116

Kaifūsō 懷風藻, 206
Kangxi, Qing Emperor 清康熙帝 (r. 1654–1722), 10
Kant, Immanuel (1724–1804), 152–54
Kojō Teikichi 古城眞吉 (1866–1949), 225–26
Kong Shangren 孔尚任 (1648–1718), 128
Kuaikui 蒯瞶 (Duke Zhuang of Wei 衛莊公, r. 480–478 BCE), 55–57, 68, 70
Kuhn, Thomas (1922–1996), 156n11, 163
Kurzweil, Ray (b. 1948), 253

Lady Ban. *See* Ban Jieyu
Lam, Agnes (b. 1972), 239
Lambeck, Peter (1628–1680), 218
Leishuo 類説, 114n24
Li Ao 李翺 (772–841), 101, 123, 161, 162, 165; and "Yang liefu zhuan" 楊烈婦傳, 101–3, 104–9 passim, 121–24 passim
Li E 李諤 (fl. 580s), 71, 79–80, 97
Li He 李賀 (790–816), 164; and "Su Xiaoxiao mu" 蘇小小墓, 164–65
Li Shangyin 李商隱 (ca. 812/813–858), 93, 165; and "Fude yue zhao bingchi bayun" 賦得月照冰池八韻, 93–96; and *Jinyao* 金鑰, 93; and "Wuti" 無題, 165–66
Li Yu 李煜 (ca. 937–978), 201

Li Yu 李漁 (1610–1680), 126, 148, 149. See also *Yizhongyuan* 意中緣
Li ji 禮記, 185
"Li Wa zhuan" 李娃傳, 99–100, 106–10, 112, 113, 114, 121–24
Liang Chenyu 梁辰魚 (1519–1593), 127
Liang Qichao 梁啓超 (1873–1929), 227
Lienü zhuan 列女傳. *See* Liu Xiang 劉向
Lin Chuanjia 林傳甲 (1877–1922), 4, 221, 226–28
Lingguai ji 靈怪集, 66n38
Liu An 劉安 (179–122 BCE), 36n37. See also *Huainanzi* 淮南子
Liu Cixin 劉慈欣 (b. 1963), 255–56
Liu, James J. Y. (1926–1986), 17–18
Liu Kezhuang 劉克莊 (1187–1269), 174
Liu Xiang 劉向 (79–8 BCE), 81; and *Lienü zhuan* 列女傳, 100
Liu Xie 劉勰 (ca. 460s–ca. 520s). See *Wenxin diaolong* 文心雕龍
Liu Xiyi 劉希夷 (651?–680?), 201
Liu Yong 柳永 (987–1053), 244
Liu Yuxi 劉禹錫 (772–842), 163
Liu Zongyuan 柳宗元 (773–819), 109
Lu Cai 陸采 (1497–1537). See *Yu Chu zhi* 虞初志
Lu Gui 盧瓌 (fl. early tenth century), 188n22
Lu Ji 陸機 (261–303), 84; and "Ni 'Mingyue he jiaojiao'" 擬明月何皎皎, 84–85, 87–88, 92, 95; and "Wen fu" 文賦, 194–95
Lu Ji 陸輯 (1515–1552). See *Gujin shuohai* 古今説海
Lu Qinli 逯欽立 (1910–1973), 59, 68, 69, 180
Lu Xun 魯迅 (1881–1936), 11–12, 118–20, 122–24, 237, 250; and *Tang Song chuanqi ji* 唐宋傳奇集, 119–20; and *Zhongguo xiaoshuo shilüe* 中國小説史略, 12, 119n36, 122, 124
Lu You 陸游 (1125–1210), 171, 173
Lü Yanzuo 呂延祚 (fl. ca. 718), 195–96
Lunyu 論語. *See* Confucius

284 *Index of Personal Names and Titles of Works*

Mandelbaum, Maurice (1908–1987), 150–51, 176

"*Mao Shi* daxu" 毛詩大序, 28–30, 31, 32, 35, 37–38, 42, 58, 157, 185, 190n27, 192, 205

Mao Shi zhengyi 毛詩正義. See *Shi jing* 詩經

Marx, Karl (1818–1883), 142

McCunn, Ruthanne Lum (b. 1946), 245n22

Mei Dingzuo 梅鼎祚 (1549–1615), 57–59, 68

Meltzl, Hugó (1846–1908), 213–14

Meng Jiao 孟郊 (751–814), 163, 164, 166, 202n60

Mikami Sanji 三上參次 (1865–1939), 228

Min Mafu 閔馬父 (fl. 522 BCE), 33–36

Mitrev, Dimitri (1919–1976), 210

Mudanting 牡丹亭, 139. *See also* Tang Xianzu 湯顯祖

Murasaki Shikibu 紫式部 (d. ca. 1014). See *Genji monogatari* 源氏物語

Murong Chui 慕容垂 (325–396; Later Yan Emperor Chengwu 後燕成武帝, r. 384–396), 10, 54, 65–69, 70

Nihon bungakushi 日本文学史. *See* Mikami Sanji 三上參次; and Takatsu Kuwasaburō 高津鍬三郎

Nihon kaika shōshi 日本開化小史. *See* Takuchi Ukichi 田口卯吉

Ouyang Xiu 歐陽修 (1007–1072), 167

Ouyang Xun 歐陽詢 (557–641), 75. See also *Yiwen leiju* 藝文類聚

Pan Yan 潘炎 (fl. 708), 186

Pan Yue 潘岳 (247–300), 86; and "Daowang" 悼亡, 85–86, 89

Pang Yuanying 龐元英 (fl. 1082). See *Tansou* 談藪

Pi Rixiu 皮日休 (ca. 834–883), 93

Powell, Patricia (b. 1966), 245n22

Prince Zhao (Wangzi Zhao 王子昭), 32–33, 35, 36, 39, 47

Qian Zhongshu 錢鍾書 (1910–1998), 38n44

Qu Yuan 屈原 (fl. fourth to third centuries BCE), 18

Quan Tang shi 全唐詩, 10, 59, 68–69, 178, 180

Reimmann, Jacob Friderich ([Jacob Friedrich] 1668–1743), 218

Ruan Dacheng 阮大鋮 (1587–1646), 129

Ruan Ji 阮籍 (210–263), 85; and "Yonghuai" 詠懷, 85–86, 89

Sanguo zhi yanyi 三國志演義, 238

Sasagawa Rinpū 笹川臨風 (1870–1949), 226, 227

Selections of Refined Literature. See *Wen xuan* 文選

Shang Yang 商鞅 (ca. 390–338 BCE), 224

Shang shu 尚書, 27–32 passim, 38n42, 186, 223; and "Yao dian" 堯典, 27–28, 29, 31–32, 35, 37

Shang shu dazhuan 尚書大傳, 186

Shen Quanqi 沈佺期 (ca. 656–ca. 716), 1

Shen Yue 沈約 (441–513), 1–2, 4, 10, 61–65. See also *Song shu* 宋書

Shenzong, Song Emperor 宋神宗 (r. 1067–1119), 137n8

Shi Jie 石介 (1005–1045), 167

Shi ji 史記. *See* Sima Qian 司馬遷

Shi jing 詩經, 26, 28–29, 30, 33–40 passim, 41n49, 56–57, 58, 73–74, 75, 167, 185, 189–92, 195n39, 196, 199, 205; and *Mao Shi zhengyi* 毛詩正義, 190; and "Guanju" 關雎 (Poem 1), 28n15; and "Mian" 綿 (Poem 237), 55n14, 57; and "Wo jiang" 我將 (Poem 272), 33. See also "*Mao Shi* daxu" 毛詩大序

Shi Kuang 師曠 (fl. sixth century BCE), 40–41, 46–47

Shi ming 釋名, 80, 82

Shina bungakushi 支那文学史. *See* Kojō Teikichi 古城貞吉; and Sasagawa Rinpū 笹川臨風

Shina kobungaku ryakushi 支那古文学略史.
See Suematsu Kenchō 末松謙澄
Shiping 詩評, 199
Shuihu zhuan 水滸傳, 226n28, 244
Shuofu 説郛, 120n37
Shuowen jiezi 説文解字, 52
Siku quanshu zongmu tiyao 四庫全書總目
提要, 78, 87
Sima Qian 司馬遷 (ca. 145–ca. 86 BCE),
73–74
Song Zhiwen 宋之問 (d. 712), 1
Song shu 宋書, 61–62, 180, 183, 187. *See also*
Shen Yue 沈約
Soushen ji 搜神記, 186
Su Shi 蘇軾 (1037–1101), 24n5, 167–68, 171,
202n60; and "Zhouzhong yeqi" 舟中夜
起, 168–70
Suematsu Kenchō 末松謙澄 (1855–1920),
222–24, 225, 226
Sui shu 隋書, 180, 187

Taiping guangji 太平廣記, 114–20, 122, 124
Taiping yulan 太平御覽, 58
Taizong, Tang Emperor 唐太宗 (r. 626–
649), 10, 54, 65–69, 70, 88, 97
Takatsu Kuwasaburō 高津鍬三郎 (1864–
1921), 228
Takuchi Ukichi 田口卯吉 (1855–1905), 225
Tang Xianzu 湯顯祖 (1550–1616), 128, 139
Tangshi leixuan 唐詩類選, 190
Tansou 談藪, 201
Tao Hongjing 陶弘景 (456–536), 187
Tao Zongyi 陶宗儀 (1329–1410). See
Shuofu 説郛

Vasilyev, Vasily (1818–1900), 226n29

Wallerstein, Immanuel (1930–2019), 235
Wang Bao 王褒 (513–576), 97
Wang Chong 王充 (d. ca. 100 CE), 186,
194
Wang Li 王力 (1922–1996), 56n19
Wang Mao 王楙 (1151–1213), 193
Wang Yi 王逸 (ca. 89–158), 198
Warren, Austin (1877–1962), 231

Wei Hong 衛宏 (fl. first century CE), 29.
See also *"Mao Shi* daxu" 毛詩大序
Wei Liangfu 魏良輔 (1522–1573), 127
Wei Shou 魏收 (507–572), 7
Wei Yuansong 衛元嵩 (fl. 570), 187
Wei Zheng 魏徵 (580–643), 8
Wellek, René (1903–1995), 150, 231
Wen Daya 溫大雅 (d. 629), 187
Wen Yiduo 聞一多 (1899–1946), 8, 25n6
Wenguan cilin 文館詞林, 6–7
Wenxian tongkao 文獻通考, 178
Wenxin diaolong 文心雕龍, 157–58, 194–95
Wen xuan 文選, 74–75, 78, 85–86, 195–98,
206. See also *Xiao Tong* 蕭統
Wenyuan yinghua 文苑英華, 114–15,
120n37, 122, 124
Wu Chuhou 吳處厚 (fl. 1087), 191–92
Wujing tongyi 五經通義, 81, 83

Xian Qin Han Wei Jin nanbeichao shi
先秦漢魏晉南北朝詩. *See* Lu Qinli
Xiao Gang 蕭綱 (503–551; Liang Emperor
Jianwen 梁簡文帝, r. 549–551), 8
Xiao Tong 蕭統 (501–531), 74, 75, 206.
See also *Wen xuan* 文選
Xiao Yan 蕭衍 (464–549; Liang Emperor
Wu 梁武帝, r. 502–549), 64n35
Xiao Yi 蕭繹 (508–555; Liang Emperor
Yuan 梁元帝, r. 552–555), 77, 94; and
Jinlouzi 金樓子, 74–75
Xie Lingyun 謝靈運 (385–433), 2
Xie Liuyi 謝六逸 (1898–1945), 228
Xin Tang shu 新唐書, 106, 181, 183–84
Xu Ling 徐陵 (507–583), 7
Xuanzong, Tang Emperor 唐玄宗 (r. 712–
756), 76, 77n12, 117
Xue Yongruo 薛用弱 (fl. ca. 820s). See *Jiyi
ji* 集異記
Xumi She 胥彌赦 (fl. 478 BCE), 55–56
Xun Kuang 荀況 (ca. 310–235 BCE). See
Xunzi 荀子
Xunzi 荀子, 31n22, 154–57, 159, 160, 161, 185

Yan Zhitui 顏之推 (531–590s), 76–77, 97
Yang Shuqing 楊樹清, 252

Index of Personal Names and Titles of Works

Yang Wanli 楊萬里 (1127–1206), 171–73
Yanshi jiaxun 顏氏家訓. *See* Yan Zhitui
Yao He 姚合 (ca. 779–ca. 855), 164
Yi jing 易經, 189–90
Yiling 懿靈 (b. 1964), 239
Yiwen ji 異聞集, 112–14, 115–16, 120n38, 121
Yiwen leiju 藝文類聚, 6–7, 73, 75, 76, 78–88, 96–97
Yizhongyuan 意中緣, 126, 132–49. *See also* Li Yu 李漁
Yu Dafu 郁達夫 (1896–1945), 238
Yu Xin 庾信 (513–581), 97
Yuan Zhen 元稹 (779–831), 93, 163
Yu Chu zhi 虞初志, 116–17, 119, 122
Yuefu shiji 樂府詩集, 63, 68
"Yue ji" 樂記. *See Li ji* 禮記

Zhang Dai 張岱 (1597–1684), 129
Zhang Heng 張衡 (78–139), 81
Zhang Jian 張薦 (744–804). *See Lingguai ji* 靈怪集
Zhang Yue 張說 (663–730), 76, 186–87

Zhang Zhengjian 張正見 (527–575), 89
Zhen Dexiu 真德秀 (1178–1235), 174–75
Zheng Xia 鄭俠 (1041–1119), 137n8
Zhongguo wenxue shi 中國文學史. *See* Lin Chuanjia 林傳甲
Zhou Zizhi 周紫芝 (1082–1155). *See Zhupo shihua* 竹坡詩話
Zhouli 周禮, 37n39
Zhu Tanlin 竺曇林 (Eastern Jin), 187
Zhu Xi 朱熹 (1130–1200), 24n5, 171, 173–74
Zhu Ziqing 朱自清 (1898–1948), 22–27, 29–32, 38n44, 39–40, 47–48; and *Shiyanzhi bian* 詩言志辨, 22–24, 26–27, 29–31
Zhuang Zhou 莊周 (ca. 369–ca. 286 BCE). *See Zhuangzi*
Zhuangzi 莊子, 31n22, 37, 154, 160, 226
Zhupo shihua 竹坡詩話, 201–2
Zichan 子產 (of Zheng), 34–36, 39, 47
"Ziye ge" 子夜歌, 54, 60–65, 70
Zuo zhuan 左傳, 28, 30–36, 39–41, 48, 53–58, 185

Harvard-Yenching Institute Monograph Series
(most recent titles now in print)

118. *Imperiled Destinies: The Daoist Quest for Deliverance in Medieval China,* by Franciscus Verellen
119. *Ethnic Chrysalis: China's Orochen People and the Legacy of Qing Borderland Administration,* by Loretta Kim
120. *The Paradox of Being: Truth, Identity, and Images in Daoism,* by Poul Andersen
121. *Feeling the Past in Seventeenth-Century China,* by Xiaoqiao Ling
122. *The Chinese Dreamscape, 300 BCE–800 CE,* by Robert Ford Campany
123. *Structures of the Earth: Metageographies of Early Medieval China,* by D. Jonathan Felt
124. *Anecdote, Network, Gossip, Performance: Essays on the* Shishuo xinyu, by Jack W. Chen
125. *Testing the Literary: Prose and the Aesthetic in Early Modern China,* by Alexander Des Forges
126. *Du Fu Transforms: Tradition and Ethics amid Societal Collapse,* by Lucas Rambo Bender
127. *Chinese History: A New Manual (Enlarged Sixth Edition),* Vol. 1, by Endymion Wilkinson
128. *Chinese History: A New Manual (Enlarged Sixth Edition),* Vol. 2, by Endymion Wilkinson
129. *Wang Anshi and Song Poetic Culture,* by Xiaoshan Yang
130. *Localizing Learning: The Literati Enterprise in Wuzhou, 1100–1600,* by Peter K. Bol
131. *Making the Gods Speak: The Ritual Production of Revelation in Chinese Religious History,* by Vincent Goossaert
132. *Lineages Embedded in Temple Networks: Daoism and Local Society in Ming China,* by Richard G. Wang
133. *Rival Partners: How Taiwanese Entrepreneurs and Guangdong Officials Forged the China Development Model,* by Wu Jieh-min; translated by Stacy Mosher
134. *Saying All That Can Be Said: The Art of Describing Sex in* Jin Ping Mei, by Keith McMahon
135. *Genealogy and Status: Hereditary Office Holding and Kinship in North China under Mongol Rule,* by Tomoyasu Iiyama
136. *The Threshold: The Rhetoric of Historiography in Early Medieval China,* by Zeb Raft
137. *Literary History in and beyond China: Reading Text and World,* edited by Sarah M. Allen, Jack W. Chen, and Xiaofei Tian